Tamed Power

TAMED POWER

Germany in Europe

EDITED BY

Peter J. Katzenstein

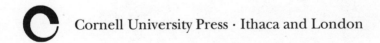 Cornell University Press · Ithaca and London

First published 1997 by Cornell University Press.
First printing, Cornell Paperbacks, 1997.

Printed in the United States of America

Library of Congress Cataloging-in-Publication Data
Tamed power : Germany in Europe / edited by Peter J. Katzenstein.
 p.   cm.
 Includes index.
 ISBN 0-8014-3429-7 (alk. paper). — ISBN 0-8014-8449-9 (pbk. : alk. paper)
 1. Germany—Relations—Europe.   2. Europe—Relations—Germany.
 3. European Union—Germany.   4. Europe—Economic integration.
 5. European Union countries—Economic policy.   I. Katzenstein, Peter J.
 DD290.3.T36 1997   97-30056
 303.48'24304-dc21

Cornell University Press strives to utilize environmentally responsible suppliers and materials to the fullest extent possible in the publishing of its books. Such materials include vegetable-based, low-VOC inks and acid-free papers that are also either recycled, totally chlorine-free, or partly composed of nonwood fibers.

Cloth printing   10 9 8 7 6 5 4 3 2 1
Paperback printing   10 9 8 7 6 5 4 3 2 1

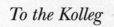

To the Kolleg

Contents

CONTENTS

Contributors

Jeffrey J. Anderson, Associate Professor, Brown University

Włodek Anioł, Associate Professor, Warsaw University

Daneš Brzica, Institute of Economics, Slovak Academy of Sciences

Simon J. Bulmer, Professor, University of Manchester

Timothy A. Byrnes, Associate Professor, Colgate University

Péter Gedeon, Associate Professor, Budapest University
of Economics

Christine Ingebritsen, Assistant Professor, University
of Washington (Seattle)

Hynek Jeřábek, Associate Professor, Charles University, Prague

Peter J. Katzenstein, Walter S. Carpenter, Jr., Professor
of International Studies, Cornell University

Paulette Kurzer, Associate Professor, University of Arizona

Michael P. Marks, Assistant Professor, Willamette University

Zuzana Poláčková, Institute of Political Science, Slovak Academy
of Sciences

Ivo Samson, Slovak Institute of International Studies and University of Giessen

František Zich, Institute of Sociology, Czech Academy of Sciences

Preface

The end of the Cold War and bipolarity has elevated the importance of the role that international regions play in world politics. This is one of two volumes. *Network Power: Japan and Asia* is a companion to *Tamed Power: Germany in Europe* which also explores the role of regions in world politics.

Although this book is about European politics, it is informed by a comparative perspective. What in Germany and Europe looks quite natural is from a non-European vantage point noteworthy. Although neither peace nor prosperity requires it, Germany and Europe are seeking an ambitious level of formal, institutional unity. General models focusing on the balance of power in the international system or the effects of global markets are unlikely to help us understand what seems distinctive about the politics of specific world regions. Contextualized, regional analyses that link regional factors to global, national, and local ones are more likely to prove useful.

There exist two views of the relationship between Germany and Europe. Robert Harris in his thriller *Fatherland* (New York, 1992) depicts Germany ruling Europe indirectly. Although in Harris's novel Germany won World War II, military domination is less important than political and economic hegemony:

> In the West, twelve nations—Portugal, Spain, France, Ireland, Great Britain, Belgium, Holland, Italy, Denmark, Norway, Sweden and Finland—had been corralled by Germany, under the Treaty of Rome, into a European trading bloc. . . . People drove German cars, listened to German radios, watched German televisions, worked in German-owned factories, moaned about the behavior of German tourists in German-dominated holiday resorts. (p. 176)

Not indirect but creeping rule characterizes a second view of the relationship between Germany and Europe. It is expressed tongue in cheek by a story that Gary Herrigel, Uday Mehta, and David Laitin sent me:

Having chosen English as the preferred language in the European Union (EU), the European Parliament has commissioned a feasibility study in ways to improve efficiency in communications between government departments. European officials have often pointed out that English spelling is unnecessarily difficult. What is clearly needed is a phased program of changes to iron out the anomalies. The program would be administered by a committee appointed by the participating nations. In the first year, for example, the committee might suggest using "s" instead of the soft "c." Sertainly, sivil servants in all sities would reseive this news with joy. The hard "c" could then be replased by "k" sinse both letters are pronounsed alike. This would klear up a lot of konfusion in the minds of klerikal workers. In the sekond year, bekause of growing enthusiasm, "ch" would be replaced by "c." This would make words like "whic" 20 percent shorter. Similarly, it will be announsed that the troublesome "ph" would henseforth be replased by "f." In the third year, publik akseptanse of the new spelling kan be expekted to reac the stage where more komplikated canges are possible. Governments would enkourage the removal of double letters, which have always ben a deterent to akurate speling. We would al agre that the horible mes of silent "e"'s in the languag is disgrasful. Therfor, we kould drop thes and kontinu to read and writ as though nothing had hapend. By this tim, it would be four years sins the skem began, and peopl would be reseptiv to steps suc as replasing "th" by "z." Perhaps zen ze funktion of "w" kould be taken on by "v," vhic is, after al, half a "w." Finaly, ze unesesary "o" kuld be dropd from words kontaining "ou." Similar arguments vud of kors be aplid to ozer kombinations of leters. Kontinuing zis proses yer aftr yer, ve vud eventuli hav a reli sensibl riten stil. Aftr tventi yers zer vud be no mor trubls or difikultis and evrion vud find it ezi to understan ec ozer. Ze drems of ze EU vud finali kom tru.

Although this book shares an institutional focus with interpretations that stress indirect or creeping rule as the fundamental cause shaping the relations between Germany and Europe, it insists on two important points. First, the Germanization of Europe is indissolubly linked to the Europeanization of Germany. And second, the smaller European states are not simply silly putty in the palms of a German or European giant. These states also have deeply rooted institutional structures that are expressed politically in domestic politics and issue-specific policy regimes. Interpretations exclusively stressing Germany's indirect or creeping rule overlook important factors that counter Germany's institutional power.

Prior work had made me recognize these factors, but I had not explored them. My research on the viability of the smaller European states traced the effects of their international vulnerability rather than investigating its character. My writing on German politics highlighted the domestic brakes on power without analyzing the international dimensions of this topic. Research on Japanese and German security policies focused primarily on the effects of domestic rather than international norms and identities. This book picks up on these themes and explores their connections.

The project that has resulted in this book began to take shape in November 1989. Because it is difficult to conduct social science research in the middle of a revolution, I decided to proceed slowly and to cast my net widely. Investigating the intersection of German unification and European integration on the basis of fieldwork and numerous case studies required careful preparation. It took me several years to raise the necessary funds and to assemble a team of researchers to collect the data.

On the way, teaching helped greatly to clarify my mind. Together with my colleague and friend Jonas Pontusson, in the early 1990s I developed a new undergraduate lecture course dealing with the political changes brought about by European integration. Eventually, I taught that course myself, reorganizing it to focus on the interaction between German unification and European integration. Over the years I tried out most of the ideas that have shaped this book in lectures that I prepared for that course.

The initial design for this book and short research memoranda were discussed at a workshop convened at Cornell University in May 1992. Draft papers were written and revised for subsequent workshops held at Cornell (February 1994), Budapest (June 1995), and Bratislava (March 1996). I thank all of the participants for their comments and criticisms, which have helped improve the individual chapters and the overall focus of the book.

Without the necessary financial support, it would have been impossible to convene these workshops. I acknowledge, specifically, the generosity of the Council for European Studies, which supported this project with two different grants; the German Marshall Fund (Grant A-0063); the American Council of Learned Societies; the Friedrich-Ebert-Foundation; the Friedrich-Naumann-Foundation; the Greek Institute for International and Strategic Studies; the Institute of European Studies at Cornell's Center for International Studies; and Cornell's Walter S. Carpenter, Jr., Chair of International Studies.

Going well beyond support of a specific book project, a number of these organizations showed generosity and flexibility in reconnecting worlds of scholarship that for too long had been forced to exist in isolation. My specific thanks go to all the authors who have contributed to this book. Throughout the last four years, they have remained interested and committed to this project under occasionally trying personal circumstances. They were good-natured to a fault in meeting my numerous requests for revisions. And they exemplified how joint scholarship can evolve into a deeper sense of intellectual companionship and enduring personal friendships.

Roger Haydon expedited this manuscript through the review process. His presence only a short walk down East Hill has been a special boon for years. Kay Scheuer steered it through the various stages of production. Finally, my special thanks go to Jeffrey Lockridge, whose careful editing improved greatly every page of this book.

Launched in 1993, the project ended where it had begun, in Berlin. I was extremely fortunate to have spent the academic year 1995–96 at the Wissenschaftskolleg Berlin. An oasis for scholars the world over, the Kolleg offered an ideal environment for thinking through all aspects of the project, for writing the framing chapters for this book, and for doing the necessary editorial work on chapter 7. I thank Wolf Lepenies, the director, and the entire staff of the Kolleg for having treated me much better than I could ever have dreamed and than I deserved. It is only fitting that I dedicate this book to the Kolleg, whose broad vision places Germany in Europe and Europe in the world.

PETER J. KATZENSTEIN

Ithaca, New York, and Berlin

CHAPTER ONE

United Germany in an Integrating Europe

Peter J. Katzenstein

Revolutionary changes in global and in European politics have reawakened old fears about Europe's domination by an unpredictable German giant. But these changes have also fueled new hopes for Germany and Europe as models of political pluralism in a more peaceful and prosperous world. In a different era, Thomas Mann distinguished between the specter of the "Germanization" of Europe and the vision of the "Europeanization" of Germany. It is a mistake to let fears from the past or hopes for the future decide between these two views. It is more useful to treat them as templates that may help us discern a more complicated pattern linking Germany and Europe.

German unification and European integration were indissolubly linked in 1989–90. Chancellor Helmut Kohl's European partners gave their grudging, basic support for German unification in Strasbourg in December 1989. In return, Kohl agreed to back President François Mitterrand's

For critical comments and suggestions on earlier drafts, I thank David Cameron, James Caporaso, Nikiforos Diamandouros, Barry Eichengreen, Peter Gourevitch, Joseph Grieco, Helga Haftendorn, Peter Hall, Gunther Hellmann, Stanley Hoffmann, Mary F. Katzenstein, Robert O. Keohane, Beate Kohler-Koch, Stephen Krasner, Michael Kreile, David Laitin, Andrei Markovits, Gary Marks, Stefan Leibfried, Harald Müller, Henry Nau, Elizabeth Pond, Simon Reich, Judith Reppy, John Ruggie, Gian Enrico Rusconi, Wayne Sandholtz, Fritz Scharpf, Gebhard Schweigler, Anne-Marie Slaughter, Wolfgang Streeck, Bengt Sundelius, and Michael Zürn; seminar participants at the University of Bremen, Darmstadt, Geneva, Göttingen, Manchester, Mannheim, the European University Institute at Florence, the Humboldt University Berlin, and the Wissenschaftszentrum Berlin; the project participants; and two anonymous readers for Cornell University Press. Portions of this chapter have been published with the same title in *Current History* 608 (March 1997): 116–23.

proposal to have the intergovernmental conference on the European Monetary Union (EMU) start in December 1990, rather than at some later, unspecified date, as Germany had preferred. And when it became clear, by March 1990, that pressure for Germany's early unification was building much more quickly than Kohl, Mitterrand, or most of Europe's leaders had expected, French support for accelerating the unification process was predicated on German commitment to a second intergovernmental conference on political union, which would encompass not only monetary and economic affairs but also foreign and security policy. This deal was politically approved by the European Council in Dublin in April 1990, and it was ratified in the Treaty on European Union (TEU), which amalgamated the proposals for economic and political union in Maastricht in December 1991. United Germany was thus to be embedded in an integrating Europe.[1]

These diplomatic bargains point to two underlying questions. Why does Germany, the most powerful state in Europe, appear bent on giving up its newly won sovereign power? And why have long-standing institutional inefficiencies of the European polity not blocked advances in European integration? The answer this book offers to these two questions has to do with a historically important shift in the institutionalization of power in Germany and Europe, power conventionally measured in terms of material resources or bargaining strength.

The Germans have eliminated the concept of "power" from their political vocabulary. They speak the language of "political responsibility" instead. Hans-Peter Schwarz has referred to a new forgetfulness of power, which has replaced Germany's old obsession with power.[2] Some observers view this rhetorical turn as little more than a cynical ploy in which the old wolf has put on new sheepskin. This book contends instead that it indicates a deeper transformation in both the style and substance of German and European politics. The culture of restraint that characterizes Germany's foreign policy and the conscious avoidance of assuming a high profile and

[1] Philip Zelikow and Condoleeza Rice, *Germany Unified and Europe Transformed: A Study in Statecraft* (Cambridge: Harvard University Press, 1995); Elizabeth Pond, *Beyond the Wall: Germany's Road to Unification* (Washington, D.C.: Brookings Institution, 1995); Stephen F. Szabo, *The Diplomacy of German Unification* (New York: St. Martin's Press, 1992); Wolfgang Schäuble, *Der Vertrag: Wie ich über die deutsche Einheit verhandelte* (Stuttgart: Deutsche Verlags-Anstalt, 1991); Horst Teltschik, *329 Tag: Innenansichten der Einigung* (Berlin: Siedler, 1991); and Hans-Dietrich Genscher, *Erinnerungen* (Berlin: Siedler, 1995). For preunification history, see Timothy Garton Ash, *In Europe's Name: Germany and the Divided Continent* (New York: Random House, 1993); and Wolfram F. Hanrieder, *Germany, America, Europe: Forty Years of German Foreign Policy* (New Haven: Yale University Press, 1989); A. James McAdams, "Germany after Unification: Normal at Last?" *World Politics* 49 (January 1997): 282–308.
[2] Hans-Peter Schwarz, *Die Gezähmten Deutschen: Von der Machtbesessenheit zur Machtvergessenheit* (Stuttgart: Deutsche Verlags-Anstalt, 1985).

seeking a strong leadership role in the European Union emanate from the same institutional source. Jeffrey Anderson quite appropriately dubs this Germany's "reflexive support for an exaggerated multilateralism."[3]

The German approach to power, and the practices that sustain and reformulate it, emphasizes its "soft" elements.[4] Other views interpret power differently, as a form of domination from which actors can escape only by breaking the shackles that bind them, or as an aspect of contractual bargaining, in which the different parties gain to different degrees from making deals. Such views underline the "hard" elements of power. In reality, soft and hard elements always blend. For example, in the summer of 1996, British tabloids characterized an English-German soccer match as a new "war" and viewed Germany and Britain as principal adversaries in a diplomatic war over beef derivatives. But at the same time, British and German foreign offices swapped officials as part of ongoing, practical efforts to further European integration through an integrated European Embassy.[5]

The institutionalization of power, this book contends, is the most distinctive aspect of the relationship between Europe and Germany. Germany's willingness to give the smaller EU members disproportionate power is puzzling, especially for Anglo-Saxons, Elizabeth Pond writes. "The efficient Germans reason that it is worth subordinating swift unilateral action today to the cumbersome forging of EU coalitions for the sake of institution-building tomorrow."[6] Only when we move institutional power to center stage can we hope to understand why Germany is willing to give up its new sovereign power or why institutional inefficiency has not stopped European integration. The institutionalization of power matters because it takes the hard edges off power relations. Over time, institutions constitute actors rather than merely constraining their preferences. They do so within particular norms (collective expectations for the proper behavior of actors with a given identity) or for specific collective identities (varying constructions of statehood). Norms and identities typically have two effects. They constitute actors and thus shape their interests. And they constrain actor preferences.

Over the past decades, European states, and in particular Germany, have acquired collective identities that are significantly more international than before. In this situation, power is a variable quantity. Parents may act against their individual interests to further the family's interest. What may seem ir-

---

[3] Chapter 3, this volume, p. 85.

[4] For the concept of "soft power," see also Joseph S. Nye, *Bound to Lead: The Changing Nature of American Power* (New York: Basic Books, 1990).

[5] Nora Boustany, "European Envoys Breach Some Old Embassy Walls," *International Herald Tribune* (July 6–7, 1996): 1.

[6] Elizabeth Pond, "Germany Finds Its Niche as a Regional Power," *Washington Quarterly* 19 (Winter 1996): 30.

rational for them as individuals can be quite rational from the perspective of the family, with which they identify. So it is for the individual member states and the European Union (EU) family. "The term which captures most accurately the dominant character of the relationship between states and the region," concludes Paul Taylor, "is *symbiosis* . . . there is no evidence to suggest that common arrangements could not be extended a very long way without necessarily posing any direct challenge to the sovereignty of states."[7] James Caporaso concurs: "Regional integration is not a zero-sum process. . . . Analysts should not have to choose between intergovernmentalism and international forms of political activity. Both logics operate in the European polity."[8] Nation-states are simultaneously "throwing out" functions to the supranational level and devolving responsibilities to subnational regions. In this view, power relations do not sum to a fixed quantity that either resides in national states or gets transferred to a supranational center of decision making. Thus institutionalized power is "soft," compared to other types of power.

The softness of German power in Europe is also the result of institutional similarities. In institutional terms, the EU and Germany are quite similar. In both polities, power is pooled, creating what I call below a European system of "associated sovereignty" and German "semisovereignty." In both systems, it is possible to exploit superior material resources and advantageous bargaining positions to exercise hard power. But such behavior is the exception, not the rule. As Elizabeth Pond explains, German interests are advanced, not in balance of power clashes, but in "tedious bureaucratic maneuvering in the confederation-plus of the EU and the confederation-minus of the transatlantic community."[9] Hence, what is distinctive about Germany is not its "unintentional power," which, like all larger states, it possesses in good measure, but that its political leaders exercise power only in multilateral, institutionally mediated systems—in Germany, the EU, the Atlantic Community, and broader international fora—that soften sovereign power.

This book explores the institutionalization of power relations in two domains. It inquires into the relations between the EU and Germany (primarily in chapters 1–3) on the one hand and the relations of Germany and the EU with some of the European states that surround them in all four directions of the sundial (primarily in chapters 4–8). This introduction focuses on the relations between Germany and Europe; the concluding chapter analyzes the relations between the smaller or more peripheral

[7] Paul Taylor, "The European Community and the State: Assumptions, Theories and Propositions," *Review of International Studies* 17 (1991): 125.

[8] James A. Caporaso, "The European Union and Forms of State: Westphalian, Regulatory or Post-Modern?" *Journal of Common Market Studies* 34 (March 1996): 46–47.

[9] Pond, "Germany as a Regional Power," p. 36.

European states, Germany, and the EU.[10] The chapter authors inquire into the institutional practices and state policies that can help explain why a strong Germany is willing to cede its new sovereignty and why the smaller states continue to back an integration process despite its numerous institutional inefficiencies. To varying degrees, often affected by the strength of different conceptions of national identity, institutionalized power can be seen to mold the identity of the states themselves and thus the interests they hold. For example, in sharp contrast to Britain, Germany has a remarkably internationalized state identity. As a result, Germany is an ardent champion of a Europeanization process through which it seeks to promote German state interests.

Several readers of earlier drafts of this book have pointed out a long list of serious omissions. I agree that detailed examination of, among others, Switzerland and Austria, Finland and the Baltic states, Slovenia and Croatia, Bulgaria and Rumania, and, particularly, Turkey would have enriched the book's analysis. But from my own research on some of these states (for example, Switzerland and Austria) and broad reading on others (for example, Finland and Turkey), I venture the guess that it would not have changed the book's central message.

Even more serious, in the view of other colleagues, is the omission of France and Britain. Without denying in any way the importance of the institutional effects of other states, such as Britain's in Scandinavia and Greece, or France's in Italy and Spain, this book focuses its attention on the effects Germany and Europe have on the smaller European states. Does the exclusive focus on Germany in Europe not lead to premature conclusions that overestimate the importance of Germany by underplaying the role of Britain and France? Perhaps. But because this book rejects the argument that Europe is succumbing to German "domination" or "exploitation," as these concepts are conventionally understood, the omission of France and Britain tends to strengthen, not undermine, its central argument.[11]

---

[10] Some of these states, like the Netherlands, are small but not peripheral. Others, like Poland, are peripheral but not small. For the sake of simplicity, this chapter refers to all of them as "smaller."

[11] This volume seeks to advance a sociological-institutional argument that bridges domestic and international levels of analysis and that differs from rationalist (realist and liberal) perspectives. With the inclusion of France and Britain, the book's twenty-six illustrative case studies, reported in chapters 3–7, would have increased greatly, far exceeding the project's limited financial resources and research capacities. Most of the existing academic and policy literatures dealing with Germany's influence in Europe are speculative and based on anecdotal evidence. The case studies this book reports provide an empirical base that, despite its unavoidable inadequacy, permits a preliminary exploration and testing of a particular analytical stance. Should this approach merit future work, researchers with, one hopes, larger and better data sets are likely to replicate, extend, reformulate, or reject the line of argument and evidence that this book offers.

Although the authors occasionally address other European or international institutions, "Europe" in this book refers to the European Union and its direct predecessors. The chapters examine this relation from the perspective of both Brussels and Bonn/Berlin as well as from the vantage points of northern, western, southern, and central Europe. To what extent are important developments in these European states shaped directly by Germany or Europe, or by Germany acting through Europe? What are the political consequences of different forms of influence? And do these forms suggest a clear answer to whether Germany will prevail over Europe or Europe over Germany? The answers this book offers derive from the premise that we can adequately understand the world of power and interest in Europe only when we see power and interest not simply as attributes of distinctive actors, Germany *and* Europe, but as aspects of relationships that place Germany *in* Europe, through institutions that tame power.[12]

REALISM, LIBERALISM, AND INSTITUTIONALISM: GERMANY AND EUROPE OR GERMANY IN EUROPE?

European integration during the last forty years has occurred in major cycles. Each cycle has created its own climate of Euro-optimism and Euro-skepticism, which was reflected on the editorial pages of daily newspapers, in the columns of weekly and monthly magazines, and in the world of scholarship. The early success of the European integration movement at the beginning of the 1950s came to a stop with the defeat of the European Defense Community in the French Assembly in 1954. The European Community in 1957, the Fouchet Plan, which aimed at creating a European union of states that included foreign and security policy (1962), and the timely completion of the customs union were halted abruptly by the crisis of the "empty chair" (1965–66), through which President Charles de Gaulle succeeded in blocking plans for a system of qualified majority voting by the end of the 1960s. Eventually, under the new leadership of President Georges Pompidou and Chancellor Willy Brandt, European integration was launched once more in the late 1960s and early 1970s. But adverse economic developments, including flexible exchange rates, the oil crisis of 1973, and a renationalization of European markets through discriminatory national regulations, effectively beached the Werner plan (1970) for achieving economic and monetary union within a decade. The relaunching of the European project with the Single European Act (SEA) in 1985 and the Treaty on European Union (TEU) in 1991 signaled another up-

---

[12] See also Elizabeth Pond, "Germany in the New Europe," *Foreign Affairs* 71 (Spring 1992): 114–30.

swing in response to economic globalization, the ending of the Cold War, and German unification.

An understanding of the dynamics of European integration must be informed by this historical evolution. Snapshots of momentary constellations, whether in the distribution of power or in the bargaining position of states or societal actors, easily skew perceptions of what is significant and make us hostage to quickly changing climates of opinion. Historical sociology helps us avoid this trap. In the 1950s and 1960s, for example, scholars such as Stanley Hoffmann and Karl Deutsch were bears in a bull market of integration studies.[13] Hoffmann argued that the closer the integration process came to the core of national sovereignty, the more difficult integration would become. Early successes in the "low politics" of commercial policy thus gave an inaccurate picture of the road ahead. Deutsch looked to mass behavior and attitudes and argued that the structural barriers to European integration were very large, as reflected in the measurement of the differential between higher national and lower international growth rates of economic transactions and social communications. Although, with Hoffmann and Deutsch, this book takes a historical and sociological approach, its main message three decades later is more optimistic.

Since the mid-1980s, U.S. scholars have analyzed the politics of European integration primarily from two perspectives, realism and liberalism, which seek to explain the actor choices that have shaped the waxing and waning of the European integration process during the last four decades. Realism and liberalism are not theories but analytical perspectives, which can be formulated in different ways.[14] Some variants of liberalism, for example, insist on the primacy of social groups in domestic politics and are fundamentally opposed to variants of realism that insist on the primacy of the effects of international anarchy. Stressing the reduction of anarchy

[13] Stanley Hoffmann, "Obstinate or Obsolete? The Fate of the Nation-State and the Case of Western Europe," *Daedalus* 95 (Summer 1996): 862–915; Karl W. Deutsch et al., *Political Community and the North Atlantic Area: International Organization in the Light of Historical Experience* (Princeton: Princeton University Press, 1957); Philip E. Jacob and James V. Toscano, eds., *The Integration of Political Communities* (Philadelphia: Lippincott, 1964).

[14] For a fuller development of this point, see Peter J. Katzenstein, ed., *The Culture of National Security: Norms and Identity in World Politics* (New York: Columbia University Press, 1996); and Peter J. Katzenstein, *Cultural Norms and National Security: Police and Military in Postwar Japan* (Ithaca: Cornell University Press, 1996). Theoretically sophisticated reviews of different analytical perspectives on European integration include James A. Caporaso and John T. S. Keeler, "The European Union and Regional Integration Theory," in Carolyn Rhodes and Sonia Mazey, eds., *The State of the European Community*, vol. 3, *Building a European Polity?* (Boulder: Lynne Rienner, 1995), pp. 29–62; Alec Stone, "What Is a Supranational Constitution? An Essay in International Relations Theory," *Review of Politics* 56 (Summer 1994): 441–74; and Thomas Risse-Kappen, "Exploring the Nature of the Beast: International Relations Theory and Comparative Policy Analysis Meet the European Union," *Journal of Common Market Studies* 34 (March 1996): 53–80.

through international institutions, other formulations of liberalism are in some ways closer to international realism than to their liberal cousins, which emphasize the primacy of domestic politics. Conversely, traditional realist perspectives, which emphasize the power of nationalism in international politics, have some affinity with liberal theories that focus on the influence of domestic groups in society. But they differ greatly from variants of liberal analysis that emphasize international institutions. In short, these analytical perspectives are not precise. Hence their different formulations can either complement or contradict each other.

Widely known in the 1960s as "intergovernmentalism," the first perspective is a version of political realism that incorporates both international and domestic levels of analysis. It focuses on the interaction of states in an international system constrained by the preferences of actors.[15] This version of realism abandons the idea that international anarchy and calculations of relative gains of governments define the national interest. It emphasizes instead the continuity of diplomatic bargains among governments intent on preserving their sovereignty. Far from denying the importance of European integration, this brand of realism sees in integration an additional arena of competition among self-interested states. European integration was part of a larger diplomatic maneuver that was designed, as Lord Ismay said of NATO, "to keep the Russians out, the Americans in and the Germans down." Governments are willing to compromise on issues of state sovereignty as long as they see such compromises as serving their interests. In the intergovernmentalist view, European integration does not modify or transform but suffuses international anarchy.[16]

German unification and European integration in the early 1990s provide plausible illustrations for this perspective. The "two-plus-four talks" that accompanied German unification involved the two German states as well as the four victorious powers in World War II. These talks rapidly changed into bargaining between the Federal Republic, the Soviet Union, and the United States, however, with Britain, France, and the GDR playing no more than a secondary role. Furthermore, the acceleration of the European integration process, illustrated by the Treaty on European Union, signed in Maastricht in 1991, was, among other things, also a self-conscious

[15] Stanley Hoffmann, *The European Sisyphus: Essays on Europe, 1964–1994* (Boulder, Colo.: Westview Press, 1995); Alan S. Milward with the assistance of George Brennan and Federico Romero, *The European Rescue of the Nation-State* (Berkeley: University of California Press, 1992); Andrew Moravcsik, "Preferences and Power in the European Community: A Liberal Intergovernmental Approach," *Journal of Common Market Studies* 31 (December 1993): 473–524. For a critical discussion, see Geoffrey Garrett and George Tsebelis, "An Institutional Critique of Intergovernmentalism," *International Organization* 50 (Spring, 1996): 269–99.

[16] Intergovernmentalism differs from neo-realism, another variant of realism that self-consciously neglects the role of domestic and transnational politics in favor of the putatively strong effects of anarchy on state behavior even in peaceful environments.

French attempt to harness the enhanced power of a united Germany to an international institution that promised to grant France partial control and thus keep the European power balance from shifting too rapidly against France.

Furthermore, in that process the Bundesbank and Germany's Constitutional Court have had no trouble distinguishing, when necessary, between their institutional, German, and European interests. The Bundesbank has always regarded German interests paramount in the determination of its monetary policy. And in ruling on the constitutionality of the Treaty on European Union on October 11, 1993, the Constitutional Court held that it, not the European Court of Justice, would determine whether EU institutions were operating within their competence. "It defined the European Union as a 'Staatenverbund,'" writes William Paterson, "a type of association of states falling somewhere between a federation and a confederation and stressed that member states remained 'Herren der Verträge' (masters of the treaties). It also argued that any significant steps in further unification needed to be legitimised by the Bundestag."[17]

But German unification and European integration also create obvious anomalies for a realist interpretation. For example, there are virtually no traces of Germany's return to realist "normalcy," to balance of power politics in an anarchical international system. Germans shun the concepts and practice of power politics (*Machtpolitik*) and balancing (*Schaukelpolitik*). Only in a few restricted intellectual quarters has German unification led to a renewed interest in the theory and practice of political realism. To date, this intellectual interest has remained without any apparent wider political resonance in Germany, even though Germany's leading conservative newspaper, the *Frankfurter Allgemeine Zeitung*, offers ample space on its editorial page for the airing of realist views.[18] In addition to historical, psychological, and political reasons for their current lack of appeal, we need to consider also the intellectual shortcomings of realist analyses. For example, proponents of Germany's national interest have failed to derive any concrete strategies from realist maxims that promise new solutions to some of Germany's foreign policy dilemmas. Peter Pulzer's critical review of a mod-

[17] William E. Paterson, "Beyond Bipolarity: German Foreign Policy in a Post Cold-War-World," in *Developments in German Politics*, vol. 2 (London: Macmillan, 1996), p. 144. For a scathing review of the Federal Constitutional Court's conservative, central European conceptions of *ethnos* and *demos* and its understanding of the requirements of democratic legitimacy in pre- and post-Maastricht Europe, see Joseph H. H. Weiler, "The State "über alles": Demos, Telos and the German Maastricht Decision," EUI Working Paper RSC 95/19, Badia Fiesolana, San Domenico (FI), European University, 1995. See also Juliane Kokott, "The European Court and National Courts Doctrine and Jurisprudence: Legal Change in Its Social Context: Report on Germany," EUI Working Paper RSC 95/25, Badia Fiesolana, San Domenico (FI), European University, 1995.

[18] See John Ely's extremely critical essay, "The *Frankfurter Allgemeine Zeitung* and Contemporary National Conservatism," *German Politics and Society* 13 (Summer 1995): 81–121.

est revival of conservative writings on German foreign policy thus concludes that even contemporary German conservatives do not "advocate a radical departure from institutional anchoring in the West. Least of all do they disavow the ideological and geopolitical experience of the Federal Republic. . . . The new calls for national pride have earned only a limited response."[19]

Realist interpretations sometimes fail to acknowledge the importance of the historical experiences of the Federal Republic since 1949. Hence some realists skip across decades or centuries to seek support for propositions that often disregard fundamentally different historical contexts. European integration is a process by which states and societies interact over time. This process does not pit unchanging states bent on maximizing fixed objectives, such as security, as some variants of realism have it, or on pursuing national interests determined solely in domestic politics, as other realists argue. Because historical time is more than the repetition of sameness, we cannot afford to overlook sources of change and innovation.

The realist approach to history is illustrated by John Mearsheimer's bold interpretation of the end of the Cold War. In his pessimistic assessment, a new post–Cold War system of European international relations will not emerge for decades. The Cold War will truly end only when the last American soldier has left Europe; it is immaterial whether the intervening period is filled with war or peace in Europe. Consistent with the realist assumption that history is sameness, that throughout the ages states have only sought to maximize their security, Mearsheimer restricts his analysis of history to comparative statics and neglects the dynamics of change. Where, however, the realist assumption is unwarranted or the definition of security does not match physical survival, as is true of Europe after the Cold War, political analysis suffers.[20]

Furthermore, as Elizabeth Pond has pointed out, an integration process that aims at pooling state sovereignty calls into question the very foundation of a realist perspective, where states, locked into a struggle for survival in an anarchic world, seek to defend their existence to the end.[21]

[19] Peter Pulzer, "Nation-State and National Sovereignty," *Bulletin* 17 (London, German Historical Institute, 1995): 9, 13. See also the theoretically sophisticated and comprehensive survey of recent German writings on foreign policy in Gunther Hellmann's, "Goodbye Bismarck? The Foreign Policy of Contemporary Germany," *Mershon International Studies Review* 40 (1996): 1–39, and a series of articles published between April 18 and August 4, 1994, under the heading "What's right" in the *Frankfurter Allgemeine Zeitung*.

[20] John Mearsheimer's original article and some of the debate it elicited are contained in Michael E. Brown, Sean M. Lynn-Jones, and Steven E. Miller, eds., *The Perils of Anarchy: Contemporary Realism and International Security* (Cambridge: MIT Press, 1995). See also John J. Mearsheimer, "The False Promise of International Institutions," *International Security* 19 (Winter 1994/95): 5–49, with a set of rejoinders in the Summer 1995 issue of the same journal.

[21] See Elizabeth Pond's exchange with Kenneth Waltz, "International Politics Viewed from the Ground," *International Security* 19 (Summer 1994): 195–99, and Elizabeth Pond and

Some realists have attempted to explain European integration through the concept of "self-binding," at least for the case of France, but even they remain silent in the face of German foreign policy or abandon neorealist theory when addressing domestic politics.[22] Why is Germany, as Europe's most powerful state, so intent on furthering integration and relinquishing its advantage in relative power and bargaining strength?

Known as "neofunctionalism," the second perspective is a version of political liberalism. It draws attention to the context of integration.[23] European welfare states have a profound effect on how actors, such as interest groups and bureaucracies, define their interests and thus shape the course of the European integration process. What matters primarily is not power but interests. Liberal theory thus focuses not only on governments and states but also on the aggregation of interests in private and transnational actors.

Liberals focusing on the primacy of domestic politics see the driving force not in the condition of international anarchy but in the dynamics of interest formation in domestic politics, the process that translates private interests into public policy. Neoliberals agree with those realists who insist on the primacy of international anarchy. For them, the institutionalization of European integration does not eliminate but civilizes anarchy. Like their domestic analogues, international institutions have this salutary effect through the reduction of uncertainties and the lowering of transaction costs. Because institutions enhance both political predictability and efficiency, they shape the interests of relevant actors in ways that often tend to favor integration. But there is nothing inevitable about this process. The logic of anarchy and exogenous shocks can always override the effects of institutions and lead to a partial or total unraveling of past achievements.

With its powerful insights into important episodes of German unification and European integration in the early 1990s, liberal analysis captures an important strain in German foreign policy.[24] And it also explains some

---

David Schoenbaum, *The 'German Question' and Other German Questions* (New York: St. Martin's Press, 1996).

[22] See especially Joseph M. Grieco, "Understanding The Problem of International Cooperation: The Limits of Neoliberal Institutionalism and the Future of Realist Theory," in David Baldwin, ed., *Neorealism and Neoliberalism: The Contemporary Debate* (New York: Columbia University Press, 1993), p. 338, n. 14; and Joseph M. Grieco, "The Maastricht Treaty, Economic and Monetary Union, and the Neo-Realist Research Programme," *Review of International Studies* 21 (January 1995): 21–40.

[23] David Mutimer, "1992 and the Political Integration of Europe: Neofunctionalism Reconsidered," *Journal of European Integration* 13 (Fall 1989): 75–101.

[24] Hanns W. Maull, "Germany and Japan: The New Civilian Powers," *Foreign Affairs* 69 (Winter 1990–91): 91–106; James Sperling, "German Security Policy after the Cold War: The Strategy of a Civilian Power in an Uncivil World," *Arms Control* 12 (December 1991): 77–98.

of the imperatives that are driving European integration. For example, because they saw European integration as a partial solution to overregulated national markets threatening corporate competitiveness in the global economy, chief executives of large European corporations pushed hard for the initiative to create a single European market by 1992.[25] Pressures for greater efficiency and predictability also came from within the European integration process, rather than from global markets without. In his speeches and articles, former Chancellor Helmut Schmidt used to point out that, when he traveled through the twelve member states of the EU in the early 1990s, exchanging a one-hundred deutsche mark bill each time he crossed national borders would leave him with only fifty deutsche marks at the end of the journey, without his having bought a thing. For reasons of efficiency, the largest corporations tend to favor the creation of the European Monetary Union (EMU), which many envisage as a step to political union, one of the ambitious goals of the TEU.

With their insistence on the efficiency-enhancing effects of institutions, however, liberal analyses confront serious empirical and analytical problems. Although frequently at odds on the issue of European integration, neither the ordinary citizens nor the elites of EU member states view the Brussels bureaucracy as increasing some aggregate measure of political or social efficiency. Indeed, the story of the EU is also a story of the growth of overregulation and institutional inefficiency. It is partly because of Brussels' inefficiency in long-distance governance that opposition to harmonizing divergent national regulatory regimes throughout the EU is growing, even though this inefficiency has not stopped integration.

Analytically, the focus on the efficiency effects of institutions is also problematic. It is a great weakness of neoliberalism, and the branch of institutional economics on which it builds, that, to date, it assumes rather than measures the additional information that institutions provide about the preferences of actors and their record of compliance. If the institutional effects of the EU were actually reducing transaction costs among democratic states in western Europe, rather than increasing them through an oversupply of information, these beneficial effects are likely to be small. Western European societies are democratic and open; extensive media coverage and governmental as well as nongovernmental bureaucracies provide ample information about the preferences of actors and the compliance records of states with international agreements. In short, the important thing about institutions, at least in this setting, is not that they enhance efficiency but that they offer a normative context that constitutes actors and

[25] Wayne Sandholtz and John Zysman, "1992: Recasting the European Bargain," *World Politics* 42 (October 1989): 95–128; Maria Green Cowles, "Setting the Agenda for a New Europe: The European Round Table and EC 1992," *Journal of Common Market Studies* 33 (December 1995): 501–26.

provides a set of norms in which the reputation of actors acquires meaning and value.[26] Furthermore, a library filled with books dealing with the politics of policy implementation has established that, contra liberal theory's neat separation of private from public actors, the European welfare state is defined by the deep mutual penetration of state and society. This finding creates serious analytical difficulties for variants of liberalism that hold autonomous social groups and the private sector chiefly responsible for shaping the preferences that determine government policies in the European integration process.[27]

For example, empirically, the case of German business does not fit liberal expectations. Survey data collected among European business executives indicate that economic and industrial structures shape perceptions of expected gains and losses. Thus support for the 1992 single-market program was strongest among European executives working in export-oriented rather than state-owned sectors.[28] Because of Germany's large export sector, on economic grounds alone, German business support for the single-market initiative should have been particularly strong. But, as Maria Green Cowles explains, "the handful of German companies that did publicly support the 1992 project did so primarily for *non-economic* reasons. They did not tout the Single Market program as an important means to liberalize the market. Rather, the firms endorsed the European project on *political* grounds—they wanted to assure their industrial colleagues that German companies were 'good Europeans' and committed to further integration."[29]

A careful empirical study of the position of a number of German unions on the issue of the European single market also undercuts liberal expec-

[26] The normative aspect of institutions is developed at greater length in Ronald L. Jepperson, Alexander Wendt, and Peter J. Katzenstein, "Norms, Identity, and Culture in National Security," in Katzenstein, *Norms and National Security,* chap. 2. See also the trenchant critique by Wayne Sandholtz, "Rules, Reasons and International Institutions," paper prepared for presentation at the Annual Meeting of the International Studies Association, San Diego, April 15–21, 1996, pp. 2–12.

[27] These analytical difficulties are addressed in a compelling manner by Renate Mayntz and Fritz W. Scharpf, "Der Ansatz des akteurzentrierten Institutionalismus," in Mayntz and Scharpf, eds., *Gesellschaftliche Selbstregelung und Politische Steuerung* (Frankfurt: Campus, 1995), pp. 39–72.

[28] Neil Fligstein and Peter Brantley, "The 1992 Single Market Program and the Interests of Business," Working Paper 1.27, University of California, Center for German and European Studies, Berkeley, December 1994.

[29] Maria Green Cowles, "German Big Business and Brussels: Learning to Play the European Game," Seminar Paper 15, American Institute for Contemporary German Studies, Johns Hopkins University (November 1995), pp. 1–2. Michael G. Huelshoff shares this view in arguing that "German support for 1992 is based mostly on ideological grounds rather than on German interests." See his "German Business and the 1992 Project," in Carl F. Lankowski, ed., *Germany and the European Community: Beyond Hegemony and Containment?* (New York: St. Martin's Press, 1993), p. 23.

tations. Andrei Markovits and Alexander Otto report that the position of the German unions was strongly positive, and that member attitudes were not affected by sectoral variation. "We were surprised," they write, "how relatively insignificant sectoral economic expectations and potential changes, which very well might have concrete effects on the unions' world of collective bargaining, were in shaping the unions' positions."[30] In a situation of uncertainty, ideology shaped position more than concrete economic interests. More generally, "the striking aspect of Germany's stance," writes Elizabeth Pond, "is the regularity with which the popular consensus chooses enlightened, long-term self-interest over short-term gain, especially in European Union (EU) matters."[31]

Liberalism is attuned to recognize historical processes of change. Social interests evolve in response to domestic or international change, and institutions evolve to facilitate different kinds of political bargains. In the 1950s, important segments of German industry were critical of Chancellor Adenauer's policy and not convinced that European economic integration would serve their interests well. Two decades later, in the world of finance, Chancellor Schmidt favored the creation of the European Monetary System (EMS), while the Bundesbank and important elements of German finance did not. Over time, German industry and finance redefined what they considered to be in their interests. European governments, including Germany's, subsequently were free to strike new bargains that defined new focal points for compromise in an increasingly dense environment of European institutions.

This dynamic conception of historical change is an improvement over realism's insistence on history as mere repetition. But all variants of liberalism underestimate seriously the effects institutions have on politics. Bargaining theory typically overlooks a central aspect of all bargaining—the framework or context in which a particular issue should be seen. A richer conception thus emphasizes not only how institutions facilitate bargains among political actors. It also investigates how institutions affect the context of bargaining, primarily through the effects they have on the identities of the political actors who make political choices. In the case of Germany, for example, it is plausible to argue that the European option, which in the 1950s had been a clear instrumental calculation of Chancellor Konrad Adenauer and the business elite, became for Chancellor Kohl, Adenauer's "grandson," and the German business elite in the 1980s an unquestioned assumption of policy. This is not to argue that German policy reflected idealist motives in the 1980s or 1990s. It did not. It reflected Ger-

---

[30] Andrei S. Markovits and Alexander Otto, "German Labor and Europe '92," *Comparative Politics* 24 (January 1992): 169.
[31] Pond, "Germany as a Regional Power," p. 30.

man interests. But those interests, pursued through power and bargaining, were fundamentally shaped by the institutional context of Europe and the Europeanization of the identity of the German state that had taken place in the preceding decades.

This helps explain why it matters so little to the German government that on an issue of vital importance to its export-oriented trade policy, it is in a minority position in the European Union. Klaus Günter Deutsch, for example, calculates that the coalition favoring, with Germany, "open regionalism" controls only 28 votes in the Council of the EU, a clear minority, compared to the 48 votes of the coalition backing "closed regionalism" in the EU's common commercial policy.[32] Similarly, the internationalization of Germany's state identity made it quite natural for the German government to insist in the early 1980s that Siemens, one of Germany's industrial giants and one of its largest semiconductor producers, cooperate with a Dutch firm, Philips, on the submicron circuit technology necessary for the production of advanced memory chips in the government-initiated Megaproject.[33] Institutions make certain political realities more or less natural. That is, they endow them to different degrees with the quality of being taken for granted. In Bonn and Berlin in the 1990s, it appears, Germany's embeddedness in Europe has acquired this aura.

Thus the central insight of a sociologically inclined analysis highlights the importance of "thick" identity-forming effects of institutions, as opposed to their "thin" uncertainty-reducing effects. The first wave of theories of European integration in the 1960s was largely sociological. In mapping the evolution of the social foundations of integration, Karl Deutsch and some of his students analyzed mass interactions and elite attitudes.[34] These studies did not seek to replace intergovernmental and neofunctional explanations. They looked instead at the broader social context that framed and influenced the negotiations between governments and the bargaining among interest groups in Brussels and in national capitals. The conclusions of this research, shaped by the communications theory and behaviorist bent that inform all of Deutsch's work, pointed in two directions. On the one hand, they suggested the growth of a security commu-

[32] Klaus Günter Deutsch, "The Politics of Freer Trade in the European Community, 1985–93," Ph.D. diss., Free University Berlin, June 1995, p. 150.

[33] J. Nicholas Ziegler, *Governing Ideas: Strategies for Innovation in France and Germany* (Ithaca: Cornell University Press, 1997), chap. 5.

[34] Karl W. Deutsch, Lewis J. Edinger, Roy C. Mactidis, and Richard L. Merritt, *France, Germany and the Western Alliance: A Study of Elite Attitudes on European Integration and World Politics* (New York: Scribner's, 1967); Hayward Alker, Jr., and Donald Puchala, "Trends in Economic Partnership: The North Atlantic Area, 1928–1963," in J. David Singer, ed., *Quantitative International Politics: Insights and Evidence* (New York: Free Press, 1968), pp. 287–316; Bruce M. Russett, *International Regions and the International System: A Study in Political Ecology* (Chicago: Rand McNally, 1967).

nity, in western Europe and within the North Atlantic area, that made war highly improbable. On the other, they pointed to structural limitations in European integration. In Deutsch's language, the integration process favored pluralism and loose organizational coupling in pluralistic security communities over homogeneity and tight coupling in amalgamated security communities.[35]

Shorn of behavioralism, the sociological perspective is alive and well in contemporary theories of international relations generally and in the analysis of European integration specifically. In international relations theory, both on questions of national security and political economy, the sociological perspective seeks to link the materialism and rationalism of mainstream theorizing to the processes of communication and social discourse that constitute actors and help define their interests. The analysis of institutional forces has retained an even stronger appeal in the analysis of domestic politics. The "new" institutionalism encompasses a broad array of approaches. Prominent among them is the historical-sociological approach that seeks to understand how institutional norms and identities shape policies and politics.[36] Applied to European integration, a variety of formulations have described and explained in different terminology some of the structures and processes characterizing the acceleration of European integration since the mid-1980s.

Compared to an earlier generation, the language of sociological approaches has changed more than its central message. That message moves to center stage what realist and liberal accounts tend to neglect, a partial pooling of sovereignty into multilevel governance systems that vary by problem area. "Euro-speak" or "Euro-babble" hints at this important shift. It has invented a large number of concepts that describe ad hoc and de jure political solutions to the problems of the EU, among them "subsidiarity," "co-decision," "variable geometry," "opting out" and "opting in," "comitologie," and "concentric circles."[37] John Ruggie sees in the EU a novel

[35] Deutsch et al., *Political Community*.

[36] Peter A. Hall and Rosemary C. R. Taylor, "Political Science and the Three New Institutionalisms," MPIFG Discussion Paper 96/5, Max-Planck Institute, Cologne, 1996; James G. March and Johan P. Olsen, *Democratic Governance* (New York: Free Press, 1995); Sven Steinmo, Kathleen Thelen, and Frank Longstreth, eds., *Structuring Politics: Historical Institutionalism in Comparative Analysis* (New York: Cambridge University Press, 1992); Walter W. Powell and Paul J. DiMaggio, eds., *The New Institutionalism in Organizational Analysis* (Chicago: University of Chicago Press, 1991); George M. Thomas, John W. Meyer, Francisco O. Ramirez, and John Boli, *Institutional Structure: Constituting State, Society, and the Individual* (Newbury Park, Calif.: Sage, 1987).

[37] See Philippe Schmitter, "Speculation about Alternative Futures for the European Polity and their Implications for European Public Policy," paper prepared for presentation at the Conference on Quo Vadis Europa 2000, Center for European and Russian Studies, UCLA, Los Angeles, March 16–19, 1995, pp. 6–7.

international form not well described in the familiar terms of national, intergovernmental, or supranational relations. Because politics no longer starts simply from separate, fixed national viewpoints, the give-and-take by which states are defining their "own identity—and the identities are logically prior to preferences—increasingly endogenize[s] the existence of the other. . . . Within this framework European leaders may be thought of as entrepreneurs of alternative political identities."[38] Viewing the same process from the perspective of Europe, Walter Mattli and Anne-Marie Slaughter find that "in lieu of standard models of the unitary state, the picture that emerges is one of 'disaggregated sovereignty.'"[39]

Building on the English school of international society theorizing, Ole Wæver points out that the European polity emerging on the international scene is both a global competitor and a barrier against a possible remilitarization of intra-European rivalries; this polity is not a state but a socially constituted force in the complex, multilayered politics of Europe.[40] One reason why, in this view, all attempts to integrate Europe as a state are doomed to failure lies in deeply rooted societal insecurities about the future viability of established national and state identities.[41] Hence the integration process is encroaching on national sovereignty without creating a new sovereign unit. And the link between statehood and exclusive territorial control is weakened. From a similar constructivist perspective but with a different twist, Emanuel Adler comes to roughly similar conclusions. Building on the sociological approach of Karl Deutsch and his collaborators, Adler focuses his attention on a historically grounded concept of security communities that can be measured not only through the numerous social indicators Deutsch has ingeniously specified but also through an analysis of changes in discursive practices.[42]

[38] John Gerard Ruggie, "Territoriality and Beyond: Problematizing Modernity in International Relations," *International Organization* 47 (Winter 1993): 172.

[39] Walter Mattli and Anne-Marie Slaughter, "Constructing the European Community Legal System from the Ground Up: The Role of Individual Litigants and National Courts," unpublished paper, Columbia University and Harvard Law School, 1996, p. 3.

[40] Ole Wæver, "Europe's Three Empires: A Watsonian Interpretation of Post-Wall European Security," paper prepared for delivery at the Thirty-sixth Annual Convention of the International Studies Association, February 21–25, 1995. With specific reference to Germany and France, see Ole Wæver, "With Herder and Habermas: Europeanization in the Light of German Concepts of State and Nation," Working Paper 16/1990, Centre for Peace and Conflict Research, Copenhagen, 1990.

[41] Ole Wæver et al., *Identity, Migration and the New Security Agenda in Europe* (New York: St. Martin's Press, 1993).

[42] Emanuel Adler, "Europe's New Security Order: A Pluralistic Security Community," in Beverly Crawford, ed., *The Future of European Security* (Berkeley: University of California, International and Area Studies, Center for German and European Studies, 1992), pp. 287–325; Emanuel Adler, "Seizing the Middle Ground: Constructivism in World Politics," *European Journal of International Relations* (forthcoming).

Philippe Schmitter tries to escape the misplaced dichotomy between national and supranational forms of legitimate governance through his typology of territorial and functional elements in the emergence of polities.[43] Markus Jachtenfuchs and Beate Kohler-Koch examine in greater depth the process of governance in the European polity, which they conceive of as a multilevel system that responds to conditions of an increasing globalization of problems and a growth in transnational systems of governance.[44] And in their writings on European regionalism, Gary Marks and Alberta Sbragia have done much to articulate a similar analytical perspective.[45] In a similar vein, Paul Pierson makes the case for a "historical-institutional" rather than an "intergovernmental" perspective on integration even for issues, such as social welfare, where the European polity has relatively small direct, financial effects. European integration unfolds over time, during which governments, motivated by short-term bargains, face both the ubiquity of the unintended consequences of their actions and the "lock-in" effects of historical trajectories. These consequences and effects make it very costly for national governments to reassert national control. In this historical perspective, European integration results in a fragmented, discernibly multi-tiered European polity.[46]

Finally, Johan Olsen articulates an institutionalist perspective in arguing that the analytical focus on coalition building and policy development normally rests on the implicit assumption, appropriate only for stable periods, that "political processes maintain, rather than change, existing ac-

[43] I am basing this presentation on the most recent iteration of a set of ideas that Schmitter has developed in a series of papers dating back at least to 1990. See, most recently, Philippe Schmitter, "If the Nation-State Were to Wither Away in Europe, What Might Replace It?", unpublished paper, 1996. Schmitter distinguishes territorial constituencies (which are variable or fixed, tangential or contiguous, egalitarian or hierarchical, differentiated or identical, reversible or irreversible) and functional ones (which are variable or fixed, dispersed or cumulative, shared or separate, overlapping or coincident). On the basis of these distinctions, Schmitter delineates four different types of polities: "condominio," "consortio," "conferderatio," and "stato" or "federatio."

[44] Markus Jachtenfuchs and Beate Kohler-Koch, "The Transformation of Governance in the European Union," Working Paper 11, Mannheimer Zentrum für Europäische Sozialforschung, 1995.

[45] Gary Marks, "Structural Policy and Multilevel Governance in the European Community," in Alan W. Cafruny and Glenda Rosenthal, eds., *The State of the European Community* (Boulder, Colo.: Lynne Rienner, 1993), pp. 391–410; Liesbet Hooghe and Gary Marks, "Birth of a Polity: The Struggle over European Integration," unpublished paper; Alberta M. Sbragia, "Thinking about the European Future: The Uses of Comparison," in Alberta M. Sbragia, ed., *Euro-Politics: Institutions and Policymaking in the 'New' European Community* (Washington, D.C.: Brookings, 1992), pp. 257–91; and Gary Marks, Fritz Scharpf, Philippe C. Schmitter, and Wolfgang Streeck, eds., *Governance in the European Union* (Beverly Hills, Calif.: Sage, 1996).

[46] Paul Pierson, "The Path to European Integration: A Historical Institutionalist Analysis," *Comparative Political Studies* 29 (April 1996): 123–63.

tors and institutional and cultural frameworks."[47] But in unstable periods this assumption is problematic because political conflicts and discourse work to fix the boundaries that define a political community as well as the identity of the actors that operate within it. An institutionalist perspective is then necessary to address these important political processes.

While realist and liberal perspectives capture important elements of the manifold relationships between Germany and Europe, they tend to overlook the institutionalization of power that softens much of the hardness in contemporary Europe's international relations. This oversight is not mitigated by the fact that both perspectives are often complementary in their insights. Liberalism's insights can make up for realism's discounting of the importance of domestic politics, transnational relations, and international institutions. Liberalism's neglect of the distributional consequences and power can be complemented by realist accounts. Yet in the analysis of Germany and Europe neither perspective pays sufficient attention to the effects that institutional similarities and the internationalization of state identities have in jointly "softening" "hard" relationships frequently marked by great asymmetries in material power and bargaining positions. That is, they neglect the institutional forces that have transformed a relationship between Germany *and* Europe to one of Germany *in* Europe.

THE INTERNATIONALIZATION OF IDENTITIES: EUROPEAN AND GERMAN

In the fall of 1989, the voices of leading German, European, and U.S. politicians such as Helmut Kohl, Oskar Lafontaine, Hans-Dietrich Genscher, Mikhail Gorbachev, François Mitterrand, and James Baker were seeking to articulate new concepts—such as "unification through association" and a "common European home"—with which to describe this new political reality in often muffled voices. Willy Brandt, Margaret Thatcher, and Henry Kissinger captured these changes with the more familiar political terminology of "national unification" and "national power." Both sets of voices describe important aspects of reality. National power and state interests have not become irrelevant in Europe's new political context. But the Europeanization of that context has itself become very important for how states such as Germany conceive of their national interests, and for how they pursue their political strategies. The title of this chapter conveys the central message of this book. In times of revolutionary change, the ex-

[47] Johan P. Olsen, "Europeanization and Nation-State Dynamics," ARENA Working Paper 9, Oslo, March 1995, p. 2. See also James G. March and Johan P. Olsen, "Institutional Perspectives on Governance," ARENA Reprint 94/2, Oslo, 1994.

tension of a partly internationalized German state is in many German and European quarters accepted as a natural response.[48]

European Collective Identities

State identities are primarily external; they describe the actions of governments in a society of states. National identities are internal; they describe the processes by which mass publics acquire, modify, and forget their collective identities. While national identities in Europe have probably not decreased during the last decades, to date they have not posed an insurmountable barrier to European integration. The permissive consensus among national mass publics is reinforced by the gradual growth of ambiguous and contested collective European identities that are beginning to complement national identities among some social strata. Illustrative examples include cultural policy, language use, currency, citizenship, and anthem as ambiguous symbols of collective identity that mirror in the social sphere the intermingling of a "multiperspectival" polity with "multitiered" governance systems through which traditional state identities have been partly internationalized.

The institutional presence of Europe as a set of norms and a source of collective identity has been the subject of explicit political considerations. For example, the Adonnino committee, debating how to make Europe more accessible to its citizens, in 1985 recommended the extension of student exchanges and an all-Europe TV channel.[49] The Franco-German bicultural "arte" television channel, with an estimated budget of DM 250 million, has broadcast since 1991. Student exchanges have blossomed. Between 1995 and 1999, the EU is planning to spend about $2.5 billion on all types of programs. Student applications for the largest of these programs

[48] In a flood of publications on this topic see, for example, Simon Bulmer and William Paterson, "Germany in the European Union: Gentle Giant or Emergent Leader?" *International Affairs* 72 (January 1996): 9–32; Commission of the European Communities, "The European Community and German Unification," *Bulletin of the European Communities,* Supplement 4/90; Michael Kreile, "Will Germany Assume a Leadership Role in the European Union?" *American Foreign Policy Interests* 17 (October 1995): 11–21; Carl Lankowski, *Germany and the European Community: Beyond Hegemony and Containment?* (New York: St. Martin's Press, 1992); Michael G. Huelshoff, Andrei S. Markovits, and Simon Reich, eds., *From Bundesrepublik to Deutschland: German Politics after Unification* (Ann Arbor: University of Michigan Press, 1993); Jeffrey J. Anderson and John B. Goodman, "Mars or Minerva? A United Germany in a Post–Cold War Europe," in Robert O. Keohane, Joseph S. Nye, and Stanley Hoffmann, eds., *After the Cold War: International Institutions and State Strategies in Europe, 1989–91* (Cambridge: Harvard University Press, 1993), pp. 23–62; Lily Gardner Feldman, "Germany and the EC: Realism and Responsibility," *Annals of the American Academy of Political and Social Science* 531 (January 1994): 25–43. For an earlier era preoccupied with a similar issue, see Karl W. Deutsch and Lewis J. Edinger, *Germany Rejoins the Powers: Mass Opinion, Interest Groups, and Elites in Contemporary German Foreign Policy* (Stanford, Calif.: Stanford University Press, 1959).

[49] See *Europa-Archiv* 22 (1985): D606–21. "Eurolotto" and a "Europe-day" have not yet been adopted.

increased from 3,000 in 1987–88 to 146,000 in 1994–95.[50] And the trade conflict between Europe and the United States over movies and television programming was resolved only in the last hectic hours of the Uruguay Round. Against the wishes of most national governments and the entertainment and media industry, the European Parliament has since demanded more than nonbinding quotas. "Culture is not a commodity," argues Luciana Stellina, the Italian Communist chairing the parliament's culture committee. "What is at stake is the survival of the cultural identity of Europe."[51] And that culture is plural.

In terms of language, for example, Europe is not rationalizing around one standard, as did Spain and France in the eighteenth and nineteenth centuries. Contemporary European integration instead resembles twentieth-century India, with its strong preference for retaining national languages and the growing trend toward globalization.[52] David Laitin contends that a 2±1 standard language repertoire is consolidating in Europe. English is the lingua franca, state languages tenaciously defend their position in the educational systems of EU members, and regional languages have made successful incursions into national language regimes.[53] A European living in southern England will be able to function effectively with one (2–1) language; other Europeans will need command of their mother tongue and English; Europeans living in regions with their own distinctive languages, such as Catalonia or Scotland, will speak three (2+1) languages. In their language use, Europeans are institutionalizing a stable multiple-language regime, which they accept as natural and normal. But this regime is not efficient. States will retain separate state languages in a European and global language regime increasingly centered on English. And about one-third of the European Commission's staff work in translation and interpretation services. This constitutes about two-fifths of the EU's administrative budget, approaching a billion European Currency Units (ECU) annually.[54]

[50] Andrei S. Markovits and Carolyn Höfig, "Germany as a Bridge: German Foreign Cultural Policy in a Changing Europe," paper prepared as part of the seminar series of the American Institute for Contemporary German Studies "Germany's Role in Shaping of the New Europe: Architect, Model, Bridge," Washington, D.C., January 9, 1996, pp. 30–34.

[51] *International Herald Tribune* (February 15, 1996): 1.

[52] See the compelling argument that David Laitin develops in "The Cultural Identities of a European State," paper prepared for delivery at the conference "European Identity and its Intellectual Roots," Harvard University, May 1993, revised July 22, 1994.

[53] Fifty-one percent of the EC citizens reported in 1987 as having learned English, compared with 42 percent for French and 33 percent for German. The percentages of those speaking a foreign language well enough to take part in a conversation are, respectively, 36%, 27%, and 25%. See *Eurobarometer* 28, pp. 76–78. (December 1987): and quoted in Laitin, "Cultural Identities," p. 9.

[54] Laitin, "Cultural Identities," pp. 16–17. Laitin reports data from Florian Coulmas, ed., *A Language Policy for the European Community: Prospects and Quandaries* (Berlin: Mouton de Gruyter, 1991), pp. 22–26. See also Caporaso, "European Union," p. 39.

Much debated in the 1990s, the EMU also has an important symbolic dimension that touches Europe deeply.[55] As with language, the outcome points to multiple collective identities. With German national identity closely linked to the deutsche mark, as is implied in the concept of DM-nationalism, the choice of a name and the look of a future European currency was vigorously contested. While the French favored sticking to the French-sounding "ecu" (identical in sound but not in orthography to the ECU, the European Currency Unit), which they had used several centuries ago, Chancellor Kohl objected because this currency sounded in plain German too much like *Kuh* (cow). For a while, there was talk of calling the new currency a Euro-franken or Euro-franc, a concession to France, and with the association of a stable currency derived from both German history and present Swiss practice. Britain, however, vetoed the idea, dubbing the franken a Frankenstein.

At the December 1995 EU summit meeting in Madrid, the choice was made in favor of the "Euro." The look of the new currency still remains to be decided. The choice of Euro leaves open the possibility of a hyphenated European-national currency, as in "Euro-pound," "Euro-franc" or "Euro–Deutsche mark," and a look for the currency that will somehow integrate the blue colors or design of the European flag. The division of the Euro into cents foreshadows such a solution; countries adopting the common currency will be permitted to put their own designs on one side of the coins.[56] Judging by a number of other institutional practices, such a combination of European and national symbols would be compelling not only for a transitional period but as a long-term solution for a polity in which citizens may retain some aspects of their national currencies in a future EMU. New automobile license plates in Europe are a daily reminder of what a Euro coin might look like. National plates are now adorned with a blue strip on the left-hand side showing both the European emblem, twelve golden stars against a blue background, and the national origin of the car.[57]

[55] *Der Spiegel* 23 (1995): 102; Nathaniel C. Nash, "What Fits in Europe's Wallets?" *New York Times* (July 11, 1995): D1, D5; *Frankfurter Allgemeine Zeitung* (October 30, 1995): 13.

[56] *International Herald Tribune* (April 15, 1996): 13; *Süddeutsche Zeitung* (December 16/17, 1995): 19; *Frankfurter Allgemeine Zeitung* (January 3, 1996): 11. The issue can get very complicated in specific cases. Greece, for example, has been very enthusiastic about the choice of the name "Euro" because of its ancient Greek origins. But a big controversy remains whether the new coins will be inscribed with "Euro" only in Latin letters or also in Greek letters, and, if the latter, whether this will apply only to coins minted in Greece or throughout the EU. I would like to thank Susannah Verney for bringing to my attention the specifics of the Greek case.

[57] The Council of Europe adopted a European flag in 1955, which the European Parliament accepted in 1986: a circle of twelve golden stars on a dark blue background. By accident for some years the membership of the EC also matched the number 12. With the enlargement of the EU to fifteen, the number of stars has not changed. On Berlin's streets in 1996 I saw cars

The new EU passport, issued in identical format and red color, but embossed with the names of the different member states, is another example of the same practice. Arriving at European airports and having to stand in longer and slower queues, travelers who are not citizens of a EU member state quickly notice that European citizenship has become a practical reality, even though the Europeanization of border controls remains one of the most controversial aspects of the European integration process in the 1990s.[58] Social and economic rights that were once restricted only to national citizens are gradually being extended to immigrants.[59] And movement toward a European citizenship that is partly distinct from national citizenship has become a definite possibility.[60]

The adoption of the "Ode to Joy" finale to Beethoven's Ninth Symphony as Europe's anthem points in the same direction.[61] A well-known publicist for European unity in the interwar period, Count Coudenhove-Kalergie, had in 1949 been one of the first to suggest the "Ode to Joy" as a possible anthem. Between 1952 and 1964, East and West Germany used the "Ode" as their joint victory hymn at the Olympic Games. Overcoming a number of potential rivals, the "Ode" gradually established itself as the most widely accepted European hymn, especially in local communities. Building on many unsolicited, private suggestions, the Council of Europe made its first formal plea for an official European anthem in June 1971. The 1971 resolution recommended the tune of the "Ode," without the words, as Europe's anthem.[62] Herbert von Karajan was commissioned to make the musical arrangements and provided them in 1972 for orchestra and brass.

---

from Poland, Ukraine, and Hungary that had also added the EU symbol to their national plates, probably a combination of a political statement and a good way to get on the right side of the German police.

[58] On passports, see Antje Wiener, "European Citizenship: Practice and Parameters of a New Policy," Ph.D. diss., Carleton University, September 1995; John Torpey, "'The Surest Thermometer of Freedom': The Evolution of Passport Controls in Europe," unpublished paper, Badia Fiesolana, San Domenico (FI), European University, February 1996; and Reiner Luyken, "Ihren Pass, bitte!" *Die Zeit* 37 (September 17, 1993): 24.

[59] Yasemin Nuhoğlu Soysal, *Limits of Citizenship: Migrants and Postnational Membership in Europe* (Chicago: University of Chicago Press, 1994).

[60] Paul Close, *Citizenship, Europe and Change* (London: Macmillan, 1995). Because of the long-standing differences in the policy of recognizing nationality based on place of birth, as in Britain or France, or on descent, as in Germany, the possibility of recognizing a distinctly European citizenship is more remote for Germany than for other states. For an analytically sophisticated comparative treatment of this question, see Jeffrey Checkel, "International Norms and Domestic Institutions: Identity Politics in Post–Cold War Europe," paper prepared for delivery at the 1995 Annual Meeting of the American Political Science Association, Chicago, August 30–September 3, 1995.

[61] My discussion here follows Caryl Clark, "Forging Identity: Beethoven's 'Ode' as European Anthem," *Critical Inquiry* 23 (Summer 1997).

[62] Clark, "Confronting Ninth," p. 9.

In 1986, the European Parliament took "formal note of the current practice concerning the European anthem" in the hope that it and other symbols would "strengthen the concept of European identity."[63] Although the issue of language was not explicitly debated, the tune was consigned to wordlessness, not so much because of the global rather than regional appeal of Schiller's verses, but because of the simple, widely understood, and undebated fact that this was a German-language text.[64] Reflecting on the ambiguities surrounding the adoption of this anthem, Clark concludes, "here was truly a bastard-child of the Enlightenment: a song without words; hope without a text . . . at a basic level the Council of Europe acted out of ignorance, was seduced by commercialism, fell prey to an ideology which espoused the superiority of German music, and (unwittingly or not) succumbed to the powerful force exerted by the Beethoven myth itself."[65]

The wordlessness of the European anthem speaks volumes about the ambiguities created by the regional, national, European, and international admixture of elements that constitute an evolving collective European identity. The weakness of the European media, European public discourse, and the European Parliament point to the fact that the European polity is not a democratic state-in-becoming that currently suffers from a democratic deficit. Rather, its system of multilevel governance reflects primarily a transnational growth of public and private bureaucracies. This constrains the growth of a European collective identity and guarantees the persistence of strong national and subnational identities in an integrating Europe. Europe's collective identity has been sustained by a permissive consensus among mass publics and by a strong commitment among political and social elites. Just as Beethoven continued to rework the ending to his Ninth Symphony, so, too, are European states continuously reworking a collective identity, which now contains more international elements, in particular in Germany, than it has at any time in this century.

Internationalizing German State Identity

Symbols of collective identity contain a diversity of national and international elements. In Britain and France, for example, traditional national and state identities are much stronger than in Germany, where collective identities have changed many times; in the decade preceding unification,

---

[63] European Parliament, Document A 2–0104/88 (June 9, 1988), pp. 7, 9, as quoted in Clark, "Confronting Ninth," p. 12.

[64] Sometimes even Beethoven's music is associated with nationality. During the 1996 European soccer cup games, BBC was heavily criticized for its choice of a German tune for a British-based tournament. BBC had been too European in thinking of the "Ode" not as a German tune but as the European anthem. See *Sun* (May 27, 1996): 4.

[65] Clark, "Confronting Ninth," pp. 13, 15.

for example, the "Federal Republic" was already often equated with Germany in common parlance. German receptivity for ambiguous identities that incorporate new, internationalized forms is arguably greater than British or French. Thus, as Klaus Goetz observes, "the Europeanisation of the German state makes the search for the national, as opposed to the European, interest a fruitless task. The national and the European interest have become fused to a degree which makes their separate consideration increasingly impossible."[66] That Germany's Europeanization serves Germany's broad interests, as first Simon Bulmer and then (with modifications) Jeffrey Anderson contend in chapters 2 and 3, reinforces the important point that, far from undermining interests, institutions are of critical importance in helping to shape the conceptions of interests that inform policy in Germany and elsewhere.

Between 1949 and 1990, Germany's division and European integration were closely connected in a Cold War setting. Within the context of the U.S. security guarantee for West Berlin, the Federal Republic, and Europe, West Germany's integration into Europe was, in Germany and in Europe, a calculated reaction to historical memories of the disastrous consequences of Germany's bid for European and global supremacy in the first half of the twentieth century. The gradual fading of these memories and the sudden end of the Cold War posed once again the issue of how a united Germany should relate to Europe. The answer, before and after 1989–90, was the same—through European integration.

Constitutive politics in the EU, Simon Bulmer tells us in chapter 2, mediates German power. Rare in contemporary Europe is what Bulmer calls "deliberative" power, a direct international projection of German interest and power, as for example in the rules for the European Central Bank (ECB). The Bundesbank's high-interest-rate policy soon after unification is instead an instance of "unintentional power" that had strong effects on Germany's European neighbors. The economic consequences of German unification thus illustrates how Germany exercises power not so much strategically as by its sheer weight. Finally, what matters most often is Germany's "indirect institutional" power. In shaping the rules of the game, Germany tends to mobilize a bias favoring its policy in the long term. Indirect power eventually translates into regulative power. This is generally evident, Bulmer notes, in the constitutional politics of the EU, as well as in some of its specific governance regimes.

Indirect institutional effects derive partly from similarities. For example, multitiered governance arrangements are very typical of both the EU and Germany. To be sure, lacking an accretion of power at the top, the Euro-

[66] Klaus Goetz, "Integration Policy in a Europeanized State: Germany and the Intergovernmental Conference," *Journal of European Public Policy* 3 (1996): 40.

pean version of "cooperative federalism" resembles Germany's only super-ficially. The importance of legal institutions in the EU flows from the weak-ness, not the strength, of the state administration; the EU commands only a very small fraction of the financial resources that are at the disposal of the German government; and the European Commission does not have access to a field system of administration. More importantly, enveloped by strong legal institutions, both the EU and Germany have many multitiered governance arrangements that institutionalize consultative bargaining and consensual decision-making procedures between different centers that are jointly involved in deliberation, decision and implementation.

It is noteworthy, Jeffrey Anderson observes in chapter 3, that German political elites initially embraced the European Community as a means for reestablishing Germany's national sovereignty. Subsequently, Germany used its sovereign power to project onto its European partners a markedly different, internationalized state identity. The signing of the Maastricht treaty, however, may have been a high point of Germany's internationalization. This is illustrated by the increasing importance of the *Länder* for some policy issues and by the limits that the Federal Constitutional Court's 1993 judgment imposed on possible future constitutional reforms of the EU.

Germany's indirect institutional power, Bulmer argues further, is rein-forced by the agenda-setting role that it has played in the European Coun-cil. The Council provides for biannual summit meetings of the EU's heads of state. It combines elements of intergovernmentalism, cooperation, and supranationalism through, respectively, the institutions of the Common Foreign and Security Policy (CFSP), Justice and Home Affairs (JHA), and the Council of the EU and the Committee of Permanent Representatives.

Chancellors Helmut Schmidt and Helmut Kohl, as well as Foreign Min-ister Hans-Dietrich Genscher, have played central roles in the European Council: in launching the idea of the EMS during the 1978 Copenhagen summit; in the initial outline of the budget compromise and the Solemn Declaration for the longer-term prospects for European integration at the Stuttgart summit in June 1983; in relaunching the EMU at the Han-nover summit in June 1988; and in the joint letter that Chancellor Hel-mut Kohl and President François Mitterrand sent in April 1990 to the Council's Irish president calling for an intergovernmental conference on political union to parallel the proposed EMU. Significantly, Germany started none of these initiatives on its own. Typically, it cooperated with France, and occasionally with Italy, and thus avoided the temptation of try-ing to set the European agenda unilaterally. Indeed, when Germany found itself isolated, as it did unexpectedly in its opposition to the MacSharry proposals for reforming the Common Agricultural Policy (CAP) in 1991–

92, German officials described the situation as "unacceptable" and made a drastic, last-minute change in policy.

Germany's internationalist orientation is reflected, after the early 1960s, in its consistently strong support of successive enlargements of the EU. In the late 1950s and early 1960s, Chancellor Konrad Adenauer and Economics Minister Ludwig Erhard were still divided over the benefits of a "smaller" Europe, integrated around Germany and France, and of a "larger" Europe, more loosely structured to include Britain and most of the other European Free Trade Association (EFTA) members. But from then on, Germany was a strong supporter of enlargement: British, Danish, and Irish accession in the 1970s, the joining of the three Mediterranean states in the 1980s, and the proposed eastern enlargement of the EU by the end of the 1990s. Put differently, in line with the internationalization of the identity of the German state after World War II, Germany's approach to European institutions since the 1960s has been based on a broad definition of European identity.

Without touching on Germany's underlying strong commitment to multilateralism or a long-term definition of its political interests, Jeffrey Anderson notes in chapter 3 that unification has had noticeable effects on Germany's European policy.[67] Underneath the "soft" power of constitutive politics, in the area of regulative politics newer, "hard" economic interests express serious, internal resource scarcities. They are beginning to supplant older, "hard" political interests that had aimed at the general stabilization of Germany's external environment. This shift has disturbed what Anderson calls a "comfortable equilibrium" that existed between constitutive and regulative politics before 1990. In four case studies (the Common Agricultural Policy or CAP, foreign trade, competition, and structural funds), Anderson illustrates the full range of Germany's response to changed circumstances. Because they absorb three-quarters of the EU budget, the areas covered in these cases are substantively important. Anderson concludes that, since 1992, the German government has tended to look much more closely at the bottom line, paying more attention to who gets what. This is not surprising. Germany is by far the largest net contributor to the EU budget, measured both in absolute and per capita terms. While unification has made Germany drop from the second to the seventh rank in the per capita income of the EU members, its net contribution has increased from DM 10.5 billion in 1987 to DM 22.0 billion in 1992, and is estimated to rise to DM 30.0 billion by 1997. A German household with four members paid about DM 2,000 in 1993–94 for the EU,

---

[67] See also Jeffrey J. Anderson, *Unification and Union: The Domestic Sources of Germany's European Policy* (forthcoming).

more than the special solidarity tax levied after unification.[68] By 1996, Germany's financial contribution to the EU amounted to about two-thirds of the net revenue of the EU, double its share of the combined GDP of the EU; Germany's annual excess payment of about $9 billion, the leaders of all major parties agreed, would have to stop.[69]

This shift reflects new conditions at home and abroad and increases the weight of short-term interests in German policy. The issue that is likely to reflect this new condition most clearly is the eastern enlargement of the EU. Germany favors enlargement more strongly than any of the other main powers in the EU. But for enlargement to work, the EU and Germany will have to allocate additional funds. Considering Germany's postunification budgetary and economic difficulties, playing the accustomed role of Europe's paymaster will become increasingly difficult.[70] Enlarging Europe toward the east and paying off the southern European countries, which worry over a shift in the EU's funding priorities, will seriously test established patterns of conducting political business in Europe. Budgetary conditions thus are likely to dictate the pace and direction of Europe's future enlargement. This change in Germany's traditional stance will rob the European polity of a traditional, important shock absorber.

The evolving relationship that has placed Germany in Europe during the last forty years has been furthered greatly by a transformation of Germany's nationalist and neo-Nazi right. The dynamics of party competition in the Federal Republic, reinforced by the electoral strategy of the Christian Democratic Union/Christian Social Union (CDU/CSU), led in the 1950s to the gradual absorption of a traditional nationalist protest vote by refugees and former Nazis into a staunchly anti-Communist conservative camp that favored European integration. The revival of a neo-Nazi right in the mid-1960s was no more than a brief interlude. The alarming increase of neo-Nazi social movements, like the skinheads, with their xenophobic and racist violence directed against foreigners in the 1990s, had little resonance among the established political parties or major institutions in society. After Chancellor Kohl reacted to these attacks with a thunderous si-

[68] Deutsche Bundesbank, *Monatsbericht* (November 1993), pp. 61–65. *Der Spiegel* 47 (1994): 29.

[69] "Grössere Ausgewogenheit angestrebt," *Frankfurter Allgemeine Zeitung* (July 22, 1996): 5.

[70] The best data available suggest that the four Visegrad states (Poland, Hungary, the Czeck and Slovak Republics) would need between 60 and 90 percent of the annual 18 billion ECU transfer flowing in the mid-1990s from the structural and cohesion funds to the four Mediterranean member states of the EU. Economic growth in central Europe during the coming years and cutbacks in Germany's bilateral economic assistance may reduce transfer payments in a few years' time to perhaps below the annual estimate of 10–16 billion ECU. See András Inotai, "From the Association Agreements to Full Membership? The Dynamics of Relations between the Central and Eastern European Countries and the European Union," paper presented at the Fourth Biennial International Conference of the European Community Studies Association, May 11–14, 1995, Charleston, South Carolina, p. 13.

lence, it was countered by a largely spontaneous social movement and an eventual crackdown by the *Länder* governments.

Finally, it is a happy accident of German history that the post-Communist Party of Democratic Socialism (PDS), absorbs in the five new *Länder* not only the votes of old Communists but also of most of those who normally would vote for a protest party on the Right. Hence despite extraordinarily high unemployment rates and totally disorienting changes, a nationalist Right has been unable to draw sizable popular support in the new eastern *Länder* of the Federal Republic. History, institutions, strategy, and luck all have left Germany with an extreme Right that is weak, if measured by the standards of other European states such as France, Belgium, and Italy. This fact has enhanced the trust of other European states in German politics and policies. And it has created space for an expansion of the international elements that have gradually become part of Germany's identity as a state. Hence developments inside Germany and in Europe have run parallel, not just in terms of government policy and transactions in markets, but also in the institutions that constitute the identity of political actors and prescribe norms of conduct that help define their political interests.

Internationalization of European State Identities

The Europeanization of state identities extends well beyond Germany. The European model that helped shape Germany after 1945, at various times and in various places, has been important also for other states that have had to make a transition from authoritarian to democratic government. For these European states, a "return to Europe" seems more natural, for example, than for the United States, which was reattached to Europe in the late 1940s through the deliberate ideological construction of a "North Atlantic" region. Numerous examples illustrate this point.

After the colonels had relinquished power in 1974, for example, beyond all reasons of national security and normal politics, Greece was helped in its rejoining Europe by being widely viewed as the foundational civilization of Europe. In this historical construction, it mattered little that for centuries Greece had been part of the Ottoman Empire and that the structure of the Greek state was not well suited to the European integration process.[71] Similarly, during their transition from autocracy to democ-

---

[71] This is not to deny the importance of political conflicts over identity inside Greece. Historically, such conflicts occur between those who assign primary importance to the ancient rationalism of the Hellenic civilization as an ideological pathway to Europe, on the one hand, and those wishing to explore Orthodoxy and the dream of Constantinople and a Balkan or Middle Eastern identity of Greece, on the other. See Susanne Hoeber Rudolph, "Dehomogenizing Religious Formations," in Susanne Hoeber Rudolph and James Piscatori, eds., *Transnational Religion and Fading States* (Boulder, Colo.: Westview Press), p. 245. In the 1970s and 1980s, political debates centered on Greece's competing west European, Balkan, and national roles. I thank Susannah Verney for this clarification.

racy in the 1970s, Portugal and, in particular, Spain de-emphasized their traditional Iberian–Latin American identity and, for domestic and international reasons, highlighted their European role instead.[72] And after the revolution of 1989–90, the central European democracies are looking to "Europe" more than to any other model for their domestic politics and international relations. This is true not only in terms of general ideological orientation but, specifically, for human rights and political citizenship, which are more strongly institutionalized at the regional level in Europe than in any other world region. German policy has been highly sympathetic toward these efforts at political reform and reorientation among the southern and central-eastern European states, for after 1945, this was precisely the European path that Chancellor Konrad Adenauer and his successors had charted for the Federal Republic.

European collective identities are also defined negatively. To be European in southern France and Spain means not to be from North Africa, and in eastern Germany, not to be from central-eastern Europe. Which is to say, European identity contains a good dose of xenophobia. Turkey, for example, is arguably less "European" than Greece in its geography, history, and current political practices. Hence it has had a much more difficult time negotiating terms by which it, too, could be part of the European integration process. Beyond history, where the European powers moved to block the western expansion of the Ottoman Empire, Europe's collective, Christian identity has been intimately bound up with the perception of Turkey as something alien to Europe.[73]

Russia occupies an even more important position for post–Cold War Europe. Will Russia stretch from Vladivostok to San Francisco, from the Urals to the Atlantic, or only to the near abroad? Because Russian identities remain still tied primarily to an empire lost, rather than a state gained, Europeans are watching Russian domestic politics carefully. An international or European Russia would diminish and a nationalist Russia would increase the external pressure for a further development of a collective European identity, especially in central Europe.[74] The political conflicts about how Russia should relate to Europe will have profound influence on the depth of collective European identity.

"Europe" stands not only for formal human and democratic rights. It also expresses a substantive commitment to human welfare in capitalist markets. For this, the Germans have coined the term *social market economy*. It was

[72] Michael P. Marks, *The Formation of European Policy in Post-Franco Spain* (Brookfield, Vt.: Avebury, 1996).

[73] Iver B. Neumann and Jennifer Welsh, "The Other in European Self-Definition: An Addendum to the Literature on International Society," Norsk Utenrikspolitisk Institutt (Norwegian Foreign Policy Institute) Paper 445, Oslo, May 1991.

[74] Iver B. Neumann, *Russia and the Idea of Europe* (London: Routledge, 1996); idem, "Russia as Central Europe's Constituting Other," *East European Politics and Societies* 7 (Spring 1993): 349–69.

first articulated by the Freiburg school of economics and implemented in the 1950s, most importantly with the indexation of social security payments in 1957, thus eliminating the structural poverty that afflicted the old in earlier German welfare regimes. Since then, the institutions of the welfare state have had a phenomenal success throughout Europe.

At no place has the power of this state identity been more evident than in Germany. The unification process illustrates that collective assertion has given way to individual entitlement. Sensing this momentous change, Chancellor Kohl did not promise the Germans what the economic expertise of the Bundesbank was telling him: blood, sweat, and tears. Instead, he promised the German voters business as usual: national unification without individual sacrifice. Combined with a by now firmly anchored welfare state identity, this nationalism of individual entitlement typifies not only Germany but all western European states.

The process of a Europeanization of state identity has been considerably weaker in France and Britain than in Germany. Prime Minister Thatcher's persistent and public and President Mitterrand's wavering and covert opposition to Germany unification in 1989–90 are a reflection of this important fact. But it was France, rather than Germany or the smaller European democracies, that accelerated the European integration process in the 1980s. Once it had recognized that national strategies were becoming too costly, France turned toward Europe as the most promising way for defending a now redefined, more international identity. Put bluntly, France was prepared to sacrifice a measure of control in Paris in expectation of gaining new instruments of control in Brussels. France has thus begun to follow what had become Germany's postwar foreign policy strategy: seeking to regain national sovereignty through international integration. The end of the Cold War and German unification reinforced Germany's traditional and France's newfound stance. Hence the SEA, the TEU, and moves toward the creation of an EMU were carried forth by a strong French-German consensus on the advantages that derive from a more international definition of state identities and interests.[75]

In contrast to France, Britain has had a more distant relation to Europe. The traditional identity of being a global power and a victor in World War II has made it harder to accept Britain's descent to the position of an important medium-sized state in Europe. The special partnership with the United

[75] David R. Cameron, "National Interest, the Dilemmas of European Integration, and Malaise," in John T. S. Keeler and Martin A. Schain, eds., *Chirac's Challenge: Liberalization, Europeanization, and Malaise* (New York: St. Martin's Press, 1996), pp. 325–82; idem, "Transnational Relations and the Development of European Economic and Monetary Union," in Thomas Risse-Kappen, ed., *Bringing Transnational Relations Back In: Non-State Actors, Domestic Structures, and International Institutions* (Cambridge: Cambridge University Press, 1995), pp. 37–78; and Gregory Flynn, ed., *Remaking the Hexagon: The New France in the New Europe* (Boulder, Colo.: Westview Press, 1995).

States retains a strong hold over British policy, reflected in Britain's adamant opposition to developing a common security and foreign policy
within the EU. The Europeanization of British identity is undercut also by
the traditional British role of playing off one European state against another from a position of splendid isolation. And British politicians are
deeply committed to maintaining national sovereignty and to protecting
Parliament's power as the guarantor of British democracy. Furthermore,
many of Britain's economic interests remain global (for example, direct foreign investments and financial services, which are totally separate from the
EU; and oil, which the EU imports and Britain exports), or are a source of
profound financial and political irritation (for example, agriculture). For
numerous reasons, then, Britain's relation to Europe has remained awkward.[76] The United Kingdom's halfhearted commitment to an integrated
Europe stems from the prospect of a diminished global rather than an enhanced national role.

By contrast, Germany and some of the smaller European states have
embraced Europe as a means of strengthening and projecting existing
state identities. "Hence for many states," Brigid Laffan concludes, "there
has been a high degree of compatibility between the national project and
European integration."[77] This difference in orientation is both reflected
in and reinforced by an internationalization of Germany's position in European and Atlantic institutions that is more far-reaching than France's
or Britain's. France has become a strong supporter of European integration
while taking a cautious attitude towards NATO and the role of the United
States in European defense matters. Britain is deeply divided over the issue of European integration but remains an avid supporter of NATO. In
contrast to both Britain and France, Germany's position has been to further political integration in Europe, specifically by enhancing the power
of the European Parliament and by extending the principle of qualified
majority voting. And Germany has not lacked in its fervor for NATO. The
first survey of the German elite taken since the end of the Cold War showed,
as Ronald Asmus writes, that "today's German leaders are overwhelmingly
pro-European Union and pro-NATO; strongly favor enlargement to Eastern Europe, are sober about Russia's future, and are increasingly willing
to deploy the Bundeswehr under a NATO flag in 'out of area' missions to
defend common Western interests."[78]

---

[76] S. George, *An Awkward Partner: Britain in the European Community*, 2d ed. (Oxford: Oxford University Press, 1994); S. George, ed., *Britain and the European Community: The Politics of
Semi-Detachment* (Oxford: Clarendon Press, 1992).

[77] Brigid Laffan, "The Politics of Identity and Political Order in Europe," *Journal of Common
Market Studies* 34 (March 1996): 87.

[78] Ronald D. Asmus, "In Germany, the Leadership's Vision Goes Beyond the Border," *International Herald Tribune* (April 12, 1996): 10.

German political controversies concern which international context to choose, the United Nations for peacekeeping operations, as the center-left prefers, or NATO for peace enforcement, as the center-right maintains. That the context for military action must be international is, however, beyond dispute in Germany. This is true neither of the unabashedly realist approach with which Britain seeks to defend its national sovereignty against an encroaching European Union nor of the instrumental-institutionalist one with which France seeks to defend national interests using supranational instruments. Only Germany is a strong supporter of both the EU and NATO and appears ready to push ahead with a deepening institutionalization of Europe. Germany, writes Elizabeth Pond, "is thoroughly European in a way that none of its allies yet is. Germany is increasingly comfortable with its role as a medium-sized power. It no longer aspires either to be a big, cuddly Switzerland abstaining from Europe, or to any more global reach. It has found its niche."[79]

An institutional perspective on Germany's place in Europe does not have to neglect the effects of power and interest. Institutional effects shape identities and thus help define actor interests that inform the exercise of material power and efforts to coordinate conflicting objectives. An institutional perspective highlights how institutions connect national and international levels and thus avoids reifying analytical distinctions. It does not negate the importance of power but inquires into the meaning of power. It does not disregard actors but inquires into the political processes that define their identities and thus condition their political choices. It does not overlook interests but examines how they are defined. And it draws our attention to the importance of both historical time and the possibility of change.

INSTITUTIONAL SIMILARITIES: EUROPE'S ASSOCIATED SOVEREIGNTY AND GERMANY'S SEMISOVEREIGNTY

The hard edges of power relations between Germany and Europe are also softened by the overlap of competencies that characterize the institutionalization of power relations within each. Although distinctive, the institutional practices that mark the European polity resemble Germany's on this score. The system of governance in the European polity is based on what one might call "associated sovereignty," pooled competencies in overlapping domains of power and interest, which is characteristic also of Germany's "semisovereign" state.[80]

---

[79] Pond, "Germany as a Regional Power," p. 38.
[80] Peter J. Katzenstein, *Policy and Politics in West Germany: The Growth of a Semisovereign State* (Philadelphia: Temple University Press, 1987).

The overlapping of competencies and powers that mark different European governance systems resembles the politics of the smaller European states and Germany more than those of France or Britain. In some instances, such as the strong political role of the judiciary, this is the result of German and European developments that have happened to run parallel. In others, such as the blueprints for an independent European Central Bank (ECB) committed to the goal of price stability, the assertion of German power has been crucial. And there are numerous instances of institutions that fall between sheer coincidence and strategic calculations backed by power. More than thirty "Euroregions," for example, express a political commitment to the principle of subsidiarity and the strength of local and regional interests. The formal institutions of the EU—the Council of the EU (formerly the Council of Ministers), the European Commission, the European Parliament, and the European Court of Justice—are hybrids that share powers with national governments and with each other.[81]

As representative of the national governments, the EU's general and twenty-two specialized councils deal, respectively, with foreign policy and a variety of specialized issues.[82] The Council of Ministers is assisted by the Committee of Permanent Representatives (COREPER). Although the councils have many executive prerogatives, they are also the most important legislative body of the EU. In the execution of policy, the councils are linked closely to national bureaucracies; they are arenas for the creation of transgovernmental coalitions. And because they deal with mostly technical issues, the councils also provide access to the committees of the European Parliament and interest groups operating at national and, increasingly, at European levels. Furthermore, the Council of the EU is involved in policy implementation through "management" committees on which some of its members sit and which operate by weighted voting. Operating mostly by consensus, the councils shroud their proceedings in a secrecy that reinforces the democratic deficit characterizing EU institutions at large. In their political practice, they illustrate how in the EU power is combined across different levels of governance and among different centers of power.

[81] Some of the best analyses of the European polity include Robert O. Keohane and Stanley Hoffmann, eds., *The New European Community: Decisionmaking and Institutional Change* (Boulder, Colo.: Westview Press, 1991); Sbragia, ed., *Euro-Politics;* Jeffrey J. Anderson, "The State of the (European) Union: From Single Market to Maastricht, from Singular Events to General Theories," *World Politics* 47 (April 1995): 441–65; Helen Wallace and William Wallace, eds., *Policy-Making in the European Union,* 3d ed. (Oxford: Oxford University Press, 1996); Nicholas Colchester and David Buchan, *Europower: The Essential Guide to Europe's Economic Transformation in 1992* (London: Economist Books, 1992).

[82] The TEU has put the EU's general and specialized councils under the jurisdiction of the Council of the EU, which comprises also the second and third pillars of the EU, dealing with issues of external and internal security. Martin Westlake, *The Council of the European Union* (New York: Stockton, 1995).

With its twenty members meeting as a cabinet, the European Commission acts in concert with the Council of the EU.[83] It supervises the 13,000 civil servants who work in Brussels, and initiates most important legislation. Issued largely in the form of regulations and decisions, the total legislative output of the Commission more than doubled between 1970 and 1987, from 3,209 to 8,471 items.[84] The Commission also supervises implementation by member states but does not act as an enforcement agency.[85] Commissioners are appointed by their national governments; the Commission often relies on the expertise of national bureaucracies, both in the development of new policies and in the implementation of existing ones. And because it seeks also to lessen its dependence on national governments, it is also a voracious consumer of information provided by nongovernmental sources. Thus the institutional practices of the Commission reflect a merging of legislative and executive as well as supranational and national power.

Between 1985 and 1994, Jacques Delors was at the helm of the European Commission and arguably its most important President since 1957. The Delors team's approach was, in the words of François Lamoreux, a "Russian doll" strategy: "You take the first doll apart and then, inside is another one, which leads you to another and so on . . . until it is too late to turn back."[86] Delors's ambition went beyond the liberalization embodied in the Single European Act (SEA). He was interested in advancing the institutionalization of the European polity along several fronts. German unification presented both a great challenge and an opportunity. Delors welcomed unification without any hesitation, and he worked hard and successfully at facilitating the early integration of the five new *Länder* into the EC. "The wisdom of Delors's course on Germany," writes George Ross, "seemed self-evident. A Germany anchored at the center of the EC was the *sine qua non* of the Community's future."[87]

---

[83] Geoffrey Edwards and David Spence, *The European Commission* (New York: Stockton, 1994).

[84] The 1987 numbers refer to roughly equal numbers of regulations and decisions, overwhelmingly issued by the European Commission, not the Council of the EU, formerly the Council of Ministers; the Council of the EU issued two-thirds of the sixty-three directives. See Peter Ludlow, "The European Commission," in Keohane and Hoffmann, eds., *New European Community*, p. 100.

[85] In 1992 the European Commission sent 1,210 letters of formal notice, issued 248 reasoned opinions, and brought 64 cases before the European Court of Justice. See Tenth Annual Report to the European Parliament on Commission Monitoring of the Application of Community Law 1992, COM(93) 320 final, April 28, 1993. I thank Simon Bulmer for providing me with these data.

[86] Jacques Delors, quoted in George Ross, *Jacques Delors and European Integration* (New York: Oxford University Press, 1995), p. 39.

[87] Ross, *Jacques Delors*, p. 49.

The members of the European Parliament, elected directly since 1979, caucus along ideological rather than national lines.[88] But the Parliament's power has remained largely advisory. It can delay actions, and it has the right to impeach members of the Commission. But its power is restricted to the approval of noncompulsory spending items, which amount to only about two-fifths of the European budget. It is excluded from exercising any significant budgetary control over the largest item, agriculture. The absence of a European public and media, of strong transnational links between parties, and of important issues to be decided in European electoral politics explains why elections to the European Parliament are often plebiscites on unrelated national issues, rather than on the substance of the European polity.

The cooperation and assent procedures introduced by the SEA have, however, considerably enhanced the power of the European Parliament.[89] The result has been an intensification of bargaining within the Parliament prior to the introduction of proposals by the EU Council or Commission and thus a partial merging of legislative and executive powers. In the eyes of the German government, though not of the French or British, these reforms fall far short of remedying the democratic deficit of the EU. Any future evolution of the powers of the European Parliament is likely to derive largely from the forging of stronger links between it and national legislatures. Parliamentary practice thus brings together legislative and executive powers and, more weakly, national and supranational elements of power.

The European Court of Justice is marked by judicial activism.[90] The Court's judicial identity shields it from political interference as it pursues

[88] The European Parliament's smaller parties, however, look at times more like a conglomerate with somewhat similar leanings than corporate actors subscribing to a similar world view. I thank Beate Kohler-Koch for pointing this out to me. See also Richard Corbett, Francis Jacobs, and Michael Shackleton, *The European Parliament,* 3d ed. (New York: Stockton, 1995).

[89] The cooperation procedure stipulates that for two-thirds of the proposals contained in the Single European Act, on a second reading the European Parliament can amend or reject a European Commission proposal with 50 percent of the votes. If the Commission agrees with the Parliament, the EU Council can override that Parliamentary vote only with a unanimous vote of its own; if the Commission disagrees, the Council can override with a simple majority vote. The assent procedure requires that the Parliament must agree to any future enlargement of the EU through full or associate members, as well as to certain trade agreements. The TEU institutionalized the co-decision procedure, which has tended to further increase the power of the parliament.

[90] J. H. H. Weiler, "The Transformation of Europe," *Yale Law Journal* 100 (June 1991): 2403–84; Thijmen Koopmans, "The Birth of European Law at the Crossroads of Legal Traditions," *American Journal of Comparative Law* 39 (Summer 1991): 493–507; Francis Snyder, "The Effectiveness of European Community Law: Institutions, Processes, Tools, and Techniques," *Modern Law Review* 56 (January 1993): 19–54; Anne-Marie Burley and Walter Mattli, "Europe before the Court: A Political Theory of Legal Integration," *International Organization* 47 (Winter 1993): 41–76. See also a series of working papers written under the auspices of the European University Institute, Badia Fiesolana, San Domenico (FI), for the project

its objectives. In contrast, courts and executives at the national level openly contest the institutional prerogative to define the balance of power among government institutions and the pace, scope, and manner of integrating a European polity.[91] The Commission's right to sue member states (Article 169), the right of member states to sue each other (Article 170), and the Court's right to review the legality of all actions taken by the EU Council and the Commission (Article 173) aim at securing compliance with the obligations of the Treaty of Rome. But it is the principal task of the Court to enforce a uniform interpretation and application of European law (Article 177) throughout the EU. Furthermore, as part of its evolving practices, the Court monitors national laws for possible incompatibilities with the Treaty of Rome, deciding cases in which individual citizens sue national legislatures and executives. Finally, as specified in Article 177, the Court also rules on general issues involving the validity of European Community law. It is an indication of how strongly supranational and national levels of governments are linked that the Court does not decide these issues directly. Rather it issues "preliminary rulings" and thus seeks to guide national courts in their judgments.[92] There is ground for reasonable disagreement on whether the Court's decentralized method of enforcement is a source of weakness, strength, or both. But it is evident that the Court's activism relies heavily on an admixture of supranational and national powers.

A substantial overlap of powers also characterizes the three mainstays of Germany's semisovereign state—federalism, parapublic institutions, and coalition governments[93]—which combine the competencies of different actors in a broad array of different institutions. First, in Germany's strong federal system the dispersal of power is reflected in the overlapping competencies of *Länder* and federal authorities, in the structure of the German bureaucracy, in the financing of different levels of government, and in a regional diversity that has been reinforced by German unification. Second, Germany's parapublic institutions, found in most major arenas of public policy, concentrate decision-making power in the hands of those most qualified, not necessarily those most affected, to deal with specific issues. Finally, at both federal and *Länder* levels, the German state pools the

---

"The European Court and National Courts—Doctrine and Jurisprudence: Legal Change in its Social Context," directed by Anne-Marie Slaughter, Martin Shapiro, Alec Stone, and Joseph H. H. Weiler.

[91] Mattli and Slaughter, "Constructing Legal System," pp. 24, 28–29.

[92] Lower national courts may appeal such preliminary judgments; national courts of last resort must appeal. In 95 percent of the cases, lower and national courts tend to follow the judgments of the European Court.

[93] Katzenstein, *Policy and Politics*. In this book, the concept of "semisovereignty" refers to the organization of power in domestic politics, rather than to the loss of sovereignty resulting from European integration or Allied prerogatives.

powers of different coalition governments. The logic of coalition government is reflected also in the relations between the Bundesrat and the Bundestag. Political parties are themselves often statist in outlook, illustrated, for example, in their dependence on public funds. In Germany there is no clear concentration of power. Rather, political bargaining takes place in a system that fuses executive and legislative functions in the process of policy formulation and federal, state, and local centers of power in the process of policy implementation.

Remarkably, the process of unification has done little to change these basic features of Germany's political institutions.[94] At the time of unification, many observers and activists inside and outside of Germany worried about the possibility that the "Berlin republic" would differ as much from the "Bonn republic," as "Bonn" had differed from "Weimar." Even those who avoided apocalyptic messages were united in the belief that the increasing heterogeneity in Germany's federal system would make a greater centralization of power inevitable. But the record of the first seven years after unification did not support those views. Consensual governance sustained by the same overlapping domains of power has remained the dominant trait of German politics after unification. Neocorporatist tendencies, for example were illustrated by the "Solidarity Pact" and the way unions proposed a "Job Alliance." In Germany's federal system the individual states have become no less important. Distrustful of a central government that pushed the mounting costs of unification increasingly also on their shoulders, the states have forged alliances across all partisan and denominational cleavages. And they have fought successfully for stronger rights of co-determination in the affairs of the European Union. And Germany's tradition of loyal opposition has been continued by a Social Democratic Party (SPD) that has been meek, even by German standards, while facing a government that has enjoyed only a four-seat majority in the Bundestag since the 1994 election. While the SPD moves gingerly to explore the possibilities of alliances at the state level with the post-Communist Party of Democratic Socialism (PDS), the CDU is eyeing with growing interest a Green Party that is rapidly transforming itself from a single-issue social movement party to the "third force" in the party system. With or without the Free Democratic Party (FDP), the German party system is likely to continue the practice of coalition government and loyal opposition.

The institutions of the EU and national systems of governance are linked in transnational policy networks that vary according to the particular issue

[94] The case for the limited impact of unification on Germany's political institutions is argued forcefully by Douglas Webber in "The Second Coming of the Bonn Republic," IGS Working Paper 95/1, University of Birmingham, Institute for German Studies, 1995. In many respects, social conditions in unified Germany are considerably more homogeneous than widely believed. See Wolfgang Zapf and Roland Habicht, eds., *Wohlfahrtsentwicklung im vereinten Deutschland: Sozialstruktur, sozialer Wandel und Lebensqualität* (Berlin: Sigma, 1996).

at hand.[95] Marked by an admixture of "hard" and "soft" regulatory styles that Adrienne Héritier calls a "policy patchwork, these networks are the locus for the reconciliation and synchronization of European and national policy processes."[96] The passing of time has altered some political practices and not modified others. In the early 1960s, European interest groups were relatively unimportant, no more than liaison groups with the secretarial function of coordinating the view of different national groups.[97] But it was clear even in the early days of the EC that a shift of power to Brussels would change the nature of lobbying. Research on interest group politics and the process of policy implementation illustrates this point. In the 1990s more than ninety regional and local governments, representing more than half of the EU's population, have opened offices in Brussels.[98] The accretion of power in Brussels has created an important new arena for lobbying even though it is still quite unstable, remarkably open, and at times highly unpredictable.[99] The industrial employer organizations, food and agriculture, commerce, and the professions account for the vast majority of EU associations. These are exceptionally well placed for influencing the consultative bodies of the EU, whose number doubled in the 1980s, to about 1,200.[100] The expansion in the scope of EU policies and in the role of the European Parliament has intensified lobbying at the European level. Europe's emerging system of interest group representation tends toward pluralism, in contrast with neocorporatist arrangements and stable policy communities at the national level. Business, not labor, has become the international actor par excellence.[101]

[95] The discussion of transnational policy networks draws on the overview and various case studies in Svein S. Andersen and Kjell A. Eliassen, eds., *Making Policy in Europe: The Europeification of National-Policy-Making* (London: Sage, 1993).

[96] Adrienne Héritier, "The Accommodation of Diversity in European Policy Making and Its Outcomes: Regulatory Policy as a Patchwork," EUI Working Paper SPS 96/2, Badia Fiesolana, San Domenico (FI), European University, 1996. Adrienne Héritier, Christoph Knill, Susanne Hingers, *Ringing the Changes in Europe: Regulatory Competition and the Transformation of the State: Britain, France, and Germany* (New York: Walter de Gruyter, 1996); Adrienne Héritier, ed., *Policy-Analyse: Kritik und Neuorientierung* (Wiesbaden: Westdeutscher Verlag, 1994).

[97] Leon Lindberg, *The Political Dynamics of European Economic Integration* (Stanford: Stanford University Press, 1963), pp. 287–88.

[98] Gary Marks, François Nielssen, Leondard Ray, and Jane E. Salk, "Competencies, Cracks, and Conflicts," *Comparative Political Studies*, 29 (April 1996): 164–92.

[99] Sonia Mazey and Jeremy Richardson, eds., *Lobbying in the European Community* (Oxford: Oxford University Press, 1993); Svein S. Andersen and Kjell A. Eliassen, "Complex-Policy-Making: Lobbying the EC," in Andersen and Eliassen, eds., *Making Policy*, pp. 35–53. William Averyt, "Eurogroups, Clientela and the European Community," *International Organization* 29 (Autumn 1975): 949–72.

[100] Philippe C. Schmitter and Wolfgang Streeck, "Organized Interests and the Europe of 1992," in Norman J. Ornstein and Mark Perlman, eds., *Political Power and Social Change: The United States Faces a United Europe* (Washington, D.C.: AEI Press, 1991), pp. 52–53.

[101] Franz Traxler and Philippe C. Schmitter, "The Emerging Euro-Polity and Organized Interests," *European Journal of International Relations* 1 (June 1995): 191–218.

Change has been less noticeable in the area of social movement politics. National social movements deal primarily with national rather than European institutions. Ordinary Europeans and their domestic groups, as Sidney Tarrow observes, do not react directly to decisions at the European level. Grassroots collective action remains primarily focused on national structures of political opportunity. While interest groups have to some extent shifted their focus from national to European institutions, with the exception of the environment, most other social movements have not. "The EU," writes Tarrow, "has not yet become a fulcrum for movement organisations as the national state did before it."[102] The absence of this shift is not surprising. The EU's emphasis on regulatory policy making leaves a multitude of competency venues for national governments and bureaucracies, especially in the process of national implementation of EU directives; movement organizations seek access to these national venues, where they feel they will have the biggest impact. Taking stock of both the theory and practice of European integration in 1970, Leon Lindberg and Stuart Scheingold referred to Europe as a "would-be polity."[103] In the 1990s, most students of European integration see the European polity as internationalizing, not replacing, the identity of European states in transnational governance systems.

The system of associated sovereignty in the European polity and semisovereignty in the German state are both distinguished by overlapping competencies, not by their concentration or division. This is not to say, however, that the growing links between associated sovereignty and semisovereignty were part of an overarching plan to bring about a domination of Europe by Germany. German institutional practices have evolved from a relatively coherent political vision expressed in the Basic Law. European institutional practices have evolved as the result of often contradictory ideological and state perspectives. In the deregulation and reregulation of national and European politics, complex political bargains between national governments and Brussels have created numerous opportunities for political creativity in the implementation of partial plans. Despite differences in historical origin, the similarity between European and German institutions and practices (such as multilevel governance systems, subsidiarity, an activist court, and an autonomous central bank) creates a milieu in which German political actors can feel at home.[104] This provides a strong

---

[102] Sidney Tarrow, "The Europeanisation of Conflict: Reflections from a Social Movement Perspective," *West European Politics* 18 (April 1995): 238.

[103] Leon N. Lindberg and Stuart A. Scheingold, *Europe's Would-Be Polity: Patterns of Change in the European Community* (Englewood Cliffs, N.J: Prentice Hall, 1970).

[104] This similarity extends to the smaller European states as well. See Arnold Wolfers, *Discord and Collaboration: Essays on International Politics* (Baltimore: Johns Hopkins University Press, 1962), pp. 73–74.

anchor for Germany in Europe. Internationalization creates national, regional, and local countercurrents, but because of a structural congruence in how power is exercised, Europe's institutional setting is remarkably familiar and natural for Germany. In brief, two historical processes, German democratization and European integration, came to be linked, thus making it possible for German and European political elites to reinforce and exploit an institutional fit that had emerged fortuitously. Historical accident and human agency interacted in the creation of the institutional congruence of Germany and Europe.

Other political systems mesh less well with the European polity. The U.S. system of government, for example, has no more than a surface similarity with Europe's associated sovereignty and Germany's semisovereignty. It is true that the separation of power between different branches of the U.S. government and its layer cake federal system divides and diffuses power; it offers interested actors, groups and institutions sharing power numerous veto points to shape the formulation and implementation of policy, backed by a U.S. version of the practice, not the ideology, of subsidiarity. But in contrast to the European Union, the United States has in the presidency a strong center of power that accentuates political fissures. And in contrast to Germany, the United States lacks a system of political parties as the central political institution, folded into a marble cake system of federalism that brings all the affected actors together in problem-focused negotiating arenas. In short, the division and diffusion of power in the U.S. political system reflects institutional practices that differ greatly from the partial pooling of sovereignty in the European polity and in Germany.

In contrast to the United States, Britain and France concentrate rather than divide power in their polities. Britain is organized around a system of parliamentary government and a strong two-party system. The British system of winner-take-all elections creates decisive majorities that provide the basis for strong leadership. A "neutral" civil service, the absence of a written constitution and of judicial review, and a society with a relatively decentralized system of interest groups support the concentration of power in the majority party in Parliament and in the hands of the prime minister. French politics revolves around a system of presidential rule and a powerful state bureaucracy. Parliament is relatively uninvolved in policy making. The courts and the National Bank occupy subordinate, though important, positions, while interest groups are relatively decentralized and marginal.

Britain's late entry, in 1973, policy clashes on agriculture and budgetary contributions, persistent political divisions between and within the political parties, and the strong tradition of parliamentary government have made for an uncomfortable fit in terms of policy, politics, and institutions, which accounts for Britain's position as a relative outlier in the European integration process. On questions of investment and finance, British economic interests have remained closely tied to the global economy. Conversely, on questions of agriculture and its disproportionately large contribution to the EU budget, Britain has had compelling national concerns. Beyond economic matters, British officials have tended to view Europe as a poor second cousin to the global empire they were relinquishing. Britain's traditional role had been to balance the affairs in Europe, not to get engaged in Europe. And Britain's "special relationship" with the United States valued U.S. entanglement in European affairs more than the growth of an autonomous center of power in Europe. Most important, strong conflicts within and between its major political parties, reinforced by the adversarial style of the House of Commons, mobilized strong opposition against foreign attempts to encroach on the political prerogatives of the oldest parliament in the world, a parliament that had never seen its power checked either by a written constitution or by a constitutional court. Britain's troubled relationship with Europe thus results from numerous sources.

Like Britain, France retains a clear state and national identity, but in its policies, politics, and institutions, France has been more European. Seeking to regain some of the national sovereignty it gave up at the supranational level, France has based its commitment to the European project on relatively clear calculations of long-term interest rather than a partial merging of identities, as in Germany. Key bargains between France and Germany on important political initiatives have defined the structure of opportunities and constraints for other European states; like Germany, France has benefited from exercising its coalitional power. Furthermore, the institutionalization of Franco-German relations in the Elysée treaty has begun to embed this coalitional power in a new social reality marked by a growth in social interactions. Since its creation in 1964, the German-French Youth Association, for example, has sponsored under its various programs six-week visits for about 4.6 million French and German participants in the neighboring country. At the level of elites, Franco-German consultations have intensified even more dramatically. During the 1980s, for example, Bjørn Sverdrup estimates that President Mitterrand and Chancellor Kohl met from six to eight times a year on a bilateral basis; if one includes their meetings in multilateral fora, they met, on average, once a month during a period of a dozen years.[105] Thus interests and institutions have brought France much closer to Germany and Europe than they have Britain.

Clearly, British and French political elites must make far greater adjustments to the organization of power in the European polity than their Ger-

[105] Bjørn Otto Sverdrup, "Institutionalising Cooperation: A Study of the Elysée Treaty and Franco-German Co-operation 1963–1993," University of Oslo, Department of Political Science, 1994, pp. 58–59, 100–01.

man counterparts. For Britain, what matters is will, not institutions; realism or intergovernmentalism captures much of the British approach to Europe. France takes an instrumental approach to Europe that stresses a combination of short- and long-term French interests. Furthermore, in contrast to Germany and the EU, both Britain and France exercise independent military power; this makes them players on important issues in world politics from which Germany and the EU are excluded. Thus neither the British nor the French political system is fully compatible with Germany's institutional approach to Europe, which emphasizes long-term interests rooted in a Europeanization of state identity, and which, like the European polity, is grounded in a system of diffused power.

In sharp contrast to Britain and France, several of the small European states diffuse power and thus operate quite easily in a system of associated sovereignty. The legitimacy of corporatist bargains tends to matter in these small states more than the efficacy of popular participation in politics, which remains restricted to regular electoral certification of the major political parties.[106] Analogously, the legitimacy of the European polity rests substantially on voluntary compliance and the effectiveness of the policy machinery rather than on authoritative, central control and public participation in the policy process. Indeed, Paul Taylor argues convincingly that for some of the smaller European democracies, consociational arrangements, rather than intergovernmental bargains or functional pressures, most accurately describe the European integration process.[107] Within the power systems of both these smaller states and the European polity, individual parts enjoy considerable autonomy, which compromises the sovereign control of the center within the consociation. Political consensus supports common arrangements that aim at increasing the welfare of both parts and collectivity. The parts are represented by the principle of proportionality, and government is dominated by a cartel of elites that operates by consensus, avoids majoritarian decision making, and seeks to protect the autonomy of the parts.

Furthermore, the preferences of these smaller states for legal rather than political ways of organizing international affairs match well with the German *Rechtsstaat* tradition after 1945 and the importance of legal norms in the process of European integration.[108] Indeed, the institutional prac-

---

[106] Peter J. Katzenstein, *Small States in World Markets: Industrial Policy in Europe* (Ithaca: Cornell University Press, 1985). It should be noted that Denmark, for example, is much concerned about the democratic deficit in the core institutions of the EU and has, through the use of popular referenda, slowed the process of European integration. More generally in the small states, public referenda check the power of governments that are opting for European integration and supranational policy coordination.

[107] Taylor, "European Community and State"; idem, "The European Union in the 1990s: Reassessing the Bases of Integration," in Ngaire Woods, ed., *Explaining International Relations since 1945* (Oxford: Oxford University Press, 1996), pp. 283–308.

[108] I thank Ulrich Preuss for this insight.

tices of its smaller European neighbors more closely resemble Germany's than they do any other larger European state's.[109] It is therefore not surprising to find an affinity between the institutional practices of associated sovereignty and semisovereignty, on the one hand, and those of democratic corporatism, on the other. Furthermore, a weakening of the corporatist arrangements in some of the smaller states in northern and western Europe has further increased their institutional similarity to Germany, which has never featured fully developed corporatist arrangements.[110]

Semisovereignty and associated sovereignty are systems of power that are closely linked. Looking at it from the perspective of important political institutions in Germany, specifically the government, the ministerial bureaucracy, the Bundestag, the *Länder,* the Bundesrat, and the courts, Dietrich Rometsch concludes that "an increasing 'Europeanization' . . . a *fusion* of national and European institutions can be observed clearly in the German case."[111] The product of material power, strategic bargaining, and historical accident, the institutional practices of associated and semisovereignty in Germany and Europe have evolved in mutually supportive ways. Whatever the precise mechanisms that have shaped this evolution, it is an important consequence that, from the perspective of Bonn and Berlin, the European political milieu is largely taken for granted. Politicians deviating from a strong European policy tend to do poorly at the polls.[112]

The meshing of European associated sovereignty and German semisovereignty is not well analyzed in terms of universal categories that describe the relationship among actors whose identities are fixed. And the relations between Germany and Europe cannot simply be viewed as a contest over the maximization of relative power or a bargaining process to coordinate conflicting policies. Such views conceal what is distinctive about

---

[109] Katzenstein, *Small States.*

[110] For an in-depth discussion of political and economic changes in the 1980s in a number of smaller European states, see Paulette Kurzer, *Business and Banking: Political Change and European Integration in Western Europe* (Ithaca: Cornell University Press, 1993). See also Christine Ingebritsen, "As Europe Changes, Will Scandinavia Remain the Same?" *Scandinavian Studies* 64 (Fall 1992): 641–51 and *The Nordic States and European Union* (Ithaca: Cornell University Press, 1998).

[111] Dietrich Rometsch, "The Federal Republic of Germany and the European Union: Patterns of Institutional and Administrative Interaction," IGS Discussion Paper 95/2, University of Birmingham, Institute for German Studies, 1995, p. 39.

[112] This poor showing in the polls holds for both ends of the political spectrum. A conservative who once worked for the European Commission in a high-ranking position, Manfred Brunner, was unsuccessful in contesting the constitutionality of the TEU before the German Constitutional Court; his attempt to compete for votes with a right-wing splinter party of the FDP, the League of Free Citizens (Bund Freier Bürger), on an anti-EU plank was a flop. On the left, the SPD suffered defeat in three important state elections in the spring of 1996 in which, for short-term electoral reasons, it sought to articulate a modulated, anti-European stance.

Germany in Europe. The concepts of associated and semisovereignty alert us to a structural congruence in power arrangements at different levels of governance, as well as to a partial pooling of German sovereignty in an emergent European polity. Coexisting with its member states, that polity to some extent modifies the identities of those states, the interests they hold, and the policies they pursue.

CONCLUSION AND PREVIEW

Regional integration is nothing new for either Germany or Europe. History is replete with examples of a variety of leagues, commonwealths, pacts, associations, and councils. German unity in the nineteenth century emerged from one such construction, the Zollverein, which in 1834 brought under one roof a variety of smaller customs and commercial unions. Subsequently, the German states formed a tax and a monetary union, although German unity came only in 1871, after three bloody wars in less than a decade. This mixture of voluntarism and violence also marked to different degrees subsequent European experiences with regional integration. At the end of the nineteenth century, for example, numerous proposals made for regional economic integration at the European level were quite similar to those made after World War II. By contrast, the "New Order" that Germany sought to impose on Europe in the 1930s and 1940s used the old instruments of economic coercion, exploitation, occupation, and war. Seen against this historical background, the degree of institutionalization that places united Germany in an integrating Europe is quite remarkable.

A comparison with integration processes in other regions reinforces this point. In terms of geography and politics, Germany, China, and the United States are central, respectively, to the developments of all of the various subregions in Europe, Asia, and North America.[113] They are more important than France, Britain, or Italy; Japan, India, Indonesia, or Russia; and Canada or Mexico. Asian integration occurs through markets and informal corporate, ethnic, and familial networks. The elites of many of Asia's developmental states remain deeply suspicious of relinquishing sovereignty to an international bureaucracy that cannot easily be held accountable. Market integration in North America follows a shallow path, seeking to create little more than a free trade zone. In both regions, political attempts to further integration have accelerated only in the 1990s.

---

[113] This geographic and political argument speaks to the centrality of Germany for the developments in various European subregions, *not* to a domination of Germany over Europe. Put in realist terms, the EU is dominated by a "Big Three," not a "Big One."

Compared to Asia and North America, the formal institutionalization of the relations between different states is Europe's most defining characteristic.[114] At the inception of an integrated Europe in the 1950s, political elites in favor of integration aimed at internationalizing the core of Germany's military-industrial complex and army through the creation of the European Coal and Steel Community (ECSC) and the European Defense Community (EDC). After the political defeat of the EDC in the French Assembly in 1954, the European Economic Community (EEC) became an important political instrument to prevent backsliding into the traditional pattern of European state-to-state diplomacy. Put differently, in its moment of defeat the political architects of European integration planned for a denser set of institutions (including a customs union) than did North America when its moment of creating a regional free trade zone arrived, more than three decades later. And unlike Asia, from the very beginning the EEC institutionalized the pooling of sovereignty in some policy sectors (foreign trade, agriculture, and transportation) rather than relying on informal integration through markets. Although political leadership and grand bargains mattered intermittently, in subsequent decades the European integration process was full of unintended consequences that further strengthened a high degree of formal institutionalization. Accompanied and interrupted by multiple political crises over successive decades, the growth of European institutions has continued to shape state identities and norms of conduct and thus has influenced the conceptions of the national interest that political elites seek to further.

This book investigates the institutionalized taming of Germany's power in Europe through a set of empirical case studies that seek to uncover different patterns of influence linking Germany with the EU, on the one hand, and Germany, the EU, and a number of smaller European states, on the other. Instead of projecting past experiences onto the future, this volume develops its insights based on specific institutional and policy episodes in different European states. Specifically, chapters 2–3 present an analysis of the interaction between Germany and the EU, viewed from the vantage points of both Bonn/Berlin and Brussels. And chapters 4–7 offer twenty-two case studies of how European and German influences manifest themselves in different institutions and policy sectors in ten states clustered around Germany at all points of the compass.

The book focuses on countries that have been core members of the EU since the 1950s (Netherlands and Belgium), that joined in the 1980s and 1990s (Greece, Spain, and Sweden), that are hoping for membership in

[114] Peter J. Katzenstein, "Introduction: Asian Regionalism in Comparative Perspective," in Peter J. Katzenstein and Takashi Shiraishi, eds., *Network Power: Japan and Asia* (Ithaca: Cornell University Press, 1997), pp. 7–44.

the coming years (Poland, Hungary, the Czech and Slovak Republics), and that decided not to join but to adjust unilaterally (Norway). The specific country case studies include economic-regulatory issues central to the European integration process, as well as social, cultural, and security issues less central to the EU than to either broader (continental, transatlantic, or global) or narrower (national or subnational) concerns. In brief, absent established facts on which we might directly base our judgments about Germany's effects on Europe, this book has had to include a broad range of political institutions and policy issues.

The next two chapters analyze Germany in Europe from the perspective of Brussels (chapter 2) and Bonn/Berlin (chapter 3). They show how the political norms that have evolved in the European polity are creating a milieu in which Germany exercises indirect institutional, rather than direct deliberative, power, and how, in the aftermath of unification, the growing economic constraints that Germany faces call for a set of "harder" economic goals favoring short-term tangible returns over long-term political benefits.

Chapters 4–7 analyze German and European influences on the institutions and policies in ten smaller states on the northern, western, southern, and eastern periphery of Germany and Europe. Specifically, these chapters point to variability within each of four subregions by offering a comparative analysis of the Netherlands and Belgium (chapter 4), Spain and Greece (chapter 5), Sweden and Norway (chapter 6), and Poland, Hungary, and the Czech and Slovak Republics (chapter 7).[115] These chapters illustrate the different ways in which German and European effects are jointly shaping some of the institutions and policies in these ten states.

Chapter 8 concludes by drawing together some of the main findings of the case studies, namely: (1) international effects are pervasive but not overly constraining; (2) depending on the policy sector, the soft German and European institutional effects can be parallel, countercurrent, mutually reinforcing, and independent; and (3) neither the political ambitions expressed in the Maastricht treaty nor a unified Germany exercising hegemonic leadership, whether singly or in combination, are likely to meld these diverse national states into one European polity or protostate anytime soon. Instead, Europe, Germany, and the smaller European states will most likely continue to forge pervasive institutional links at the domestic, regional, and international levels.

---

[115] Chapter 7 summarizes thirteen case studies that illustrate the political experiences of Poland, Hungary, and the Czech and Slovak Republics. They are abbreviated versions of full chapters of a related volume dealing with the role of united Germany in central Europe. See Peter J. Katzenstein, ed., *Mitteleuropa: Between Europe and Germany* (Providence, R.I.: Berghahn Books, forthcoming).

Our initial question—Will Germany dominate Europe or Europe Germany?—does not identify converging or crosscutting political processes that we can analyze solely in terms of material or bargaining power. The domination of one state by another and the coordination of conflicting objectives of different governments occur frequently in the European polity. But they acquire a different meaning in different historical and institutional contexts. And those contexts have changed greatly since 1945, as the identity of the German state has been internationalized. This historical development is distinctive and noteworthy viewed both from the perspective of modern German history and contemporary European affairs. By themselves, analyses that focus on the importance of material or bargaining power fail to recognize how institutions have softened the effects of German power in Europe. Far from denying the existence of German power, this book points to important changes that have affected how German power in Europe is exercised, arguing that we need to think not of Germany *and* Europe but of Germany *in* Europe. Because the European polity offers a familiar political stage, it is highly improbable that German political elites will any time soon turn their back on European institutions that have served German interests so well both at home and abroad. Germany in Europe is a political fact that is defining the national and international politics of the new Europe.

CHAPTER TWO

Shaping the Rules? The Constitutive Politics of the European Union and German Power

Simon J. Bulmer

The Federal Republic of Germany (FRG) has been of central importance to the process of European integration since the May 1950 Schuman Plan. The resultant European Coal and Steel Community (ECSC), designed to prevent (West) German heavy industry from providing the basis for expansionism, was the first step in a faltering but ongoing integration process that has multilateralized German diplomacy. Cumulatively, the issue of German power and predominance in western Europe and, from 1989, in the wider post–Cold War Europe, has become intertwined with the integration project.

Of the founding six member states, France and the Benelux countries, as Germany's neighbors, were able to gain at least some assurance that German power was being tamed. For their part, German elites came to see the material benefits that flowed from a deepening involvement in integration, including at first international rehabilitation, an important economic market, and subsequently a valuable multilateral arena for the conduct of German diplomacy. But Germany's commitment to integration was more than a matter of material benefit. German political elites developed a robust attachment to the institutions of integration, incorporating a strong European identity in their diplomacy. Has the unified Germany's role in the "new" Europe changed to the extent of raising concerns about Ger-

I am grateful, for their comments on earlier drafts, to Peter Katzenstein, other project participants, Beate Kohler-Koch, Willie Paterson, Lowell Turner, and the anonymous referees. I am also grateful to Cornell University and the British Economic and Social Research Council (award no. R000234004) for financial support of the research.

49

man dominance? Does Germany's institutional embeddedness in the European Union (EU) allay the concerns held by fellow European states and partners—small and large alike—about German power?

In addressing these questions and the wider concerns of the volume, this chapter is concerned specifically with Germany's role in the European Union. It contends that there is a good fit between German and EU interests, institutions, and identities, and that to fully appreciate the FRG's role and diplomacy within the EU, all three of these dimensions have to be taken into account. Germany's interests in integration, defined by its strong institutional embeddedness in the EU, have changed significantly since the early 1950s, as the supranational institutions have been given new tasks in response to new challenges. The indirect institutional influence of Germany and the strong European and multilateral "mission" of its political elites have come to shape the rules and norms of the EU and the integration process itself.

As its subtitle suggests, this chapter will focus on how German power has influenced the rules, norms, and framework of integration ("constitutive politics") rather than its specific policies ("regulative politics").[1] The two forms of politics are, of course, connected. If the EU's broad fit with the FRG's interests, institutions, and identity is good, then Bonn/Berlin's conduct of European policy should be facilitated, which brings us specifically to the analysis of German *power* in the EU.

The FRG's power in the EU cannot be captured by a simple examination of the forceful articulation of German interests. In embracing an "exaggerated multilateralism," Germany has avoided a realist, unilateral projection of power.[2] To capture the extent of German power in the EU, it is therefore necessary to be conscious of other faces of power, including indirect institutional power.[3] In advancing multilateral, integrative solutions to its problems, the federal government may suggest institutional arrangements that reflect domestic norms. To the extent that these arrangements are adopted at the EU level, they may mobilize a bias that will favor German interests. German involvement in the EU institutions may consequently—to overstate and generalize a more subtle story—resemble a warm bath, whereas a more reluctant United Kingdom may find involvement closer to a cold shower.[4] Hence it is not just interests that shape a multilateral form of

---

[1] On "regulative politics," see chapter 3 in this volume.

[2] The term *exaggerated multilateralism* is coined by Jeffrey Anderson in chapter 3, this volume.

[3] More generally on the different faces of power, see Steven Lukes, *Power: A Radical View* (London: Macmillan, 1974).

[4] I return to a comparison of German and British projections of power in the conclusion to the chapter.

governance like the EU but norms and ideas, too.[5] In short, it is important to be aware of what might be called "social power" or "institutional power."

There should be no illusion that Germany plays a powerful role in European integration. What this chapter seeks to show, however, is that German power is projected indirectly and in a diffuse manner. It is "soft" power. It rarely is a mere reflection of naked German interests and, as such, is satisfactory for German elites socialized into reflexive multilateralism. Equally, its "soft" character, mediated by the EU, is much more acceptable to other European states, especially the smaller ones dependent upon Germany in the various ways outlined in later chapters.

The chapter is divided into four sections. The first outlines the EU in terms of its general institutional framework, normative context, policy program level, and policy profile. The second contrasts the fit with Germany on these points. The aim in these two sections, therefore, is to identify the level of congruence between the EU, as a multilateral framework for the articulation of German interests, and patterns of domestic German governance. The third section assesses the meaning of these findings in terms of power: how the pattern of institutional interaction mediates or facilitates the exercise of German power. And the concluding section offers some brief contrasts with Britain, to show how a member state less at institutional ease with the EU has greater difficulty "playing the integration game" than Germany.

THE EUROPEAN UNION AND GERMANY: THE FRAMEWORK OF INSTITUTIONAL INTERACTION

The relationship between the EU and the FRG is one of considerable interdependence. Trade flows with EU partners are in excess of 50 percent of German trade; the EU represents the principal international focus of German policy; and the institutional penetration of the German political system by European integration is deep. Even so, it is important to keep this in perspective. The FRG is not merely an economic force within the EU but has substantial export flows to other advanced industrial states. Thus the international purview of the FRG is not confined to Europe,[6] although in both political and economic terms the EU is the principal multilateral policy framework used by the FRG.

[5] See James Caporaso, "International Relations Theory and Multilateralism: The Search for Foundations," in John G. Ruggie, ed., *Multilateralism Matters: The Theory and Praxis of an Institutional Form* (New York: Columbia University Press, 1993), pp. 73–81.

[6] The constitutional constraint upon the deployment of the armed forces outside the NATO area was redefined in 1994 through a ruling of the Federal Constitutional Court. German forces are now permitted to conduct certain "out of area" activities, such as peacekeeping, subject to approval by the Bundestag.

The European Union has become a highly encompassing international framework for action. Its member states, in consequence, are located in a dense set of relationships, not only with the EU and its component institutions but also bilaterally with other member states, such as the Franco-German relationship. While it is possible to see the FRG as "ensnared" in a cobweb of institutional ties, this is only one side of the picture. The other is that the EU offers additional possibilities for Germany to solve domestic policy problems. Thus member governments can solve domestic matters of common concern through package deals such as the single market/Single European Act (SEA) or the Treaty on European Union (TEU). Hence Germany's ties with the EU must not be seen as a straitjacket for Germany, or as automatically creating a "joint-decision trap."[7] The EU's institutions and policies offer opportunities for Germany to project its changing material interests, policy norms, and social goals. These need to be addressed in turn.

The governance of the EU has a particularly unusual profile. In some respects it resembles the upper tier of a federal or confederal order. Although Article C of the TEU states that "the Union shall be served by a single institutional structure," the framework for that structure is highly complex. Economic policies are subject to a supranational system of governance, with a system of European Community (EC) law and a judicial framework as essential components. By contrast, foreign and security policy, together with justice and home affairs, are subject to a more orthodox intergovernmental system. Since the mid-1980s, supranational governance has made two quantum leaps in its constitutional evolution. Thus the SEA (and the related single-market program) transformed the governance capacity of the EC,[8] and it extended (or codified) the boundaries of supranational and intergovernmental governance. The TEU brought further reconstruction along these two parameters. These two treaties brought major reconfigurations in the responsibilities and detailed goals of supranational governance.[9]

What the SEA and the TEU did not do, however, was reconfigure the *pattern* of supranational governance. This remains characterized by limited budgetary resources; a major (institutionalized) reliance on member states in the policy-making and, particularly, the policy-implementing stages; a dense network of committee-based intergovernmental relations;[10] and the

---

[7] Fritz Scharpf, "The Joint-Decision Trap: Lessons from German Federalism and European Integration," *Public Administration* 66 (1988): 239–78.

[8] See Simon Bulmer, "Setting and Influencing the Rules," in D. Mayes, ed., *The Evolution of Rules for the Single European Market* (Aldershot, U.K.: Edward Elgar, 1997).

[9] At the time of writing, a further intergovernmental conference was considering supplementary constitutional reform.

[10] "Intergovernmental" is used here to denote the predominance of governmental agencies of whatever level, at the expense of legislative bodies.

preeminent role of producer groups in the regulation of socioeconomic issues.[11]

In terms of policy profile, the EC pillar of the EU is centered on economic activities and based largely on the EC Treaty, which establishes a framework for collective action by the member states.[12] The European economic "constitution" set by the founding treaties afforded considerable discretion to the member states; indeed, the goal of a true common market slipped from view until revived in the 1980s. In the meantime, the EC's principal policy was the Common Agricultural Policy (CAP), which also incorporated a range of devices enabling member states discretionary action, while retaining the appearances of a common policy. Although the extension of collective governance in the 1970s to include cooperation on foreign, environmental, and regional policies broadened the policy profile, it was the single-market program, with the much wider package of policy measures embodied in the SEA, which invigorated the EC in the mid-1980s. Further extension of collective governance through the TEU has created an encompassing framework within which the FRG is located.

How can this European context for German institutions and policy be outlined in a manner that allows us to appraise the constraints and opportunities European integration affords the FRG? To do this in a manner consistent with this volume's emphasis on institutional power, we must take into account four aspects of the EU: its broad constitutional order; its normative context; its differentiated patterns of mesolevel governance; and its policy profile. Each of these structures Germany's role in the EU. Each is important to developing our argument about how German power is mediated institutionally through the EU.

The Constitutional Order of the European Union

One means of understanding the broad structure of the EU is to examine its institutional configuration. The principal structural characteristic of European integration is its cooperative (con-)federalist nature: the upper (European Union) tier has relatively few exclusive competences but many policy areas entail cooperation between the two levels of the system.

[11] For a new institutionalist account, see Simon Bulmer, "The Governance of the European Union: A New Institutionalist Approach," *Journal of Public Policy* 13 (1993): 351–80. For more on the regulatory character of the EU, see the review and analysis of existing literature by James Caporaso, "The European Union and Forms of State: Westphalian, Regulatory or Post-Modern?" *Journal of Common Market Studies* 34 (March 1996): 39–44.

[12] The EC Treaty corresponds to the earlier European Economic Community Treaty, which was amended and renamed as part of the constitutional engineering associated with the TEU. See Clive Church and David Phinnemore, *European Union and European Community: A Handbook and Commentary on the Post-Maastricht Treaties* (Hemel Hempstead, U.K.: Harvester Wheatsheaf, 1994).

Thus it is much more in line with the characteristics of German federalism than with the greater insulation between the federal and state levels of government that characterizes the U.S. model of federalism.

How has this pattern of European cooperative federalism come about? One explanation is that it reflects the way the member states have responded to domestic challenges to governance. Thus, in differing ways, Alan Milward and Wolfgang Wessels have seen supranational governance develop as a means of addressing intransigent domestic problems, including the insatiable appetite of voters for ever higher living standards.[13] The important point is that the cooperative federalist framework of the EU has come about as a result of the consent of the member governments, which has not, of course, eliminated dissatisfaction with the framework of action, as the policies of, most notably, President Charles de Gaulle (the 1965 "empty chair" crisis) and Prime Minister Margaret Thatcher (on the budget) have demonstrated. Nevertheless, it makes it very difficult for a member state to free itself from its obligations to adhere to the rules of the game.

If the evolution of the EU takes place along cooperative federalist lines, what about the day-to-day decision-making process? For many years this level of action was characterized by unanimity, for the EC's institutional apparatus was frozen by the 1966 Luxembourg Accords.[14] From the 1980s, matters have moved on, with the provision for qualified majority voting (QMV) in the annual budgetary process (already agreed upon in the 1970s), further extension of QMV as a result of the Single European Act, and still wider provision following ratification of the TEU. In addition, the Luxembourg Accords are deemed to have been superseded.[15] But the voting procedure in the EU Council of Ministers remains highly nuanced; treaty provision is of limited assistance in illuminating matters. There remains a strong logic of consensus, in part with an eye to ensuring subsequent compliance with the law. In consequence, resort to QMV is as much a threat against obstructionist governments as it is regular practice in the Council. One principle often observed is that "significant minorities" are not overruled, even where this is constitutionally permitted.[16] Overall, then, the decision-making arrangements represent a balance between

[13] Alan Milward, *The European Rescue of the Nation-State* (London: Routledge, 1992); Wolfgang Wessels, "An Ever Closer Fusion? A Dynamic Macropolitical View on Integration Processes," *Journal of Common Market Studies* 35 (June 1997): 267–99.

[14] See Scharpf, "Joint-Decision Trap."

[15] See Anthony Teasdale, "The Life and Death of the Luxembourg Compromise," *Journal of Common Market Studies* 31 (December 1993): 567–79. Also see Fiona Hayes-Renshaw and Helen Wallace, "Executive Power in the European Union: The Functions and Limits of the Council of Ministers," *Journal of European Public Policy* 2 (1995): 559–82.

[16] See Neill Nugent, *The Government and Politics of the European Union* (Durham: Duke University Press, 1994), pp. 142–48.

rules and conventions, where successful implementation depends upon the constructive cooperation of the member governments, beginning with the transposition of EC directives into national law.

A further feature of this cooperative federalist framework concerns the participants in the multitiered governance structure. The participants are overwhelmingly from the executive branch of government. Policy making is largely "precooked" in negotiations between civil servants in the Committee of Permanent Representatives (COREPER) and its specialist subcommittees. This is analogous to what happens in Germany's extensive array of cooperative federalist committees. The common feature is the intergovernmental nature of the negotiations. The counterpart to this situation is the EU's democratic deficit. The European Parliament has gained powers both through the SEA and the TEU but continues to lack a clear profile among the European electorate. In addition, most national parliaments lack the structures necessary to call to account national negotiators in EU bodies.

Prior to the TEU, this multitiered system of intergovernmental relations had been extended downward to national governments only. However, it is worth noting that, largely in response to the pressure of the German *Länder,* the supranational institutions are increasingly aware of the importance of subnational government as a potential partner. Under the TEU, not only was a Committee of the Regions set up but also Article 146 was amended to facilitate the participation of ministers from subnational government in the delegations to the Council. With Article 3b (EC) setting out the principle of subsidiarity, these changes gave the EU a greater regional sensitivity. But the EU commitment to a decentralized approach is not without difficulty because of the uneasy balance with member states averse to the notion of subnational subsidiarity, in particular, the United Kingdom Conservative government.[17] Furthermore, several states have experienced difficulties in identifying with a "regional" level of governance in the EU.

In horizontal terms, the pattern of governance in the EU is differentiated between that prevailing in the EC pillar and that prevailing in the other two. The EC pillar is characterized by a strong reliance on the law as an instrument. This reliance arises primarily because of the lack of commission field agencies and the lack of a substantial EC budget. Thus supranational governance has a limited set of policy tools. In consequence, it is dependent upon a regulatory approach. A framework of rules is put forward in EC legislation, but policy execution and the judicial dimension are largely left to national and subnational procedures. These character-

---

[17] Andrew Scott, John Peterson, and David Millar, "Subsidiarity: A 'Europe of the Regions' v. the British Constitution?" *Journal of Common Market Studies* 32 (March 1994): 47–67.

istics are consistent with, and indeed reinforce, the administrative pattern of federalism that prevails in Germany.

By contrast, in the arenas of foreign policy and home affairs cooperation, the EU's activities are rather different. Common Foreign and Security Policy (CFSP) is based much more on declaratory diplomacy with a much looser supporting set of instruments, such as sanctions, that are almost wholly in the hands of the national governments. By contrast, cooperation in the Justice and Home Affairs (JHA) domain is achieved in a predominantly covert manner. It entails extensive collaboration on policing, immigration, and judicial matters. Decisions are dependent upon the consent of all member governments, which also possess the key policy instruments.

Diversity within the EU manifests itself also in the persistence at the fringes of the EU of differentiated integration.[18] Characterized in the 1980s by the incomplete participation of member states in the European Monetary System, it has been extended by the TEU's provision, in the Protocol and Agreement on Social Policy, for social policy that does not apply to the United Kingdom; further scope exists for its application if only an inner core of countries proceeds to the third stage of European Monetary Union (EMU).

The one institution that has come to unify the diversity of the EU is the European Council: the twice-yearly meetings of the heads of state or government and the president of the European Commission. Over the past twenty years or so, the European Council has taken on the role of shaping the EU's constitutional order. Two characteristics of the European Council are particularly worthy of mention for present purposes. First, it is not concerned with legislative work (unlike the Council of the EU), for it is political in character. By the same token, and in contrast with other forms of summitry, it is supported by an extensive institutional substructure. Both by design and in consequence, the European Council offers an important opportunity for the exchange of ideas between the chief executives of the member states.[19]

The institutional configuration of the European Council is important to the integration process. Conducted on the basis of consensus, its intergovernmental approach is regarded as privileging the larger member states; the smaller states originally regarded the European Council as a cuckoo in the EC's nest.[20] It might be argued, then, that large member

[18] For a valuable typology of differentiated integration—namely, according to time, space, and matter—see Alexander Stubb, "A Categorisation of Differentiated Integration," *Journal of Common Market Studies* 34 (June 1996): 283–95.

[19] On the importance of the exchange of ideas to international relations, see, for example, Judith Goldstein and Robert O. Keohane, eds., *Ideas and Foreign Policy: Beliefs, Institutions and Political Change* (Ithaca: Cornell University Press, 1993).

[20] Simon Bulmer and Wolfgang Wessels, *The European Council: Decision-Making in European Politics* (Basingstoke, U.K.: Macmillan, 1987), p. 40.

states, particularly if working in concert, may have an enhanced position in shaping the constitutive politics of the EU. If they are able also to generate creative political ideas and articulate them in the European Council, they have the potential to assume a powerful, but subtle, agenda-setting role in the integration process. We shall return to Germany's role in the European Council in the second section of this chapter. What, then, of the role of institutional norms?

The Normative Setting

Cultural analysis has been criticized for underspecifying the factors that explain the distinct practices of different political systems. Nevertheless, distinct normative values do apply in different systems. It is assumed here that these normative values are an intrinsic part of their institutional setting. Institutional interaction also entails a coming together of bureaucratic and political norms.

A major problem arises in identifying at a general level what exactly these norms are in a multinational political system as relatively young as the European Union. Michael Shackleton has demonstrated that quite divergent values are held by different actors within the EU.[21] Thus recent British Conservative governments have tended to pursue *individualism* in the EU, with their emphasis on a market-based EU and their opposition to transferring further power to the EU level. By contrast, the European Commission has pursued a line more closely identified with *egalitarianism,* through its emphasis on the EU's social and economic cohesion. Some common values may be developing as part of the EU's institutional arrangements, but it is not yet possible to refer to political or administrative traditions at the EU level.

Potentially more valuable is the identification of "rules of the game" within EU policy making. Member governments' preference to agree on policy in the Council of Ministers by consensus rather than necessarily following the treaty rules on QMV represents one normative aspect. Subsidiarity may be seen as a procedural norm of EU governance since the TEU. Another apparent norm is not to challenge the *acquis communautaire,* or EU "policy inheritance," in any fundamental way, for instance in the way that Prime Minister Thatcher challenged EC budgetary arrangements at the start of her premiership. The tendency to cloak national interests in pro-European language is another apparent characteristic of the EU, although one not open to member governments with a significant grouping of Euro-skeptics (such as Britain). Sometimes dismissed as "Euro-babble," pro-European rhetoric may reflect deeply held Europeanist norms.

[21] Michael Shackleton, "The European Community between Three Ways of Life: A Cultural Analysis," *Journal of Common Market Studies* 29 (December 1991): 575–601.

Mesolevel Governance

If these characteristics form the broad context of institutional interaction between Germany and the EU, they do not amount to a full picture. Generalizations can be arrived at from interaction at the macro level, but a full understanding necessitates appreciation of the policy program level.

The identification of differing sectoral dynamics in EU policy making is scarcely a new development,[22] although commentators have begun to emphasize the procedural diversity within EU policy making, particularly since the Single European Act. The diversity was magnified with the implementation of the TEU/Maastricht treaty, which created three distinct pillars of integration—each with different procedures—and even greater procedural differentiation within the most developed pillar, namely, the EC.

What are the kinds of procedural differentiation that exist within the European Union? Foreign policy cooperation has largely been based on the member states' reaching unanimity and this continues for the time being under the TEU; the European Commission is in a relatively weak position and is eclipsed by the member state holding the presidency of the Council of Ministers; decisions and actions are not justiciable before the European Court of Justice (ECJ); and the European Parliament (EP) has very limited influence. A similar situation applies to JHA cooperation on combatting terrorism, cross-border fraud, drug smuggling, and other transfrontier crime. Following implementation of the TEU, JHA forms a separate pillar of the European Union, with a number of quite specific procedural options.

It is within the EC pillar that the greatest degree of differentiation is to be observed. Only the key variables need be identified here. What is the treaty basis for action? In particular, does it provide for exclusive EC or mixed EC/national legislative competence? What form of legal act—if any—is to be undertaken: directive, regulation, or decision? What is the nature of the European Parliament's involvement? Is it by the consultation, cooperation, assent, co-decision, or budgetary procedure? What is the treaty provision regarding voting in the Council of Ministers in the policy area, and what is the predominant *practice* on voting? Is the Committee of the Regions to be consulted? Is the policy area legislation-led or, as in the case of competition or mergers policy, regulation-led? The answers to these and similar questions determine the profile of the policy sector. They also determine the potential influence of individual supranational institutions, the way in which the member governments must prepare for policy making and, indirectly, how nongovernmental actors relate to the key institutions.

[22] See, for example, Helen Wallace, William Wallace, and Carole Webb, eds., *Policy-Making in the European Community*, 2d ed. (Chichester: John Wiley, 1983).

This picture reflects the differentiated nature of decision making in the European Union, to which individual member states must orient themselves. The EU gathers a set of rather discrete governance structures under one umbrella. The relative independence of the governance structures from one another is reinforced by the rather poor cross-sectoral coordination arrangements within the EU institutions. This situation is true within the European Commission, where vertical coordination within the directorates general is much stronger than horizontal coordination between them. It is also true of the various formations of the Council of Ministers, of which there are over twenty: they tend to confine themselves to their individual provinces. The (General) Council of Ministers (foreign ministers) has an overburdened agenda and, consequently, is unable to pursue one of its original tasks, namely, the coordination of policy. Coordination at the level of minister or head of government tends to occur by default, usually in the event of a crisis.

An example of the impact of this institutional form of EU policy making is the shape of the Common Agricultural Policy (CAP). The CAP has developed incrementally since its establishment. The normal fiscal counterbalance to the agriculture minister in an exclusively national setting would be the finance minister, who has control over the purse strings. In the supranational case, the Council of Budget Ministers was until 1988 virtually a decision *taker:* control over the deliberations of the Council of Agriculture Ministers was limited, and, within budgetary policy making, CAP price support spending had a privileged position as "compulsory expenditure." It is striking that the three occasions when CAP reform has been undertaken resulted from pressures external to agricultural policy makers. In 1984 and 1988 the threat of bankruptcy for the EC led to reform measures (including in 1988 the introduction of greater financial discipline over CAP expenditure). The 1992 MacSharry reforms owed their origin to pressures emanating from the Uruguay Round of GATT negotiations. This pattern of policy differentiation within the EU can be explained in terms of the different institutional frameworks that apply to each policy program. Although the result is a diverse set of institutionally defined governance regimes,[23] it is also relevant to consider the congruence between the policy emerging from these governance regimes and the FRG's domestic policy interests.

Policy Content

Textbooks have been written on the policies of the EU; thus only a skeletal profile can be offered here. One key parameter is the notion of

---

[23] See Bulmer, "Governance of European Union."

state-market relations in the EU context. Although the founding European Economic Community Treaty represented a relatively market-oriented framework (apart from the CAP—see below), in reality, its objectives were undermined by state intervention of two forms. First, nontariff barriers (NTBs) became an alternative means whereby national protectionism was conducted; second, state subsidies, especially to state-owned enterprises, were also widespread. And even though both NTBs and state subsidies fell within the parameters of the treaty, it was not until the single-market program that treaty rules were enforced, with the assistance of the 1992 goal of completing the internal market and the procedural improvements of the SEA. The spirit of the single-market program represented the high point of neoliberal influence on the EC. However, this was achieved through a package deal that entailed concessions in the form of increased structural funds to benefit the poorer member states and a commitment to social cohesion through supranational legislation on working conditions.

Although the core of the EC Treaty is concerned, at least at the textual level, with facilitating the creation of European markets, other forms of economic governance have been promoted. For instance, the gradual development of technology policy (formalized in the SEA) encourages research and development alliances between European companies. Environmental policy, also formalized in the SEA, introduces a further element of social regulation into EU policy concerns. The TEU placed EMU at the core of its agenda for the late-1990s, although the program is in question as a result of questions about sufficient states meeting the criteria to ensure EMU's viability.

The CAP has remained distant from the objective of creating a "common" market in agricultural produce. State aid by member governments continues to distort the common funding of the European Agricultural Guidance and Guarantee Fund. Even following the MacSharry reforms, the CAP continues to be an expensive policy, although the form of subsidies has moved toward principles established within GATT, where the EU has played a somewhat ambiguous role. Although supporting efforts at tariff reduction, the EU has also been protective of member states' special interests, as the negotiations during the Uruguay Round demonstrated.

The origins of the second pillar of the EU, the Common Foreign and Security Policy (CFSP), can be traced back to 1970. Its operation on the basis of consent has on occasion hampered effective representation of common interests. Nevertheless, the member states are now much less inclined to undertake unilateral foreign policy démarches, preferring instead to coordinate and respond through common declarations or common action. Following the ratification of the TEU and with an eye on the 1998 expiration of the founding treaty of the Western European Union, a creeping movement in the direction of security policy is under way.

The third pillar of the EU, covering Justice and Home Affairs (JHA) cooperation, was formalized in the TEU itself and is at a somewhat earlier stage of development. The JHA pillar's origins lie in an initiative of the mid-1970s known as TREVI (Terrorism, Radicalism, Extremism, Violence International). Under the TEU, judicial and home affairs cooperation has been extended to include asylum policy; immigration into the EU by nationals of third countries; civil and criminal proceedings; customs matters; police work associated with the European Police Office (Europol); and action against drug misuse and cross-border fraud. Some of these activities have their origins in TREVI; others are a response to the removal of frontier controls as part of the single-market program. The wish to isolate the EU from migration flows or criminality originating from "the outside" was heightened by the lifting of the Iron Curtain.

MEASURING INSTITUTIONAL INTERACTION IN PRACTICE

To assess, from a European perspective, the extent to which the EU mediates German power entails measuring Germany's fit in terms of the four aspects of the EU's character outlined above. I will show that there is a strong correspondence between the EU's constitutional order, norms, patterns of mesolevel governance, and policy profile and Germany's institutionalized identity and interests, setting the scene for a dissection of German power in the EU in the third section of this chapter.

Congruence in Constitutional Order

At the macro level, a large measure of congruence between German and EU institutional arrangements may be identified. Cooperative federalism applies as well to the domestic reordering of responsibilities in Germany as it does to patterns in the EU. Indeed, of the original states, the FRG has the greatest experience domestically with a pattern of multitiered governance of the type familiar in the EU. Just as in the EU, so in the FRG the goals of economic and policy efficiency have resulted in the reorganization of state activities.[24] Indeed, in the 1970s and 1980s, the need for more effective delivery of environmental policy entailed a transfer of authority to both the federal government and the EU from the *Länder*. There was no fundamental major challenge to "German interests" at the federal level in all this because these were guaranteed by the underlying consen-

[24] See Simon Bulmer, "Efficiency, Democracy and West German Federalism: A critical analysis," in Charlie Jeffery and Peter Savigear, eds., *German Federalism Today* (Leicester: Leicester University Press, 1989), pp. 103–19.

sus needed for the creeping restructuring of governmental authority. Thus German perceptions of political institutions as forums for the management, or even avoidance, of conflict find an echo within the EU.

Germany's approval of institutionalized power sharing in domestic policy making finds an echo in another respect within the EU, namely, as a result of the strong corporatist traditions that are enshrined in German institutional arrangements. The commitments to economic and social cohesion (Article 130a, EC), set down in the Single European Act, along with the commitment to developing the dialogue between the social partners (Article 118b), bear testimony to this. Thus the Kohl Government has found no serious difficulty with the organic view of society that lay behind the Community Charter of Fundamental Social Rights for Workers (the "Social Charter"). It also supported the incorporation of social rights into the TEU, in the Social Chapter, and was frustrated by the British government's wish to opt out of any such provision.[25] The German practice of including the social partners, most notably at the meso and micro levels of industrial relations, is beginning to find reflection in EU legislation, for example, on works councils.

One area of institutional conflict—at least until the negotiation of the TEU—concerned the way European integration represented a centralizing process that permitted no real participation of the *Länder*. This situation predated the emergence of a concern with a "Europe of the Regions" and the EU's emphasis on the principle of subsidiarity. Partly promoted by the *Länder*, EU policies are taking on an increasingly region-sensitive dimension, most notably in structural policy.[26] This trend has been reinforced by European regions perceiving the need to promote themselves as destinations for inward investment in the competitive context of the single market.[27] The TEU's creation of a Committee of the Regions is the most striking institutional manifestation of these developments; German federalism is highly congruent with this emergent trend. A unitary state, such as the United Kingdom, has severe difficulties with identifying the territorial boundaries of its own "regions."

The legal/regulatory character of the governance of the EU is also largely congruent with the arrangements prevailing in the domestic Ger-

[25] Some social policy regulation in the labor market domain is being undertaken, under the terms of the Protocol and Agreement on Social Policy appended to the TEU, by legislation governing all member states with the exception of the United Kingdom.

[26] On German pressure in regional matters, see Joachim Bauer, ed., *Europa der Regionen: Aktuelle Dokumente zur Rolle und Zukunft der deutschen Länder im europäischen Integrationsprozess* (Berlin: Duncker und Humblot, 1991); and Charlie Jeffery, "The *Länder* Strike Back: Structure and Procedures in the German Federal System," Discussion Papers in Federal Studies, no. FS 94/4, University of Leicester: Centre for Federal Studies, 1994.

[27] See Martin Rhodes, ed., *Regions in the New Europe: New Patterns in Core and Periphery Development* (Manchester: Manchester University Press, 1995).

man arena.[28] Much of the integration process has occurred through legal means, although this dimension is often neglected by political scientists.[29] The legal component is also important in German politics and public administration.[30] This coincidence of approach creates a close correspondence between Germany and the EU in the way in which policy is executed. By contrast, Britain has tended to rely on self-regulation in several key EU policy areas, although these have become increasingly juridified, in part as a consequence of European legislation, for instance, in the financial services sector.

The one area of tension concerned human rights. In the "Solange Beschluß" of 1977, the Federal Constitutional Court questioned the supremacy of EC law over German law, given that the former did not embody a catalog of rights. Although a clash between the norms of the two legal systems was subsequently headed off, with the European Court developing its own jurisprudence on rights, the Federal Constitutional Court's judgment on the compatibility of the TEU with the Basic Law raised the possibility of a future clash by setting out certain domestic preconditions for the transfer of further powers to the EU.[31]

Another aspect of the legal/regulatory character of EU governance is illustrated in Peters's analysis:

> The Community's impact on its constituent nations is increasingly through law and integration. This choice of policy instruments may be wise because regulative instruments tend to mask the effects of policies and to make winners and losers less visible than expenditure programs do. Regulatory policy may thus minimize (although not eliminate) national, regional and even class conflicts over Community policy.[32]

It is possible, therefore, that the particular instruments of integration used may limit awareness of, and interstate conflict over, the benefits derived

[28] On Germany's domestic regulatory arrangements, see Gerhard Lehmbruch, "The Institutional Framework of German Regulation," in Kenneth Dyson, ed., *The Politics of German Regulation* (Aldershot, U.K.: Dartmouth, 1992), pp. 29–52.

[29] On the legal dimension of integration, see Anne-Marie Burley and Walter Mattli, "Europe Before the Court: A Political Theory of Legal Integration," *International Organization* 47 (Winter 1993): 41–76.

[30] See Nevil Johnson, "Law as the Articulation of the State in Western Germany: A German Tradition Seen from a British Perspective," *West European Politics* 1 (1978): 177–92.

[31] On the Federal Constitutional Court's TEU judgment, see W. Kaufmann-Bühler, "Deutsche Europapolitik nach dem Karlsruher Urteil: Möglichkeiten und Hemnisse," *Integration* 18 (1994): pp. 1–11; H. H. Hahn, "Maastrichter Vertrag und nationale Verfassungsgerichtssprechung," Interne Studien und Berichte, no. 66/1993 (Sankt Augustin, Germany: Konrad-Adenauer-Stiftung, 1993).

[32] B. Guy Peters, "Bureaucratic Politics and the Institutions of the European Community," in Alberta Sbragia, ed., *Euro-politics: Institutions and Policymaking in the "New" European Community* (Washington, D.C.: Brookings Institution, 1992), p. 93.

by Germany from integration. As it is, because Germany's surplus in trade with her EU partners cannot directly be adduced to EU policy, this particular indicator cannot be used as the basis for demanding greater German sacrifices for the collective good.

Overall, the way that state-market relations are institutionalized at the supranational level has been highly congruent with the character of German policy. Thus the treaties serve as a kind of economic constitution along the lines of the FRG's "Ordnungspolitik." Moreover, both the EU and the FRG adopt a regulatory approach for putting this framework into effect. In the EU case, as noted, this approach is the result of the Union's peculiar set of policy instruments; in the FRG, the lack of a Keynesian tradition biases economic legislation toward the goal of promoting the functioning of markets through regulation. A further point is that both the EU and the federal government in Germany tend in important areas to define framework legislation, while leaving the administration of policy to lower levels of government. This congruence of approach has proved to be a valuable reference point for German negotiators in EU organs. One area where institutional congruence has failed to develop concerns redistributive policy instruments because the EC budget remains very small. As will be seen below, however, a small EC budget reflects the substantive policy interests of the FRG.

The structural characteristics of the CFSP warrant some comment. Because, for historical reasons, the Federal Republic has been hampered from pursuing a forceful unilateral foreign policy, the European level of foreign policy cooperation has augmented German policy capacity. Expectations to the contrary, unified Germany has continued to feel the need to place its foreign policy in a multilateral context.[33] It should also be pointed out that the pattern of European foreign policy cooperation has hitherto been based on the idea of civilian power. The absence of a defense component avoided potential structural clashes with German constitutional constraints upon its armed forces, although these constraints have now been relaxed following the Federal Constitutional Court's 1994 ruling.

As argued earlier, the European Council has been the principal institution shaping the constitutive politics of the EU. Two characteristics of the EU's regular summit meetings were advanced as relevant to Germany's role: the importance of the exchange of ideas; and the importance of large states, particularly when acting in concert. With these points in mind, it is worth reflecting upon the role played by the federal government in the European Council.

[33] Jeffrey Anderson and John Goodman, "Mars or Minerva? A United Germany in a post–Cold War Europe," in Robert O. Keohane, Joseph Nye, and Stanley Hoffmann, eds., *After the Cold War: International Institutions and State Strategies in Europe, 1989–1991* (Cambridge: Harvard University Press), pp. 45–51.

Certainly, in terms of ideas the two chancellors whose tenure has co-incided with the regular summit meetings have made a significant impact. Chancellor Helmut Schmidt was instrumental in the creation of the European Council (with French President Valéry Giscard d'Estaing). He launched the idea of the European Monetary System (EMS) at the informal, after-dinner session of the April 1978 Copenhagen summit: the perfect opportunity for launching ideas because there was no agenda. The idea had been discussed in advance with Giscard.

Chancellor Helmut Kohl assumed office in the midst of an EC crisis surrounding British budgetary contributions, but it was his Foreign Minister, Hans-Dietrich Genscher, whose long period in office gave him experience in shaping the work of the 1983 German presidency of the European Council. Although the declarations at the June 1983 Stuttgart European Council did not resolve the budgetary problem, they did put forward the contours of the settlement reached a year later during the French presidency, and they also set out a longer-term agenda for European integration. Lord Cockfield, the European commissoner (1985–88) responsible for the internal market program, states: "If any specific event can be regarded as 'relaunching the Community' it was undoubtedly the Solemn Declaration."[34] Included in the Solemn Declaration were support for European Monetary Union (EMU), strengthening of social policy and of the EC institutions: issues that were central to the EC of the mid-1980s onward. The Solemn Declaration was derived from an initiative dating from 1981 on the part of German Foreign Minister Hans-Dietrich Genscher.[35] It was subsequently turned into a joint initiative with the Italians (the Genscher-Colombo "European Act"). Although the Solemn Declaration was non-binding and thus an initial disappointment to the federal government, it played an important agenda-setting role.

Genscher was again at the fore with relaunching European Monetary Union at the Hanover European Council in June 1988. This proposal was influential in getting the momentum to EMU under way with the establishment of the Delors Committee, which was to develop concrete proposals.[36]

These examples are not exhaustive. Nevertheless, they give a flavor of the way in which informal German proposals or ideas have come to shape the European agenda. To be sure, other member states have played an active role in shaping the EU, particularly in the context of the intergovern-

[34] Lord Cockfield, *The European Union: Creating the Single Market* (Colorado Springs, Colo.: Wiley, 1994), p. 23.

[35] Gianni Bonvicini, "The Genscher-Colombo Plan and the 'Solemn Declaration on European Union,'" in Roy Pryce, ed., *The Dynamics of European Union* (Beckenham, U.K.: Croom Helm, 1987), pp. 174–87.

[36] Kenneth Dyson, *Elusive Union: The Process of Economic and Monetary Union in Europe* (Harlow, U.K.: Longman, 1994), pp. 125–29.

mental committees on treaty reform. However, it is one thing to table proposals once the agenda has been set; it is another to use the European Council to set the agenda itself. With a domestic political consensus supporting the principle of integration, it has been possible for the German chancellor or his foreign minister to do that. Within the European Council, it is questionable whether the smaller states carry sufficient weight to do so. Successive British governments have been hampered from playing such a role because of domestic divisions over European integration; successive Italian governments have lacked sufficient stability more generally. Perhaps only the French have had comparable possibilities, which they have used, often in conjunction with the federal government.[37] There is a suggestion that the German government has been a disproportionate source of demand for supranational policies. If that were so, then it would have significant implications for an analysis of German power in the EU.

If German ideas have been influential via the European Council in setting the supranational agenda, they have often been put forward bilaterally, thus strengthening their resonance. The creation of the European Council; the launching of the EMS; and the Solemn Declaration on European Union have already been mentioned. Similarly, one could mention the joint letter sent by Kohl and Mitterrand to the Irish president of the European Council in April 1990. In that letter they called for the convening of an intergovernmental conference on political union to parallel the one proposed for EMU. The Dublin European Council meeting in June of the same year finally agreed to that action.[38] The prominence of creative bilateral initiatives in the European Council represents a striking contrast with the British record of *unilateral* appeals *against* existing policy (e.g., over contributions to the EC budget, reform of the CAP); or obstructionism against reform (the attempt by Prime Minister Thatcher in both June 1985 and in October 1990 to stop the convening of intergovernmental conferences); "opt outs" from the Social Charter (1989), EMU and the Social Chapter (Maastricht 1991).[39]

In short, the European Council has proved to be a useful vehicle for the projection of German interests at the all-important agenda-setting stage of the policy process. Schmidt, Genscher, and Kohl have been among a very

[37] See David Cameron, "National Interest, the Dilemma of European Integration, and *Malaise*," in John Keeler and Martin Schain, eds., *Chirac's Challenge: Liberalization, Europeanization, and Malaise* (New York: St. Martin's Press, 1996).

[38] A similar but less convincing joint initiative was undertaken by Chancellor Kohl and President Chirac before the December 1995 European Council, at which the 1996 intergovernmental conference was discussed.

[39] Paradoxically, the Milan European Council of June 1985 not only saw Prime Minister Thatcher defeated over the calling of an intergovernmental conference; it also saw a rare British triumph in the government heads' agreement to the single-market program, which Thatcher favored.

small group of participants able to exploit the European Council for the furthering of integration.

Congruence in Norms and Conventions

As regards the norms and conventions of the EU, the supranational rules of the game present no fundamental problems for Germany. Above all, Germany's "reflexive multilateralism" represents the ideal match with the supranational rules of the game. As noted earlier, Germany's commitment to multilateralism both as an idea and as a means to achieve specific policy goals is firmly embedded in German elites. Klaus Goetz has argued that it has entered the elites' "genetic code."[40] Although the expression of Germany's European identity to be found in the speeches of successive chancellors and foreign ministers is sometimes dismissed as pro-integration rhetoric, it is seen here as the product of deeply held values concerning the rules of the game of postwar European politics.[41] Thus it is argued that Germany seeks to project its norms and model of community at the supranational level. This model of international society held by German elites shapes the presentation of German interests.[42]

Leaving aside the congruence of supranational integration with the norms embedded in German policy-making elites, there are other, more specific areas of correspondence. The reliance in the domestic arena on coalition building predisposes the government to finding consensus. The well-established domestic principle of "bundestreues Verhalten" (loyalty to the federation) also facilitates a constructive approach to solving problems within the EU: dogmatic positions are avoided. Moreover, as a founding member of supranational integration, Germany has not needed to challenge the rules of the game or the policy inheritance, for it shaped them from the very outset.

A further normative aspect refers back to the legal and constitutional setting of the EU, familiar to German participants from domestic experience. Just as the EU's institutions and practices are based on treaty and rule, so is the law in Germany a "structuring instrument defining institutions and the rights and duties of citizens, and equally . . . a statement of political and so-

---

[40] K. Goetz, "Integration in a Europeanized State: Germany and the Intergovernmental Conference," *Journal of European Public Policy* 3 (1996): 24.

[41] *Pace* rationalists who see Germany as merely concealing its interests through "dressing them up" in European rhetoric and thereby allaying neighbors' fears about a German *Sonderweg*, the argument here follows a constructivist approach.

[42] This reflects the position adopted by James Caporaso in explaining the phenomenon of multilateralism, namely, that "shared understandings and communicative rationality are as important as instrumentalist rationality." See James Caporaso, "International Relations Theory," p. 82.

cial values to which the society as a whole is committed."[43] The importance of the legal dimension in the EU presents no problems for German civil servants functioning at the supranational level.

Congruence in Patterns of Mesolevel Governance

At the meso level, there is a strong correspondence between the segmentation of EU policy making and the sectorization inherent in German public policy. Two possible scenarios arise from this. One is the development of highly specialized governance regimes comprising EU and national (and, potentially, subnational) policy makers. The mutually reinforcing nature of the policy specialization and the creation of a set of rules of the game specific to a group of policy makers generates considerable scope for discrete governance regimes to develop. Thus German and European policy may become incremental and somewhat uncoordinated. A lack of coordination in German European policy would imply a reduction in German influence. In this scenario, one would point to the domestic constraints imposed by the need to consult the *Länder* on certain issues; the emergence of the Bundestag's Committee on EU Affairs, established after the 1994 federal elections to strengthen domestic democratic control; the need to establish liaison with parapublic agencies (e.g., the Bundesbank); and the conditions set for further integration in the 1993 Maastricht judgment of the Federal Constitutional Court. Above all, however, the considerable autonomy held by individual federal ministries, sometimes reinforced by coalition politics, can lead to the confused articulation of German policy in Brussels.[44]

The alternative scenario would regard these weaknesses as a form of "soft power." Thus apparent weaknesses in domestic policy coordination can translate into useful bargaining resources in interstate negotiations. Federal ministers or officials may find it a useful negotiating strategy to argue in interstate negotiations that the *Länder* governments or similar would not accept a certain position. German bargaining positions within the EU may be reinforced if they are a product of domestic institutional stipulations.

Germany, the member state that can least be seen to exercise its national influence in the EU, also may derive particular benefit from having its interests obscured by a fragmented policy process. Although Germany might be highly influential in many discrete EU-FRG policy communities, no particular actor in the process—perhaps not even the federal government itself—has an overview sufficient to establish the cumulative effect of this. In addition, the technical nature of negotiations in discrete gover-

[43]Johnson, "Law as Articulation," p. 178.
[44]See S. Bulmer and W. Paterson, *The Federal Republic of Germany and the European Community* (London: Allen and Unwin, 1987), chaps. 2 and 3.

nance regimes may "mask potentially divisive issues beneath a proliferation of professional and expert language."[45] Cumulatively, as a result of the institutional framework of FRG-EU interaction, the extent of "German power in the European Union" receives very unsystematic attention. Put another way, because of its internal institutional pluralism, Germany may not articulate its policy interests in the centralized manner characteristic of Britain, but it avoids taking on extreme negotiating positions and bargaining styles that (mistakenly) presume member state–EU relations are a zero-sum game. In the more subtle institutionalized politics of the EU, there is more to power than the realist articulation of national interests.

Congruence in Policy Goals

How far does the EU policy profile correspond to that of the FRG? German economic policy has been something of a conundrum. On the face of it, the social market model provides an "Ordnungspolitik" designed to help economic markets work, while providing a safety net where market failure occurs. The rhetoric of the social market does not coincide with reality, however; Germany provides considerable state support for industry.[46] Further, criticism arose in the early 1980s about German technical standards (DIN) being employed as a barrier to intra-EU trade. Although at the liberal end of member states on economic policy issues, Germany was undertaking mercantilist measures itself, albeit through a diffuse set of domestic agencies.

The situation changed somewhat in the context of the single-market program. First, the British government took on the mantle of neoliberalism, resulting in greater transparency of German intervention in the market. On a range of measures, from air transport to financial services, the German government was noticeably less enthusiastic about liberalization. Given the new domestic agenda of financing economic reconstruction in the former German Democratic Republic (GDR), however, the changed EU context for German policy—which includes seeking to meet the convergence criteria for EMU—has offered a useful alibi for the more economically liberal (or financially restrictive) parts of the government in their attempts to cut German budgetary commitments. Unification has also caused some limited changes in German European policy; for example, Germany, traditionally an opponent of steel subsidies, found itself arguing the opposite case in order to save the Eko Stahl plant in the east (see chapter 3 for elaboration and case study evidence).

[45] Peters, "Bureaucratic Politics," p. 80.
[46] See Simon Bulmer, "Completing the European Community's Internal Market: The Regulatory Implications for the Federal Republic of Germany," in Kenneth Dyson, ed., *The Politics of German Regulation* (Aldershot, U.K.: Dartmouth, 1992), pp. 53–77.

In the domain of technological cooperation, Germany may be regarded as the member state with the least need to rely on EU programs. Nevertheless, such support is offered at the domestic level, so there is no fundamental clash of policy direction. In the context of environmental policy, the FRG and Denmark have been the prime movers in policy development. In many respects, Germany has been able to shape the policy agenda by virtue of having addressed issues and developed ideas ahead of a number of the other states. Although it is difficult to portray this action as part of a strategy, for there were too many agencies involved as well as the Greens, it gave Germany "first mover" advantage once the EU started to regulate the policy area.

Despite the initial reservations of the Bundesbank, EC monetary policy coordination was suited to German economic objectives. The wish to secure a zone of trading stability, through restraining appreciation of the deutsche mark, explains why the EMS was launched by Chancellor Helmut Schmidt in 1978. Debate about German dominance of the system was brought sharply into focus following German unification. With the costs of unification imposing a heavy burden on the domestic economy, the Bundesbank was obliged to follow a policy of comparatively high interest rates, which in turn forced other member states in the EMS exchange rate mechanism to raise their interest rates as well. Not only did this situation have a depressing effect on partners' economies, but the asymmetric shock of German unification was a major contributor to the virtual breakdown of the EMS in 1992–93.

If the EMS had served German interests so well, how is it that Germany signed the Maastricht accord on EMU, which would entail a fundamental weakening of the power of the Bundesbank and the replacement of the deutsche mark? In short, for two reasons. First, Chancellor Kohl felt the need to demonstrate "reflexive multilateralism" in the new, postunification context for fear that neighbors would be concerned at the Bonn government looking east rather than west. Second, Germany secured its particular objectives, namely, tight convergence criteria and an independent European Central Bank. Dyson expresses matters thus:

> Quite simply, given the domestic priority to low inflation, German officials had little economic incentive to see countries with weak currencies in an EMU; every incentive to ensure that the final EMU bargain reflected German economic priorities and institutions writ large; and the capability, resting on the structural power of its economy and currency and its role as the anchor of the ERM, to get its way in negotiations.[47]

[47] See Dyson, *Elusive Union,* p. 149; more generally, pp. 154–59. Apart from emphasizing Helmut Kohl's importance in securing the final agreement at the Maastricht European Council, Dyson's subsequent analysis shows how German preconditions were met.

The move to the third stage of EMU is likely to lead to a call for further strengthening of the redistributive policy instruments of the EU. Hitherto these have remained small because of the modest size of the supranational budget. Much of the spending, particularly on the Common Agricultural Policy (CAP), has been allocative, and with perverse distributive consequences. German interests have favored a tight rein on the budget, for the FRG has been the main net contributor. German concern at the level of contributions has at times become an issue of political concern at the domestic level, and it is likely that any substantial increase in contributions could be achieved only at the cost of major public dissent. The experience with funding the reconstruction of the former GDR economy is illustrative of this. Indeed, there was increasing concern among German politicians and in the Bundesbank during 1993–94 at the level of German contributions to the EC budget (1993: DM 22 billion), particularly because the costs of unification had the effect of pushing Germany down the EU "league table" of affluence.[48]

Because German agricultural policy had never been run on a market-led basis, German policy makers saw no problem with a protectionist CAP. Indeed, the discretion afforded by the CAP to agriculture ministers within the European Community redounded to the benefit of Germany's agricultural sector. This situation was assisted by the creative use of CAP policy instruments (green currencies, monetary compensatory amounts, etc.). Behind this lay regulatory capture of the agriculture ministry in Bonn and the dynamics of electoral politics at federal and *Länder* levels. (All this despite the resulting higher German contributions to the EC budget!) The inclusion of agriculture in the Uruguay Round of GATT negotiations meant that some of the autonomy enjoyed by that sector was lost. Quite simply, the more economically significant interests of the German manufacturing and service sectors found they could not be jeopardized by obstructionism from the agricultural lobby.

Finally, in economic policy, the EU framework has not significantly constrained German industry's global trading role. Although on occasion there have been times of tension, when threats of a "fortress Europe" have been in the air, these times have been relatively infrequent.

What of the correspondence between German and EU policy interests in the CFSP and JHA pillars of the EU? In Europe, both during and after the Cold War, Germany's geopolitical location has given it a vested interest in European stability. Foreign policy cooperation in the European Community/European Union has served as an important vehicle for securing

---

[48] See "Die Finanzbeziehungen der Bundesrepublik Deutschland zu den Europäischen Gemeinschaften seit dem Jahr 1988," *Deutsche Bundesbank Monatsbericht* (November 1993): 61–78.

this and other German foreign policy goals. It has emancipated the FRG from the shadow of the past, particularly in dealing with the Middle East situation.

JHA cooperation was particularly supported by Helmut Kohl in the period immediately preceding the TEU. Although German unification had gone hand-in-hand with the lifting of the Iron Curtain, the result was not simply a "peace dividend." New problems emerged: criminality infiltrating the EU from the east; and additional cross-border economic migrants. The JHA pillar was advocated strongly by German ministers and Chancellor Kohl as a response to these developments, which affected the FRG particularly, owing to its location and borders with numerous states. Germany hoped that, in return for cooperation on immigration matters, other member states might share the burden of responsibility for regulating the rapid increase in those seeking asylum in the FRG at the end of the 1980s. Subsequent work within JHA cooperation has added important new policy instruments to the domestic ones available in the FRG. Although, in the end, the German asylum issue was resolved domestically, the moves toward European cooperation served as a useful means for trying to limit domestic opposition.

MEDIATING GERMAN POWER IN THE EUROPEAN UNION: FOUR FACES

Thus far, we have looked at the pattern of institutional interaction between Germany and European integration: at how the constitutive order of the EU provides a profile of governance that the FRG has come to embrace. Congruence between the profile of the governance of the EU and that of the FRG does not automatically relate to any conception of power, which, as a contested concept in the methodology of political science, cannot be examined in detail here.[49] What follows, rather, is a discussion of four faces of German power based on the work of Guzzini,[50] whose "dyadic" understanding of power appears particularly valuable precisely because Germany and the EU are in *inter*action. The character of the EU is not only the product of Germany (and the other states) but has its own dynam-

[49] See, generally, Lukes, *Power;* Peter Morriss, *Power: A Philosophical Analysis* (Manchester: Manchester University Press, 1987); and Brian Barry, *Democracy, Power and Justice* (Oxford: Clarendon Press, 1989).

[50] Stefano Guzzini, "Structural Power: The Limits of Neo-Realist Analysis," *International Organization* 47 (Summer 1993): 443–78. For a different systemization of German power, see Andrei S. Markovits and Simon Reich, *The German Predicament: Memory and Power in the New Europe* (Ithaca: Cornell University Press, 1997); also Anne-Marie Le Gloannec, "The Purpose of German Power," in Z. Laïki, ed., *Power and Purpose after the Cold War* (Providence, R.I.: Berg, 1994), pp. 35–53.

ics and can, in turn, offer opportunities for, and constraints upon, German (and other states') elites to redefine their interests and identity. In other words, the character of the EU can empower Germany (and other member states) in different ways.[51]

One face of German power would see it as a function of the forceful articulation of interests, combined with valuable power resources for articulating leverage (e.g., the FRG's strong economic position; its governmental stability; its well-established domestic consensus on integration; and a largely effective administrative organization). This neorealist perception of utilizing power in multilateral negotiations might be termed *deliberate power*. It corresponds to a perception of power politics that holds particular sway in the United Kingdom, reinforced by institutional peculiarities like the institutional and normative importance of national and parliamentary sovereignty, the adversarial values of parliamentary politics, and so on.[52] The contrast between Germany and Britain is striking, for the FRG's institutions and institutional norms are strongly oriented toward power sharing and consensus building. Anderson and Goodman encapsulate the situation thus:

> Over the course of forty years, West Germany's reliance on a web of international institutions to achieve its foreign policy goals, born of an instrumental choice among painfully few alternatives, became so complete as to cause these institutions to become embedded in the very definition of state interests and strategies.[53]

Under these circumstances, it is possible to understand why this more naked form of power is seldom exerted by Germany within the EU. Germany's prior history constrains the federal government from projecting national interests in a nakedly self-interested manner. Thus the internal institutional diffusion of power and the strong commitment to external multi- or bilateral diffusion of power mean that the German approach is more subtle.

A second face of German power relates to influencing the structure, norms, and policy principles of the EU indirectly. Thus, in certain central areas of policy, it has been possible for the FRG to play an active role in

---

[51] A primitive comparison of Britain and Germany in the EU reveals this situation. For an initial attempt at an Anglo-German comparison, see Simon Bulmer, "Britain and Germany in the European Union: British Realism and German Institutionalism?" paper presented at the Conference of Europeanists, Chicago, March 14–16, 1996.

[52] See Bulmer, "Britain and Germany"; also Kenneth Armstrong and Simon Bulmer, "The United Kingdom," in Dietrich Rometsch and Wolfgang Wessels, eds., *The European Union and Member States: Towards Institutional Fusion?* (Manchester: Manchester University Press, 1996), pp. 253–90.

[53] Anderson and Goodman, "Mars or Minerva?" p. 60.

shaping institutional development in such a way as to mobilize a bias in the character of EU governance. Following Guzzini, we term this *indirect institutional power*.[54] This form of power may be exercised through efforts to shape the broad framework of the EU (its constitutive politics), or through shaping one of its governance regimes, such as relating to monetary cooperation. Once shaped—if German efforts succeed—a bias is mobilized in the character of the governance of the EU. From the standpoint of the smaller European states such power is less threatening than a more realist form of deliberate power, for the latter is associated with an international system where the rules of the game privilege large states. Where, however, the federal government advocates the deepening of integration, it is presenting a view of integration compatible with the interests of smaller member states, which fear a looser EU would be dominated by the larger states.

Germany is well placed to utilize power in this manner because of the continuity of the consensus among political parties and elites supporting European integration. These circumstances facilitate the playing of a constructive role in the design of supranational integration. Germany's voice is generally articulate when constitutive politics are on the agenda of the EU. The negotiations on EMU leading up to the Maastricht treaty are a case in point. First, Germany was seeking to deepen European integration, in line with its *Staatsräson* (reason of state). But, more specifically, negotiators could point to the requirements of domestic law concerning the Bundesbank's autonomy or concerning fiscal prudence in order to exert leverage in technical negotiations on the economic criteria for the third stage of EMU and on the constitutional-legal situation for the European Central Bank. This negotiating position was enhanced by traditional power resources (for example, the strength of the deutsche mark and the organizational prestige of the Bundesbank), such that Germany was in a strong position to influence both the terms of transition to an EMU and its subsequent evolution. Indirect institutional power was important to this episode.

Moreover, the new domestic constitutional commitments that Germany undertook after signing the Maastricht treaty have imposed significant constraints on the future pattern of integration (e.g., the need to satisfy the *Länder,* the Bundestag, and so on). The Federal Constitutional Court's 1993 judgment on the Maastricht treaty has set further tests for the acceptability of future constitutional reform within the EU. It is important not to underestimate the indirect power that can be exerted in this fashion.[55] This second face of German power alludes to what Susan Strange (in

---

[54] Guzzini, "Structural Power," pp. 451–56.

[55] Standard setting by European agencies, in which Germany is strongly represented because of its extensive record, is another domain where German indirect influence may be exerted, with important implications for industrial competitiveness. I am grateful to Willie Paterson for pointing this out.

a different context) referred to as the "power to set the agenda of discussion or to design . . . the international 'regime' of rules and customs."[56]

A third face of German power in the EU arises from unintended consequences of domestic political and economic power. We term this *unintentional power*. This form of power is dispositional rather than the product of deliberate action.[57] Guzzini gives the specific illustration of the unintended effects of the Bundesbank's domestic monetary policy following German unification.[58] As indicated earlier, its actions had the unintended consequence of exporting higher interest rates to other member states in the exchange rate mechanism of the EMS, paving the way for economic problems in those states and, eventually, the currency crises of 1992 and 1993. German power had come into play as a capacity, but in an unintended manner. The Bundesbank was simply following its script, the 1957 Bundesbank Act, which is concerned with the conduct of domestic monetary policy, not foreign economic relations. As the largest in the EU, the FRG's economy is likely to influence the economic variables in fellow member states through its unintentional power, which is less acceptable to the FRG's neighbors and EU partners because it is particularly associated with economic indications of German predominance.

In each of these three faces, Germany agent power may be facilitated by various resources, such as authority, money, legitimacy, information, or organizational capability.[59] Military capacity—a traditional power resource in realist analysis—is of limited value for the articulation of German European policy interests because it is not the "currency" the EU deals in (except on the fringes, with respect to peacekeeping activities in the CFSP pillar).

Finally, it is important to think of the character of the EU itself. Might this character provide a fourth face of German power? As argued above, German power is not just the product of forces emanating *from* Germany. The assumption here is that Germany's institutional interdependence with the EU means that the exercise of power is not all one-way traffic, that is, from Germany as "agent" to the EU as "structure." Rather, the EU

---

[56] Susan Strange, "The Myth of Lost Hegemony," *International Organization* 41 (Autumn 1987): 565.

[57] It is an open question whether this unintentional form of power is power or luck. See Brian Barry, *Democracy, Power and Justice,* chap. 9; and Keith Dowding, *Rational Choice and Political Power* (Aldershot, U.K.: Edward Elgar, 1991), pp. 63–68. My thanks to Vittorio Bufacchi for assistance on these matters.

[58] Guzzini, "Structural Power," p. 457.

[59] The resources listed here are drawn from Rod Rhodes's analysis of multitiered governance in Britain: Rod Rhodes, *Beyond Westminster and Whitehall: The Sub-Central Governments of Britain* (London: Unwin Hyman, 1987). However, following the work of Baldwin, power resources may be delimited in their utility, that is, they are nonfungible. Money, therefore, may not be a resource for Germany in policy areas where there is no budgetary dimension. See R. Baldwin, *Economic Statecraft* (Princeton: Princeton University Press, 1985).

as an evolving system of governance represents a framework within which Germany, as "agent," manages its power dispositionally. Empirically, such an assumption presumes that the EU institutions possess their own institutional dynamics, independently of the member states. Given these assumptions, the argument is that the EU is characterized by a bias that facilitates the disposition of German agent power. This assertion is difficult to substantiate because the routine mobilization of bias is difficult to document. Nevertheless, it is suggested that it can be identified in two ways. First, for a state such as Germany, with its limited ability to employ neorealist, nation-state-based forms of projecting its power, the EU has an empowering capacity. Thus the dynamics of integration emanating from the EU itself systemically represent a mobilization of bias that matches Germany's Europeanized definition of state interests. Second, the adoption of German institutional rules (e.g., on EMU) and norms (e.g., subsidiarity) mobilizes a procedural bias that should facilitate the articulation of German interests. There is, of course, a time lag in how this institutional power comes into play. Shaping the EU's constitutive politics in one time period will enable Germany to advance its interests in the regulative politics of the EU only in a subsequent time period. For example, German insistence on fiscal rectitude in the Maastricht convergence criteria comes into play when it is decided who is to proceed to stage three of EMU. This fourth face of power means that the close congruence between the EU's character and Germany's institutions and identity has a passive, dispositional power dimension: a kind of *empowerment*.

The cumulative effect of Germany's institutional power in the EU is that, for German policy makers, participation in the institutions of the EU resembles a warm bath. This situation is illustrated in Jeffrey Anderson's examination in chapter 3 of how the management of German unification was handled in the regulative politics of the EU.

CONCLUSION

This chapter has sought to outline how German power is mediated institutionally by the EU. It is not that the institutions of the EU represent some kind of external "imposition" on the FRG, designed to constrain its power. Rather, those institutions—their broad constitutional order, norms, governance regimes, and policy activities—are also shaped by Germany as a member state. German interests, institutions, and identity have a strikingly good fit with the character of the EU.

Is the fit better for Germany than for France and Britain, and if so how? To answer these questions, let us briefly compare the interests, institutions, and identities of the three states vis-à-vis the EU.

Of the three, Britain has the experience of integration most different from Germany's. Joining the European Community only in 1973, it found some of the policies to be out of step with national interests, notably the burden of budgetary contributions and the form of the CAP. Economically, Britain's interests came much more into line with EU policies with the launching of the single-market program, while its mixed experience with fixed exchange rate systems has contributed to reservations on EMU. The Conservative Government's labor market policy also set Britain apart from the thrust of supranational social policy.

Divergences of interests such as these are sharpened by Britain's domestic political system. There has been a persistence of divisions within governing parties throughout the period since 1973. These divisions have become most critical when the governing party has had a small working majority because the adversarial norms of British parliamentary democracy encourage their exploitation in the pursuit of high office. Thus the Labour Party was willing to sabotage the ratification of the TEU, despite its support for the contents, in order to topple Prime Minister John Major's government from power.[60] British parliamentary institutions have not facilitated the main parties' adoption in office of a European identity of the type displayed by their German counterparts. Arguably, the best adaptation to EU institutions has occurred in Whitehall's European policy-making machinery.[61]

It is revealing, then, that there has only been one major British initiative for integration that has found support from its EU partners, namely, the single market. Otherwise, Britain's record under both Labour and Conservative governments has been that of an "outlier": renegotiation of the terms of membership (1974–75); refusal to join the EMS in 1979; the budgetary crisis (1979–84); refusal to sign the Social Charter (1979); insistence on opt-out provisions for EMU and the Social Chapter in the TEU (1991); and noncooperation in the Council in protest at the other member states' failure to agree on a program for the lifting of the ban on the British export of beef which arose from concerns about "mad cow disease." This is not the diplomacy of a state that experiences the EU as a warm bath. It reflects continuing domestic political divisions that hamper the projection of British interests, institutional models, and identity in the EU context.

France occupies a position between Britain and Germany. In common with Britain, it seeks to retain its strong national identity, based on former grandeur as a colonial power. Combining a strong national identity with a

---

[60] D. Baker, A. Gamble, and S. Ludlam, "The British Parliamentary Siege of Maastricht 1993: Conservative Divisions and British Ratification," *Parliamentary Affairs* 47 (1994): 37–60.
[61] See Armstrong and Bulmer, "United Kingdom."

European one has been a difficult balancing act. Failure to maintain a balance was the underlying reason why de Gaulle's diplomacy in the European Community led to the 1965 "empty chair" crisis, which remains the episode that most fundamentally challenged the integration process. France is still not averse to pursuing its interests unilaterally or in terms of a nationalist language, as was shown by President Jacques Chirac's suspension of aspects of the Schengen Accords and his resumption of nuclear testing in the South Pacific. The TEU was divisive in French politics, and recent public opinion has shown a decline in support for integration.[62] Party fragmentation has also become sharper over integration during the 1990s. Pursuing a strong identification with integration has been more problematic for French political leaders than their German counterparts.

Institutionally, France has proven to be well adapted to the EU, both on its own and through use of the Franco-German relationship. Moreover, presidential power normally enables the thrust of European policy to be above day-to-day political difficulties. The administrative machinery of France's European policy making is centralized and geared toward an efficient projection of French interests in the EU, which, in general terms, have been well served by European integration, given France's central role in defining the founding treaties. In terms of interests, institutions, and identity, France has a fairly good fit with the EU, but there are some challenges ahead: the domestic dilemma of how to meet the EMU convergence criteria without engendering further domestic protest; the challenge to the French model of state-market relations emerging from the EU's single-market program; and a possible tilt away from French interests in the EU with projected eastward enlargement.[63] Overall, France is closer than Britain to the kind of relationship with the EU enjoyed by Germany, but it is not as comfortable with reflexive multilateralism and giving up a national identity.

The institutional mediation of German power is, I argue, distinctive in form. The situation has not come about as a result of Germany conducting a hard-nosed, centralized defense of its national interests. Indeed, until the 1970s German negotiators tended to back down if isolated in negotiations in the Council. Almost all German initiatives in the EU—from the EMS on—have been presented bilaterally, usually with the French government of the day. It is precisely for this reason that German diplomacy over the recognition of Croatia and Slovenia at the end of 1991 was so striking: for once, Germany *did* deploy its bargaining resources unilater-

[62] See Cameron, "National Interest."

[63] On the first two challenges, see, respectively, Cameron, "National Interest"; and Vivien Schmidt, "Loosening the Ties That Bind: The Impact of European Integration on French Government and Its Relationship to Business," *Journal of Common Market Studies* 34 (June 1996): 223–54.

ally to achieve its objectives.[64] This case remains the exception, and for the time being Germany remains a "gentle giant" within the EU.[65]

"Gentle giant" expresses two important facets to Germany's role in the EU. As noted, German diplomacy is "gentle": it is not characterized by unilateral, deliberate power, the first face of German power examined above. This is not to suggest that German negotiators do not defend their corner in Council negotiations. They do, but they take care not to be isolated, and not to conduct themselves in a manner that challenges the consensual norms upon which the EU rests. On the other hand, Germany *is* a giant, particularly in the economic sphere. In consequence, smaller European states—both within the EU and outside—may experience the dispositional form of unintentional power. More congenial to them, however, is the pursuit of German diplomacy through indirect institutional means. To the extent that Germany's governments continue to embed themselves in the EU, as has been the case hitherto, the smaller states are comfortable with the resultant taming of its power.

[64] See Beverley Crawford, "German Foreign Policy and European Political Cooperation: The Diplomatic Recognition of Croatia in 1991," *German Politics and Society* 13 (Summer 1995): 1–34; also Anderson and Goodman, "Mars or Minerva?" 49–51.

[65] See S. Bulmer and W. Paterson, "Germany in the European Union: Gentle Giant or Emergent Leader?" *International Affairs* 72 (January 1996): 9–32.

CHAPTER THREE

Hard Interests, Soft Power, and Germany's Changing Role in Europe

Jeffrey J. Anderson

Between 1958 and 1989, the European Community frequently provided a backdrop to the clash of national interests and the exercise of raw power by the large member states. President Charles De Gaulle and the "empty chair" crisis; Prime Minister Margaret Thatcher and the British rebate— these are just two of many possible examples. Conspicuous by their absence on the list, however, are the six German chancellors whose combined tenure in office spanned this brief but eventful period. Clearly, Germany influenced the integration process, often decisively. Yet it did so in an unusual manner for a large member country. Germany projected its power softly, revealing a firm preference for normative and institutional over material interests, an ingrained support for multilateralism, and a greater inclination than its large European partners to delegate sovereignty to supranational institutions.[1]

I thank Simon Bulmer, András Inotai, Peter Katzenstein, Beate Kohler-Koch, Andrew Moravcsik, and Lowell Turner for their helpful comments and suggestions. Research support was provided by the German Marshall Fund of the United States and Cornell University.
[1] I refer to "soft" power in a behavioral sense; thus my usage differs from resource-oriented discussions, such as Joseph Nye, *Bound to Lead: The Changing Nature of American Power* (New York: Basic Books, 1990). For a more complete discussion of the distinction between "hard" and "soft" power, see Katzenstein's introduction to this volume.

Multilateralism is an institutional form that "coordinates relations among three or more states on the basis of generalized principles of conduct." Two corollaries follow from multilateralism: (1) the generalized principles of conduct "logically entail an indivisibility among the members of a collectivity with respect to the range of behavior in question"; and (2) expectations of diffuse reciprocity among members generally flow from successful multilater-

What effect will unification have on Germany's unique European vocation? Will a unified Germany—larger in terms of territory, population, and economic resources and free of Cold War international constraints—eventually abandon soft power for a harder realpolitik? And if so, with what consequences, for Germany and for Europe?

This chapter's analysis rests on the conceptual distinction between constitutive and regulative politics in the European Union. "Constitutive politics" relates to processes and outcomes that establish or amend EU rules of the game and is largely coextensive with the high politics surrounding the periodic "grand bargains" like the Treaty of Rome, the Single European Act, and the Treaty on European Union. "Regulative politics" relates to processes and outcomes that take place within established, routinized areas of EU activity. Constitutive and regulative politics are not mutually exclusive phenomena; each influences the other in complex ways.

This simple typology allows for a more differentiated analysis of Germany's power at the supranational level. As briefly discussed below, German influence over European Community/European Union constitutive outcomes has been substantial. The aim of this chapter is to examine the regulative side of Germany's EC/EU policies, both before and after unification. How, if at all, are German approaches to regulative politics connected to the realm of constitutive politics? Does the projection of German power in constitutive politics mobilize bias in its favor within discrete regulative policy sectors? If not, what logic underpins the relationship?

To address these questions, the first section briefly discusses the preunification period, the political challenges that unification presented to the link forged by German leaders between constitutive and regulative politics, and the content of their responses to date. The analytical thrust of this section is embodied in four intrinsically important case studies of regulative politics in the EC/EU: the Common Agricultural Policy (CAP), trade, the structural funds, and competition policy. Together, the CAP and the structural funds constitute approximately 75 percent of the EU budget and, as such, encompass the bulk of the visible benefits allocated by European institutions from day to day. Furthermore, these regulative policy areas are intimately connected to constitutive politics in the EU, figuring prominently in negotiations over the single-market initiative and the Maastricht treaty.

My basic argument is as follows. Until 1989, Germany's modal approach to European Community regulative politics was not to maximize its return of material benefits under the prevailing rules of the game, although this certainly occurred in some instances such as the CAP. Rather, German

---

alism. John Gerard Ruggie, "Multilateralism: The Anatomy of an Institution," in Ruggie, ed., *Multilateralism Matters* (New York: Columbia University Press, 1993), p. 11.

behavior revealed a profound concern with two other "hard" interests: (1) strengthening the broader framework of European multilateralism and Germany's self-defined role within it; and (2) creating a supportive external environment within which the German domestic model of political economy could flourish. Germany's largely successful pursuit of these interests remained politically viable throughout the period because it satisfied the expectations of other EC members as to the acceptable face of German power, and because it could draw on a stable domestic consensus about Europe and the German model. As a result, German approaches to constitutive and regulative politics stood in lagged harmony with respect to one another, with constitutive politics setting strong parameters for regulative politics, and the latter reinforcing the principles underpinning the former.

Unification has unsettled this comfortable equilibrium. Between 1990 and 1992, the German government attempted to conduct business as usual, and willingly submitted to—indeed, requested the application of—established EC procedures and related outcomes despite the huge costs imposed on domestic actors, especially those in the former German Democratic Republic (GDR). Since then, as a result of changes in domestic politics flowing from unification, the German government has shifted its approach to regulative politics in Brussels, paying more attention to issues of distribution and redistribution. This has been accompanied by a more visible, assertive projection of power, one that has achieved short-term successes, but often at the expense of damage to Germany's long-term interests in both the regulative and constitutive realms of EU politics. In sum, a new set of hard interests, overlaid on the old ones, has shaken the foundations of soft power.

PREUNIFICATION GERMANY AND THE EC: CONSTITUTIVE-REGULATIVE HARMONY

As Simon Bulmer has pointed out in chapter 2, by the time the Berlin Wall collapsed in November 1989, a striking congruence had emerged between the Federal Republic and the European Community. Institutionally, both were characterized by variants of cooperative federalism that encompassed a diverse set of subsystem governance patterns. Similar ideational principles underpinned the rules of the game in each system, such as subsidiarity and consensualism. And finally, the content of many policies overlapped sufficiently to preclude major clashes between European and German objectives.

To say that congruence resulted directly from German attempts in the 1950s to construct the European Economic Community (EEC) in its own image would be to misrepresent the interests and capabilities of not just the Germans, but all the participants in this process. Nevertheless, as Hitler's shadow faded somewhat in the late 1960s, Germany began to shape constitutive outcomes in Europe more directly, in terms of both the evolving institutional and ideational architecture of the Community and the content of policies carried out under its aegis.

Several things are notable about the German projection of power in Community constitutive politics. First, Germany rarely if ever exercised solitary leadership or sought to impose its will on fellow members. Indeed, German governments were extremely averse to political isolation in Brussels, preferring instead to build consensus from within and, if necessary, offer concessions to preserve that consensus. German initiatives invariably were launched in tandem with other major powers in the Community, usually France.[2] Second, Germany was less concerned than its major partners about the diluting effects of integration on national sovereignty, behaving much more like the smaller member states than France or Britain.

The origins of this distinctive European policy are complex. In no small part, they lie in the reordering of German interests that took place after 1945, amid the smoldering ruins of the Third Reich. The total military defeat of the Nazi dictatorship had removed not only fascists from the postwar picture, but also those wedded to Germany's authoritarian past. The deepening Cold War marginalized the champions of an eastward-looking, socialist future. Thus postwar Germany was not just a truncated version of its former self but a new polity.

That said, the new Germany was a country with tender democratic roots and uncertain economic prospects. And so, on the basis of hard-headed instrumental calculations, German elites embraced multilateralism. International organizations like NATO, the European Coal and Steel Community (ECSC), and the EEC offered the Federal Republic concrete opportunities to gain access to foreign markets and to win back its forfeited sovereignty, thereby achieving an "equality of rights" with its European neighbors.[3] In short, early German support for multilateralism can be linked directly to domestic interest politics.

---

[2] The two most recent initiatives, the Single European Act (SEA) and the Treaty on European Union (TEU), resulted largely from Franco-German initiatives. On the broader subject of Germany's European policy, see S. Bulmer and W. Paterson, "West Germany's Role in Europe: 'Man-Mountain' or 'Semi-Gulliver'?" *Journal of Common Market Studies* 28 (December 1989): 95–117; and J. Anderson and J. Goodman, "Mars or Minerva? A United Germany in a Post-Cold War Europe," in R. Keohane, J. Nye, and S. Hoffmann, eds., *After the Cold War: International Institutions and State Strategies in Europe, 1989–1991* (Cambridge: Harvard University Press, 1993), pp. 23–62.

[3] Alan Milward, *The European Rescue of the Nation State* (Berkeley: University of California Press, 1992), p. 197.

Interest politics alone, however, cannot account for Germany's pacifist military security policy, nor does it provide a satisfactory explanation of Bonn's approach to national sovereignty or its aversion to unilateralism. One must look beyond material and political interests to the politics of national identity in postwar Germany, which unfolded in searing domestic political debates over rearmament, reunification, and European integration carried out under the watchful eyes of neighboring countries and allies.[4] Initially, the new collective identity defined itself far more in terms of what Germany was not: an expansionist state pursuing a predatory foreign policy. It also reflected foreign expectations about acceptable German behavior on the international stage.[5]

European integration took on immediate importance for Germany not only because it served the country's interests but because it reinforced the country's reconstituted national identity. The multilateral frameworks of the ECSC and the EEC provided welcome constraints: liberal-democratic swaddling clothes for the infant democracy. They also allowed Germany to signal to Europe and to the outside world its changed and ultimately benign identity and intentions. Over time, as the Federal Republic established a reputation for economic prowess, new dimensions appeared in its identity, characterized more by what the country now embodied than by the negation of what it once was. This evolving collective identity manifested itself in Germany's approach to constitutive politics; Bonn was keen to erect institutional and normative frameworks at the supranational level that would nurture or otherwise support its successful domestic economic formula.

In sum, the intersection of international opportunities, constraints, and expectations, on the one hand, and a transformed and ultimately supportive domestic context, on the other, explain Germany's distinctive European policy in the postwar period.[6] German-EEC relations soon established a resonance frequency that resulted in the amplification of mul-

---

[4] "National identity" refers to "(a) the nationally varying ideologies of collective distinctiveness and purpose . . . , and (b) country variation in state sovereignty, as it is enacted domestically and projected internationally." Ron Jepperson, Alexander Wendt, and Peter Katzenstein, "Norms, Identity, Culture, and National Security," in Peter J. Katzenstein, ed., *The Culture of National Security: Norms and Identity in World Politics* (New York: Columbia University Press, 1996), p. 59. On German debates pertaining to security, see Thomas Berger, "Norms, Identity, and National Security in Germany and Japan," in the same volume, pp. 317–56.

[5] Scholars working in this tradition emphasize the extent to which collective identity is shaped by the broader environment, including the expectations of other actors. See Jepperson, Wendt, and Katzenstein, "Norms, Identity, Culture," p. 19.

[6] The domestic context for Germany's European policy comprised the outcomes of interest and identity politics alluded to earlier, as well as the adoption of institutional mechanisms like administrative federalism, which necessitates a high degree of coordination and consensus building among national and subnational actors. The importance of the domestic environment to the viability of multilateralism is stressed by Ruggie, "Multilateralism."

tilateralism both in Brussels and in Bonn. As a member of the Community, Germany consistently sought to intensify and expand the multilateral principles on which the European project rested. This resulted in one of the splendid ironies of postwar European history: German political elites originally embraced the European Economic Community as a means of establishing an equality of sovereign rights between Germany and its neighbors, but then used membership to help project a markedly different conception of those rights onto their European partners. Parallel to the projection of German identity and interests onto Europe during this period, European multilateralism diffused throughout Germany and became embedded in the very definition of German state interests and strategies.[7]

Germany's reflexive support for an exaggerated multilateralism in the constitutive politics of the Community colored its approach to regulative policy too. In general, Germany rarely if ever adopted the accountant's yardstick, but sought to maintain the viability of the German domestic model within a complex, overarching multilateral framework of common policies. Preserving multilateralism meant satisfying partners' expectations about appropriate German conduct, which included footing the bill with little regard for the net return. This often led Bonn to bankroll expensive supranational policy efforts even though German domestic actors stood to receive few material benefits.

THE CHALLENGE OF UNIFICATION: FOUR CASE STUDIES OF REGULATIVE POLITICS

The constitutive politics surrounding the Treaty on European Union was driven in no small way by German unification. In early 1990, as the policy of "two German states, one German nation" looked increasingly untenable, voices—some official, some less so—across Europe and beyond began to express public concerns about the intentions of a united Germany. Fears ranged from the absurd—unification as the precursor to a renaissance of predatory fascism—to the cynical: many of Germany's European Community partners worried that Bonn planned to erect a new Hong Kong in the soon-to-be former GDR, replete with low taxes, low wages, and minimal regulatory frameworks. The ghosts of Germany's past, as well as a few conjured up from the present, roamed the continent, and for many, a deepening of European integration promised a solution.

Within Germany, political debates over the internal and external aspects of unification revealed little in the way of a mounting collective identity crisis. Indeed, official promises of a rapid, painless transition to democratic

---

[7] Anderson and Goodman, "Mars or Minerva?", p. 60.

capitalism in the former GDR revealed the brimming (over)confidence of western German elites in their sense of collective self. Economic unification on July 1, 1990, and political unification three months later represented the transfer not only of institutions but also of identity from west to east.[8]

This ambitious and complex system transfer found expression in the Federal Republic's approach to the external dimension of unification. In negotiations with the European Commission and member governments over the terms of EC accession for the former GDR, the Bonn government expressly eschewed a Mediterranean strategy, which called for a long transition period and significant exemptions from the Community's "rules of the game."[9] Instead, the Bonn government sought a rapid transition to western German, EC-consistent standards within a remarkably short period of time. More broadly, Germany's commitment to multilateralism offered an appropriate vehicle to signal continuity in its intentions vis-à-vis Europe, with the Maastricht treaty as the eventual outcome.[10]

Thus the constitutive politics flowing from unification—eastern German accession to the EC and adoption of the Maastricht treaty—represent a reaffirmation of Germany's collective identity. Yet the Federal Republic's approach to constitutive politics also masked important challenges building in the realm of regulative politics. Linked directly to changes in domestic interest politics brought about by unification, these challenges threaten the comfortable fit between constitutive and regulative politics achieved by West Germany.

Competition Policy (State Aid) and the Treuhandanstalt

West Germany enthusiastically supported stringent application of the EC's competition rules, which prohibit state aid likely to distort intracommunity trade. Nevertheless, Bonn officials were not above accepting EC sectoral aid for industries in crisis, like steel or shipbuilding. In practice, they distinguished between assistance to cushion the social dislocation caused by industrial decline, which they held to be consistent with the basic

[8] In many respects, identity transfer was much more problematic than its institutional counterpart. On eastern German public attitudes toward NATO and western integration, see Ronald Asmus, "Germany in Transition: National Self-Confidence and International Reticence," RAND/N-3522–AF (Santa Monica: Rand, 1992).

[9] See Barbara Lippert et al., *Die EG und die neuen Bundesländer* (Bonn: Europa Union Verlag, 1993).

[10] The Maastricht bargain consisted of limited French (and to a lesser extent) British concessions on political union in exchange for substantial German concessions on economic and monetary union. See Stanley Hoffmann, "French Dilemmas and Strategies in the New Europe," in Keohane, Nye, and Hoffmann, eds., *After the Cold War,* pp. 127–47; and Anderson and Goodman, "Mars or Minerva?"

tenets of the social market economy, and aid to prop up inefficient producers, which they regarded skeptically. Bonn pursued two objectives in Brussels: (1) to keep the level of state aid across the Community as low as possible, on the premise that German firms were well equipped to prosper in a relatively subsidy-free environment; and (2) to ensure, in the interests of preserving a level playing field, that German firms and regions retained access to subsidies as long as these were tolerated by the Community.

Unified Germany's position on state aid was called into question by the privatization policies of the Treuhandanstalt (THA Trust Agency).[11] Even though the German government expected the agency to carry out its mission swiftly and profitably, with an eye to the bottom line, the European Commission saw in the THA a potential for distortions to intracommunity trade, and sought to bring the agency within the EC competition framework.

After protracted negotiations with German officials, the European Commission issued a set of procedural guidelines designed to create a transparent privatization process in which the THA would adhere to "best offer" criteria in selling off its assets and guarantee that foreign buyers were not disadvantaged. Certain categories of assistance that normally would be considered questionable, such as the cancellation of old debts and state financing of environmental cleanup costs, were declared acceptable a priori. The Commission also pledged to evaluate preprivatization financing by the THA more flexibly than standard regulations permitted, provided that privatization remained imminent. In return, the THA was required to notify the Commission when a privatization case involved a "sensitive" sector (automobiles, steel, shipbuilding, textiles, synthetic fibers), or when the "best offer" criteria were not followed. Notification was also required whenever the THA provided one of its firms with credits or grants above a certain specified amount.

On the whole, German officials were satisfied with the September 1991 decision, although they would have preferred to keep the EC out of the picture altogether, fearing that the additional layer of bureaucracy would hamper an increasingly difficult privatization process. According to one THA official in Berlin, the decision evoked "no elation, but no horror either."[12] Both Bonn and Brussels affirmed that the EC's competition policy, a fairly flexible framework in itself, should apply immediately and completely to the eastern *Länder*. Available evidence suggests that the THA and the Commission quickly developed an appreciation of each other's

---

[11] For an excellent overview of the THA, see W. Seibel, "Strategische Fehler oder erfolgreiches Scheitern? Zur Entwicklung der Treuhandanstalt, 1990–1993," *Politische Vierteljahresschrift* 35 (1994): 3–39.

[12] Interview with THA official, Berlin, October 28, 1992.

interests and expectations. An official with the Treuhandanstalt stated confidently, "We believe we have a firm understanding of what the Commission categorically will not accept."[13] Although individual privatization cases were subjected to intense Commission scrutiny owing to the size and manner of public financing, by the middle of 1993 only one case had failed to win EC approval.

In 1992, as the THA turned to the most difficult privatization cases, the European Commission's competition policy directorate-general (DG-IV) reassessed the terms of its September 1991 decision. Brussels officials were concerned about several new developments: (1) the increasing likelihood of negative sale prices, as the THA sought to rid itself of its least desirable (and typically largest) holdings; (2) the use of cluster sales, in which the THA assembled mixes of desirable and less desirable firms in a single package to sweeten the deal for potential buyers; (3) the greater risk of illegitimate state aid, as the THA opted to hold on to large concerns with remote privatization prospects rather than close them down. Under the prevailing notification criteria, DG-IV was not seeing many of these cases.

New notification criteria, which supplemented rather than replaced the old ones, were announced in November 1992 and accepted by Bonn shortly thereafter. Designed to increase the number of notifications sent to the European Commission, these criteria were reformulated once again in 1994 to accommodate the transfer of remaining privatization functions from the THA to its successor organizations in 1995.

The European Commission's ability to set the basic parameters and even specific terms of privatization was often manifest and explicit. For example, during the privatization of the shipbuilding industry in 1992, a proposal to create a giant, state-owned holding company for the myriad enterprises awaiting privatization was quickly dropped when the Commission signaled through back channels that it would frown on such a solution. In the end, the Commission sanctioned the THA's preferred privatization scheme, but linked support to a substantial reduction in sectoral capacity.

In the vast majority of such cases, the policy line represented by the Commission paralleled that of the federal government, which was usually more than willing to let the Commission take the blame for the perceived hardship inflicted on eastern German interests. With regard to the privatization of the shipbuilding sector in 1992, a finance ministry official, claiming to speak for all the relevant ministries involved in the decision, explained at the time, "Our ministers were not at all upset with this outcome. Indeed, without Brussels, things could have turned out to be much more expensive." Under the prevailing fiscal climate in Germany, he added, "we

---

[13] Ibid.

have to use every brake possible [on public expenditure]."[14] Thus, up until 1992, relations between Bonn and Brussels in this policy area remained on an even keel, one consistent with Germany's long-standing approach in this regulative policy area. Thereafter, however, at least two interrelated developments, one at the *Land* level, the other at the national level, began to inject friction into the equation.

After mid-1992, as the specter of deindustrialization in the former GDR began to take shape, large unprivatized firms often became the sites of protests organized by unions, municipal authorities, and local political representatives. Responding to this pressure, the eastern *Land* governments stepped up their demands for a more direct role in THA decision making.[15] Their efforts eventually led to the creation of new institutions at the regional level that increased the potential for repeated conflicts with Brussels over its competition rules. Among the new *Länder,* Sachsen was the pacesetter with its "Atlas Program." Under the terms of a formal agreement with the THA in May 1992, Sachsen determined on a case-by-case basis "regionally significant" firms in the *Land.* When the THA opted to invest in one of these firms with an eye toward modernization and eventual privatization, Sachsen agreed to provide the firm with supplemental resources via *Land* policy instruments. This experience was replicated in other eastern *Länder.*

The public commitment on the part of the *Land* governments to target specific firms and locations for special treatment obviously exposed them to local political pressure, something state officials were acutely aware of. Commission officials were loathe to see the eastern *Länder* drawn into long-term financial relationships with privatized or unprivatized firms.[16] One DG-IV official, commenting at the end of 1992, expressed concern about the "Italianization" of eastern Germany.[17] In early 1993, Commissioner for Competition Sir Leon Brittan, commenting on Germany's overall subsidy practices since unification, declared, "I fail to see market order and discipline in the new *Länder.*"[18] Many officials in Bonn voiced similar concerns, fearing an explosion of subsidy programs particularly at the *Land* level.

---

[14] Interview with official in the Federal Ministry of Finances, Bonn, October 2, 1992.

[15] See Seibel, "Strategische Fehler?"; R. Czada, "Die Treuhandanstalt im politischen System der Bundesrepublik," *Aus Politik und Zeitgeschichte* 43–44 (28 October 1994): 31–42; and F. Nägele, "Strukturpolitik wider Willen? Die regionalpolitischen Dimensionen der Treuhandpolitik," *Aus Politik und Zeitgeschichte* 43–44 (28 October 1994): 43–52.

[16] By 1994, various forms of public enterprise were growing increasingly prevalent in the eastern *Länder* as the THA prepared to turn over its remaining functions and responsibilities to its successor organizations.

[17] Interview with European Commission official in DG-IV, General Directorate for Competition Policy, Brussels, December 1, 1992.

[18] European Parliament, "Die Treuhandanstalt und die Gemeinschaft," April 1992; reprinted in Treuhandanstalt, *Dokumentation 1990–94,* vol. 10, pp. 24–25.

Efforts to preserve eastern German core industries and their production locations in the new *Länder* received official sanction in late 1992, when Chancellor Kohl announced that his government and the THA would support this approach. His remarks signaled a public shift in the privatization program that had been under way for the better part of a year. This change in policy was finalized in the Solidarity Pact of March 1993, when the government pledged to provide the THA with additional financial resources to preserve eastern Germany's industrial cores in exchange for a union commitment to exercise wage restraint.[19] As such, the option of liquidation moved further into the background, and the prospect that unprivatized firms would spend several years under public or parapublic tutelage in preparation for eventual privatization became very real.

Bonn's public commitment to an employment-oriented sectoral policy in the eastern *Länder,* which extended beyond the formal dissolution of the THA in 1994, did nothing to reduce the likelihood of run-ins with Brussels over state aid. Both sides usually managed to reach mutually acceptable compromises on difficult cases, such as Eko Stahl, but only after protracted negotiations. The European Commission, concerned about adding subsidized production capacity in the midst of one of the worst postwar steel crises, cast a critical eye on the string of privatization proposals presented to it by the THA over the course of 1993–94. The German government, publicly committed to the retention of the Eisenhüttenstadt complex, agreed in November 1994 to implement additional capacity cuts in the eastern German steel sector in exchange for Commission approval of a massive rescue package crucial to the eventual sale of the company to the Belgian steel producer Cockerill Sambre. Still, after 1995 Brussels demonstrated a growing willingness to reject or withdraw questionable aid practices in the new *Länder.* Celebrated cases include subsidies paid out to the shipbuilder Bremer Vulkan in Mecklenburg-West Pomerania, and a Saxony aid package to Volkswagen. Needless to say, these and other Commission challenges placed the German government in an uncomfortable and indeed unprecedented position.[20]

Germany has yet to formally repudiate its long-standing position on state aid. Bonn officials, perhaps more out of hope than conviction, characterize their departures from social market orthodoxy as necessary but temporary, and maintain that these will have no long-term effects on German economic policy, either at the national or supranational level. Yet DG-IV officials point to evidence that Bonn is adopting a less stringent line in Brussels: preoccupied with eastern German aid cases, German ministers

[19] Razeen Sally and Douglas Webber, "The German Solidarity Pact: A Case Study in the Politics of the Unified Germany," *German Politics* 3 (April 1994): 18–46.

[20] I have just finished a book manuscript, provisionally titled "Unification and Union: The Domestic Sources of German Policy toward Europe," which addresses the Bremer Vulkan and VW cases in more detail.

are more reluctant to upbraid their partners for questionable practices than in the past. Because many EC decisions regarding eastern Germany, from structural funds to steel aid to CAP derogations, must be made in the Council of Ministers, the Germans are fully aware that they risk undermining their own position if they challenge other member governments.

The Eko case again provides a good example. Having to go hat in hand to the European Commission and ultimately to the Council of Ministers to get approval of a subsidy package designed to facilitate the sell-off of Eko, Germany found itself grouped with Spain and Italy, two chronic subsidizers who were seeking special treatment for their ailing nationalized firms. As a result of its public commitment to Eko, Bonn was able to give only tepid support for the European Commission's 1994 plan to manage capacity reductions in the European steel industry. The resulting delays, as well as the ire raised in the nonsubsidized parts of the steel sector, led to the plan's eventual collapse.[21] Moreover, the Eko case left Germany vulnerable to other members' demands for a more lenient approach to state aid vis-à-vis their own pet projects, a practice that Commission officials describe as "hostage taking."[22]

In this regulative policy area, the trade-off between long- and short-term objectives has been severe. With unification, Germany has become the largest state subsidizer of industry in the EC/EU, measured in both aggregate terms and in per capita assistance rates to the eastern region. This truly was, in Lehmbruch's words, "state interventionism with a bad conscience."[23] The emergence of Germany as a leading subsidizer has inflicted serious damage to its credibility in this policy area; Commission officials frequently mention the Federal Republic and Italy in the same breath. A DG-IV official offered this sober reappraisal in 1994: "The Germans believed that unification would generate a few skeletons in the closet where competition policy was concerned, but that they would remain in the closet. . . . Well, I'm here to tell you that the skeletons are spreading. . . . Bonn first has to restore discipline on its home front before it can turn to Europe and demand a rigorous approach from the Commission and its member governments."[24]

---

[21] Western German steel producers criticized the German campaign on behalf of Eko for allowing the far more egregious instances of subsidization in Spain and Italy to go forward with the EC's blessings.

[22] In November 1994, France held up final approval of the Eko package to win Council of Ministers support for an extension of shipbuilding subsidies, which were due to be phased out at the end of the year, a position Germany had supported.

[23] Gerhard Lehmbruch, "Die deutsche Vereinigung: Strukturen und Strategien," *Politische Vierteljahresschrift* 32 (December 1991): 597. On the trajectory of German subsidies since 1990, see Emma Tucker, "Commissioner Promises Crackdown on State Aid," *Financial Times*, January 23, 1997, p. 2.

[24] Interview with European Commission official in DG-IV, General Directorate for Competition Policy, Brussels, March 3, 1995.

Trade Policy

The Federal Republic's postwar trade policy can be described succinctly as western-oriented and liberal. West Germany's strategy of export-led growth presumed an expanding and increasingly barrier-free European market, which enabled German firms to achieve scale economies and successfully penetrate international markets. Within this basic trade orientation, a complex mixture of security interests and domestic politics drove West Germany's foreign policy toward the Soviet bloc. *Ostpolitik,* launched by the Brandt-Scheel government in 1970, sought to institutionalize a regional détente capable of promoting the cause of unification by drawing the German Democratic Republic into an ever-deepening web of contacts and ties.[25]

Since 1990, there has been no appreciable change in Germany's liberal orientation. Indeed, many officials argue that German interest in free trade intensified after 1990 because the mounting costs of unification could only be financed through increased exports.[26] This commitment did not always manifest itself in resolute action, however. In the Uruguay round of GATT, the Kohl government was very reluctant to isolate the French, which in effect allowed Paris to determine the pace and outcome of the negotiations, at least from the European Community side. The desire to preserve the Franco-German partnership, coupled with an almost ingrained reluctance to take the reins of leadership on a controversial issue in the EC/EU, is nothing new in Germany's European policy. Although Chancellor Kohl worked assiduously behind the scenes to bring about a meeting of minds between the American and French negotiating teams in December 1993, there is no denying the considerable gap between the free trade rhetoric of the German government and its silence when confronted with French brinkmanship.

Although unification did not call into question Germany's broader trade policy, it framed the trade dimensions of *Ostpolitik* in new ways. In the words of an official in the Federal Ministry of Economics, interviewed in 1992, "the fact that Germany now has a piece of the former Comecon [Council for Mutual Economic Assistance] system within its borders has created additional nuances in Ostpolitik."[27] In the past, *Ostpolitik* had served foreign policy goals almost exclusively, but it now contained an explicit domestic economic rationale. In short, the trade-based promotion

---

[25] See Wolfram Hanrieder, *Germany, America, Europe: Forty Years of German Foreign Policy* (New Haven: Yale University Press, 1989); and, most recently, Garton Ash, *In Europe's Name* (New York: Random House, 1993).

[26] Interview with official in the Federal Ministry of Finances, November 11, 1992, Bonn; interview with official in the Federal Ministry of Economics, October 7, 1992, Bonn.

[27] Interview with official in the Federal Ministry of Economics, October 2, 1992, Bonn.

of economic and political liberalization in the former Soviet bloc would contribute to regional stability *and* rejuvenate the economy in the five new *Länder,* thereby securing a broader foundation for the country's export-led growth strategy.

The new *Ostpolitik* proceeded along several fronts after 1990. Germany spearheaded the EC initiative to negotiate trade and cooperation treaties with its Eastern European neighbors.[28] To preserve Soviet export markets, the German government requested EC exemptions from the common external tariff for existing contracts between Comecon countries and the former GDR. Italy, France, and Britain expressed concerns about a flood of substandard, low-priced goods that would endanger the health of their citizens and the markets of their firms. After pledging to undertake administrative measures to ensure that Comecon goods imported into eastern Germany would be consumed within the region, the Germans received their exemptions.[29]

What is perhaps most remarkable about Germany's eastern trade policy since 1990 is Bonn's decision not to employ overt export credits or subsidies to prop up trade with the USSR and its successor states, which was estimated to support anywhere from 400,000 to 700,000 jobs in the eastern *Länder.* Instead, the federal government opted for a program in operation since 1949—Hermes export credit guarantees—as the principal trade policy instrument for the eastern *Länder.*[30] After obtaining approval from the European Community and the Organization for Economic Cooperation and Development (OECD), the government implemented a set of special conditions, valid during the 1991 calendar year, for which only eastern German firms trading with the Soviet Union were eligible.[31]

The government resorted to Hermes orthodoxy on the basis of an optimistic assessment of the challenges facing manufacturing industry in the

---

[28] These trade and cooperation treaties include existing and proposed "Europe Agreements" with Poland, Hungary, the Czech and Slovak Republics, Bulgaria, Romania, and the Baltic republics, and partnership agreements with Russia and Ukraine. According to the OECD, the Federal Republic had contributed fully half of all international aid to the former eastern bloc up through 1992. "Deutschland ist einer der größten Zahler," *Frankfurter Allgemeine Zeitung* (October 1, 1994): 15.

[29] Interview with official in the Europe Division of the Federal Ministry of Economics, July 9, 1992, Bonn.

[30] Hermes is administered by a state-backed agency, Hermes Kreditversicherungs-AG (Hamburg), which pledges to reimburse commercial loans for exports in the event the purchasers default on payment. For a technical discussion of government-funded export credit insurance in Germany, see I. Hichert, *Staatliche Exportabsicherung* (Cologne: Deutscher Instituts-Verlag, 1986).

[31] Bonn originally asked for a longer duration and an extension of the conditions to cover trade with Eastern European countries. The EC and OECD poured cold water on these demands, and Bonn settled for the temporal and geographical limitations contained in the final arrangements.

new *Länder* and of the adjustment process in their far-flung markets to the east. The flaws in this reasoning became apparent by the end of 1991. First and foremost, markets in Eastern Europe and above all the Soviet Union deteriorated rapidly, leaving many eastern German firms floundering. Second, the assumption that the Soviets would continue to purchase products "Made in [eastern] Germany" proved unfounded. Soviet importers could now readily compare goods offered by the ex-GDR with the more sophisticated—and often cheaper—products available on world markets.

In January 1992, the federal government decided to place a DM 5 billion ($3.2 billion) cap on the annual Hermes budget for the former USSR, bowing to concerns expressed in interministerial discussions about the increasingly subsidy-like character of assistance. In response to the precipitous decline in exports to the former Soviet republics and related complications in the THA-led privatization process, the government announced a few months later that it would undertake a review of trade policy toward the east, and in particular consider alternatives to Hermes. Many of the more ambitious or unorthodox proposals came from the eastern *Länder*. They included measures to enable the countries from the Commonwealth of Independent States (CIS) to mortgage raw materials like crude oil and natural gas against immediate deliveries of manufactured goods from eastern German firms, and to allow the CIS to pay for eastern German exports in rubles, which would be placed in a federal account used to finance German direct investment or joint ventures in these countries, with eastern German firms compensated by indirect federal payments in deutsche marks.

The government announced the results of the review in September 1992. The various unorthodox alternatives or complements to Hermes were considered and ultimately rejected on the grounds of cost and their fundamental incompatibility with existing trade commitments to the EC, OECD, and GATT. Instead, the government called on firms in the former GDR to reorient toward western markets with the help of the THA. Bonn stated that because almost 40 percent of the original DM 5 billion ($3.2 billion) remained unclaimed, there would be no increase in the Hermes budget for the time being, although it left open the option to raise the budget ceiling in the future. Existing Hermes guidelines were modified to include barter-exchange, and certain guarantee deadlines for the CIS countries were extended into 1993. Bonn also funded several flanking measures in the areas of foreign advertising, industry shows, and export advisory services. The government described the entire package as "revenue-neutral."

Thereafter, the government approved Hermes guarantees on a case-by-case basis, with preference given to viable THA firms central to the regional economy, and gave no sign of reconsidering the basic thrust of the September 1992 decision. The Hermes budget for the CIS states continued to shrink over the course of 1993–96, and a major overhaul of the program in 1994 raised insurance premiums for eastern trade to reflect the greater risk of default for export contracts to that part of the world. Thus, in the face of considerable domestic pressure and a deteriorating situation in the former Soviet Republics, Bonn continued to hold to a basically liberal, market-oriented trade policy out of budgetary considerations and its obligations to international and EC trade regimes.

The Common Agricultural Policy

Bonn's policy toward the CAP was predicated on the relative homogeneity of the West German farming sector.[32] German governments pursued a consistent CAP course that centered around the maintenance of high prices for its farmers, and structural assistance for the small- to medium-sized farms in the sector. The introduction of Europe's agrimonetary system after the collapse of Bretton Woods, based on so-called green exchange rates, proved to be an important vehicle for Bonn, which it used to shield German farmers from the agricultural price reductions otherwise demanded by the appreciation of the deutsche mark.[33] Whenever the issue of CAP reform took center stage in Brussels, Germany's preferred position was to address chronic agricultural surpluses through set-asides and co-payment procedures, "which would leave reasonable scope for increases in prices during annual farm prices reviews."[34]

The challenge posed by unification to Germany's position on CAP resided in the distinctiveness of eastern German agriculture. Property relations on the land were dominated by state-owned farms and collectives.[35] The level of East German employment in the sector stood at approximately 825,000 in 1989, or 10 percent of the total workforce—double the figure

[32] The following discussion of preunification Germany and the CAP is based on Gisela Hendriks, *Germany and European Integration: The Common Agricultural Policy* (New York: St. Martin's Press, 1991).

[33] With the collapse of fixed exchange rates in 1972, the EC implemented a grid of green exchange rates to neutralize the impact of shifts in exchange rate parities on national agricultural prices; it employed a system of export refunds and regulatory levies on imports to preserve the target prices reached by the Agricultural Council. Studies estimate that because of the use of the "green mark," prices for agricultural products in Germany during the 1970s were 10 percent and more above the average EC price level. Ibid., p. 60.

[34] Ibid., p. 75.

[35] In 1989, they employed over 95 percent of agricultural workers, and accounted for 87 percent of annual output and almost 90 percent of total acreage. Presse- und Informationsamt der Bundesregierung, *Unsere Landwirtschaft* (Bonn, 1992), p. 20.

for West Germany. Average farm size in the GDR (11,120 acres) dwarfed the typical western farm of just over 40 acres.[36] Thus convergence to the western mean would entail a wrenching upheaval, accompanied by massive downsizing and a radical contraction in the amount of land devoted to farming.[37] Moreover, the prospect of large, efficient producers in the five new *Länder* was bound to elicit concern among the smaller, family-owned farms in western Germany, located primarily in the south. Any regional conflicts between eastern and western German farmers would in all likelihood spill over onto the CAP agenda, which, largely but not exclusively at Bonn's insistence, had been tailored to accommodate its mix of small- to medium-sized farms. Amending the CAP and national agricultural programs required approval by the Council of Ministers. As in other policy areas, Bonn negotiated limited exemptions from existing CAP guidelines to cushion the transition to a market-based agricultural sector in the east.

The recasting of Germany's agricultural sector occurred amid a sweeping reform of the CAP initiated by the European Commission and protracted negotiations over the Uruguay round of the GATT, both of which put additional strains on Bonn's traditional preference for a high-price, supply-side, small-farm approach to agricultural policy. In 1991, European Commissioner for Agriculture Ray MacSharry published a set of reform proposals that broke with past CAP orthodoxy, which had sought to use the price mechanism as the principal means of insulating EC farmers from the economic vagaries of their chosen calling. At the center of the MacSharry reforms was a substantial reduction in the price support for cereals. Farmers were to be compensated for resulting income losses by means of direct transfer payments, the receipt of which was conditional on their participation in compulsory set-aside schemes. According to the principle of "modulation," small farms were to receive full compensation, whereas larger farms would be eligible only for partial compensation.[38] Combined with GATT-related pressures to further reduce EC production and export subsidies for agricultural products, the MacSharry initiative challenged Germany's traditional position on the CAP.

After the publication of the MacSharry proposals, Germany's agriculture minister, Ignaz Kiechle, stated publicly on numerous occasions his principled opposition not just to cereal price cuts but to the conceptual

[36] Grit Viertel, "Gemeinsame Agrarpolitik und neue Bundesländer," in Lippert et al., *EG und neuen Bundesländer,* p. 211.

[37] By mid-1994, employment in the eastern agricultural sector had dropped to 20 percent of its preunification level. "Agrarstrukturen noch im Wandel," *Frankfurter Allgemeine Zeitung* (January 7, 1994): 12.

[38] See Alan Swinbank, "CAP Reform, 1992," *Journal of Common Market Studies* 31 (September 1993): 359–72.

foundations of the reform package—direct income transfers. Kiechle's statements drew angry responses from various industry associations at home and on more than one occasion elicited open disagreement from the federal minister of economics, yet they were never disavowed by the chancellor. Kiechle advocated additional set-aside programs, quota schemes, and co-payment programs to address the problems of overproduction.

Germany approached the final negotiating round in Brussels firmly opposed to a price reduction of the magnitude proposed by the European Commission, and was counting on the French to hold the line at a 20 percent reduction or less. However, in the weeks prior to the decisive Council of Ministers meeting in May 1992, France signaled a willingness to accept much larger reductions, a conversion designed to take the steam out of the GATT export subsidy spat with the Americans by bringing European grain prices much closer to the world price. This course of action, which would not necessarily harm the comparatively more efficient French grain farmers, was intended to cast Paris in a progressive light.[39]

Abandoned by the French, the German delegation found itself isolated in the Council, a position that officials described as unacceptable. This assessment was grounded in the specific issues facing the twelve agriculture ministers; Germany would be perceived as blocking any possible agreement on GATT, something to which its leaders were publicly committed. For the German government, said one ministry official, "GATT and CAP have been from the beginning two sides of the same coin." Yet this internal evaluation of what constituted acceptable behavior drew on more general norms to which German officials had always been extremely sensitive. Remarking that the Council veto had become an option devoid of legitimacy, the same ministry official explained that Kiechle's only option was to change tack.[40] Resigned to the inevitable, Kiechle sought full compensation for farmers through the direct transfer mechanism, as well as additional flanking measures to cushion the shock. Bonn's assent represented not just a sharp break with its past position in the Council, but also a last-minute, public U-turn by its minister.

Thus, after long and often acrimonious negotiations, the EC's agricultural ministers agreed to a CAP reform that bore a strong familial resemblance to the original MacSharry model. The agreement provided for a 29 percent reduction in the price support for cereals over a four-year period; compensatory direct income transfers, linked to a compulsory set-

[39] Interview with official in the Federal Ministry of Food, Agriculture, and Forestry, June 11, 1992, Bonn.

[40] Interview with official in the Federal Ministry of Food, Agriculture, and Forestry, June 11, 1992, Bonn. Apparently, the agriculture ministry and (by implication) the German government were willing to write off a GATT agreement if this was the will of the Council of Ministers, but they were unwilling to take the blame alone.

aside scheme, were also approved. The Council of Ministers rejected the principle of modulation; all farms, and not just smaller enterprises, would receive full compensation for lost income. Moreover, small farms were exempted from the set-aside requirement.

The new *Länder* surfaced during the negotiations; the subject of discussion was the way in which the original MacSharry proposals discriminated against eastern German farms. The principle of modulation, as well as acreage premium formulas and various eligibility criteria for product categories like grains and beef, would have seriously disadvantaged large farms in the former GDR at a critical point in their transition to capitalist agricultural production. Bonn, motivated by intense pressures emanating from the eastern *Land* governments, won concessions from the Commission and Council members because German officials decided not to press for EC-wide changes in the various offending regulations, but to seek narrow exemptions of limited duration for its eastern German farmers.[41] Although Bonn officials denied the linkage, it appears that Germany's willingness to support the larger aims of the MacSharry reforms was tied at least in part to the package of exemptions secured for the new *Länder*.

Alongside the CAP reform initiative, a comprehensive reassessment of German agricultural objectives unfolded in the aftermath of unification. The slow, painstaking move toward a policy based on an efficiency rationale, under way since the early 1980s, gained momentum. In the words of a federal official interviewed in 1992, "The new *Länder* have given added impetus to the principle of competitiveness, as opposed to the preservation of the farming way of life, in agricultural policy."[42] The shift is reflected in a number of areas, from intangibles like the national "discourse" on agricultural policy[43] to concrete domestic reforms to bring national agricultural programs in line with the needs of larger, more efficient farms.

Given the linkage between the CAP regime and domestic policy, Bonn has been forced into the role of reluctant champion of limited reform in Brussels. The shift in emphasis is clearly relative and applies much more to policies designed to reshape the structure of the agricultural sector than to pricing policy. Overall, the German government shows no signs of adopting a zealous, missionary approach to the reform of the CAP. Since 1992,

[41] The one exception was the abandonment of modulation, which was brought about by EC members with significant numbers of farms above the full-compensation threshold (e.g., Germany and Britain).

[42] Interview with official in the Federal Ministry of Food, Agriculture, and Forestry, May 11, 1992, Bonn.

[43] According to an official in Bonn, the current agriculture minister, Jochen Borchert, makes many more references to efficient farming structures and far fewer allusions to the "bäuerliche Familienbetrieb" (small family farm) than did his predecessor, Ignaz Kiechle. Interview with official in the Federal Ministry of Food, Agriculture, and Forestry, May 16, 1994, Bonn.

the agriculture ministry has consistently resisted attempts by the European Commission to push through price reductions on cereals and other products that go beyond the letter and spirit of the May 1992 Council of Ministers decision. The federal agriculture ministry has recommended "a phase of tranquillity and consolidation" following the 1992 decision and has rejected calls for "a reform of the reform."

Thus German support for members of the efficiency-oriented coalition in the Agricultural Council—Britain, the Netherlands, Denmark, and now possibly Sweden—has been and will continue to be episodic in the near term. Germany's approach to the CAP will be shaped by forces at both the domestic and supranational levels, including the ongoing transition in the eastern German agricultural sector, GATT commitments, stringent budget ceilings on EU agricultural expenditure, and the anticipated financial and administrative strains of EU expansion to Eastern Europe. Germany, motivated by altered domestic parameters and by its intense support for eastern enlargement of the EU (a goal not unrelated to unification), could well become an increasingly important swing vote on EU agricultural policy.

The Structural Funds

Of the four regulative policies discussed here, the structural funds[44] provide the clearest evidence of the triumph of West Germany's long-term over its short-term interests. Strong German opposition to this European Community policy could have been expected for several reasons. As the EC's wealthiest member and de facto paymaster, Germany footed the bill for the structural funds yet received a trifling share of the outlays designed to improve the spatial distribution of investment and social capital within the internal market. Germany also found itself targeted by the EC's competition rules, which the European Commission used to reduce the amount of territory covered by federal and state regional assistance programs.[45] Finally, the evolution of the funds in the 1980s, in particular the strengthening of the Commission's role and its links to subnational actors, placed great strains on intergovernmental relations within the Federal Republic.[46]

[44] The structural funds consist of the European Social Fund (ESF), the Guidance section of the Common Agricultural Policy, the European Regional Development Fund (ERDF), and (as of Maastricht) the cohesion fund.

[45] In 1988, Bonn bowed to European Commission pressure and reduced the percentage of the population covered by federal and state assisted areas from 45 percent to 39 percent.

[46] Jeffrey Anderson, "Skeptical Reflections on a Europe of Regions: Britain, Germany, and the European Regional Development Fund," *Journal of Public Policy* 10 (October–December 1990): 417–47.

In spite of these drawbacks, German governments endorsed the official rationale underpinning cohesion policy, as well as its unofficial role as the principal mechanism by which grand bargains were struck in exchange for side payments.[47] In short, the structural funds addressed both socio-economic and political cohesion, and the latter in particular was central to Germany's conception of EC constitutive politics. Germany gave voice to its financial concerns by demanding improvements in the efficacy of the structural funds and a consistent focus on the EC's neediest areas. The government accepted the implications of Community regional priorities, which resulted in a negligible share of fund expenditure for Germany, and provided wary yet ultimately crucial support for the Commission's efforts to reform the structural funds in the 1980s.

These tensions within an otherwise consistent German approach to the structural funds were exposed by unification. The Bonn government, in accord with its rosy estimates of the time frame for economic takeoff in eastern Germany, regarded EC cohesion policy not as an additional source of development assistance but as a potentially disruptive factor in Germany's relations with other EC members and in domestic intergovernmental relations. With unification increasingly likely, Chancellor Helmut Kohl offered in April 1990 to waive structural fund assistance for the ex-GDR in exchange for permission to restructure the region on the basis of domestic initiatives consistent with EC law. In this manner, Bonn hoped to dispel the concerns of southern members about a potential competitor for structural assistance and to minimize the European Commission's influence over the economics of unification.

The EC never gave serious consideration to this offer; in August 1990, the European Commission budgeted an additional 3 billion European Currency Units (ECU) ($3.8 billion) for the ex-GDR over the period 1991–93, and listed the region as an assisted area sui generis in the absence of reliable data on the economic situation there. The Commission made final approval of the assistance package contingent on Bonn's enactment of promised reductions in the proportion of the western German population covered by the national program, which occurred in January 1991.

Soon thereafter, demands emanating from the new *Länder* created more strains on Bonn's traditional approach to the structural funds, which eventually caused the government to reorient its approach to this policy area. The impetus resided in the Maastricht treaty's pledge to institute a new cohesion fund and to consider substantial increases in expenditure

[47] See Simon Bulmer and William Paterson, *The Federal Republic of Germany and the European Community* (London: Allen and Unwin, 1997), pp. 202–22, for a case study of Germany's role in the formation of the largest of the structural funds, the ERDF. On the structural funds and side payments, see Gary Marks, "Structural Policy in the European Community," in Alberta Sbragia, ed., *Euro-Politics* (Washington, D.C., 1992), pp. 191–224.

levels for the three original structural funds. The so-called Delors II budget proposal envisioned a doubling of structural assistance (defined as structural funds plus cohesion) for Spain, Portugal, Greece, and Ireland over the period 1994–97. For eastern Germany, the European Commission proposed a continuation of its special status, and a 66 percent increase in its allotment of the three principal structural funds, a figure in line with proposed increases for the "Objective 1" regions.[48] The eastern *Länder* cried foul, arguing that because their region had been underfunded in 1991, an across-the-board increase would lock in the original inequity. Bonn, joined by other wealthy member governments, voiced strong dissatisfaction with what it viewed as an unacceptable increase in the EC budget ceiling from 1.2 to 1.37 percent of Community GDP.

Soon after the publication of the original Delors II package, the new *Länder* launched a campaign for Objective 1 status and a commensurate increase in funding. Regional advocates sought to build an objective case based on unemployment rates, infrastructure, and per capita GDP, and asked that current data be incorporated into the statistical base used by the European Commission to designate Objective 1 regions.[49] This seemingly innocuous proposal would have lowered the EC's per capita GDP average by three percentage points, which in turn would have left a handful of existing Objective 1 regions above the program's eligibility threshold. Both Brussels and Bonn reacted with consternation: to support this demand would have required German officials to backtrack on their pledge not to advance eastern German interests at the expense of poorer Community members.

The second contentious demand tabled by the eastern German *Länder* was for a two- to threefold increase in their allocation, placing the region on a par with assisted regions in the Mediterranean periphery such as Greece or Portugal.[50] Once again, Bonn reacted with embarrassed silence, while representatives of the poorer EC members pointed out that such comparisons omitted a very important variable—the size and wealth of the German *national* economy, which bestowed on the eastern *Länder* a considerably higher development potential over the long run than that enjoyed by the Objective 1 "regions" of Portugal and Greece.

---

[48] About two-thirds of the proposed doubling of assistance for the poor four (Spain, Portugal, Greece, and Ireland) was to come via the three main structural funds, with the other third contributed by the new cohesion fund. Germany is not eligible for cohesion fund assistance.

[49] "Objective 1 regions," which enjoy the highest assistance priority within the structural funds, are defined as those in which per capita GDP is 75 percent or less of the European Community average.

[50] The 1991–93 structural fund package for the eastern *Länder* worked out to 64 ECU per capita, which compared unfavorably to the EC average for Objective 1 regions (130 ECU per person), to say nothing of Portugal's figure (over 200 ECU per person).

The German government found itself in an increasingly difficult position, especially with regard to the question of funding. On the one hand, it had no desire to permit a dramatic expansion of the EC budget at a time when public support for a more perfect European union was on the decline, along with Germany's ability to pay the bill. On the other hand, the government was drawn increasingly into open support for the demands of the eastern *Länder*, as the scale of economic misery in the east (and the fragility of economic assumptions in the west) became apparent. Thus, a new role, namely that of supplicant, began to take shape alongside the Federal Republic's traditional one of Community paymaster. The federal government's torn loyalties threatened to play into the European Commission's hands; although favorably inclined to the region's demand for Objective 1 status, Delors argued that if Germany wanted more money for the east, it would have to support an increase in the EC's budgetary ceiling. Germany countered by recommending internal shifts in budgetary spending priorities to free up the necessary resources for the eastern *Länder*. This strategy also aimed to calm fears on Europe's southern periphery.

Germany's dilemma eased with the Danish rejection of the TEU in June 1992, which threw the European Commission on the defensive and killed the original Delors II package, thereby freeing Bonn to support eastern German demands without fear of falling prey to Delors's budgetary logic. Within two months, the Bonn government had gone public with its support for comparable treatment of the new *Länder* to that received by Objective 1 regions. Officials in the Federal Ministry of Economics confirmed that Germany was seeking an ECU per capita figure for the eastern *Länder* consistent with the EC average for an Objective 1 region.[51]

At the Lisbon summit in June 1992, the heads of government agreed that the five new *Länder* and east Berlin would gain Objective 1 status as of 1994. This was in effect a political decision; the European Commission, backed by the poorer EC members, argued strenuously against the inclusion of the eastern German data on technical grounds, and Germany declined to press the issue for fear of setting off a crisis in Brussels. At the Edinburgh summit in December 1992, Germany entered the negotiations having put forward no concrete numbers as to the budget ceiling or any specific line items, including the structural fund allotment for the new *Länder*. This strategy placed Germany in its preferred role of consensus builder; indeed, Chancellor Kohl was instrumental in forging a compromise between the more spendthrift Spanish and the more austere British proposals. In the end, the EC Twelve decided to extend the five-year bud-

---

[51] Interview with official in the Europe Division of the Federal Ministry of Economics, July 22, 1992, Bonn.

get plan to seven years (1993–99), and to increase the budget ceiling from 1.2 to 1.27 percent of Community GDP over that same period.

Within the larger settlement, the budgetary parameters for the four structural funds were also discussed. Bargaining snagged on a last minute reversal in Bonn's negotiating position; the German delegation pushed for the inclusion of eastern Germany in the European Commission's database. German officials appeared to have reached the conclusion that the former GDR should no longer be treated as a special case. In their view, increased assistance for eastern Germany was entirely consistent with the fund's long-standing goal of targeting the neediest regions in the EC, which called for an allocation based on objective data. Bonn officials also believed that inclusion of the data would bolster Germany's claims to the maximum possible allotment for the new Objective 1 region. In return for the inclusion of the eastern German data, the Commission and Council insisted that any region receiving Objective 1 status prior to the inclusion of the data be so designated for the period 1994–99.

Final agreement on the structural funds occurred in July 1993. The outcome effectively doubled assistance levels for the poorer member governments. The eastern *Länder* received approximately DM 27 billion ($15.7 billion) over the seven-year period beginning in 1994, which placed Germany's Objective 1 region squarely on the EC mean. An official in the Federal Ministry of Finances stated that Germany had asked for more, in the range of DM 34–38 billion, but "we did not get it."[52] Reports out of Brussels suggested that the award level was in part motivated by concern within the European Commission over growing anti-EC sentiment in Germany, centered around the feeling that Brussels was abandoning (western) Germany to deal with the problems in its eastern region alone.

The Federal Republic's achievements on behalf of the new *Länder* came with a price tag. In 1991, the federal government agreed to a reduction in area coverage in western Germany to 27 percent of the population by the end of 1993; this figure declined to 22 percent in 1994. As area coverage in Germany's national regional policy continued to shrink in the face of continued pressure from EC competition policy, the stage was set for east-west territorial conflicts. Moreover, soon after the 1994 decision, inter-ministerial conflicts over access to EC funds for the Objective 1 region in the east broke out in the federal government; stoked by the European Commission, these conflicts pitted the ministries of transportation, environment, and research and technology against the ministry of economics, and resulted in a small though significant loss of the latter's control over distribution of the funds. The Commission, drawing on the support of a domestic coalition in Germany that included parts of the federal and east-

---

[52] Interview with official in the Federal Ministry of Finances, May 17, 1994, Bonn.

ern *Land* governments, used the opportunity to export what it viewed as a more appropriate southern European development model, focusing on the creation of basic infrastructure and the improvement of human capital, to Germany.[53]

At the supranational level, the German delegation paid for its Objective 1 region with an increase in the EC budget at Edinburgh, albeit one well below the target set out in the original Delors II package. More central to the regulative policy in question, though, German officials achieved a technically sound decision for their new Objective 1 region, but at the price of strained relations with southern members and some damage to the principles underpinning the structural funds. Specifically, Germany agreed to turn a blind eye to compensatory political decisions that expanded Objective 1 area coverage from 21.7 percent to 26.6 percent of the EU population, and that resulted in the incorporation of six new designated regions in which GDP per capita lay markedly above the 75 percent threshold.[54] Bonn's approach to reform has also grown more tentative. Commission proposals to overhaul the EU's regional aid regime to improve policy efficiency and efficacy have met with expressions of concern on the part of German officials, who fear that any changes in current practice might complicate ongoing restructuring efforts in the new *Länder*.

ANALYSIS AND CONCLUSIONS

Unification did not precipitate a major domestic reevaluation of Germany's role in Europe. Amid the domestic and international upheaval associated with unification, the factors contributing to Germany's distinctive blend of constitutive and regulative politics remained largely intact; these include domestic conceptions of interest and identity, as well as international expectations of appropriate German behavior on the world stage. Thus key ingredients of soft power remain in place, and it is still possible to interpret Germany's approach to the EC/EU in terms consistent with the preunification period, as outlined earlier in this chapter. Germany's exaggerated multilateralism and culture of restraint have endured (see Peter Katzenstein's introduction to this volume).

Nevertheless, the preceding case studies, taken together, suggest that to describe the united Germany's relationship toward Europe in terms of seamless continuity would be inaccurate. Something has changed since 1990, as attested to in numerous journalistic accounts of a more assertive

[53] For an extended discussion, see Jeffrey Anderson, "Germany and the Structural Funds: Unification Leads to Bifurcation," in Liesbet Hooghe, ed., *Cohesion Policy and European Integration: Building Multi-Level Governance* (Oxford: Oxford University Press, 1996), pp. 163–94.

[54] See R. Waniek, "EG-Regionalpolitik für die Jahre 1994 bis 1999," *Wirtschaftsdienst* 1 (1994): 43–49.

German posture on issues ranging from the budget to the status of the German language in official EU business. This new phenomenon warrants close inspection.

Initially, the German government, buttressed by broad public support in both the western and eastern parts of the country, sought continuity regarding its place in Europe. This followed naturally from Bonn's approach to German economic and monetary union, which envisioned a rapid transfer of West German institutions and identity to the east. The federal government sought limited exemptions and other forms of special treatment from the EC, and did not to attempt to bring Community regulative policy regimes in line with eastern German requirements, to say nothing of a new postunification domestic economic model. Generally speaking, the Federal Republic acted as a "policy taker" in Europe between 1990 and 1992; that is, it submitted to established procedures and outcomes. Bonn held to the preunification formula: EC regulative politics as a means to constitutive ends and to domestic system requirements.

During this period, however, domestic pressures were building that would eventually call into question the preunification equilibria established in several EC regulative areas. These pressures originated in the east—specifically, from actors whose short-term material interests were ill served by Bonn's priorities in Brussels. The demands of the new *Länder*, employers and trade unions in the unprivatized sector, and farmers began to resonate in an increasingly charged political environment in Bonn. The deterioration of domestic consensus can be traced in part to the events of 1989–90; for example, budgetary strains generated by the mounting costs of unification led to a full-scale debate about Germany's contribution to EU financing, which soon spilled over onto the EU agenda. It can also be attributed to widespread public disillusionment and frustration over recent European developments, from economic and monetary union to Bosnia.

Although eastern German pressures for change surfaced in each of the four regulative policy areas, they did not translate into uniform changes in Germany's approach; what emerges is a mixed pattern of change and continuity. By far the most visible and formal national policy shift has occurred in the structural funds, whereas a more nuanced and drawn out change is under way in the CAP. On the question of state aid, Germany's official position remains unchanged, although its actions suggest an amended set of operating principles at work. In trade, continuity reigns.[55]

To explain this cross-policy variation would take us well beyond the bounds of this chapter. Factors such as the political resources available to

---

[55] The puzzle of continuity in trade is taken up in Jeffrey Anderson and Celeste Wallander, "Interests and the Wall of Ideas: Germany's Eastern Trade Policy after Unification," *Comparative Political Studies* (forthcoming December 1997).

eastern German actors[56] and the degree of congruence between German and EU policy practice[57] conceivably contributed to these outcomes. While, overall, Germany's European policies after 1989 continue to be driven by concerns about process and principles, more and more attention is being paid to distributive outcomes and the immediate net payoff to Germany. Is the exercise of soft institutional power compatible with the increasing resort to harder forms of power based on bargaining?

Let us begin with the specific areas of regulative politics in question. In some cases, Bonn / Berlin's pursuit of short-term returns is unlikely to generate long-term damage to its established objectives. For example, Germany justified its demand for an Objective 1 region in the east in terms of its long-held position that the funds should be targeted at the poorest of the EC's poor regions. Which is to say, as long as Germany contains the poorest region in the Community, it is entitled to a commensurate level of assistance.

In other cases, however, long-term negative consequences are far more likely. German weaknesses—the extreme economic vulnerability of key THA firms and the crushing political pressure for action that results— have led to a more assertive and self-regarding exercise of German influence on questions of state aid for individual privatization cases.[58] Yet Germany continues to pay a price for its assertiveness on behalf of eastern German firms—namely, an increasingly tarnished reputation and weakened leverage on the subsidization practices of other member countries. This in turn could undermine the broader EU regulative regime govern-

---

[56] In the two instances of official policy change, the eastern German *Länder* are formal participants in the domestic policy process and enjoy institutionalized access to EU arenas. In competition policy, where an unofficial shift occurred, the *Länder* enjoyed privileged access to the THA. In the one case of regulative continuity, eastern German pressure took the form of a classic lobby led by producer groups. On the basis of this limited selection of regulative policy areas, *Länder* participation appears to be crucial to effecting a change in the federal government's position. I explore these issues in detail in my book-in-progress, "Unification and Union."

[57] If one compares the degree of congruence between German and EU principles underlying the four major regulative policy areas, the following rank ordering emerges, in descending order of congruence: (1) trade, (2) agriculture, (3) state aid, and (4) structural funds. This list roughly parallels the observed pattern of change and continuity. It is possible that where established EU frameworks closely mirror German practice, Bonn has been able to resist much more effectively eastern demands that challenge orthodoxies of the prevailing West German economic model.

[58] Approximately 10 percent of THA concerns ended up in foreign hands. However, in key industrial sectors such as chemicals and steel the proportion of non-German ownership is much higher. A case in point, the public wrangling over Eko Stahl tended to obscure the fact that a Belgian firm assumed control of the former flagship of the GDR steel sector. This suggests a rather different conception of "national interest" than that prevailing in contemporary France or Britain. I am grateful to Peter Katzenstein for encouraging me to develop this point.

ing state aid, with negative consequences for the competitiveness of German export sectors.

Perhaps even weightier dilemmas loom in the realm of constitutive politics. Up to and including the Maastricht treaty, European integration thrived on an implicit bargain between Germany and the other members. In exchange for the invisible benefits provided by the internal market and democratic multilateralism, Germany agreed to underwrite the European project and to wield its influence in an unobtrusive manner. Unification challenged the foundations of this bargain by injecting a potential contradiction into Germany's comfortable fusion of regulative and constitutive politics. At the level of interstate relations, the uniting of the two Germanys accentuated deeply entrenched anxieties among its neighbors about German power and intentions. Perhaps more than ever, Germans were expected to walk, talk, and act softly. At the same time, however, unification reshuffled the cards within Germany, thereby changing the domestic context in which European policy is made. New, hard material interests, overlaid on the older institutional and normative interests, render it more difficult for the German government to satisfy domestic constituencies with the exercise of soft power in Brussels.

The implications of this development, both for Germany and for the European Union, have yet to sort themselves out. Yet they do not bode well for the next phase in European integration, which entails both widening (the eastern enlargement) and deepening (institutional reform). The simultaneous achievement of both will depend, in all likelihood, on package deals involving expensive side payments to the prospective losers. Germany's declining interest in footing the bill, coupled with a growing interest in securing a fair share for itself, will introduce heretofore unseen complications in EU grand bargaining, slowing the pace of integration and raising the level of interstate conflict along the way.

Chapter Four

Placed in Europe: The Low Countries and Germany in the European Union

Paulette Kurzer

The findings in this chapter dispute the contention that a newly assertive Germany influences the developments and affairs of its smaller neighbors through its pivotal position in the European Union. Indeed, Germany's influence over Belgium and the Netherlands, whether direct or indirect, must be considered marginal on at least three different grounds.

A first ground relates to the institutional compatibility between the Low Countries and Germany. Institutional convergence, primarily a product of historical forces, makes it impossible to speak of Germany imposing its will on the Low Countries. "Dominance" is simply not an accurate way of describing the complex relations between Germany and the Low Countries. Two examples will elucidate this point. First, the countries' institutions and objectives are convergent with regard to monetary policy. Although Germany determines the shape and terms of European monetary integration, Belgian and Dutch officials do not, as a rule, complain about the tyranny of the deutsche mark and the Bundesbank. They approve of German monetary leadership because they fully share German goals of stable prices and currencies. Invariably, they follow the decisions of German monetary authorities because doing so bolsters the credibility and reputation of their own policy course. Basic compatibility of domestic institutions and goals

I thank the many individuals in Belgium and the Netherlands who have provided me with data and background information. Erik Jones, Lars Mjøset, Andrew Moravcsik, Christine Ingebritsen, and Peter Katzenstein have been instrumental in improving the flow and content of my argument. The InterNetKrant (ink@splinter.rad.usf.edu) and Elis MailServeR (msr@elis.rug.ac.be) have been indispensable sources of news and information.

mutes any criticism whether it involves German goals in the monetary sphere or the apparent subservience of Dutch and Belgian monetary authorities to the Bundesbank. A better description of the relations between Germany and the Low Countries is an (unequal) alliance, with the Dutch and the Belgians relying upon German determination to keep inflation at bay and exchange rates strong. Second, the countries enjoy basic institutional compatibility with regard to their social welfare systems. Social Catholicism and Christian Democracic influences figured prominently in the drafting and execution of social legislation in Belgium, the Netherlands, and Germany; moreover, in the postwar era, labor-management consultation stood at the center of the industrial relations systems in all three countries. The combination of extensive, generous Christian-Democratic social welfare systems and workers' codetermination rights goes a long way toward explaining why Germany and the Low Countries frequently speak with one voice during the often unproductive debates over a "European social dimension."

A second ground is that Belgium and the Netherlands are fully committed to the European Union (EU). Their enthusiasm for Europe reflects their export dependency, flows from their decision to renounce any further claims to an independent foreign or security policy after World War II, and represents their positive experiences as core members of the EU. Because they know that European integration can coexist with national models of social intervention and democratic governance, both states are willing to forgo immediate short-term interests for the sake of long-term goals of closer political union and further market integration. The European Union obviously limits independent action and decision making. For example, more than 70 percent of all laws passed by the Dutch parliament in 1992 concerned EU regulations and directives. Germany, too, displays a strong identification with Europe and pursues its national interests consistently through the institutions of the European Union. Because all three countries converge on their preferences for a solid and viable supranational Europe, Belgium and the Netherlands are sympathetic to many of Germany's most ambitious designs for Europe. They agree with Germany's Europe policy, and they welcome German assertiveness, which they hope will result in stronger multilateral frameworks.

A third ground for considering German influence marginal is that Belgium and the Netherlands are far from being defenseless and powerless. Certainly, neither country follows Germany's policy toward Europe blindly. However infrequently, Belgium and the Netherlands do on occasion oppose a particular European strategy or project supported by Germany. Generally, the three countries think alike because of similar institutional structures and processes, which is partly a function of their convergent commitments to Europe and partly the product of historical contingencies. But Belgian and Dutch acceptance of European multilateralism and German leadership coexists with particular national agendas or interests. Although the number of times that Belgium and the Netherlands disagree sharply with German long-term goals for the European Union is small, both countries have in the past opposed a German agenda.

The above conclusions are based upon an analysis of three different policy regimes. My first policy regime is monetary and economic integration. Monetary integration is one of the success stories of the European Union; the centerpiece of the Maastricht treaty is the European Monetary Union (EMU). By all accounts, Germany exerts much control over the terms, pace, and final contours of the EMU; if there is any direct German influence on Belgium and the Netherlands, monetary policy is the most likely place to find it. In addition, the rush to meet the EMU convergence criteria gives us, plausibly, a direct example of how German monetary targets shape the budget debates and retrenchment programs in these two core participants in the EMU. My analysis of monetary integration, however, finds scant reason to support the thesis that Germany dominates and influences its smaller neighbors.

My second policy regime is social welfare policy. I decided to include social welfare policy because virtually every EU government must institute far-reaching social welfare reforms in light of rising demographic and competitive pressures. Does Germany provide a source of inspiration for Belgium and the Netherlands? What role does the European Union play, and does Germany affect welfare state retrenchment in Belgium and the Netherlands through the EU? Moreover, because global economic pressures and EMU membership may bring about further convergence in social welfare systems and thus even greater correspondence with the German model, social welfare policy provides another useful test for addressing the themes of this book.

In my final policy regime, judicial policy and policing, I look at the third pillar of the Treaty of European Union and follow attempts to achieve greater coordination, if not harmonization, there. Institutionalized police cooperation at the European level (in contrast to international collaboration through Interpol) is a relatively new issue for the European Union and reflects a rising concern with transnational crime and international migration. As with monetary and economic policy, absolute national control over law enforcement is no longer either possible or desirable. Germany is the most vocal champion of increased judicial integration and of "federalizing" criminal systems and procedures, yet the future of the third pillar is uncertain as other member states of the EU persist in delaying further steps toward judicial and legal integration.

This chapter will show that Germany does not dominate Belgium and the Netherlands, and that neither of the two smaller countries has to fear a new, assertive Germany, either directly or indirectly. Although monetary policy is of course dictated by the Bundesbank, the policy establishment in both Belgium and the Netherlands welcomes this "domination" in order to strengthen and reinforce its pursuit of a stable exchange rate. It is more appropriate to speak of a "partnership" where the smaller countries "exploit" the reputation of the Bundesbank to protect price stability and a strong exchange rate. The case of judicial integration and coordination in home affairs and justice demonstrates what happens when a "European" agenda, advocated by Germany, requires contentious changes in the basic structure of law enforcement of a sovereign state. At that point, even the most committed multilateralists—Belgium and the Netherlands—have second thoughts. When these countries cooperate and undertake joint action with Germany, they therefore do so on the basis of institutional convergence and shared identification with Europe—not because Germany has imposed its priorities on their agendas.

MONETARY INTEGRATION

It is widely accepted that Germany determines the process of monetary integration. In the 1980s, more and more European countries followed the German example, favoring economic growth and jobs over price and exchange rate stability. Many of these countries, however, have not been willing or able to refashion institutions or instruments to meet the new objectives of low inflation, low budget deficits, and fiscal moderation. For example, the Netherlands follows the German monetary regime very closely. Yet certain aspects of its macroeconomic management conform to their own logic and, indeed, seem to clash with the hard currency option. Belgium decided to peg its currency directly to the deutsche mark in order to import "anti-inflation credibility." Yet its economic and social institutions have not been aligned to safeguard the renewed emphasis on price and exchange rate stability. Thus the European Monetary System (EMS) is less of a straitjacket or disciplinary device than is often assumed, and most member states are not yet "pseudo-*Länder.*" Final decisions with regard to budget expenditures and monetary policy are just as likely to be motivated by a prior commitment to pursue a stable exchange rate and low inflation as they are by the need to comply with German demands for price stability and fiscal rectitude. Certainly in the Netherlands and Belgium, the overall objective of the EMS (and future EMU) complements priorities first elaborated in the late 1940s.

Dutch Monetary Regime

Since the EMS's founding in 1979, the Netherlands has narrowly interpreted its rules so as to avoid automatic exchange rate adjustments and to preserve its strong currency policy. Subsequently, in 1989, six years after the Netherlands, Belgium also adopted a harder stance by seeking closer economic convergence with Germany. In June 1990, the Netherlands and Belgium, which had been able to bring down their inflation rates close to that of Germany, gradually tightened their involvement in the system beyond what its rules demanded.

In the 1990s, Dutch interest rates were among the lowest in Europe. At the time of the Exchange Rate Mechanism (ERM) crisis in 1992–93, because the Netherlands experienced neither capital flight nor pressure on the guilder, it did not have to raise interest rates. When speculators bought guilders, however, the Dutch central bank intervened extensively in July 1993 to prevent further upward pressure on the guilder in the ERM. Considering the stability of the Dutch guilder, we would expect an overall fiscal and economic framework highly supportive of a rigid exchange rate policy. Indeed, Dutch officials have tailored economic intervention instruments with the aim of conserving price stability and of protecting the value of the guilder by steering toward chronic current account surpluses. It is therefore counterintuitive and surprising to discover that net public debt in the Netherlands was close to 80 percent of GDP in 1996, which is above the threshold agreed upon during the Maastricht summit. This points to a relatively relaxed fiscal policy and suggests a greater degree of fiscal autonomy to pursue national objectives than we might have expected, considering the constraints imposed by a hard guilder.

Public debt consolidation has been difficult to achieve although it is dropping to 74 percent of GDP in 1997 because the Netherlands faces two major challenges: low rates of employment and a very generous social welfare system. Twenty-six percent of the labor force receives some form of social welfare benefit[1] and the rate of nonemployment (or the proportion of employed to the population of working age) is around 50 percent. Plausibly, the strong guilder and restrictive monetarism are the reasons for the high rate of labor force inactivity although it is remarkable that the large outlays on social programs (and high public debt) have not harmed the fixed exchange rate pegged to the deutsche mark. Can the exchange rate regime be blamed for the Netherlands' low level of employment? And why have the ensuing social expenditures not forced a change in exchange rate policy?

[1] This includes all unemployed and inactive individuals of working age who receive social security benefits or who are working in a special job creation program.

The combination of a strong guilder and comparatively high labor costs has indeed encouraged firms to invest in labor-saving machinery and has stimulated corporate downsizing. Labor costs in common currency are high because of the strong guilder and high payroll taxes. Social security contributions have risen because public revenues finance social benefits. The combined effects of high labor costs and a strong exchange rate have priced certain types of workers out of the market.[2] Dutch firms adapt to high labor costs by focusing on capital investments, thanks to which the Dutch economy enjoys high rates of productivity, while suffering from low employment rates. At the same time, cognizant of the effects of a strong currency on an export-oriented economy, union leaders have sought only modest wage increases over the years.[3]

The Netherlands finds itself in this situation because its social partners and political parties committed themselves in the late 1960s and early 1970s to building a social welfare system that underpins very liberal unemployment and disability programs. Christian Democratic cabinets passed numerous social welfare bills in the late 1960s, anticipating an era of steady economic growth, and the Labor Party refined and extended the system in the early 1970s. Tripartite consultations between unions, business, and government representatives resulted in a pay and benefits system that coupled unemployment and disability allowances to the minimum wage, which in turn was linked to wage developments in the private sector. In such a fashion, everybody would be protected against inflation, and nobody would be deprived from enjoying the fruits of economic growth. Solidarity norms, moreover, stipulated that the differential between private sector pay and the legal minimum wage should be kept small.[4] In the 1990s, the result of these decisions is, first, a narrow wage dispersion because of high pay compensation for unskilled work and, second, high labor costs because of high social security contributions.

[2] Technological shifts and rising labor costs are the main reasons for the high level of joblessness.

[3] OECD, *Economic Surveys: The Netherlands, 1993* (Paris: OECD, 1993), pp. 48–49. Labor costs in local currency have been significantly below those in trading partner countries since 1983.

[4] In 1992, a new law was passed that enabled the Dutch government to ignore the full wage-benefit coupling if unions achieved large wage increases and if the number of social security beneficiaries surged. Nevertheless, in 1993, the lowest social security allowance still equaled the minimum wage after taxes. J. de Haan and C. A. de Kam, "Arbeidsmarkt," in J. W. van Deth and J. C. P. M. Vis, eds., *Actuele politieke problemen* (Amsterdam: Instituut voor Publiek en Politiek, 1994), p. 93. In 1996, high contractual minimum wages were decreasing the importance of the legal minimum wage because sectoral wage agreements tend to follow average wage growth and the government was keeping the legal minimum wage low. The proportion of workers at the legal minimum wage was declining. OECD, *Economic Surveys: The Netherlands, 1996* (Paris: OECD, 1996), p. 49.

What is surprising is that the Dutch authorities (plus unions and employers) have failed to pursue an active labor market policy to employ unskilled labor by establishing training and job placement programs. In the Federal Republic of Germany (FRG), tight monetary policy was viewed as an opportunity to invest in quality production and in advanced manpower training. In the Netherlands, the reaction of the social partners and government to falling demand for certain kinds of workers was to ease their exit from the labor market at the expense of the taxpayer and corporate sector. Unskilled workers were the first to be laid off but were also the least likely to seek new employment because generous unemployment benefits and social assistance served as disincentives to find new work. In 1989, replacement income by the state for an individual with a family and nonworking spouse was pegged at 70 percent of previous earnings, higher than in the FRG (58 percent) or Belgium (50 percent).

In 1990, the authorities decided to set up several training and work experience programs while recertifying many disabled individuals as fit for work. Yet the public funds devoted to manpower programs are a small drop in a huge bucket. Instead of making a serious difference, the authorities have focused on bringing down government expenditures to enhance the business and investment climate and, of course, to meet the entry criteria of the EMU, which are widely supported in the Netherlands. Yet the Dutch postwar consensus is built on solidaristic transfer payments to guarantee financial security to disadvantaged groups of workers and households. Trust in and support for the welfare state remains high and accounts for the tenacious resistance to any fundamental reform in the provision of social benefits. Instead, small adjustments are implemented, although these may have the overall effect of diluting the specific structure of the Dutch redistribution regime in the long run. More selective access, lower benefits, and more provisional nature of benefits have reduced real social spending in the mid-1990s.[5]

Nevertheless, the Netherlands still copes with a labor market problem. The latter has been partly alleviated by encouraging the growth of part-time work and the expansion of temporary employment agencies. Trade unions have approved of a variety of measures to improve labor market flexibility. It would appear that a German-type monetary regime can coexist with an un-German-like labor market regime and budgetary behavior. While German officials and social interest groups have made a connection between a strong currency and an active labor market policy, the

---

[5] Godfried Engbersen, "Poverty Regimes and Life Chances: The Road to Anomia?," in Brigitte Unger and Frans van Waarden, eds., *Convergence or Diversity? Internationalization and Economic Policy Response* (Brookfield, Vt.: Avebury, 1995), pp. 200–225. OECD, *Economic Surveys: The Netherlands, 1996,* pp. 48–57.

Dutch have retained their own approach to nonintervention in the supply and demand of labor. Surprisingly, the high level of nonemployment and enormous public expenditures on social programs in the Netherlands have not eroded the confidence of international investors in the stability of the guilder. They continue to express this confidence, convinced that nothing will divert the Netherland's commitment to a strong guilder and low inflation. Moreover, like Germany, the Netherlands has as a rule a comfortable balance of trade surplus, thanks to the export of agricultural products, financial services, and energy. The current trade surplus helps sustain confidence in Dutch exchange rate targets.[6]

As in Belgium, which also adopted a hard-currency policy and a fixed exchange rate after 1949, the consensus in the Netherlands after World War II was to seek trade liberalization and to pursue a monetary policy that would be anti-inflationary in order to protect the value of the guilder. A stable currency would protect the Netherlands' overseas earnings and persuade international investors to deposit their money in Dutch banks. The Dutch central bank and the financial service sector stood behind the agenda of turning the guilder into an international reserve currency. Enjoying a large degree of independence from political meddling, the central bank embarked upon a monetary framework that yielded low inflation, a stable exchange rate, and liberalized capital flows. Wide support was given to the central bank's emphasis on monetary stability because international financial services had always been among the most dynamic economic sectors in the country. Institutional arrangements in the Netherlands also lent support to a strong currency policy. Governments in the past, and again in the 1990s, used or threatened to use special powers to declare pay freezes and push back wage increases if pay negotiations seemed too inflationary.[7] Unions, in turn, moderated wage demands and preserved the international competitiveness of export firms. High labor costs are thus a product, not of market forces, but of the legal and contractual features of the wage formation system, which automatically extends any pay agreement to the entire sector, and of the tax system with its high marginal rates and high social security charges.[8]

A long history of a strong currency and corresponding institutional arrangements accounts for the widespread perception that the guilder is as good as the deutsche mark, and perhaps in the early 1990s, better than the deutsche mark. Again, it is important to stress that this success was not achieved overnight. Originally, the Dutch central bank kept the guilder

[6] Paulette Kurzer, *Business and Banking: Political Change and European Integration in Western Europe* (Ithaca: Cornell University Press, 1993), chap. 6.

[7] OECD, *Economic Surveys: The Netherlands, 1993*, p. 20.

[8] OECD, *Economic Surveys: The Netherlands, 1996*, pp. 48–49.

close to the Belgian franc. It joined the "snake"—the currency band created in 1972 to stabilize European exchange rates with respect to each other but to let them move jointly against the dollar—for most of the 1970s. Within the EMS, the Dutch guilder devalued twice against the deutsche mark, in 1979 and 1983, by just 2 percent each time. Moreover, over the last twenty years as a whole, the inflation rate was only slightly higher in the Netherlands than in Germany, and occassionally lower than the German rate in the 1980s.[9] Changes in discount rates in Germany are almost immediately followed by changes in official Dutch rates. In terms of reputation and credibility, after Germany the Netherlands had the highest anti-inflation reputation prior to and during the EMS period.[10] Interestingly, Dutch fiscal and social welfare policies acquired their singular traits despite restrictive monetarism and even though the numerous social welfare programs were never meant to carry so many claimants. The 1994 coalition agreement between the Liberal (VVD) and Labor (Pvd A) Parties has set out a fiscal plan that, formally recognizing EMU criteria, should reduce the government deficit to 2 percent and gradually reduce the national debt after 1998. By mid-1996, strong growth in services and exports reduced the official Dutch unemployment level to 6.6 percent, but measures to reform the much-abused disability system stalled in parliament after the resignation of a junior minister in charge of drafting the new benefit structure. Nevertheless, the Netherlands is poised to join EMU on time because its budget deficit has been set to fall below the famous 3 percent target stipulated by the Maastricht treaty. This is remarkable because the Dutch government has also lowered the collective tax burden, which will help keep labor costs in line with neighboring countries, and which has restored business confidence. The Netherlands is predicted to have the fastest growing economy in 1997 and 1998 in Europe. Export growth, which is the leading factor in its strong performance, benefited from the softening of the guilder against the dollar and pound sterling. A lowering of social security charges has also increased international competitiveness.

Belgian Monetary Regime

Belgium, too, declared its intention to pursue a strong currency policy and to resist further devaluations after the massive round of devaluations in 1949. According to every observer, the historic openness of the Belgian economy would suffer from devaluations, which would raise inflation and

[9] Andrew Britton and David Mayes, *Achieving Monetary Union in Europe* (Newbury Park, Calif.: Sage, 1992), p. 107.
[10] Axel A. Weber, "Reputation and Credibility in the EMS," *Economic Policy* 12 (1991): 78.

production costs. After the turmoil in foreign exchange markets in the 1980s, Belgium's national bank consolidated the relationship between the Belgian franc and the deutsche mark by pegging the currency directly to the deutsche mark in imitation of the Dutch. Yet the reputation of the Belgian franc is weak. Belgium has presently Europe's highest debt-to-GDP ratio. The origins of the debt crisis lie with the events of the mid-1970s, when interest rates began to climb, surpassing annual rates of economic growth, even as borrowing requirements spiraled. State spending rose in the 1970s, in part to keep the country together. Widening divisions between Walloon/French-speaking and Flemish/Dutch-speaking communities were bridged by providing subsidies and extra funds to troubled industrial sectors in each region. Moreover, when the social insurance funds, controlled by labor and employer associations, began to record large deficits, these were covered by the state, which had to borrow money at ever higher costs, resulting in a gross national debt that currently exceeds GDP by 30 percent. At regular intervals, foreign exchange markets attack the Belgian franc, assuming that the Belgian monetary authorities cannot (and should not) defend the pegged exchange rate by relying upon higher and higher interest rates.

In the late 1970s, when the debt problem first emerged, Belgium shared the inflation "reputation" of France. By mid-1987, impressed by the achievements of the Dutch economy and afraid of recurrent pressures on its currency, Belgium returned to a more overt German-linked exchange rate regime. Although inflation rates in Belgium had been higher than those in the Netherlands or Germany, by 1987 they began to converge. Emboldened by the convergence, Belgian authorities announced in 1990 a new exchange rate objective of pegging the Belgian franc to the stronger currencies in the ERM and promising to preserve the parity with the deutsche mark in the event of a realignment.[11] They narrowed their bilateral margins against the deutsche mark to ±0.5 percent, while retaining their official margins in the parity grid against other currencies. The narrower margins reduced the risk premium on the Belgian franc and eliminated short-term interest rate differentials as markets learned to trust the commitment and reputation of Belgian monetary authorities.[12]

The Belgian franc's fixed parity with the deutsche mark came after Belgium had experienced some humiliating treatments by international speculators and the European Community (EC). In June 1981, Belgium

[11] Britton and Mayes, *Achieving Monetary Union*, p. 108; and Jan Willem in 't Veld, "The Diverse Experience of the Netherlands, Belgium, and Denmark in the ERM," in Ray Barrell, ed., *Economic Convergence and Monetary Union in Europe* (Newbury Park, Calif.: Sage, 1992), pp. 162–64.

[12] Kenneth Dyson, *Elusive Union: The Process of Economic and Monetary Union in Europe* (New York: Longman, 1994), p. 207.

had the dubious distinction of being the first and only member state to receive an official recommendation of the European Commission to address
its growing public finance deficits and rapidly rising wages. The Commission report noted that these trends were highly inconsistent with a proper
functioning of the EMS and submitted a list of reforms that would stem
the spiraling growth in Belgium's budget deficits and pay increases. It was
only at the end of 1981 that a newly elected Belgian government was able
to begin the painful process of reducing the budget deficit. When pressures on the exchange rate continued to mount, the government had to
request a devaluation. In February 1982, the Belgian franc was devalued
by 8.5 percent. Famous among students of monetary integration, this devaluation is often cited as an instructive example of how German authorities bully others into pursuing tighter monetary discipline and fiscal moderation. The Belgian request for a 12 percent devaluation was considered
too steep by the German delegation, which countered by recommending
only a 3 percent devaluation. After difficult negotiations, the Economic
and Financial Council of Ministers (ECOFIN) produced a 9 percent compromise. The Belgian negotiators were not sure whether 9 percent would
be acceptable to the cabinet and to the various political parties in the coalition government. The next day (Sunday), the Belgians notified the EC that
they would go along with the lower rate, but the Germans wanted to teach
them a lesson. The German delegation withdrew their earlier agreement
to the ECOFIN compromise and instead proposed a smaller devaluation
of 8.5 percent.

At first sight, it would appear that the Germans had flexed their economic muscles and pulled a humiliating trick on a much smaller member
state. What is often overlooked is that the devaluation itself was controversial in Belgium. The Christian labor movement, closely tied to the dominant Christian Democratic Party, pressed for a modest devaluation out of
fear that it would cut into the purchasing power of its union members.
The Liberal Party in a coalition with the Christian Democrats advocated a
deep devaluation (of at least 12 percent) or no devaluation at all. During
the cabinet deliberations, the Liberals won the first round. But at the EMS
discussions, thanks to the German insistence that the size of devaluation
be limited to 8.5 percent, organized labor walked away with an important
victory.[13] Thus it is not clear whether Germany "bullied" Belgium when it
unwittingly lent support to a political faction that opposed any devaluation, and which had lost the first round in the internal cabinet debates.

[13] Hugo de Ridder, *Omtrent Wilfried Martens* (Tielt: Lannoo, 1991), pp. 148–50; Erik Jones,
"The Transformation of the Belgian State," in Erik Jones and Patrick McCarthy, eds., *Disinte-
gration or Transformation? The Crisis of the State in Advanced Industrial Societies* (New York:
St. Martin's Press, 1995), p. 176, n. 44.

Wage development cooperated with the 1982 devaluation, and Belgium's competitiveness improved. After 1983, the central government gained more influence over private sector pay development and used its new powers to intervene in the wage-bargaining process. Real wages remained frozen until 1986, and a competitiveness norm was legislated in 1989 that restrained wage gains to what was recorded, in common currency, in seven trading partners.[14] In 1993, the new law on competitiveness was for the first time applied when the first Dehaene cabinet announced a three-year wage freeze coupled with social welfare reforms and changes in the cost-of-living index. Announced in October 1993, the plan contained provisions for a three-year wage freeze (till 1996), drastic cuts in social security payments, health care, and child benefits, and new taxes on property and investment income. When the Belgian trade union federations reacted by calling for a general strike, the cabinet withdrew some of the measures, although the wage freeze and some cutbacks in social spending were not rescinded.

These fiscal measures have not adequately dealt with the debt issue, however, which is why a fixed deutsche mark–Belgian franc parity sets off recurrent speculative frenzies against the Belgian franc. EMS participation did not, in the end, impose the kind of fiscal behavior associated with restrictive monetarism. In addition, past spending has not prevented downsizing because one million Belgians (25 percent of the active labor force) were unemployed, including those who found publicly subsidized jobs. Total nonemployment was 43 percent in 1996.[15] The overwhelming majority of unemployed individuals draw state allowances and keep social spending levels high.

In the 1990s, the surge in German and European interest rates constituted an impossible burden for Belgium. Furthermore, the appreciation of the deutsche mark vis-à-vis other EMS currencies and the dollar in the early 1990s pulled up the Belgian franc as well, which rose by 3 percent against other EMS currencies between August 1992 and July 1993.[16] In

[14] In 't Veld, "Diverse Experience in ERM," pp. 162–63; Servaas Deroose and Jef Vuchelen, "Budgetary Policy," in M. A. G. van Meerhaeghe, *Belgium and EC Membership Evaluated* (New York: St. Martin's Press, 1992), p. 57; Paul de Grauwe, "The Need for Real Convergence in a Monetary Union," Christopher Johnson and Stefan Collignon, eds., *The Monetary Economics of Europe* (London: Pinter, 1994), pp. 271–75.

[15] OECD, *Economic Surveys: BLEU 1995* (Paris: OECD, 1995), p. 13. "Nonemployment" in Belgium is measured as the percentage of the population of working age not employed and "employment" as the percentage of the active workforce actually employed.

[16] OECD, *Economic Surveys: BLEU 1993/1994* (Paris: OECD, 1994), p. 33. In 1993, Belgium's social partners agreed that competitiveness had deteriorated, but they could not agree on a solution. The government reduced social security charges for most firms exposed to international competition and financed the reduction in social security contributions by introducing a tax on fuel consumption for nonindustrial users.

the aftermath of the National Bank's 1990 decision to peg the Belgian franc to the deutsche mark, the decline in international competitiveness was again an issue.[17] While the Belgian franc appreciated against currencies not pegged to the deutsche mark, labor costs and wages failed to take into account the deteriorating external position. On the one hand, long-term interest rates could be kept as low as possible and thus helped reduce the servicing costs of the national debt, but on the other, the Belgian franc was frequently under pressure, which could be countered only by raising (short-term) interest rates. Moreover, export prices in common currency rose with the appreciation of the deutsche mark against devaluating currencies.

The disintegration of the EMS after July 1993 prompted a group of respected liberal economists to publish an open letter in Belgium's main financial newspaper urging the government to take advantage of the situation by unpegging the Belgian franc from the deutsche mark.[18] Pleading for a "responsible" exchange rate policy, they argued for a depreciation of the Belgian franc, with correspondingly lower interest rates, in order to stimulate investments and job creation. In their opinion, an inflation rate of 2.5 percent and an unemployment rate of 12 percent left ample room for a flexible monetary stance that could boost the economy in the short term. The economists argued further that the cost-of-living indexation should be dismantled to exploit the gains of a currency devaluation, and that the inefficient and wasteful social insurance system, administered by labor associations, should be reformed to bring about additional budget savings. No debate took place in the days following publication of the economists' letter. Not even the trade union federations joined in the call for a less restrictive monetary regime, although the switch promised a short-term increase in the creation of jobs.

Organized labor welcomed a flexible exchange rate, but not at the expense of its treasured price indexation system.[19] Nor were unions pleased to hear about their loss of control over the provision of social welfare provisions. Employer associations were also opposed to a depreciation of the Belgian franc even though many export firms had lost market shares as a result of its overvaluation. Employers had been complaining since the early 1990s that high labor costs, in common currency, were choking

[17] Paul de Grauwe, *Onze schuld: Onstaan en toekomst van werkloosheid en staatsschuld* (Tielt: Lannoo, 1994), p. 67.

[18] "Leuvens Manifest is een pleidooi voor tijdelijke monetaire versoepeling," *Financieel Ekonomische Tijd* (August 26, 1993).

[19] The Belgian labor movement was one of the few that fought for and won automatic cost-of-living increases in the 1980s. The weighting of the cost-of-living index has changed, however, and tends to underestimate actual increases in the price of average consumer expenditures.

them.[20] But when it came down to casting off the fixed and strong currency policy, employers had second thoughts. They feared that organized labor would be able to convince a four-party coalition of Christian Democrats and Socialists to save the cost-of-living indexation, which would fuel higher inflation rates. Within government circles, the open letter was ignored. Belgium's central bank and national debt bureau opposed changing monetary regime because the depreciation would result in higher inflation and require higher interest rates in the long term. A strong Belgian franc would also minimize the cost of retiring foreign debt whose burden would rise in local currency if the Belgian franc were to be devalued. Thus none of Belgium's social partners and political groups were inclined to shelve restrictive monetarism, not because of any particular liking for an appreciating currency nor because they feared the Germans. Rather, since the late 1940s, monetary policy had centered on preserving a stable and strong exchange rate. Subsequently, labor-management relations and a system of social cooperation, based upon various trade-offs and exchanges, were founded on the concept of stable exchange rates. Changing these intricate labor-business-government arrangements might conceivably spark a battle for the redefinition and redesign of the entire social structure. Nobody was ready for this eventuality.

Jean-Luc Dehaene, popularly known as the "Fixer" or "Plumber" because of his ability to repair the leaky pipes of Belgian politics, called for an early election in February 1995. He expected to be reelected with a clear mandate to pass a tough budget and, indeed, the Center-Left coalition was returned to power after the May 1995 election. The cabinet's main priority has been to reduce the budget deficit and work toward reducing the national debt. At the same time, the coalition has insisted on putting in place fail-safe mechanisms to prevent any further increases in Belgian labor costs. A new competitiveness law, extending the earlier 1993 act, urges the social partners to step in if Belgium loses market shares to its neighbors (France, the Netherlands, and Germany) and if any one of four other criteria—principally wage costs—deteriorates in relation to those of its trading partners. If the social partners fail to arrest wage growth or the decline in market shares, the government will inter-

[20] By late 1995, for the first time in ten years, businesses/employers complained openly that the exchange rate was pricing Belgian goods out of European markets. The strong exchange rate is more of a handicap for Belgian than for Dutch goods because Belgium specializes in the same categories of manufactured goods that Italy or the United Kingdom does. The central bank dismissed the complaints by stating that a cheaper currency would lead to higher inflation, higher interest rates, higher production costs, and greater public sector deficits. Bart Vinck, "Topmanager Karel Vinck verdedigt de sterke frank," *Elis/MSR* (July 31, 1995); Sophie Bourgois, "Nationale Bank wijst op gevolgen van zwakkere frank," *Elis/MSR* (August 18, 1995).

vene without consulting the social partners. Real wage increases came to 1.4 percent in 1994 and the government neutralized their impact by reducing social security charges and by adjusting the cost-of-living indexation.[21] Wage accords for 1995–96 excluded any increase in real wages. In early 1996, the cabinet initiated a round of talks with employers and unions to halve Belgium's 14 percent unemployment rate after the turn of the century. In exchange for a phased reduction in social security charges, more flexible work patterns, and wage restraint, unions were promised more jobs. The socialist trade union movement accused the government of bad faith because there were no guarantees that wage earner sacrifices would indeed translate into more jobs. The pact collapsed after two months of consultation. After the disintegration of tripartite discussions, Dehaene requested special powers for the next year to pass the "most important budget in Belgium's history." The new law would enable the government to take measures in all areas of public finance to ensure that Belgium reached the 3 percent budget deficit target set out by the Maastricht treaty.[22] Parliament passed the framing laws in July 1996, and executive measures will try to limit budget deficits to 3 percent by 1997, from the current level of 3.2 percent in 1996, while savings of nearly one billion dollars are projected to come from the social insurance system.

A single currency without Belgium's participation is for many Belgians, whether on the left or the right, too appalling to contemplate. The ambitious proposals of the second Dehaene cabinet must be seen in this light. Belgium wants to participate in the first round of monetary union because Belgium is a core member of the European Union and because it has always upheld a fixed exchange rate.

In retrospect, participation in the exchange rate mechanisms of the EMS brought about "nominal" or exchange rate convergence but no real convergence in institutional configurations. Ultimately, it is the institutional context that creates constraints and opportunities and that defines feasible policy courses. It would appear that neither Belgium nor the Netherlands suffered excessively from an "assertive" Germany because neither discarded cherished institutions or reconceptualized major policy strategies. Fixed exchange rates were incorporated into the export strategy of each country after World War II, and European initiatives on that front neatly coincided with national economic interests. Sticking to an exchange rate regime and monetary policy set by Germany did not automatically impose restrictions and strains on the postwar welfare state. It is only in the last ten years, after a steady rise in expenditures and years of slow growth, that the postwar welfare state has interfered with restrictive

[21] Belgium's new wage index excludes tobacco, alcohol, gasoline, and diesel fuel.
[22] Neil Buckley, "Decree to Pass Belgian Budget," *Financial Times* (May 10, 1996), p. 2.

monetarism. Yet social welfare reforms have been piecemeal and have not touched the core of the postwar social pact. Unless growth rates again reach levels not seen since the 1960s, social welfare programs and social solidarity will have to adjust to harsher economic environment and demographic shifts.

For now, public spending on social insurance and welfare programs compensates for the hardships and dislocations arising from the pursuit of a fixed exchange rate and an appreciating currency. Leaving aside for the moment the difficult question of whether monetary integration contributed to jobless economic growth, EMS participation brings with it major economic shifts and dislocations. Social spending induces voters to accept a genuine loss of national monetary autonomy and to acquiesce in continued participation and compliance with EMS or future EMU rules. Paradoxically, the best political strategy to achieve the unachievable, namely, to recast the postwar consensus on social redistribution, would be to encourage the free movement of labor and thereby force greater European harmonization of social security. Governments could intentionally tie their hands by promoting labor mobility and could then claim that the unrestricted movement of workers requires a totally new approach to state intervention in the social arena. Yet national governments resist at all costs relinquishing social welfare policy to the EU because it is one of their main functions and closely tied to the rise of the modern state. Even right-wing politicians refuse to endorse the free movement of labor or the harmonization of social security within the EU for fear of an electoral backlash.

SOCIAL POLICY AND SOCIAL SECURITY

In practically every country, social security is a mixture of public legislation and private arrangements organized by occupation. Firms, industries, or individuals supplement public benefits with occupational or private insurance. In theory, public benefits should be portable throughout the EU, in contrast to private benefits, which, by rewarding loyalty, hard work, and pay moderation, discourage turnover and thus impede labor mobility. Private insurance contracts are regulated by negotiating parties and come in many different forms. It follows that national coordination of multiple private insurance contracts is fraught with difficulties; international coordination is virtually impossible. Neither employers, employees, nor governments are eager to witness greater EU legislative action in this area.[23]

[23] Jef van Langendonck, "Coordination of Social Security in Europe," in Jos Berghman and Bea Cantillon, eds., *The European Face of Social Security* (Brookfield, Vt.: Avebury, 1993), p. 316.

From the beginning, national governments and the European Commission agreed on two things. First, in response to the fear that increased economic competition would lower social welfare standards in the prosperous members of the European Community, the Commission pledged to ensure high standards in environmental protection, health and safety, and general social welfare provisions.[24] Second, national governments and the Commission reached an understanding on the extent to which the principle of subsidiarity would apply to the social elements of the Treaty on European Union. Subsidiarity is popular because national governments want to retain sufficient decisional authority to act within the institutional history and normative values of their respective countries. Social security systems articulate widely accepted norms about equity, fairness, and state-society relations that make a harmonized, integrated social space at the European level difficult to achieve.[25] Yet, at the same time, financial and economic integration and capital mobility persistently pressure governments to arrest the growth of public sector deficits, social security taxes, and social regulations.

This is why elections in the 1990s in Belgium and the Netherlands have been fought over clashing views on social welfare reform. Whether participants in these national debates trace the crisis in the social security system to past domestic decisions and arrangements or to contemporary trends like a rapidly aging population and excessive health care costs, solutions are sought within a national context.[26] In the 1994 Dutch election, the Liberal Party advocated a pared-down welfare state that would guarantee a minimum level of social assistance, while the Labor Party favored preserving the current system with a few changes. The Liberal Party proposed various alternatives to the current system, such as "work-fare" programs, the privatization of certain kind of risks (disability and sickness), and the implementation of a basic income plan. None of these alternatives was weighed against its possible impact on the "European social dimension."

[24] Jacques Pelkmans, "Significance of EC-1992," *Annals of American Academy of Political and Social Science* 531 (1994): 108; Hugh Mosley, "The Social Dumping Threat of European Integration: A Critique," in Ungar and van Waarden, eds., *Convergence or Diversity?*, pp. 182–99; Paul Pierson and Stephan Leibfried, "The Dynamics of Social Policy Integration," in Pierson and Leibfried, eds., *European Social Policy* (Washington, D.C.: Brookings, 1995), pp. 432–65.

[25] See the essays in Pierson and Leibfried, eds., *European Social Policy*, on the difficulties of achieving social integration. See also Edward Moxon-Browne, "Social Policy," in Juliet Lodge, ed., *The EC and the Challenge of the Future* (New York: St. Martin's Press, 1993), pp. 152–62.

[26] Prior to the Maastricht Summit, the Dutch who held the Council Presidency in the second half of 1991 circulated a position paper to get the member states to think about political integration and the Internal Market. One topic entirely ignored was the "European social dimension." The Dutch did mention the new structure of the EU, the Internal Market, foreign policy cooperation, and so on, but not the social welfare aspects of the new Europe. George Ross, *Jacques Delors and European Integration* (New York: Oxford University Press, 1995), p. 71.

In Belgium, as mentioned earlier, the second Dehaene cabinet has aimed for deep budget cuts and institutional reforms to meet the EMU deadline. The hope is to get the budget deficit down to 3 percent of GDP, after which the other member states will, presumably, ignore Belgium's enormous public debt. But the sweeping powers of this cabinet must also be seen against the background of rising deficits in the health care and unemployment funds and deteriorating international competitiveness. Arguably, the spiraling costs of the social insurance system and the loss of international market shares alone would have prompted drastic actions by the political establishment. In 1982, another cabinet led by the Christian Democratic Party also relied upon extraordinary powers to stem inflationary pressures and impose austerity measures. Belgian politicians see the EMU as just another reason for why the executive needs extra powers to make last-minute budget adjustments and why Belgium needs to rethink its postwar social welfare state institutions. Opposition to drastic changes is fierce because elites from the trade union and employer organizations manage social welfare provisions and are reluctant to give up their control when they will be held responsible for drastic changes.

To be sure, at the beginning of the revitalization of the European Community and the launching of the Internal Market in the mid-1980s, labor market integration and free movement of labor provoked fears among Dutch and Belgian officials that their generous system of social protection would spur "social tourism." They conjured up images of migrants flocking to the Low Countries for the sole purpose of taking advantage of entitlement benefits. In retrospect, many of these fears were groundless. Presumably, employers will weed out "bad risk" employees and not employ them. Moreover, there is some serious doubt whether sick and disabled individuals are likely to uproot themselves from their community, given the psychological and financial costs of moving to another country.[27] The European Court of Justice (ECJ), while passing decisions in support of freedom of movement for EU citizens, ruled that they must carry their own health insurance and be financially able to support themselves. The ECJ has declared that an EU citizen can look for employment in another EU country for up to three months, provided the person has a place to stay and registers at the local employment office. The host country pays the unemployment benefits against later reimbursement by the job seeker's country of origin. Job seekers who have not found work after three months forfeit their right to unemployment benefits in the host country and, lacking sufficient financial resources, can be asked to return home.

Arguably, even employed individuals from other EU countries could pose a burden on the social security system of the host country. For ex-

---

[27] Antonie de Kemp and Corien Sips, *Prospects for European Integration and Consequences for Social Security Policy in the Netherlands* (The Hague: VUGA, 1994), pp. 114–15.

ample, part-time workers whose earnings fall below the legal minimum income as defined by Belgian and Dutch legislation could apply for social assistance. Other workers could lose their jobs after a short period and qualify for up to two years of unemployment benefits, or until their residence permits expired. In the Netherlands, moreover, the social security system is based on risk instead of amount or years of contribution. This is to say that the Netherlands could theoretically be responsible for the payment of social security benefits of a person who resided for only a short period in the Netherlands and primarily contributed to the social security system of another country.[28] Some changes have been made that will make social security less vulnerable to entitlement claims by non-Dutch employees. For example, since 1992, persons eligible for disability benefits receive 70 percent of their last wages for a specific duration, which is calculated by the age when they began to contribute to the insurance plan.[29] Earlier, disabled persons could draw 70 percent of their last earnings until retirement age. It is noteworthy that the Dutch parliament passed the new disability law not to prevent foreign EU nationals from exploiting the social welfare system, which is susceptible to fraud and abuse, but rather to control public expenditures and to encourage benefit recipients to look for work. At no point during the deliberations on reforming disability qualifications did legislators point out how the previous system had attracted "social tourists." Discourse on social policy questions is, by and large, a domestic affair, which explains why the involvement of the EU is limited. National governments, accountable to national electorates, wish to retain their monopoly over social welfare policies, which closely bind them to their societies.

German Influence? Europeanization of Industrial Relations

German industrial relations are built on national institutions and employment rights that bring together government, employers, and unions in a social partnership. Codetermination and works councils ensure equality between labor and management at the point of production. German labor officials and politicians have been keenly interested in establishing a European model of works councils and of co-determination since the 1970s. German participants feared that, as a result of restructuring production in the European Community, sophisticated tasks would be carried out in Germany, while labor-intensive tasks would move to low-wage countries with minimal employment laws. The European Commission

---

[28] H. A. A. Verbon, "Sociale zekerheid en 1992," *Economische en Statistische Berichten* (March 29, 1989): 17; de Kemp and Sips, *Prospects for European Integration*, p. 93.

[29] OECD, *Economic Surveys: The Netherlands, 1996*, pp. 52–54.

shared these worries; a division of labor as envisioned by this scenario would interfere with the single market and with the aim of furthering better political cooperation in the near future. The Commission also viewed a European industrial relations system as an institutional component for a stronger European economy and seized upon the social charter for employees to give that economy a "human face."[30]

A European works council proposal had surfaced in the European Commission as early as 1975, only to encounter fierce opposition from business and from the United Kingdom. The Commission advanced numerous proposals in the next two decades in the hope of overcoming national and business resistance. Finally, in the late 1980s, a new revised directive was drafted with the assistance of the German Trade Union Confederation and the Dutch Labor Federation. Both trade union confederations toiled behind the scenes to mobilize the largest majority possible in the European Trade Union Confederation (ETUC). In 1991, a new proposal for a directive to establish works councils in companies employing more than 1,000 workers with at least 100 workers in two or more member states was placed on the agenda for further deliberation.[31] During the Dutch presidency of the Council of Ministers of Social Affairs, in the second half of 1991, a diluted version of an earlier draft proposed by the ETUC was submitted for deliberations at the Maastricht summit. Not much happened in subsequent years until the Belgian delegation brokered a compromise in 1993, using several informal papers by the Christian Democratic ministers from the Netherlands, Germany, and Belgium. Although the British minister blocked adoption in late 1993, during the German presidency (June–December 1994), the Council managed to pass the works council directive in September 1994, which represented the first successful invocation of the Maastricht social protocol since the United Kingdom opted out of the "European social dimension."

It was also during the German presidency that the Council of Ministers of Social Affairs accepted a form of institutionalized social dialogue in large, multinational companies. The council directive requires all companies in Europe employing more than 1,000 workers with 150 workers in at least two member states to establish information and consultation committees for them. The exact model of a works councils is left to companies and unions in order to allow for specific national variations, although the

---

[30] Paul Teague and John Grahl, *Industrial Relations and European Integration* (London: Lawrence & Wishart, 1992), p. 77; see also Peter Cressey, "Employee Participation," in Michael Gold, ed., *The Social Dimension: Employment Policy in the EC* (London: Macmillan, 1993), pp. 85–104.

[31] Beverly Springer, *The European Union and its Citizens: The Social Agenda* (Westport, Conn.: Greenwood, 1994), pp. 61–62, 75–76. Management would be required to hold an annual meeting with the works council and consult with it on all issues likely to affect employees.

EU imposes a uniform EU model on companies failing to negotiate a works council before the deadline (September 1996). By all accounts, the EU model resembles the German one and enables German unions to influence managerial prerogatives even outside the FRG.[32]

It was logical for Belgian, Dutch, and German participants to join forces on this EU matter. Broad features of their industrial relations systems converge. Each has a tradition of strong unions, centralized wage negotiations, and legal extension of collective wage contracts to the rest of the economy. In addition, in all three countries, works councils are specifically mandated by law in firms above a certain size and are legally responsible for the implementation of collective agreements. The objective of works councils is to promote collaboration between management and employees and to exchange information on personnel issues, investment and technology decisions, health and safety. Social Catholicism has been an influential source of ideas in each country. As early as the papal encyclical *Rerum Novarum* (1891), church officials exhorted owners and workers to work together. Such a long tradition of shared cultural norms eased joint action on behalf of a system that already existed in each country. Beyond question, governments in each of the three countries were impatient to incorporate tripartism into the fabric of socioeconomic relations of the EU.

The impact of the EU on social policy and social security is weak because the European Commission focuses on social regulation to promote economic integration. Other than social regulation of health and safety issues, member states oppose the transfer of legally binding powers to the Commission, although government negotiators have usually welcomed the Commission's efforts to eliminate nontrade barriers. Hence, in contrast to an emerging set of EU regulations with regard to health, safety, and worker participation in management, there is no genuine European social space.

Direct, immediate pressures do not force countries to revise their domestic framework of social security policy. Rather, economic deregulation and the free movement of goods, services, and capital, combined with tremendous demographic shifts, oblige high-welfare countries to reassess the costs of social programs. It is widely recognized that generous benefits distort the efficient operation of labor markets and jeopardize business productivity. There is a growing sense that social security benefits and expenditures must be reduced for the sake of international competitiveness. Dutch authorities speak of "policy competition" and point to high social benefits, high volume of claimants, low employment rates, and subsequently high social security taxes as a persistent barrier to growth and fiscal stability.

[32] Robert Taylor, "How GM Sees Works Council Working," *Financial Times* (July 27, 1995): 2. General Motors claimed that if it did not set up its own works councils, it would have German advisors all over the floor telling them how to do it.

· All western European governments have cut back on the provision of welfare benefits although the structure of the social system—unemployment and health insurance, pensions, housing subsidies—has survived. The postwar welfare state is still operative because it enjoys wide and deep electoral support. In addition, welfare provisions are one of the few remaining functions of post-Maastricht governments and legitimize the existence of distinct national administration, taxation, and political systems. Not even conservative politicians are willing to set in motion the destruction of national bureaucratic agencies by eliminating one of the primary activities of national governments. Extensive social welfare systems will, for the foreseeable future, remain national institutions.

Germany upholds a particular agenda for EU social legislation, with the approval of Belgium and the Netherlands. All three countries built similar social welfare systems and legislated similar labor-management consultation frameworks; in the 1980s all three came to see that employee rights in their respective countries constrained domestic firms unfairly, while also undermining national models of labor-management consultation. As with monetary integration, German leadership was courted by Belgium and the Netherlands and endorsed because of a convergence of interests and perceptions.

Policing and law enforcement harmonization constitute my third policy regime. Here, too, European trends challenge existing legislative frameworks, yet adjustment takes place within the sphere of domestic or national administrative boundaries, norms, and previous policy compromises. Here, too, Germany provides leadership, although it must be noted that neither Belgium nor the Netherlands fully shares Germany's goals for greater institutionalized European police cooperation.

POLICE AND LAW ENFORCEMENT

One year behind schedule, in January 1994, the European Police Office (Europol) finally found a home in a stately office building in the Hague. Europol's European Drug Unit (EDU) is the very first EU-wide system for exchanging police information to fight drug trafficking and the criminal organizations involved with money laundering. Eventually, EDU will lead to the creation of a sophisticated database on drug trafficking, and will be part of the analysis of national crime prevention programs and measures related to training, research, and forensics.

The decision to improve international police cooperation was made the very last day of the Maastricht summit, at the urgent request of the German delegation. National governments reluctantly agreed to include police collaboration as one of the nine areas regarded by the member states as matters of common interest to achieve the objectives of the EU, in particular the free movement of persons.[33] The third pillar of the union, Justice and Home Affairs (JHA) operates at the intergovernmental level and requires unanimity in the Council of Ministers, which is responsible for establishing uniform positions and for promoting all forms of cooperation to actualize the EU objectives. Although resolutions and conventions require unanimity, measures to implement the principles decided upon in the Council can be adopted through qualified majority voting.

Policing and judicial policies are essential prerogatives of sovereign nation-states. In a democratic state, law enforcement represents the central instrument of government in the domestic exercise of legitimate power. Historically, there is a strong connection between nation-states, control over police forces, and the definition of state jurisdiction of police functions. It is therefore no surprise that member states continue to be divided on many law enforcement issues. Institutionalized police cooperation requires the harmonization of different criminal justice systems and procedures, common standards to protect civil liberties, a single working language, and a common definition of what constitutes a crime. Moreover, such cooperation assumes a EU with greater transparency and accountability. This short list of requirements illustrates the layers of complications to be solved before any European police agency comes into existence.

At the same time, compelling developments make European police cooperation an urgent item on the EU agenda. The mass media plays up the rise in crime that has accompanied abolition of internal frontiers. Additional developments have reinforced the need to simplify cross-border police activities. While the end of the Cold War has eliminated direct threats to the security of the state, it has at the same time fueled the explosive growth of migration and asylum seekers, mafia-style organizations, and of trafficking in arms, drugs, and toxic substances. The only sensible strategy is for countries to pool resources and information.

Interestingly, Dutch and Belgian police systems underwent substantial organizational reforms either before or directly after the Maastricht summit. While popular debates on altering police systems focused on the dangers of the unrestricted movement of people, the actual revision of laws governing police powers and procedures had little bearing on the decisions and developments taking place in Europe at that time. Much of the discussion on the inefficiency of national police organizations was shaped by the sense that the new Europe was fair terrain for organized crime. But

[33] Ellen Ahnfelt and Johan From, "European Policing," in Svein S. Andersen and Kjell A Eliassen, eds., *Making Policy in Europe* (Thousand Oaks, Calif.: Sage, 1993); see also Monica den Boer and Neil Walker, "European Policing after 1992," *Journal of Common Market Studies* 31 (1993): 3–27; Malcolm Anderson, Monica den Boer, Peter Cullen, William Gilmore, Charles Raab, and Neil Walker, *Policing the European Union* (Oxford: Clarendon Press, 1995).

the approach to the perceived surge in crime rates was based on domestic administrative, political, and legal parameters. Elected officials in Belgium and the Netherlands used new police legislation to tighten political oversight over national police activities, but they paid scant attention on strengthening transnational police cooperation. In short, the deliberations as well as the actual legislation were firmly grounded on existing administrative rules and domestic political dynamics.

Police System of Belgium

Until 1991, Belgium had three regular police forces.[34] The municipal police, with around 16,000 employees, was the largest and did not change. The gendarmerie, in charge of public order, law enforcement, and traffic surveillance, was called upon to solve serious crimes, even in large cities like Antwerp or Brussels, because its force of 13,000 was considered better trained and more professional. Originally intended to carry out military assignments as well, the gendarmerie fell under the ministry of defense. The smallest of the three forces, the judiciary police, employed 1,400 plainclothes officers and was mostly in charge of serious white-collar crime.[35]

Until the new police legislation went into force in 1991, fragmentation and intense competition among its three forces undermined the effectiveness of the Belgian police system. The rivalry was especially ferocious between the judiciary police and the gendarmerie; indeed, one force would knowingly arrest informants of the other with the specific purpose of thwarting its rival's criminal investigations. Officials from different police agencies routinely withheld information from each other in order to be in control of investigations that required collaboration. The original police laws had contributed to this situation by failing to delineate who was responsible for which law enforcement tasks. In the late 1980s, every brigade of the judiciary police and gendarmerie and every large city's municipal police force ran its own drug crime unit, but there was no central office to collect information and coordinate the findings of the many overlapping investigations.

In the 1980s, the Belgian police made several terrible blunders that propelled the political leadership to review the entire police system. After years of watching the entire array of Belgian police organizations fight among themselves and fail to solve even the most brutal and senseless crimes, the reelected Center-Right coalition (Martens VIII) appointed a parliamen-

---

[34] For an excellent summary of the differences between the police systems of Belgium and the Netherlands, see Hans Bevers and Chantal Joubert, "Politiële samenwerking in Europa," *Politiestudies* 13 (1994): 39–57.

[35] Hugo Coveliers, *Securitas Belgica: De Rijkswacht is overbodig* (Antwerp: Hadewijch, 1989); Paul Ponsaers and Gilbert Dupont, *De Bende van Nijvel* (Berchem: EPO, 1988).

tary committee in April 1988 to investigate how Belgium was dealing with crime and terrorism. Two years of research yielded a massive report with a long list of proposed reforms. The committee faulted the current system for, among others things, inadequate supervision over police activities, low standards of police training, and the cumbersome structure of law enforcement administration, which involved no less than three ministries—defense, interior, and justice. In response, the government adopted many of the committee's reforms during the legislative session 1990–91. By far the most important step was to demilitarize the gendarmerie and to phase out its military symbols and connections. The gendarmerie was turned into a regular civilian force, responsible to the ministry of interior. The twin objectives of the new police laws were to improve effectiveness, which was achieved by establishing a joint data center, better training, closer national contacts, and the modernization of municipal police, and to strengthen accountability. A permanent parliamentary committee was set up to oversee police matters.[36]

One thing the reforms failed to achieve was to eliminate the conflict and rivalry between the judiciary police and the gendarmerie. To a large extent, each is still in charge of investigating organized crime and cross-border crimes.[37] Belgian police officers continue to complain that it is harder to cooperate among themselves than with foreign authorities. Although it would have been logical to fold the much smaller judiciary police into the gendarmerie, the ministry of justice fought tooth and nail against this proposal. In the meantime, foreign police officers and services continue to wonder to whom they should turn when seeking partners or information.[38] In retrospect, the reforms have not really improved the efficiency and operation of Belgian law enforcement agencies. In the summer of 1996, the Belgian nation read with mounting shock and anger how the entire judicial and police system had failed to rescue at least five missing children from the clutches of two well-known pedophiles. A parliamentary commission wrote a report, presented to the public eight months later in April 1997, which catalogued a long list of mistakes, errors, and misjudgments on the part of three different police forces. The rivalry

[36] W. Bruggeman, "De rijkswacht en de reorganisatie van het politiebestel in België," in C. Fijnaut, ed., *De reguliere politiediensten in België en Nederland* (Arnhem: Gouda Quint, 1992), pp. 45–53; Lode van Outrieve, Yves Cartuyvels, and Paul Ponsaers, *Sire, ik ben ongerust: Geschiedenis van de Belgische politie, 1794–1991* (Leuven: Kritak, 1992), pp. 309–22.

[37] J. J. F. Engelen, "De gemeentepolitie en de reorganisatie van het politiebestel in België," in Fijnaut, ed., *Reguliere politiediensten*, pp. 3–28.

[38] Dutch and German police authorities recount how three officers from the three Belgian police forces dropped by to request identical information because they each worked on the same investigation without consulting the others. W. Bruggeman, "De vernieuwing van de wetgeving inzake de rijkswacht," C. Fijnaut and F. Hutsebaut, eds., *De nieuwe politiewetgeving in België* (Arnhem: Gouda Quint, 1993), pp. 51–64.

among the three branches of police (judicial and municipal police and gendarmerie), according to the parliamentary report, led to dangerous competition that interfered with the functioning of justice in Belgium and allowed the chief suspect to continue to operate freely because the gendarmerie did not alert the investigating magistrates of his activities. The gendarmerie withheld information because it wanted the glory of solving the crime of the missing girls. The main recommendation of the report consists of creating one federal police structure that operates both at the federal and the local level. Since Belgian voters have been outraged by the bungling of the investigation into the missing girls, the cabinet has little choice but to implement the recommendations of the parliamentary commission.

Police System of the Netherlands

The Netherlands possessed two different police forces. The municipal police was found in cities having more than 25,000 residents (148). The administration and supervision of the local police rested with the mayor, and the budget and promotions were managed by the ministry of interior. In municipalities too small to possess their own police corps (approximately 550), the state police was responsible for law and order and for crime investigations. Financed and managed by the ministry of justice, the state police employed 14,000 people, or just over half as many as the municipal police, with a staff of 25,000.[39] After years of desultory debate, the third Lubbers cabinet presented parliament with new police legislation, whose contours had been outlined in the 1989 precoalition agreement. As in Belgium, the cabinet sprang into action in response to complaints from the media and voters about the inability of Dutch law enforcement to cope with rising crime. The government reasoned that merging the two police forces into larger regional units would lower overhead costs, freeing up funds for costly investigative equipment and procedures needed to keep ahead of dangerous criminals and cross-border crimes. By 1990, politicians, speaking for their constituents, and law enforcement officials agreed that everyone stood to benefit from larger police units, which would mean higher professional standards and better equipment at lower overall costs.[40]

In 1993, the new police law went into effect. It abolished the state and municipal police, and merged them into twenty-five regional police forces. At the head of each regional police force stands the mayor of the

[39] R. F. D. Gerrand, "Gemeentepolitie en reorganisatie van het politiebestel," in Fijnaut, ed., *Reguliere politiediensten,* p. 32.
[40] D. van de Meeberg, "Korps Rijkspolitie en reogranisatie van politiebestel," in Fijnaut, ed., *Reguliere politiediensten,* pp. 55–58.

largest city within that region, assisted by a council consisting of local mayors, officials from the office of the public prosecutor, and the regional police chief. The ministry of interior continues to be in charge of disbursements for the regional forces, while the ministry of justice (office of the public prosecutor) is responsible for organizational and financial issues.[41] Twenty-five regional forces report to nineteen court districts, but to only one office of the public prosecutor. The police chief must consult with the public prosecutor (and thus the justice ministry) on decisions with organizational and financial consequences.

The dual system of management and supervision was retained because justice officials refused to sacrifice "their" state police unless the ministry received a new mandate for administering and managing police affairs. As police regions correspond to newly drawn court districts, the office of public prosecutor stands at the head of the district and wields influence over the gathering of facts and prosecution of crimes. The minister of justice is also in charge of the so-called twenty-sixth national force, which brings together many formerly independent specialized services, such as the maritime police, royal security force, road traffic police, and central criminal intelligence (which maintains international police contacts and sends liaison officers to Europol).

As in Belgium, the police reforms came in the wake of rising complaints about increased crime and decreased police effectiveness. Novel crimes (such as those related to illegal dumping of waste, trade in plutonium) received wide media coverage and heightened the sense of vulnerability. Promises to abolish internal frontiers coupled with the unstable situation in Eastern Europe convinced Dutch citizens that crime had become more pervasive and that criminals had nothing to fear. Yet reforms to improve police services were framed within the context of existing domestic institutional arrangements and national values. In addition to renovating the organizational structure of regular police forces, politicians devoted much attention to increasing democratic supervision of the police system, which is why the new system does not radically depart from the old. The new, combined Dutch police force is still accountable to two "bosses," justice and interior, which hinders the formulation and execution of coherent police objectives. Each ministry has its own agenda: interior prefers administrative decentralization, whereas justice encourages centralization and concentration of police power.[42]

Twenty-five regional police chiefs are more likely to cooperate among themselves than are 150 municipal police chiefs and various state police

[41] Hans Bevers and Chantal Joubert, "Politiële samenwerking in Europa," *Politie Studies* 13 (1994): 39–45.

[42] Gerrand, "Gemeentepolitie en reorganisatie," pp. 35–37.

divisions. Yet joint approach and action among the twenty-five regional police forces has made little progress. Tensions between the ministries of interior and justice continue to interfere with police affairs because interior controls law enforcement expenditures, while justice formulates law enforcement policies.[43] This makes one wonder why politicians did not assign the "twenty-sixth national force" more authority to form one, overarching national police force. The reason is clear. Dutch citizens and politicians favor decentralized police forces, subordinate to elected officials, because they fear concentrated police powers.

Police Systems and Judicial Harmonization

No country has been as adamant as Germany about the wisdom and utility of cross-border police cooperation, regulated by EC agreements and agencies. Repeatedly, German officials have argued that a European police agency would be extremely useful in the prosecution of crimes against the Community and in the design of joint approaches to crimes experienced by member states: drug trafficking, illegal weapon trade, and terrorism. Until very recently, other member states did not share German enthusiasm for central intelligence data banks, the right of "hot pursuit" across national borders, and joint collaborations. When Chancellor Kohl mentioned the possible creation of a Euro-FBI in 1988, an agency with executive powers, modeled after the American FBI, his proposal met with scorn from all sides and was quickly forgotten.[44] As recently as 1996, the German government was still thinking along the lines of a federal framework for a Europol with operational capabilities.[45]

In the late 1980s, German delegations skillfully used the Schengen Accords to explore the possibilities of EC-wide policing organizations, while the meetings under the Terrorism, Radicalism, Extremism, Violence International (TREVI), which had expanded their province to include drugs and international crime, provided the Germans a second pretext for initiative proposing establishment of a European clearinghouse to ease cross-border police cooperation.[46] The German draft mentioned a central bureau for information to assemble data on the fight against drugs and organized crime, with a possible addition of executive powers for this bureau after the Maastricht summit. During its presidency of the European

---

[43] Hans Bevers, "Regionalization: The Dutch Police Forces after Their Reorganization," *Police Journal* 67 (1994): 326–33; van de Meeberg, "Korps Rijkspolitie," pp. 73–75.

[44] C. Fijnaut, "Schengen Treaties and European Police Cooperation," *European Journal of Crime, Criminal Law, and Criminal Justice* 1 (1993): 55.

[45] Anderson et al., *Policing European Union*, p. 83.

[46] Monica den Boer, "The Quest for European Policing," in M. Anderson and M. den Boer, *Policing across National Boundaries* (New York: Pinter Publishers, 1994), p. 180.

Council (June–December 1994), the German government urged national governments to implement the Europol agreement by mid-1995 to establish common control of borders and therefore to move toward implementation of the Schengen Accords. After years of trying to convince its European partners, Germany had finally succeeded in adding police cooperation to the intergovernmental summits.

How to explain German eagerness to see the establishment of an EU police organization. Does this point to a new Germany, assertive and aggressive, and threatening the national sovereignty of its small neighbors? As a matter of fact, Germany's interests in EU-wide policing grew slowly over time as its attempts to deepen existing bilateral cross-border treaties among its neighbors came to naught.[47] Germany, the Netherlands, and Belgium had already signed international police agreements in the early 1960s.[48] By the late 1960s, trilingual forms to report crimes and criminals and the constant exchange of information to fight drug trafficking became routine matters. In 1975, German police officers sought to extend the existing agreements on cross-border police cooperation by suggesting that German police officers be permitted to pursue suspects across borders and to make an arrest on foreign territory within the presence of local authorities. The Dutch demurred and rejected the proposal, even though such an agreement did exist among the three Benelux countries.[49]

Neither Belgium nor the Netherlands was ready to enter into a similar agreement with Germany, in part because they recoiled from having to restructure cross-border police cooperation among themselves to accommodate a third party. Repeatedly, the German authorities tried to revive the idea of deepening police cooperation, to no avail. Lingering memories of the activities of the German police during the Nazi Occupation may also have hardened Belgian and Dutch determination not to yield to German requests. Gradually, after 1984, German politicians decided to take another road to achieve the same goal: multilateral agreements by way of Schengen.[50] Because most of Germany's overtures had been ignored by Belgium and the Netherlands, the new police laws were not influenced by typical German preoccupation with "internal security," defined as defense against internal enemies who undermine the state and society for political or philosophical reasons. Such views find no resonance in either Dutch or Belgian rhetoric or actual policy deliberations.

[47] Fijnaut, "Schengen Treaties," p. 40; Erika S. Fairchild, *German Police: Ideals and Reality in the Post-War Years* (Springfield, Ill.: Thomas, 1988).

[48] Malcolm Anderson, *Policing the World: Interpol and the Politics of International Police Cooperation* (Oxford: Clarendon Press, 1989).

[49] C. Fijnaut, *The Internationalization of Police Cooperation in Western Europe* (Gouda: Kluwer, 1993), p. 126.

[50] Fijnaut, "Schengen Treaties," p. 41.

German or European Union influence over national police systems has also been stymied by the existence of uniquely different judicial systems. One particularly illuminating example of the ability of small EU countries to preserve policy frameworks and institutions despite the objections of a powerful neighbor and structural developments at the union level is Dutch drug policy.

Drawing on strong egalitarian traditions, the Dutch criminal justice system metes out light sentences, which partly explains the Netherlands' permissive attitude toward personal drug use and why the Dutch police quietly tolerate the consumption and possession of small quantities (up to one gram or 0.035 ounce of heroin and five grams or 0.175 ounce of soft drugs). Neighboring France and Germany claim that the Dutch permissiveness toward the sale of "soft" drugs (through licensed "coffee shops") increases cross-border drug trafficking, which has become especially problematic after the elimination of border controls. Other EU member states including Belgium, have asked the Netherlands to revise its lenient approach to drug possession in accordance with the judicial standards of its neighboring countries. Dutch delegations to EU negotiations have consistently refused to compromise. During the negotiations on the Schengen Convention, the Dutch first argued that drug users are addicts and sick, and require medical attention instead of prison sentences. After this argument failed to impress other national delegations, the Dutch pointed out that the proportion of drug users in the Netherlands was more or less equal to that in other countries, which proved that permissiveness in and of itself did not increase drug use. When representatives of other countries were still unconvinced, a middle course was found that allowed each country to administer its own drug policy so long as other countries would not suffer from the effects of a differentiated approach to the prosecution of drug offenses.[51] In return, the member states agreed to take preventive measures against the import and export of drugs to the territories of other Schengen countries and to seek better coordination between customs and police authorities in the fight against hard drug trafficking in border areas.[52]

During the preliminary preparations for the Dublic summit, held in December 1996, the Council of Ministers of Justice and Home Affairs decided on a joint action program to combat the traffic in drugs. The Netherlands was the only country to object to various proposals contained in this joint action plan and threatened to veto the entire package of measures. Two

[51] Hirsch Ballin, "Criminaliteitsbestrijding over de grenzen heen," in Fijnaut, ed., *Reguliere politiediensten,* pp. 156–57.
[52] Monica den Boer, "Schengen: Intergovernmental Scenario for European Police Cooperation," Working paper 5 University of Edinburgh, 1991, pp. 26–27.

objections were raised. First, France wanted to include a section on uniform drug laws to stop cross-border trafficking. Second, the draft presented to the Council also outlined proposals to reduce drug addiction. The Netherlands is opposed to uniform drug legislation since it would compromise its tolerant policy toward soft drugs and wants to limit joint efforts to reduce drug addiction to an informal exchange of experience among member states about research methods, information, and provision for specific target groups. After much diplomatic bickering, the Netherlands was able to insert a preamble to the introduction of the joint action program which encourages each country to seek the most efficient means of coping with drug addiction. This enables the Netherlands to preserve its coffee shop system, which is regarded as a public health measure to prevent people from experimenting with hard drugs and from falling into the clutches of criminal syndicates. In response to the endless flow of criticism, the Dutch authorities are closing down 10 percent of existing coffee shops and all unlicensed ones. The cabinet is planning to reinforce border controls to stop foreign couriers from taking back cannabis products to Germany or France and is contemplating measures to forbid the sale of soft drugs to nonnationals.

Drug policy is an example of how national norms vary in the definition of what constitutes criminal activity and how even small countries do not easily yield to external pressures. Dutch authorities have stuck with their liberal approach to soft drugs because large sections of society and practically the entire law enforcement community fully approve of the current situation and see no reason to go the German, French, or Belgian way. Nevertheless, as preparations gear up for the next important intergovernmental conference, Dutch authorities are closing down coffee shops in the border areas, taking a stricter line against small-time traffickers, and sounding more conciliatory during diplomatic exchanges.

Policing may be the area least accessible to European integration and to assertions of German power. Law enforcement is an important prerogative of the state, enabling it to legitimately use force against its citizens within its national territory. Countries are suspicious of other countries' courts and police forces. They strongly believe that no system is as good as their own. Differences of principle have greatly hampered the launching of Europol and intergovernmental cooperation in Justice and Home Affairs. In theory, political agreements can remove every obstacle to institutional cross-border police cooperation. In practice, political agreements on the objectives of police cooperation, on a supervisory system to monitor and control Europol, and on giving the citizens of Europe a real stake in the EU in order to justify transferring limited police powers to a European institution remain elusive. Economic recessions and uncertainty about the situation surrounding the Schengen accords has dampened enthusiasm for legal and judicial integration.

The 1991 Belgian reform measures and the 1993 Dutch police law addressed the question of how to maintain close oversight over more efficient and effective police organizations. Questions related to institutionalized European police cooperation did not figure in the two countries' national debates. German norms of policing did not influence the final shape of their police legislation because both Belgium and the Netherlands have their own legal and judicial traditions, and neither seeks German guidance and direction in this area.

Nevertheless, I believe that the debate on European police organizations and on improved cross-border police cooperation has made an impact on the timing, but not the substance, of new police laws. Increased public awareness of transnational crime and the decision to abolish border controls (Schengen Accords) provided an extra boost to tackle police legislation. Media coverage of spectacular crimes (smuggling of plutonium) and the operation of international crime syndicates mobilized voters to demand better law enforcement protection and more sophisticated anticrime units. In this sense, changes at the European level spilled over into national political institutions.

CONCLUSION

Generally, Belgium, the Netherlands, and Germany hold similar views with regard to European integration and institutions. All three are strongly in favor of a solid multilateral foundation for the institutional structure of the European Union, and each has readily assimilated EU goals into its policy deliberations. By and large, Belgium and the Netherlands perceive a natural congruence between their respective national interests and the further evolution of the EU. In contrast to newer members like Sweden, they find that Europe supplements their national priorities and achievements, indeed, that their national and European identities are fused together. This alone explains why Germany and the Low Countries frequently speak in one voice on matters related to the future of Europe. Belgium and the Netherlands accept a certain level of European meddling in their domestic affairs and agree, in principle, with Germany's endeavors to further European institution building.

None of this, however, should be treated as a sign of weakness and subordination. If so inclined, Belgium and the Netherlands can ignore external pressures to conform to EU-wide trends or policies. The difficulties surrounding the development of the third intergovernmental pillar of the

Maastricht treaty reveal the extent to which certain national values and institutions are impervious to European initiatives and the extent to which their European identity is anchored to the economic and monetary dimension of the European Union. Despite Germany's energetic lobbying to create EU law enforcement capabilities, its small neighbors refuse to adjust their domestic systems of law enforcement and criminal law procedures to accommodate a European compromise. Policing is too sensitive an area to allow other nations or multilateral institutions to determine its powers and capabilities. Moreover, European police legislation must be accompanied by a watertight system of surveillance and supervision. The European Court of Justice and European Parliament are the logical institutions to provide democratic accountability. But member governments are not yet ready to transfer national parliamentary accountability to the EU level.

Even though Germany dominates currency and exchange rate issues, the Dutch and the Belgians do not perceive Germany's role as constraining and oppressive. German priorities for Europe's monetary regime coincide with Belgian and Dutch interests. Preexisting objectives or convergent institutional patterns led the Low Countries to decide independently to fix their exchange rates and pursue a strong currency policy. As small countries with open economies, they decided to link their currencies to the deutsche mark. Accordingly, in order to back up the credibility of their exchange rate targets, their central banks closely followed German decisions with regard to exchange rate policies. But this should not be interpreted as a manifestation of German assertiveness or dominance over Belgian or Dutch monetary policies. This "dominance" was invited by the Belgians and Dutch to meet their own goals. A convergence of interests is also apparent in incorporating workers' codetermination into European legislation. Codetermination already exists in Belgium, the Netherlands, and Germany, and its absence in other countries threatens the long-term viability of the three countries' national systems of labor-management consultation.

A marriage of convenience binds the Low Countries and Germany, a marriage that not only reflects shared preoccupation with price stability and strong exchange rates but also testifies to the common origins of their postwar social institutions. Social Catholic and Christian democratic movements were the guiding lights behind the construction of the postwar welfare state in all three countries. On many issues related to the social dimension of the European Union, the three countries take a similar position, and each relies upon the others to pressure recalcitrant member states. As Germany's neighbors, Belgium and the Netherlands have learned to live with an economy many times the size of their own. As close allies, both countries know when to rely upon the Germans to influence agenda setting and legislative initiatives. As founding members of the European Community, both have absorbed and appropriated core European goals as their own. In the meantime, they have successfully defended domestic institutions important to national contests of power against German and European interference.

CHAPTER FIVE

Moving at Different Speeds:
Spain and Greece in the European Union

Michael P. Marks

On the surface, Spain and Greece appear to be in similar situations with regard to European integration. Both countries have national security concerns about instability along Europe's periphery, both are still far from fulfilling the requirements for economic and monetary union, and both contain sizable regions in need of development funds to achieve economic convergence with the rest of the European Union. As this chapter will show, however, Spain and Greece are moving toward integration at distinctly different speeds. While Spain has shown consistent enthusiasm for the type of unification envisioned by the founders of the European Economic Community, Greece has been more hesitant, and its institutions less easily reconciled with those of European integration. Three issues—security policy, economic and monetary union, and cohesion policy—shed light on the distinct relationships Spain and Greece experience within the EU. In the case of Spain, there has been an attempt at mutual adaptation between Spanish and EU structures, and between Spain and its counterparts in Europe. In the case of Greece, the relationship between Athens and other European capitals frequently has been strained, and the fit between Greek domestic structures and European institutions difficult.[1]

Parts of this chapter were adapted for, and appeared in, Chapter 6 of Michael P. Marks, *The Formation of European Policy in Post-Franco Spain* (Aldershot, U.K.: Avebury, 1997).

[1] Portions of the material on Greece in this chapter were formulated in consultation with Susannah Verney, who was involved in the workshops that gave rise to this volume. Many of the insights about Greece's relationship with the EU were developed by her in a series of memos, correspondences, and published and unpublished articles. I am indebted to her for her contributions.

What explains these dissimilar situations? In the first place, there are many more structural and institutional similarities between the European Union and Spain than between the EU and Greece. Spain's large size and economic strength give it greater clout than Greece in European affairs; Spain's governmental bureaucracies have better adapted to EU policy practices; and thus Spain, much more than Greece, can project the sort of soft institutional power more often projected by larger, core EU states than by smaller, peripheral ones. In the second place, leaders in Spain have identified with the norms of European integration more rapidly than have their Greek counterparts. Spain has established credibility in forging coalitions with EU member states to address common European concerns, as opposed to the purely parochial concerns frequently advanced by Greece. Much as German unification and European integration were linked in 1989–90, Spanish membership in the European Community and the negotiation of the Single European Act in the 1980s served to link Spanish national interests to European Community interests in Spain's European foreign policy. By contrast, many observers agree that when Greece joined the EC in 1981, little consideration was paid to the impact of Greek membership on the community. Thus the "birthing" of Greece and Spain into the EC occurred under different circumstances and left distinctly different impressions in Madrid and Athens as to what constitute EC norms and interests. Finally, while important segments of Greece's political elite—most notably, members of the Socialist Party, PASOK—were unsure or openly doubtful of the supposed benefits of membership in European institutions,[2] opposition to Europeanization within Spanish elites has been virtually nonexistent. Of the three southern European states that joined the European Community in the 1980s—Greece, Portugal, and Spain—Spain alone developed a pro-European consensus among its national parties.[3]

In sum, because Spain is more similar than Greece to the central core of EU states in size, economic development, institutional structure, and attitudes toward European integration, Spain has adapted much more rapidly than Greece to EU policy practices. Simply put, the institutions of the European Union evoke policies in Spain designed to make the country fit into European integration. By contrast, Greece resists European integration in ways that reflect the imperfect fit between EU institutions and important Greek interests, policies, and practices. Where Spain has learned the importance of embracing interests and norms common to other states

[2] I thank Nikiforos Diamandouros for his insights on this subject.

[3] On differences among southern European leaders concerning European integration, see Susannah Verney, "Panacea or Plague: Greek Political Parties and Accession to the European Community, 1974–1979," Ph.D. diss., Kings College, London, 1994; Berta Álvarez-Miranda, "A Las Puertas de la Comunidad: Consenso y Disenso en el Sur de Europa," Center for Advanced Studies in Social Sciences, Juan March Institute, Madrid, 1995.

involved in European unification, because of its small size, its economic weaknesses, and the hesitancy of its leaders, Greece has found it harder to adopt such transnational interests and norms.

How do these dynamics relate to Spanish and Greek interactions with individual EU states, and with Germany in particular? To some extent, relations between Germany and the southern European countries have been shaped by historical factors. During the Franco dictatorship, many Spaniards looked to Germany as an example of how a former dictatorship could successfully make the transition to democracy and economic modernization. German leaders, in turn, were eager to assist post-Franco Spanish democratization, economic liberalization, and accession to the EC. As the Cold War drew to an end, Spanish leaders were very much in favor of rapid German unification, believing it was important for Germans and Europeans that Germany be united. Likewise, Germany has had an interest in cultivating Spanish leadership in the EU, especially given Spain's proximity to unrest in North Africa. Greco-German relations historically have been more strained. While German political parties have established links with fraternal parties in countries lacking a democratic tradition, their links to parties in Greece have not been strong. To the extent Greece has looked to another European state for guidance, that state has been France, not Germany. Finally, given Turkey's strategic significance, German fears of Islamic fundamentalism, and the sizable Turkish population in Germany, Greece's main military rival enjoys a special place in German foreign policy.

While the peculiarities of German relations with Spain and Greece play an important role in the dynamics of their interactions within the European Union, the institutional environment of the union itself plays an even more important role. German influence on Spain and Greece reflects the way that Spain experiences soft institutional power in the EU, whereas Greek power relationships in the union tend to be "harder." In the realm of security policy, the lack of binding institutions within the EU means that expectations are laid down through norms and anticipations of long-term interests. Because Spain, Germany, and the EU share similar perceptions of post–Cold War threats to European security, they react to foreign policy questions in a similar fashion. By contrast, because Greece's particular security interests arise from its proximity to, and historical involvement in, the Balkans and the southeast Mediterranean, there is a disjuncture between Athens, Berlin, and Brussels on foreign policy. In the area of economic and monetary union, the norms of convergence are now enshrined as a central feature of the European Union. Neither German influence nor the contours of European monetary integration directly force Spain or Greece to abide by the convergence criteria. Rather, normative expectations keep Madrid and Athens in line. But because Spanish economic structures (including central bank independence) more closely resemble those in Germany and the core EU states, adaptation to European Monetary Union (EMU) has been easier for Spain than for Greece. Finally, in the realm of cohesion policy, both Spanish and Greek leaders have increasingly learned to play by the rules and to use the institutional aspect of developmental aid to advance regional equalization of wealth as an aim of the EU. But, again, Spain has been more efficient than Greece in this regard, being better equipped to respond to the evolution of German-style multi-level governance in the EU than small, centralized countries like Greece. Throughout this chapter, we shall see that although a pro-European political will exists in both Spain and Greece, the internalization of EU norms and the ability to adapt to European institutions has been more rapid in Spain than in Greece.

SECURITY POLICY

The emerging EU security policy highlights perhaps the starkest contrast between Spain and Greece. In the two decades after Franco's death, Spain went from being ostracized by NATO and the European Community to actively participating in the promotion of Western security institutions. By contrast, Greece has gone from serving as a linchpin in the policy of containment to complicating the West's foreign and security policy in Eastern Europe. The loose nature of coordination of the EU's Common Foreign and Security Policy (CFSP) allows this sort of variation to take place.

Geographically peripheral to tensions along the Iron Curtain and relatively unimportant to the West's military strategy, Spain was never central to the East-West aspect of the Cold War. Compared with Spanish marginalization during the era of bipolar conflict, Spain's post–Cold War security situation is representative of the emerging security issues in the new Europe. Spain's traditional defense-related concerns in western North Africa (the Maghreb) resonate in Europe's newfound preoccupation with instability in the Third World as a whole, and especially along the shores of the Mediterranean. Thus Spanish security—in particular, with respect to Mediterranean policy—illustrates how issues of internal and external security are linked in Europe's new security environment, although the EU has made greater strides toward integration in the internal than the external security realm. At the EU's summit in Cannes in June 1995, European leaders agreed to the formation of the European Police Office (Europol) to coordinate police activities among member states. In addition, the information system set up by the Schengen Group to monitor immigration was put into practice in March 1995, and tighter immigration controls have been adopted by most EU states. Nonetheless, issues of internal security in the EU continue to depend to a great degree on bilateral and multilateral ties. Perhaps the best example of this is the Spanish effort to combat Basque terrorists. While Spain would like such institutions as Europol to be active in this effort, it is France—which once refused to cooperate with Spain—that has acted in concert with the Spanish government against the Basque terrorist groups.[4] Spanish leaders should not be surprised that the difficult problems facing Spanish internal security are not yet soluble through such EU internal security institutions as the Schengen Group and Europol, which were created in the first place because of "an initial mistrust of southern Europe by northern Europe."[5] Indeed, internal security coordination through the TREVI, Schengen, and Europol organizations more closely resembles traditional international treaty cooperation than it does integration along the lines of EMU.

The lack of fully institutionalized coordination of the EU's internal security functions must be considered shortsighted. European fears that instability in the largely Islamic world to the east and south would ultimately take on an external military dimension were realized with the 1990–91 Persian Gulf crisis and war. Spain participated in the war effort by deploying ships to the blockade against Iraq and by permitting the United States to use its air bases in Spain as a transit point for troop deployment to the Persian Gulf. During the war, NATO long-range bombers also relied heavily on the U.S. air base at Morón de la Frontera as a principle staging area for bombing raids on Iraq. The Spanish government's decision to support the allied mission provoked a great deal of angry response in Spain and protest over the sending of Spanish forces to their first overseas military adventure since the Spanish-American War.[6] Prime Minister Felipe González justified Spain's military assistance by connecting it to an expanded vision of Spain's place in Europe.

Making links between the EU's internal and external security functions is important for the additional reason that, to date, NATO has only minimal plans to deal with "out of area" military threats in regions like North Africa that are important for Spanish and European defense.[7] In a 1992

---

[4] In June 1995, the French government reiterated its willingness to cooperate with Spain in apprehending fugitive members of the Basque terrorist group ETA. In return, Madrid agreed to help France monitor and police Islamic fundamentalist activities.

[5] Didier Bigo, "The European Internal Security Field: Stakes and Rivalries in a Newly Developing Area of Police Intervention," in Malcolm Anderson and Monica den Boer, eds., *Policing across National Boundaries* (London: Pinter, 1994), p. 167.

[6] A poll taken by *El País* in November 1990 showed 54 percent of Spaniards were against direct Spanish military involvement in the Persian Gulf, with 35 percent supporting it. See Álvaro de Vasconcelos, "The Shaping of a Subregional Identity," in Roberto Aliboni, ed., *Southern European Security in the 1990s* (London: Pinter, 1992), p. 20.

[7] In 1988, the Defense Planning Committee of NATO detailed a threat to the alliance from the south for the first time in NATO's history. See "Las Directrices Cierran el 'Decálogo'," *Revista Española de Defensa* (December 1988): 8–9.

report on security in Africa and the Middle East, the Spanish government concluded that "the Maghreb today is a time bomb that Europe is able to deactivate."[8] Yet only two weeks prior to the hijacking by an Islamic fundamentalist group of an Air France jet from Algiers to Paris during the 1994 Christmas holiday, EU member states clashed over the issue of development aid for economically depressed regions along the union's eastern and southern borders.[9] This is not to say that northern and southern EU members disagree over whether instability in both Eastern Europe and North Africa is a problem. Indeed, at the July 1995 Cannes summit of the European Council, Chancellor Helmut Kohl and Prime Minister Felipe González were instrumental in developing a new package of increased economic aid for both Eastern Europe and the Mediterranean region. In the absence of credible institutions of CFSP, however, EU relations with Mediterranean and Eastern European states continue to be undertaken predominantly in a scattershot fashion.[10]

In short, absent binding EU foreign policy institutions, it has for the most part fallen to individual European countries to initiate a Mediterranean policy for the EU, although the union has begun to create an institutional framework to address the internal and external aspects of Mediterranean security. Spain's traditional "special relationship" with the Arab world has allowed it to pursue a leadership role in this effort. Among the most important institutions championed by Spain (and other southern EU states) to coordinate a European response to regional instability is the Conference on Security and Cooperation in the Mediterranean (CSCM). Like the Organization for Security and Cooperation in Europe (OSCE), the CSCM would operate in a fashion complementary to, but independent of, the European Union.[11] After establishing the CSCM, the Western European Union engaged in ongoing dialogue in Brussels with ambassa-

---

[8] "Europa ante el Magreb," report by the Spanish Directorate General of Foreign Affairs for Africa and the Middle East (Madrid, February 26, 1992). See Bernabé López García and Jesús A. Nuñez Villaverde, "Europe and the Maghreb: Towards a Common Space," in Peter Ludlow, ed., *Europe and the Mediterranean* (London: Brassey's, 1994), p. 141.

[9] France, Italy, Spain, and Portugal cut back from $8.5 billion to $6.6 billion the amount of aid Germany requested for Eastern Europe, so that an equal sum could be earmarked for the Maghreb. *New York Times* (December 9, 1994): A6.

[10] Whereas Germany was able to get the European Bank for Reconstruction and Development established in order to aid Central and Eastern Europe, the southern EU states are obliged to negotiate continually for economic aid for non-EU Mediterranean countries.

[11] The Conference on Security and Cooperation in the Mediterranean was first proposed by Italian Foreign Minister Gianni De Michelis, and supported by Spain, at a meeting of EC foreign ministers on Mallorca in September 1990. See Birol A. Yesilada, "The Challenge of Enlargement: The Mediterranean Perspective," paper presented at the Fourth Biennial International Conference of the European Community Studies Association, Charleston, South Carolina, May 11–14, 1995. See also Julia Olmo, "La Reunión de Palma: La CSCE y el Mediterráneo," *Política Exterior* 5 (Winter 1991): 180–87.

dors from the Maghreb states, but these talks did not yield meaningful policies beyond institutionalizing such confidence-building measures as the talks themselves.[12]

The EU increased its efforts to create a Mediterranean policy in 1994 and extending through 1996 when Greece, France, Spain, and Italy held the rotating presidency of the European Council in near succession (Germany held the council presidency during the second half of 1994, between the Greek and French presidencies). At the June 1994 Corfu summit, Greece proposed a conference on Mediterranean issues to be held during the Spanish presidency of the European Council. On October 19, 1994, the European Commission proposed an economic and security plan to lay the groundwork for the EU Conference on the Mediterranean, held in Barcelona November 27–28 of that year. The Barcelona conference produced an aid package that includes 4.7 billion European Currency Units (ECU; $6 billion) in assistance to twelve non-EU Mediterranean states between 1996 and 1999, and also guarantees the gradual lifting of trade barriers on selected products culminating in a regional free trade area by the year 2010.[13] It is an indication of Spain's European vocation that the Spanish government has attempted to make the common security interests of all EU states a basis for institutional integration. As long as traditional bilateral and multilateral ties predominate in this area, Spain's efforts will be constrained, although these limitations have diminished as EU security institutions have matured, and Spanish determination to lead the way in the creation of the CFSP has remained strong.

The disjuncture between Greek and European Union security agendas is more pronounced than in the Spanish case. For our purposes, differences in policy over the Balkans conflict and the status of Macedonia provide the best illustration of the poor fit between Greek and EU initiatives. The positions of Greece and other EU states initially overlapped when Yugoslavia began to disintegrate in 1990. In Athens and other European capitals the message went out that Europe preferred a unified Yugoslavia so as not to incite separatist movements and ethnic conflicts elsewhere in Europe.[14] Once Slovenian and Croatian independence was recognized by the European Union, however, Greece found itself increasingly isolated, which cre-

[12] See Luis Javier Casanova Fernández (Spanish Ambassador to the Western European Union), "La Aportación de la UEO a la Seguridad Europea," in *Segundas Jornadas de Defensa Nacional,* Monografías del Centro Superior de Estudios de la Defensa Nacional, no. 8 (Madrid: Ministry of Defense, 1993), p. 46.

[13] "Madrid European Council (15 and 16 December 1995): Presidency Conclusions," text of the Madrid European Council distributed by the Office of the European Commission in the United States (reference document 95/9, December 16, 1995). See Annex 11: "Mediterranean, Barcelona Declaration."

[14] See Yannis G. Valinakis, "Southern Europe between Detente and New Threats: The View from Greece," in Aliboni, ed., *Southern European Security,* pp. 59–60.

ated a degree of resentment in Athens. Historical memory plays a role in this question; the European country most willing to recognize an independent Slovenia and Croatia was Germany. Greek leaders, some of whom were old enough to remember German atrocities in Greece during World War II, found it hard to believe that Germany could again side with Croatia against Serbia when, only a half century before, the murderous Nazi puppet regime in Croatia had obliterated its Serbian enemies.

More importantly, the breakup of Yugoslavia opened the Pandora's box of Macedonian independence and revealed fundamental disagreements between Greece and the European Union over the role of the EU's CFSP. Greeks are often surprised that the international community is not sensitive to the question of Macedonia. The resolution to the First World War and the dismemberment of the Ottoman Empire left historical Macedonia divided among Yugoslavia, Greece, and Bulgaria, with the "Macedonian portion" of each of these countries containing a mixture of ethnic Slavs, Albanians, Greeks, and Muslim Turks. In addition, Athens accused the Slavs of interfering in the Greek civil war by means of the guerilla army ELAS, which went into exile in Yugoslav Macedonia in 1949.[15]

Greek leaders were thus upset when the European Union indicated that it would recognize the independence of former Yugoslav Macedonia after the breakup of Yugoslavia in 1990–91.[16] Athens protested that Skopje had not renounced its claims over the Greek portion of Macedonia, and the Greek government undertook measures to reassert the Hellenic nature of Greek Macedonia. Much was made of the proposed design for certain denominations of Yugoslav Macedonian commemorative currency, which featured the White Tower, the edifice in Thessaloniki that defines the soul of that Greek city, much as the Eiffel Tower represents Paris. Although these banknotes, which were to be issued by a private institution with government approval to commemorate Macedonian independence, were never printed or placed in circulation, the ill will caused by this incident aggravated tensions in the Balkans. In addition, the presumptive independent Yugoslav Macedonian state adopted as the central element of its flag the sixteen-pointed Macedonian "Sun of Vergina," prompting Athens to respond by issuing a new 100–drachma coin featuring this icon.

The emerging conflict was far more serious than a mere dispute over symbols. Greek concerns were focused on clauses in the Yugoslav Macedonian constitution that promoted irredentist claims over the parts of Mace-

[15] On ELAS, see James Pettifer, "The New Macedonia Question," *International Affairs* 68 (July 1992): 481; and Anastasia Karakasidou, "Fellow Travellers, Separate Roads: The KKE and the Macedonian Question," *East European Quarterly* 27 (Winter 1993): 462–63.

[16] P. C. Ioakimidis, "Greece and the European Union: Problems and Prospects," University of Reading Discussion Papers in European and International Social Science Research, no. 52, May 1994, p. 13.

donia under Bulgarian and Greek rule. The constitution also referred to the procedures by which the borders of the Republic of Macedonia could be expanded. Greece demanded that the European Union, the United Nations, and other international institutions refuse to recognize an independent Macedonian state in former Yugoslavia. Athens insisted that the EU and the UN decline even to use the name "Macedonia" for the region north of Greece, agreeing only to describe the area as the "Former Yugoslav Republic of Macedonia" (FYROM). In February of 1994, Greece imposed a trade embargo against FYROM and, for a brief period, seemed to welcome the reassertion of Serbian control over the former Yugoslav republic.[17]

Greek leaders maintain that the dispute over Macedonia is not merely a question of national pride but an example of Greece's peculiar security concerns, which have been ignored by the European Union.[18] Indeed, a partial resolution of the Macedonia issue has been engineered, not by Greece's counterparts in the European Union, but by the United States, a country with which Greece had a difficult relationship during much of the 1980s. In 1992 Washington dispatched 500 peacekeeping troops to FYROM as part of its contribution to the United Nations effort in the Balkans. In September 1995, the Greek and FYROM foreign ministers met in New York with UN representative Cyrus Vance and American negotiators Matthew Nimitz and Richard Holbrooke. As a result of these talks, Greece lifted its embargo against FYROM, agreed to allow EU aid to be sent to the region, and endorsed Macedonian membership in international organizations such as the OSCE. Nonetheless, FYROM's status remains an open question, and the international debate over how to deal with the region remains unresolved. Perhaps more important has been the Greek crisis of confidence in the EU's inaction throughout the dispute over Macedonia. The U.S.-brokered resolution to the problem of Macedonia not only revealed the weakness of EU foreign and security policy institutions but gave Athens the impression that Greek security concerns in the Balkans were meaningless to other European states.

Aside from Macedonia, Greece's most pressing defense worries have to do with Turkey. Although both states are members of NATO, the alliance has had to deal with long-standing Greco-Turkish animosity. Now that the Cold War is over and the European Union is planning to assume greater responsibility for the defense of Europe, the differences between Greece and the EU over security in the eastern Mediterranean are coming to the fore. Yet when Greece and Turkey came close to war over two uninhabited

---

[17] *Spectator* (London; April 9, 1994): 7.
[18] Dimitri Constas, "Southern European Countries in the European Community," in John W. Holmes, ed., *Maelstrom: The United States, Southern Europe, and the Challenges of the Mediterranean* (Cambridge, Mass.: World Peace Foundation, 1995), p. 145.

islands in the Aegean, it was the United States, not the European Union, that eventually resolved the crisis. The question of Cyprus also illustrates problems posed by Greek security concerns for the EU. Cyprus has been divided into two independent republics, and peace between them has been maintained by UN troops, since Turkey occupied the northern portion of the island in 1974.[19] Athens, which has maintained that the European Union has turned a deaf ear to Turkish violation of Cypriot sovereignty, recently upped the ante by sponsoring Nikosia's application to the EU for the Greek-dominated half of the island.

Many Greek leaders remain unconvinced that their European counterparts understand the severity of threats posed to Greek sovereignty by Macedonia and Turkey. The contrast with Spain is clear. Both Spain and other EU states for the most part agree on the way that threats from instability in the Mediterranean, and especially in the Maghreb, can be solved. Although the CFSP is still incomplete, Madrid has been able to win support for its initiatives to seek accommodation with non-EU Mediterranean states. No such institutional accommodation has been reached in the EU to deal with security issues in the Balkans and the eastern Mediterranean, thus highlighting Greek's peripheral status in the CFSP. In neither case is the influence of Germany or the EU particularly strong, which is not surprising, given the incomplete nature of the EU's security institutions. Spain has been able to find greater accommodation with its EU partners because security threats in the western Mediterranean are considered more soluble than those in the east and because Spanish leaders have Europeanized their concerns to a much greater degree than leaders in Athens.

ECONOMIC AND MONETARY UNION

According to its proponents, economic and monetary union offers long-term benefits to the poorer countries of the EU. Even with all barriers to the free movement of goods, services, capital, and labor removed, the absence of a single currency and a European central bank makes economic development difficult in regions of the EU that rely heavily on foreign investment to fuel their economies.[20] While this logic has its detractors, including those skeptics who claim that states left behind in a "two-speed" Europe will suffer serious negative economic consequences, Madrid and

---

[19] Turkish occupation of the northern republic of Cyprus puts in question the independence of the northern Cypriot state.

[20] The benefits from currency unification are many, ranging from reducing currency transaction costs, to creating economies of scale, to reinforcing quality competition over price competition. See Paul J. J. Welfens, "Creating a European Central Bank after 1992," in Welfens, ed., *European Monetary Integration* (Berlin: Springer, 1991), p. 40.

Athens remain committed to European Monetary Union (EMU). In this section, we shall see that while both Spain and Greece have demonstrated a desire to comply with the strictures of economic and monetary union, institutional affinities have eased Spanish efforts to a greater degree than those of Greece.

Spain's commitment to EMU can be seen at three critical junctures: (1) the decision by the Spanish government in 1989 to insert the peseta into the Exchange Rate Mechanism (ERM) of the European Monetary System (EMS); (2) Spanish actions to keep the peseta within the EMS during the crisis of 1992–93; and (3) Spain's agreement in 1995 to pursue compliance with monetary union by the year 2002. The Spanish peseta was introduced into the EMS during the summer of 1989, to coincide with Spain's presidency of the European Council, which culminated at the Madrid Summit. Countries like Germany were in favor of tying all EC currencies to a narrow exchange rate band, but were willing to wait for Spanish interest and inflation rates to fall before asking Spain to tie the peseta to the narrow fluctuation rate required by the EMS. Most EC states were eager to commit Britain to joining the EMS and viewed the peseta's entry into the exchange rate system as a way to put pressure on London. Indeed, there is some evidence that German leaders bargained with the Spanish government for the peseta's early entry into the EMS so as to put increased pressure on British Prime Minister Margaret Thatcher.[21] Prime Minister Felipe González was eager to serve as an effective host in Madrid and had his own agenda, which included passage of the so-called Social Charter, something to which the British were opposed.

The decision to introduce the peseta into the EMS in the summer of 1989 advanced Spanish economic strategy. The fixed exchange rates permitted the government to pursue an unconventional "policy mix" by relying on the "imported credibility" of the deutsche mark through the European Monetary System. As long as the deutsche mark lent credibility to the peseta through the EMS, Spanish economic policy makers were free to pursue policies that encouraged foreign investment and allowed the government to engage in social welfare spending, while holding the line on wage increases.[22] Of course, the legitimizing effect of the deutsche mark was possible only as long as the Bundesbank maintained equally high interest rates. This it did in the early 1990s, to counter the inflationary trends brought about by German unification.

[21] Whether the peseta's insertion into the EMS in 1989 was premature is debatable. While conversations with Spanish economists indicate they felt the move was undertaken in haste and only for political motives, sources within the Spanish government dispute that assertion and argue that the decision was consummate with the government's economic agenda.

[22] Sofía A. Pérez, "Imported Credibility and the 'Strong Peseta': Bundesbank Dominance and Spanish Economic Policy in the EMS," paper presented at the Ninth International Conference of Europeanists, Council for European Studies, Chicago, March 31–April 2, 1994.

Rudiger Dornbusch has noted two effects of imported credibility: "First, inflation problems of any one country became internationalized because they had an incidence on their joint performance and the cohesion of the exchange-rate regime. Second, central banks became relatively more independent in the soft-currency EMS countries."[23] This is exactly what happened in the Spanish case. Threats of inflation in Germany led the Bundesbank to raise interest rates. The increasingly autonomous Banco de España had the independence to do the same and, consequently, to force other central banks to keep interest rates high to counter an overvalued peseta that was bumping at the upper level of the ERM. The key element, then, is the way economic planners were led to pursue unorthodox policies once semifixed exchange rates were established within the EMS. Given these dynamics, the 6 percent fluctuation rate established for the peseta in 1989 turned out to be unworkable. During September 1992, and continuing into 1993, the peseta came under heavy fire in financial markets, forcing the Spanish government to undertake three devaluations of the peseta or risk having to withdraw from the EMS entirely. These devaluations resulted in a 19 percent reduction in the value of the peseta against the deutsche mark. The government was then forced to seek a wider berth for the peseta within the EMS, asking for, and receiving, a 15 percent fluctuation rate, as opposed to removing the peseta from the EMS altogether.[24] Thus, leaders in Madrid, unlike their counterparts in London and Rome, preferred the ignominy of repeated devaluations to withdrawing their national currency from the exchange rate mechanism.

During the Spanish presidency of the European Council in the second half of 1995, monetary union again was on the agenda. The Reflection Group on the 1996 Intergovernmental Conference (chaired by Spanish Secretary of State for EU Affairs Carlos Westendorp) affirmed its unanimous decision to work toward a single currency within the time frame agreed to in the amended Maastricht treaty. Specifically, EU economy and finance ministers decided that a first group of EU states should be prepared to adopt the new currency by January 1, 1999, and that the European Central Bank should also be operational on that date. The single European currency is to be in circulation in all EU states no later than December 31, 2001, with a six-month transition period during which the single currency is to circulate alongside existing currencies. In a series of appearances before parliamentary commissions and in public forums chaired by the governor of the Banco de España, Luis Angel Rojo, Span-

[23] Rudiger Dornbusch, "Problems of European Monetary Integration," in Alberto Giovannini and Colin Mayer, eds., *European Financial Integration* (Cambridge: Cambridge University Press, 1991), p. 307.
[24] Even with the 15 percent fluctuation band, the peseta was again devalued, on March 6, 1995, by 7 percent.

ish economic policy makers expressed their commitment to meet the convergence criteria. Rojo argued that Spain could be ready for the single currency by 1999, but only if it were to take measures to reduce the public deficit. Delaying these austerity measures would only mean continued inflation and higher interest rates, which would make meeting EMU convergence criteria that much harder.[25]

The expected difficulties in preparing for the single currency have been the source of domestic political tension in various EU member states. This was most notable in France during the weeks prior to the Madrid summit. Faced with a bloated public deficit, leaders in Paris proposed changes in the pension plan for state employees, leading to a mass walkout by public sector labor unions, government bureaucrats, and their sympathizers. The French government's decision to force a showdown with state employees in order to trim the budget was tied directly to the requirements for EMU. The Spanish government wished to avoid the same fate as France, and formulated an economic plan known as the "Programa de Convergencia, 1992–96," which detailed a strategy for achieving the EMU convergence criteria.[26] This plan ran into problems, and Spain's Minister of Economy Pedro Solbes warned in late 1995 that the overheated Spanish economy— brought about in part by government spending—was straining the public deficit and forcing the Banco de España to keep interest rates high to avoid inflation. Solbes hinted that public spending would have to be cut significantly if Spain was to get on track for monetary union by 1999.[27] Although most observers do not expect Spain to fulfil the convergence criteria by 1999, Spain's economic leadership claims that there is still the possibility of meeting the single-currency deadline and is making efforts to do so.

The willingness of Spain's leaders to submit the Spanish economy to short-term dislocations in expectation of long-term benefits is significant, given that economic factors important to Spain, such as low unemployment rates, are not among the convergence criteria for EMU. Indeed, fulfillment of the convergence criteria, far from lowering Spanish unemployment rates, will probably sustain high joblessness. Spanish leaders' greatest fear, then, is of the "two-speed" Europe, which would delay the benefits of EMU for the weak-currency members of the EU while still trying to comply with the convergence criteria. Having tied Spain's fortunes to the philosophy of currency stability, Spain's leaders need to make sure that the country is ready to reap the benefits of monetary union. Spanish

[25] *El País* (International Edition; November 27, 1995): 23; (December 4, 1995): 19.

[26] Kenneth Maxwell and Steven Spiegel, *The New Spain: From Isolation to Influence* (New York: Council on Foreign Relations Press, 1994), p. 51.

[27] *El País* (International Edition; December 18, 1995): 23.

leaders on both the left and right accept the logic that a single currency will, in the long run, lead to greater economic growth by lowering transaction costs and making capital more mobile. Publicly expressing their confidence in that logic, Spanish decision makers have indicated they would not veto a decision to issue the single currency even if Spain were not among the states meeting the convergence criteria.

The story of Greece and EMU is much shorter than Spain's. For Greece, economic and monetary union is inextricably bound up with attempts to rationalize other elements of the Greek economy, and because this task is expected to take quite some time to complete, Greece remains on the fringes of the debate surrounding EMU. Of course, many economists contend that Greece, which possesses among the most troubled economies in the EU, would benefit from having EMU convergence criteria imposed on it.[28] Despite steady, though gradual progress toward economic and monetary convergence with other EU states, however, Greece lags far behind Spain.

For advocates of EMU, certain recent trends in the Greek economy are encouraging. The drachma's depreciation rate slowed from 7.8 percent in 1993 to 5.3 percent in 1994; GDP expansion rates rose to 1.5 percent in 1994 and 2 percent in 1995, after negative growth in 1993; inflation by the end of 1995 fell to 8.1 percent compared with 10.8 percent in 1994 and 14.4 percent in 1993; and the government deficit fell from 9.7 percent in 1993 to 8.9 percent of GDP in 1994.[29] In addition, the Bank of Greece has enjoyed increasing independence in recent years and has pursued anti-inflationary policies in accordance with EU convergence criteria. Central bank independence was part of a larger set of financial system reforms in the late 1980s, which included liberalization of capital movements, the freeing of interest rates, and an end to capital controls.[30] Finally, a number of widely respected economic policy experts in the government of Prime Minister Costas Simitis, which assumed power in 1996, are expected to impose discipline on the Greek economy.

These recent trends notwithstanding, Greece remains quite removed from the process of economic and monetary union. The Greek drachma has never been made subject to the European Monetary System, and Greece is a long way from fulfilling the convergence criteria for EMU. There are several structural reasons why rapid attempts to keep pace with EMU would be unsound economic policy for Greece. The Greek econ-

---

[28] Daniel Gros and Niels Thygesen, *European Monetary Integration* (London: Longman, 1992), p. 259.

[29] Figures are from "Introduction," *1995 Guide to Greece* (Supplement to the September 1995 issue of *Euromoney*), p. 2, and *Economist* (February 24, 1996): 54.

[30] George Soumelis, "Greece: Reforming Financial Markets," *OECD Observer* (April–May 1995): 40–41.

omy is one of the smallest in the European Union, and Greece's per capita income is well below the EU average. As Robert Leonardi observes: "The performance of the Greek economy represents an anomaly [in Europe]. According to the data on annual changes in GDP, the economy goes from periods of boom and bust in, many cases, parallel to the course of political instability and inconclusive national election results."[31] In 1995, Greece's budget deficit was 9.3 percent of GDP, inflation rose at an average rate of 9.3 percent, and the drachma continued to fluctuate freely against the value of other European currencies.[32] Furthermore, the drachma's weight in determining the value of the ECU is negligible.[33]

Under the PASOK government of the 1980s, these structural flaws in the Greek economy were aggravated by the idiosyncracies of Prime Minister Andreas Papandreou's economic philosophy. At the same time Spanish authorities were boosting interest rates to attract foreign investment, the Greek government lowered interest rates and passed legislation enabling the Bank of Greece to assume greater responsibility for financing public sector projects, both of which severely reduced domestic savings. In addition, the PASOK government could not decide whether to maintain stable exchange rates, leading to erratic monetary policy in the early 1980s and a severe drop in foreign direct investment in Greece.[34] These problems only began to be rectified in the 1990s when Greek capital controls were relaxed and the government took steps to lower the inflation rate in accord with EMU convergence criteria.[35]

This is not to say that Greece's economic policy in the 1980s irreparably damaged its economy, making harmonization with the principles of EMU impossible, only that the interconnectedness of economic elements in the process of European integration accentuates the dilemmas posed by Greek deviance from EU norms. In the area of social policy, the European Union presents a weak institutional environment for harmonizing Greek and EU policy, especially in light of Greece's inefficient social welfare system. In the

[31] Robert Leonardi, "The Liberalization of Southern Europe Via European Integration," Paper presented at the Annual Meeting of the American Political Science Association, Chicago, August 31–September 3, 1995, p. 11.

[32] Figures are from Solomon Brothers, cited in *El País* (International Edition; February 19, 1996): 24.

[33] In 1990, the Greek drachma constituted only 0.77 percent of the value of the ECU. Only the Luxembourg franc made up less of the ECU's value (0.31 percent). Jeremiah Riemer, "The ECU as the 'Mark' of Unity: Europe between Monetary Integration and Monetary Union," *Social Education* 57 (April–May 1993): 186.

[34] Judith Kleinman, "Socialist Policies and the Free Market: An Evaluation of PASOK's Economic Performance," in Nikolaos A. Stavrou, ed., *Greece under Socialism: A NATO Ally Adrift* (New Rochelle, N.Y.: Orpheus, 1988), pp. 200–203, 212.

[35] Panayotis Alexakis and Nicholas Apergis, "Monetary Policy in Greece: The Impact of EC Membership," in Panos Kazakos and P. C. Ioakimidis, eds., *Greece and EC Membership Evaluated* (London: Pinter, 1994), pp. 80, 88.

1980s, Prime Minister Papandreou espoused a variant of dependency theory in which social welfarism in the metropolitan core is not easily (or even eagerly) transferred to the periphery because it is not possible to create the sort of worker solidarity there that it is in the core.[36] Thus, the PASOK government made no attempt to replicate western European social welfare. Moreover, the disorganized nature of the Greek social security system has created large public deficits and undermined the ability of Athens to pursue EMU convergence criteria.[37] This has further contributed to the alienation of Greek social policy from European Union labor and welfare trends. Although by the time it again took control of the government in 1993, after a three-year period in which the conservatives were in power, the PASOK government was promising a new social contract with labor.[38] Greece's social welfare system remains out of line with most of the EU, in large part because of the country's lower levels of industrialization.

That European Union social welfare policy is neither as articulated nor as institutionalized as EU economic policy has made it easier for Athens to go its own way in this area. The Greek government's push to include a "social dimension" in the Maastricht treaty was not fully realized, resulting in a situation where national governments were still primarily responsible for implementing social welfare programs.[39] Without the incentive to make alterations in social welfare economic practices, Greek leaders have been free to retain policies that protect political party bases and perpetuate wide-scale government spending on projects that benefit supporters. Finally, as noted above, despite strides toward developing a modern, European-style social welfare system, lower levels of economic development in Greece make it difficult for such a system to take hold in the short term.[40]

In sum, Spain and Greece would appear to have something to gain by defection from the convergence criteria for EMU, given that the economic adjustments necessary for monetary union are difficult. Nonetheless, they have undertaken to support monetary union despite these economic costs. In the period since the 1992–93 EMS crisis, Spanish leaders have continued to take measures to keep Spain's economy on track toward EMU.

[36] Nikolaos A. Stavrou, "Ideological Foundations of the Panhellenic Socialist Movement," in Stavrou, ed., *Greece under Socialism,* pp. 14–16.

[37] Aris Sisssouras and Gabriel Amitsis, "Social Security Policy," in Kazakos and Ioakimidis, eds., *Greece and EC Membership,* pp. 254–55; Christos Lyrintzis, "PASOK in Power: From 'Change' to Disenchantment," in Richard Clogg, ed., *Greece, 1981–89: The Populist Decade* (New York: St. Martin's Press, 1993), pp. 26–27.

[38] Kevin Featherstone, "The Greek Election of 1993: Backwards or Forwards?" *West European Politics* 17 (April 1994): 206.

[39] Susannah Verney, "The Greek Socialists," in John Gaffney, ed., *Political Parties and the European Union* (London: Routledge, 1996), pp. 181–82.

[40] See Francis G. Castles, "Welfare State Development in Southern Europe," *West European Politics* (18 April 1995): 291–313.

They have done this because they are convinced EMU will advance the cause of European integration and therefore the long-term welfare of Spain. The inheritance of difficult economic conditions by successive Greek governments constrains Athens in its pursuit of EMU; nevertheless, little by little, it has attempted to make the needed adjustments. While many of the adjustments by both Spain and Greece are a reaction to the economic shocks brought about by German unification, it is clear from looking at the Spanish and Greek cases that the European Union provides the institutional context in which these adjustments take place. We can conclude that because the Spanish economy is better equipped, and Spanish leaders more consistent in their approach to EMU, Spain is progressing more rapidly than Greece toward monetary union.

Cohesion Policy

The six original member states of the European Economic Community agreed that reducing the inequalities of wealth among regions was essential to establishing harmony in postwar Europe. When the EEC comprised only six countries with relatively high levels of economic development, it was thought that economic growth would be sufficient to erase regional disparities. When the European Community expanded, however, to include regions or entire states with levels of development significantly below the community norm, an explicit cohesion policy was developed to aid economic growth. This policy has been institutionalized within the European Union. The norm of EU-wide economic convergence is so broad that it can be substantiated through any number of ways. The rising tide of economic prosperity that lifts all boats, and welfarelike handouts directed at poor EU regions are but two extremes. The solution agreed to by EU states, whereby funds collected through revenue sharing are distributed to underdeveloped regions (and, in some cases, entire member countries) is no less than revolutionary. At no other time in modern history have a group of independent states banded together in a union and devised a system in which taxes are collected and redistributed to other sovereign states in the union. Thus, regional development funds in the EU no longer can be considered exclusively as "side payments." As Georg Sørensen puts it: "Instead of national economies, there is an increasingly integrated economic space with a measure of redistribution."[41]

[41] Georg Sørensen, "States Are Not like Units: Types of States and Forms of Anarchy in the Present International System," paper presented at the annual meeting of the American Political Science Association, Chicago, August 31–September 3, 1995, p. 22. See also Gary Marks, "Structural Policy in the European Community," in Alberta M. Sbragia, ed., *Euro-Politics: Institutions and Policymaking in the "New" European Community* (Washington, D.C.: Brookings In-

All EU member states contain regions that qualify for cohesion policy funds. Yet increasingly, attention has been directed at how cohesion policy is carried out in the four least developed member states of the union, the "poor four" of Greece, Ireland, Portugal, and Spain, which rely on development funds to help achieve economic parity with the rest of the EU. Throughout the 1990s, 50 to 55 percent of cohesion policy funds have been distributed to the poor four.[42] Funds for regional development exist in two distinct forms. "Structural Funds" are designed to assist all economically backward areas of the European Union. Because they are destined for regions of the European Union—as opposed to individual member states—the administration of the funds has led to a proliferation of interlocutors and claimants.[43] The newer "Cohesion Fund" is designed to aid the four poorest EU member states, whose GNP per capita is currently below 90 percent of the union average. Funds are restricted to domestic infrastructure and to environmental recovery projects around zones of industrial and agricultural development.

Negotiations over cohesion policy reflect the institutional nature of this issue area. Where the norm of convergence has been internalized by an EU state, its negotiating tactics reflect a genuine attempt to fashion a cohesion policy that fulfills the intent of the founders of European integration. Spanish leaders have subscribed to the idea of making cohesion a common interest, arguing that development funds are necessary if Spain is to meet the EU's convergence criteria for economic and monetary union. They are concerned about the union's financing, by which the value-added tax (VAT) and high levels of consumer spending in less wealthy EU states risk turning some of these states into net contributors to the EU's budget.[44]

Thus Spain has lobbied within the EU for an overhaul of budgetary and financial accounting. In 1990, when the European General Affairs Council was enmeshed in one of its frequent disputes over EC finances, the Spanish government was intent on ensuring there would be adequate funds "to compensate the poorer member-states for the adverse effects of greater integration. Once the formal negotiations began, Spanish demands became more open and comprehensive, culminating in May 1991 in a pro-

---

stitution, 1992): 191–224; R. Hall and D. van der Wee, "Community Regional Policies for the 1990s," *Regional Studies* 26 (1992): 399–404.

[42]*Official Journal of the European Communities* (December 15, 1992): 159–60; (November 16, 1993): 143–44; (November 24, 1994): 161–62. The two countries that together received the next highest percentage of structural funds and aid after the poor four were Italy and the United Kingdom.

[43]See Gary Marks, "Exploring and Explaining Variation in EU Cohesion Policy," in Liesbet Hooghe, ed., *Cohesion Policy and European Integration* (Oxford: Oxford University Press, 1996), pp. 388–422 (chap. 13).

[44]Dieter Biehl, "Structural Funds and Budgetary Transfers in the Community," in Achille Hannequart, ed., *Economic and Social Cohesion in Europe* (London: Routledge, 1992), p. 57.

posal that the Community develop a financial mechanism along the lines of the German Finanzausgleich."[45] In this, Prime Minister González not only was proposing the design for a possible EC compensation fund but was also appealing to the sensibilities of the community's wealthiest member.

An effort was made by EC member states to resolve the issue at the Maastricht summit in December of 1991. In April of the previous year, Spanish Prime Minister Felipe González met with German Chancellor Helmut Kohl on Lanzarote in the Spanish Canary Islands to discuss a range of issues including the community's cohesion policy. Later in Maastricht, however, EC members were unable to arrive at a satisfactory solution when some members insisted that such a solution, along with establishing strict criteria for participation in monetary union, would lead to the much-feared "two-speed" Europe.

Although regions eligible for Structural Funds are located for the most part in the poorer member states of the EU, even the wealthier nations contain underdeveloped regions, as highlighted by the reunification of Germany and the incorporation of the five former Eastern German *Länder* into the new German state. A new focus on directing development funds away from southern Europe to Eastern Europe would deal a double blow to Spain, which is already seeing foreign investments formerly destined for the Iberian Peninsula now redirected to the east.

Following Maastricht, the issue of cohesion policy came to a head again at the December 1992 Edinburgh summit. Spain's prime minister acted as the chief spokesman of the poor four. His demands were threefold: revision of the Structural Funds, modifications in the EU's system of financing its budget, and creation of the new Cohesion Fund.[46] González asked for an increase in the EU budget ceiling from the equivalent of 1.20 percent of the union's total GDP to 1.32 percent by 1999. The summit's host, British Prime Minister John Major, insisted that the increase be only 1.25 percent. A compromise of 1.27 percent was arrived at by the EU's leaders. While González failed to get everything he wanted for Spain, the cohesion policy issue became a cause célèbre in Edinburgh, and the Spanish leader made sure the attention of every EU leader was focused on the matter.

Although the amount of money devoted to the new Cohesion Fund is dwarfed by that devoted to the Structural Funds ECU (15.1 billion

[45] Peter Ludlow, "Europe's Institutions: Europe's Politics," in Gregory F. Treverton, ed., *The Shape of the New Europe* (New York: Council on Foreign Relations Press, 1992), pp. 76–77.

[46] Jeffrey Anderson contends that the creation of the Cohesion Fund and the overhaul of EU budgetary practices represented a compromise between Spain and Germany, under which Germany agreed to some of Spain's demands in return for Spanish agreement not to veto EMU, as spelled out in the Maastricht treaty. Jeffrey J. Anderson, "Structural Funds and the Social Dimension of EU Policy: Springboard or Stumbling Block?" in Stephan Leibfried and Paul Pierson, eds., *European Social Policy: Between Fragmentation and Integration* (Washington, D.C.: Brookings Institution, 1995), p. 142, n. 36.

[$17.9 billion] to the Cohesion Fund over the seven years from 1993 to 1999, versus 34.8 billion ECU [$41.3 billion] to Structural Funds and structural aid in 1993 alone),[47] that the poor four could get the Cohesion Fund established at all is evidence they succeeded in reminding the rest of the EU that cohesion policy should be a central element of the process of European integration. Instead of simply adding a new component to the existing Structural Funds program (which benefits all EU states), the poor four have institutionalized the idea that integration depends on a Europe that enjoys a roughly uniform level of economic prosperity. Although Spain was the big winner when the Cohesion Fund was established (indeed, Greece would have preferred simply to see the existing Structural Funds increased), the principle of economic aid to the least wealthy EU states was advanced by the new fund's creation.

As one senior foreign policy advisor to former Spanish Prime Minister González has pointed out, regional development funds are a good example of how individual EU states can both protect their individual interests and create community interests.[48] Although, on the surface, Spanish cohesion policy may come across as purely parochial, Spanish leaders would prefer that their efforts be seen as congruent with EU norms of equalizing living standards throughout the union.[49] They explain that, with few exceptions, most EU member states benefit in one way or another from cohesion policy, especially from the Structural Funds earmarked for underdeveloped regions. In this respect, just to take two states as examples, wealthy Germany can obtain funds for the new eastern *Länder,* and the United Kingdom can offset the deficit it incurs through the Common Agricultural Policy with funds for urban renewal and industrial revitalization. Furthermore, improved economic conditions in poorer areas can benefit economies that do business with these regions. Finally, regional policies help harmonize wage and living standards throughout the economically diverse EU, avoiding what George Ross calls a "'race to the bottom' in labor standards and labor-market regulation."[50]

As we observed in the Spanish case, Greek deviation from the norms of European integration is less pronounced where these norms are enshrined

[47] *The European Union's Cohesion Fund,* pamphlet distributed by the European Commission, Brussels, 1994, p. 7.

[48] These observations were made in an interview with Carlos Alonso Zaldívar, director of the Department of Studies, part of the cabinet of former Spanish prime minister Felipe González, Madrid, June 9, 1994.

[49] As Richard Gillespie has observed, for former Spanish Prime Minister Felipe González, "proximity to the European political heavyweights was valued more than occasional Community pay-outs to the poorer states, because in the long term what mattered was to place Spain among the 'core countries' like Germany and France." Richard Gillespie, "The Spanish Socialists," in Gaffney, ed., *Political Parties,* p. 162.

[50] George Ross, "Assessing the Delors Era and Social Policy," in Leibfried and Pierson, eds., *European Social Policy,* p. 364.

in EU institutions. Thus, although Greece's positions on cohesion policy were for the most part self-interested early in its tenure as a member of the European Community, the more cohesion policy has been made a regular feature of the integration project, the more Greek policy agrees with accepted practices and expectations. On the other hand, there still remain aspects of Greek politics that prevent a perfect fit between EU and Greek institutions of cohesion, especially in the implementation of development funds.

The early Greek position regarding cohesion policy was shaped by the economic realities of the southern enlargement of the European Community. When Spain and Portugal were negotiating membership in the community, Greece insisted that some form of economic compensation be available to entire states that would suffer short-term economic losses from the Iberian enlargement. The European Community responded to the 1982 "Greek Memorandum" by formulating the Integrated Mediterranean Programs (IMPs), which constituted a bloc grant to southern EC states. At the time, the Greek demands were perceived as purely self-interested in motivation, and Athens's agenda as not constructive to the integration process.

These perceptions, however, eventually underwent a transformation. Greek positions on cohesion policy began to change in the early 1980s and were cemented into place around the time of negotiations over the First Delors Package, which went into effect in 1989. Leaders in Athens discovered that a Greece-only vocabulary would serve merely to alienate its EU counterparts and reduce their willingness to promote development programs.[51] As Dimitri Constas explains: "The successful pursuit of the IMP marks an important turn in the policy of [Greece's] socialist government, from making unilateral claims to offset the potentially negative effects of accession on the Greek economy to acting collectively in support of broader EC policies ('Southern interests') that could eventually be beneficial to Greece."[52] In addition, once Spain and Portugal joined the EC, Greece became one of the EC's "poor four," which could and did present a common front in cohesion policy negotiations. This contributed to a sense of common purpose that would supersede a narrowly advanced Greek agenda.

While agreeing in principle on cohesion policy, Spain and Greece differ noticeably over its implementation. Despite Athens's changed style of negotiations, Greece has a history of relatively inefficient use of cohesion

---

[51] Susannah Verney, "From the 'Special Relationship' to Europeanism: PASOK and the European Community, 1981–89," in Clogg, ed., *Greece: 1981–89,* pp. 137–38. See also George A. Kourvetaris, "Greek Attitudes Toward Political and Economic Integration into the EEC," *East European Quarterly* 27 (September 1993): 381–85.

[52] Constas, "Southern European Countries," p. 140.

policy funds. Although the Greek government has improved the way it disburses these funds, the European and international communities alike have been disappointed that monies earmarked for development projects have not yielded the expected benefits. There are several reasons why cohesion policy funds have not been put to the wisest use on Greece. In the first place, there is a poor fit between the institutions of cohesion policy and Greek governmental structures. First, Greece is a highly centralized state lacking fully articulated regional governments. European Union cohesion policy has evolved so as to take into account member states with active regional governments; in Greece such governments have only recently been given any appreciable power.[53] Second, Greek politics encourages nepotism and favoritism in the disbursement of funds and the selection of development projects.[54] Third, the Greek economy has been unable to soak up available EU funds. By the early 1990s, EU outlays to Greece constituted as much as 6 percent of Greece's GDP, and that figure can be expected to rise even more. Without institutions and agencies set up to administer these monies, an economy simply cannot absorb this large an infusion of funds, nor does Greece even have an appropriate number of development projects on the drawing board to which these funds could be directed. And fourth, Greek government officials once felt free to use cohesion policy funds to provide solutions to short-term economic problems, rather than to promote the economic agenda of the EU. Although Athens has made great strides in devising projects that put development funds to their intended use (for example, the new Athens subway system), Greek administration of cohesion policy funds initially did not live up to EU visions of long-term cohesion.

Interestingly, just as German unification had repercussions for economic and monetary union, the need to direct funds to the new eastern *Länder* highlights the institutional nature of the EU's cohesion policy and its impact on Spain and Greece. Spain, like Germany, is a de facto federal state with established institutions capable of soaking up cohesion policy funds. By contrast, Greece is a small, centralized state with an economy ill equipped to efficiently utilize regional aid. Nonetheless, Spanish and Greek leaders agree that cohesion policy must be framed in the context of long-term community-wide goals; because the EU has its own institutions in this area, member states have been able to arrive at economic solutions to regional economic disparities and to enshrine long-term goals. All member states agree that European unification cannot be achieved

---

[53] Susannah Verney, "Central State–Local Government Relations," in Kazakos and Ioakimidis, eds., *Greece and EC Membership*, pp. 166–80.

[54] On nepotism in Greek politics, see KL. S. Koutsoukis, "Sleaze in Contemporary Greek Politics," *Parliamentary Affairs* 48 (October 1995): 688–96; Dimitris Stevis, "The Politics of Greek Environmental Policy," *Policy Studies Journal* 20 (Winter 1992): 695–709.

solely through negative integration and the removal of barriers to trade. Rather, critical steps toward European integration, like EMU, depend on the ability of less wealthy EU states to catch up with the rest.

CONCLUSION

A note about the departure from power of Spain's Felipe González and Greece's Andreas Papandreou is in order. Elected to office in 1982, González presided over Spain's entry into the EU and its tenure there for over a decade. While it is true that González was the central figure in Spanish politics during this time, most of Spain's politicians share his "Euro-enthusiasm." In May 1996, José María Aznar was sworn in as Prime Minister of Spain, ending over thirteen years of Socialist Party rule. Despite Aznar's lack of experience in foreign affairs and his more low-key style, it is unlikely that Spain's new conservative coalition government will deviate in any significant way from the European policy of its predecessor. On the other hand, Prime Minister Andreas Papandreou's departure from office in 1995 opened the door for a new set of Greek leaders to formulate a European policy in Athens. In contrast to Papandreou, Prime Minister Costas Simitis represents the picture of a "normal" European leader, preoccupied more with the everyday problems of governance and less with populist politics. Although at this writing it is too early to judge Simitis's interactions with his European counterparts, it is expected that he will continue the trend of pro-European agenda in Greek foreign policy.

What can we learn about the influences that lead to the pattern of differentiation we have witnessed between Spanish and Greek experiences in the process of European integration? While such things as historical memory and bilateral ties to countries like Germany play an undeniable role, most important are the institutional linkages that bind Spain and Greece to the EU. The European Union is a hybrid arrangement that is neither purely intergovernmental nor purely supranational in nature. It is therefore unreasonable to expect that each member state of the EU will affect and be affected by EU institutions in an identical fashion. With nearly 40 million inhabitants, a large economy, a political elite unified on questions of European integration, and a governmental system that is federal in practice, Spain is more or less suited to the direction of European integration. By contrast, with a population only a quarter the size of Spain's, a small and weak economy, a political elite that has been split over European integration, and a highly centralized governmental system, Greece makes a poor fit with the integration project.

With regard to the European Union, three institutional patterns are suggested from the policy areas examined in this chapter: (1) institutions that enshrine the concept of traditional state sovereignty are likely to foster agreements that will be made either bilaterally or within traditional Cold War arrangements; (2) institutions that do not yet embody an explicit expression of common interests, but do involve some erosion of state sovereignty, will serve to mediate among EU states; (3) institutions that embody an explicit expression of common interests will lead to conformity among EU states. All three of these patterns can be observed in the Spanish and Greek cases. First, many of Spain's security interests are similar to those of other European states, yet the status of the European and Western defense systems still reflects confusion about how to counter the diffuse character of new security threats; the thorny nature of Greek security has revealed to an even greater degree the lack of integration in the realm of the CFSP. Second, in the area of economic and monetary union, all EU states now accept the logic of EMU because they believe that European integration is dependent on economic convergence. While cooperation has been informally institutionalized, the incomplete nature of the institutions of EMU leaves room for country-by-country variation. Finally, with regard to cohesion policy, Spain and Greece now understand that the EU's compensatory institutions should take into account the range of regional needs in the union, while respecting the more pressing needs of the poor four. Negotiations over the funds therefore have become regularized around convergent norms, with implementation of cohesion policy based on economic circumstances.

The influence of Germany on Spain and Greece reflects the patterns observed in the three issue areas examined in this chapter. In the area of security, Germany coordinates with Spain and Greece bilaterally or within organizations such as the UN and NATO on issues of common concern when EU institutions are absent. Where there is concurrence over the general direction of policy, as in Spanish and German agreement over the need to address instability in the western Mediterranean, then coordination will be undertaken within the context of these organizations, which reflect the evolving nature of the CFSP. Where there is no concurrence, as in German and Greek disagreement over the decision to recognize the breakaway Yugoslav republics, then the lack of EU security institutions will be obvious. In the realm of economic and monetary union, the relationship between Germany and Spain and Greece is conditioned by the institutions of EMU. Thus Germany and Spain have exercised discretion over monetary policy, but only within the confines of the convergence criteria. Similarly, Greece can refrain from participation in the European Monetary System, yet still work toward fulfillment of the convergence criteria. Finally, in the realm of cohesion policy, all EU member states have reached agreement over what constitutes the EU's common interest through negotiations over cohesion policy funds. Thus, although Germany, Spain, and Greece bargain hard to create a cohesion policy that specifically benefits them, more and more this bargaining takes place within the EU's broader cohesion norms.

All of this supports the contention that European integration as expressed through institutional development influences interstate relations, and not vice versa. Institutions have a life of their own, as long as we understand the term *institution* in its broadest sense. Furthermore, it explains why Germany and Spain—both of which are large federal states in practice—are institutionally suited to the emergent shape of the EU, while Greece—which is a small centralized state—has difficulty fitting into EU practices. Based on the three issue areas examined in this chapter, we can conclude that the mechanics of European integration are less important than factors of norms and institutions. The extent to which Spain and Greece have or have not internalized these sets of norms, and do or do not fit into the institutional structures of the EU, explains why these two states differ so markedly in their progress toward European integration.

CHAPTER SIX

Pulling in Different Directions:
The Europeanization of Scandinavian
Political Economies

Christine Ingebritsen

Sweden, Norway, and Denmark have been considered model political economies. The Scandinavian "middle way" between capitalism and socialism combined a commitment to full employment, a solidaristic wage policy, a centralized system of wage determination, and national intervention in currency markets. Although there are important differences between Scandinavian political economies in the relative strength of capital and labor, the nature of dependence on the international market, the degree of centralization of the state, and in national economic policy models, these states shared corporatist institutions, collectivist political cultures, and solidaristic policies.

In the 1970s, Scandinavian political economies began to look far more like those in the European Community (EC). As Denmark followed its largest trading partner (Britain) into the EC, it was the first of the three Scandinavian states to accept European policy coordination. When Sweden and Norway decentralized wage bargaining, abandoned wage solidarity, adopted anti-inflationary policies, experienced levels of unemployment more typical of their southern neighbors, pegged their currencies to the European Currency Unit (ECU), proposed liberalizations in protectionist agricultural policies, and endorsed core provisions for multilateral political and economic cooperation outlined in the EC's Maastricht treaty, it

The author thanks James Caporaso, Eric Einhorn, Ron Jepperson, Peter Katzenstein, Stein Kuhnle, Paulette Kurzer, Ulf Lindstrom, Henry Milner, Lars Mjøset, Jonathon Moses, Jonas Pontusson, Herman Schwartz, Sven Steinmo, and Lars Svåsand for helpful comments on earlier versions of this chapter.

became increasingly difficult to differentiate Scandinavian policy regimes from EC policy regimes. Thus in the past two decades, Scandinavian political economies have evolved from national, centralized, and solidaristic to more internationalized, decentralized, and segmented systems of industrial relations. As Scandinavian political economies lost their distinctiveness, project Europe gained legitimacy in national politics—particularly in Sweden.

WHEN AND HOW EUROPE MATTERS

Leading scholars disagree over the causes of change in Scandinavian institutions and policies and the relative importance of domestic and international determinants. Torben Iversen contends that changes in structural-economic constraints during the 1970s and 1980s led to a cross-class realignment and a more rapid breakdown of centralized bargaining systems in Sweden and Denmark than in Norway.[1] Herman Schwartz argues that in response to a declining competitiveness in international markets new domestic political coalitions have sought to reform the nature of politics and the structure of the state.[2] Jonas Pontusson and Peter Swenson attribute the decentralization of Sweden's system of wage bargaining to changes in the preferences of the employer's federation.[3] Evelyne Huber and John Stephens propose that changes in the social democratic full employment welfare model emanate from the combined effect of the strengthened position of capital, the increasing diversity within the trade union movement, increasing international constraints and a decline in economic growth.[4]

This chapter focuses on the effect of Europeanization on Scandinavian political economies. Europeanization refers to the regional integration process, where changes in institutions, policies, and identities are occurring between EC states *and* within nation-states.[5] The Europeanization of Scandinavian political economies is distinct from a broader, more diffuse process of internationalization that compels all industrialized states to liberalize trade, deregulate financial markets, and cope with late-twentieth-

---

[1] Torben Iversen, "Power, Flexibility and the Breakdown of Centralized Wage Bargaining," paper presented at the European Political Economy and Institutional Analysis Workshop, Center for European Studies, Harvard University, February 18–19, 1994, p. 11.

[2] Herman Schwartz, "Small States in Big Trouble," *World Politics* 46 (July 1994): 527–55.

[3] Jonas Pontusson and Peter Swenson, "Labor Markets, Production Strategies, and Wage Bargaining Institutions," *Comparative Political Studies* 29 (1996): 223–50.

[4] Evelyne Huber and John D. Stephens, "Economic Internationalization, the EC, and the Social Democratic Welfare State," paper presented at the annual meeting of the American Political Science Association, Chicago, September 3–6, 1992.

[5] Johan P. Olsen, "Europeanization and Nation-State Dynamics," working paper, Advanced Research on the Europeanisation of the Nation-State (ARENA), Oslo, 1995, p. 2.

century changes in capitalism.[6] Europeanization represents both domestic political reform and a change in national identities. The impetus for change originates from a well-integrated group of European states that is also Scandinavia's most important trading partner.[7] Changes are both institutional and normative because the policy regimes of EC member states are less collectivist and more individualist in their orientation.[8]

Scandinavians, in contrast to other Europeans, have historically viewed European integration with skepticism. In Sweden, "full membership in the EC does not mesh with what the [Social Democratic] party has been asserting publicly since the 1950s."[9] Even as EC members, the Danes "have always preferred a purely intergovernmental EC, where the member states preserve full sovereignty and veto against Community decisions."[10] Norwegians have on two occasions (1972 and 1994) rejected membership in the EC and have tended to view European integration as compromising the Norwegian way of life.

In contrast to other European states (Spain, Greece, Belgium, and the Netherlands), internationalization and Europeanization have imposed far greater challenges to Scandinavian institutions and policies than German hegemony. In Scandinavia, Germany's political and economic influence on the direction and substance of institutional and policy change has been indirect, mediated by European institutions. In response to changes in Germany's power, Scandinavian leaders have endorsed a Danish strategy, preferring multilateral to bilateral relations with Germany, and supporting the enlargement of the EC to diffuse the independent influence of Germany.

This chapter traces the historic evolution of Scandinavian political economies, to demonstrate how European integration became a more legitimate option, and once this path was chosen, how it locked in a process of change already under way. The first section of the chapter discusses fundamental changes in Scandinavian political economies from the international oil crisis (1973–74) to the introduction of the Single European Act (1985). It was in the midst of the crisis of the Scandinavian model that Europe became a legitimate option. The second section examines the decision by Swedish and Norwegian governments to deepen integration with

[6] Ole Weaver and Morten Kelstrup, *Identity, Migration and the New Security Agenda in Europe* (New York: St. Martin's Press, 1992), p. 62.

[7] Trade with the EC accounts for 55 percent of Swedish exports, 64 percent of Norwegian exports, and 61 percent of Danish exports. *Yearbook of Nordic Statistics* (Copenhagen: Nordic Council of Ministers, 1993–94).

[8] Olof Petersson, *The Government and Politics of the Nordic Countries* (Stockholm: Fritzes, 1994), p. 148.

[9] Klaus Misgeld, Karl Molin, and Klas Amark, *Creating Social Democracy: A Century of the Social Democratic Labor Party in Sweden* (University Park: Penn State University Press, 1992), p. 443.

[10] Torben Worre, "Danish Public Opinion and the EC," *Scandinavian Journal of History* 20 (1995): 222.

the EC, as signatories of the European Economic Area (EEA) agreement. By conforming to liberalizations in the movement of capital, goods, services, and persons required under the EEA agreement, Scandinavian governments accelerated and deepened a process of reform. As Swedish and Norwegian political elites pursued a strategy of accession and set sail for Brussels, important redirections in policy were made that further undermined the distinctive institutions and policies of Scandinavian corporatism, and that increased Scandinavia's dependence on the EC and Germany.

Which policies central to the Scandinavian model have changed? With respect to social welfare policy and internal security, national governments retain primary influence over policy making (as Paulette Kurzer contends in her analysis of Belgium and the Netherlands in chapter 4 of this volume). In these policy areas, European policy regimes are relatively weak, and Nordic regional cooperation exceeds European cooperation. In other areas, however, EC-level policy regimes are comparatively well developed (agriculture) or emerging (money, external security) and infringe on the capacity of Scandinavian governments to maintain independent policies. Scandinavian identity is tied to an agrarian past, and policies have privileged producers and consumers of domestic agricultural products. National control over currency and security policy have been critical to maintaining model political economies. The third section of the chapter focuses on these three policy areas, agriculture, money, and security, where the extent of governmental control over the national polity is narrowing, and where more and more policy decisions once strictly in the hands of domestic political leaders are now subject to EC authorities.

The fourth section contrasts Swedish and Norwegian roads to Europe. There are some important differences in the capacity of Scandinavian states to internalize the imperatives of European integration. A puzzle emerges from this analysis. Why does Sweden, once the exemplar of the most successful social democratic movement in Europe, more readily acquiesce to a Europeanization of its political economy than Norway? The transformation from national solutions to EC policy regimes has varied within Scandinavia according to the structure of each state's dependence on the European economy and the political power of domestic coalitions organized around the European project.

The concluding section examines how changes in German power have played out in northern Europe. From the perspective of pro-integrationists in Scandinavia, German power should be tempered by the benign effects of multilateral cooperation (a view shared by members of Germany's own political elite). Germany has become both a potential ally within the EC and a motivation for widening the community. The emergence of Germany as a regional power in Europe has been viewed more skeptically in Norway and Denmark than in Sweden because of the legacy of the German Occupation during the Second World War. Consider first how Scandinavian institutions and policies were changing even before the introduction of the Single European Act.

The Breakdown of the Scandinavian Model of Industrial Relations

Leading political economists reject the concept of a common Scandinavian model of industrial relations.[11] Yet, in comparison to EC member states, Scandinavian systems of industrial relations have had more solidaristic national policies and stronger corporatist institutions, macroeconomic performance, and collectivist ideologies.[12]

The origins of Scandinavian exceptionalism can be traced to two historic compromises made in the 1930s. The trade unions gained formal participation in wage negotiations by agreeing to withhold their capacity to strike. The Social Democrats forged a coalition agreement with the Agrarian Party, promising agricultural supports in exchange for political support. These bargains were maintained by the Social Democratic Party, which occupied a hegemonic position in postwar Scandinavian politics.[13]

The breakdown of Scandinavian systems of industrial relations originated in the 1970s, when the historic compromises of the 1930s became less tenable. The quadrupling of oil prices undermined consensus in industrial relations and encouraged a reassessment of economic policy priorities. In Sweden, for example, the usual remedies did not work because of the length and the depth of the recession. A subsequent disillusionment with Keynesian demand management encouraged a reevaluation of economic policy. Because the oil crisis was not uniform in its effects on industry, it became difficult to retain solidaristic solutions. Conflict within unions, and between unions and employers, intensified.[14] In Norway, the government intervened after the oil crisis to compensate for the decline in exports; this contributed to higher levels of inflation and adversely affected the competitive position of the Norwegian export industry.[15] Disillusion-

[11] See Lars Mjøset, "The Nordic Model Never Existed, but Does It Have a Future?" *Scandinavian Studies* 64 (Fall 1992): 652–71.

[12] Gøsta Esping-Andersen, *The Three Worlds of Welfare Capitalism* (Princeton: Princeton University Press, 1990).

[13] Gøsta Esping-Andersen, *Politics against Markets* (Princeton: Princeton University Press, 1985), pp. 41–53; and Ulf Lindstrom, *Facism in Scandinavia, 1920–1940* (Stockholm: Almquist and Wiksell, 1985), pp. 136–77.

[14] Michael Maccoby, *Sweden at the Edge* (Philadelphia: University of Pennsylvania Press, 1991), p. 150; and Jonas Pontusson, *The Limits of Social Democracy* (Ithaca: Cornell University Press, 1992), p. 158.

[15] Torstein Moland, "The Norwegian Economy's Oil Dependence," *Economic Bulletin* 66 (June 1995): 200.

ment with how the government intervened in the economy was coupled with Norway's emergence as a net exporter of oil. Throughout Scandinavia, the oil crisis marked a turning point in how to manage the domestic economy and led to reforms in core institutions and policies.

Perhaps the most important core institution of Scandinavian industrial relations was a centralized system of wage bargaining. Yet each of the Scandinavian states has, to a varying degree, reorganized its system of wage determination. Even Sweden, once considered the model of organized capitalism, has abandoned the institution of centrally determined wages.[16] This process of decorporatization is well documented by Scandinavian political scientists.[17]

In 1980, the Swedish Engineering Employers Association (VF) demanded negotiations at the regional or branch level, with the intent to introduce firm-level negotiations.[18] In response to employer demands, important changes were made in Swedish Employer's Federation (SAF) statutes, which decentralized wage bargaining. Although efforts have been made to restore centralized wage bargaining, they have not been successful. Thus wage bargaining in Sweden has evolved from national-level wage bargaining to sectoral or industry-wide agreements.

In Norway, wage policy has also been decentralized by granting more autonomy to local authorities. The Norwegian Confederation of Trade Unions (LO) and the Norwegian Employer's Federation (NAF) have jointly determined wages and incomes since the first General Agreement (Hovedavtale) was concluded in 1935. Norway's two-tier wage negotiation system centralizes decision making at the national level, yet agreements are supplemented at the local level, and since 1980, local settlements have increased in importance. In response, Norway has followed Denmark's example and attempted to recentralize wage bargaining.[19] According to government officials, decentralization is problematic for macroeconomic performance because "the absence of binding guidelines or limits on total wage growth involves a much greater risk of wage spiral, stronger inflationary pressure and higher unemployment."[20] The Norwegian reforms centralized bargaining, with some discretion left to local authorities.

[16] See Pontusson and Swenson, "Labor Markets"; and Jonathon Moses, "The Effects of European Integration on the Institutions of Social Democracy," paper presented at the Society for the Advancement of Scandinavian Study, Minneapolis, May 1, 1992.

[17] Olof Petersson, *The Government and Politics of the Nordic Countries* (Stockholm: Fritzes, 1994), pp. 154–57.

[18] Scott Lash and John Urry, *The End of Organized Capitalism* (Madison: University of Wisconsin Press, 1987), p. 242.

[19] Carsten Strøby Jensen, Jørgen Steem Madsen, and Jesper Due, "Towards a European Industrial Relations System?" paper presented at European Community Studies Association conference, Washington, D.C., May 27–29, 1993, p. 8.

[20] Norwegian Employment Commission, *A National Strategy for Employment in the 1990s* (Oslo: 1992), p. 45.

A second core feature of Scandinavian systems of industrial relations, the policy of wage solidarity, was adopted in the 1950s to promote both the interests of employers and the largest trade union, LO. For employers, solidaristic wage policy restrained wage increases in industry; for labor, it minimized income differentials between sectors. The policy was extremely effective in equalizing wages—within the private sector, and between the public and private sectors.[21]

When the Swedish Employer's Federation (SAF) abandoned its commitment to centralized bargaining, this also marked an end to Sweden's solidaristic wage policy.[22] SAF has promoted "segmentalist practices" more typical of German labor markets, where there are more divisions within the workforce and higher wage differentials. In a centralized wage determination system, governments are better able to offset inflation. In a more segmented system, employers rely on higher wage levels, promotions, and other practices to attract and maintain labor.[23] Under a solidaristic wage policy, the relative wage spread in Sweden's blue-collar sector was reduced by about 80 percent from 1960 to 1983. Since the decentralization of wage negotiations and the implementation of a less solidaristic wage policy, the spread has been widening.[24]

A third core policy shared by Scandinavian systems of industrial relations has been a commitment to full employment. As a consequence of active labor market policies, Sweden and Norway successfully achieved the lowest levels of unemployment in Europe during the 1970s.[25] In the 1980s, unemployment never exceeded 3.5 percent of the workforce. Denmark, on the other hand, followed the pattern of other EC member states with average levels of unemployment exceeding 10 per cent of the labor force during the same period. Denmark's Conservative-led coalition government, which came to power in 1982, was the first Scandinavian regime to adopt an anti-inflationary monetary policy.[26] After 1991, Sweden's Conservative-led government followed the lead of Denmark and demonstrated a stronger commitment to anti-inflationary policies. Unemployment in Sweden increased to 13 percent of the labor force in the early 1990s, more consistent with labor markets in Denmark and other EC member states.

Scandinavian economic policies have shifted in priority—from a primary concern over unemployment to policies intended to combat inflation. For example, in the Swedish Social Democratic government's January

[21] Peter Swenson, "Managing the Managers," *Scandinavian Journal of History* 16 (1991): 352.

[22] Ibid., p. 351.

[23] Jonas Pontusson, *The Limits of Social Democracy* (Ithaca: Cornell University Press, 1992).

[24] Swedish Ministry of Finance, *The Medium Term Survey of the Swedish Economy* (Stockholm: 1992), pp. 256–57.

[25] Goran Therborn, *Why Some Peoples Are More Unemployed Than Others* (London: Verso, 1986), pp. 18, 23, 27, 101–4.

[26] Iversen, "Power, Flexibility," pp. 19–21.

1991 budget proposal, low inflation was the "overriding goal for economic policy."[27] According to a Swedish analyst, this change is a necessary response to the forces of Europeanization:

> In recent years, however, the priorities of Swedish economic policy have shifted toward the battle against inflation. Because of Sweden's extensive and growing interdependence and its rapprochement with the European Community (EC) and the future European Union (EU), its chances of pursuing an autonomous national economic policy are increasingly limited.[28]

Thus Scandinavian political economies were already undergoing a transformation when the EC launched its internal market program in 1985. All three core features of Scandinavian systems of industrial relations began to unravel during the period from 1973 to 1985: the system of centralized wage bargaining, the policy of wage solidarity, and the pursuit of full employment. As integration deepened, Scandinavian political economies shared more in common with European institutions and policies than in the previous accession period (the 1970s). With the implementation of the SEA and the adoption of the Maastricht treaty, the EC became even more important to the momentum and direction of Scandinavian political change.

FROM FREE TRADE TO FULL MEMBERSHIP

The European Community's proposal to create an internal market led the Nordic states to pursue a wider partnership with the EC, the European Economic Area (EEA) agreement. Negotiations between the members of the European Free Trade Association (EFTA)—Finland, Sweden, Norway, Iceland, Austria, Switzerland, and Liechtenstein—and the EC to create a new, expanded free trade area (the EEA) were initiated in April 1984, and approved by the EC in February 1992. The EEA agreement led to the reform of policies and institutions central to these model political economies, and has narrowed the gap between Scandinavian policy regimes and European Community policy regimes. For states with protectionist national policies limiting the free movement of capital, practices designed to ensure that nationals own and operate domestic industry, and regulations designed to meet the specific needs of their own labor markets, this marked an important step in opening up these economies to greater competition and foreign direct investment.

[27] Assar Lindbeck et al., *Turning Sweden Around* (Cambridge: MIT Press, 1994), p. 4.
[28] Pär Trehörning, *Measures to Combat Unemployment in Sweden: Labor Market Policy in the 1990s* (Stockholm: Swedish Institute, 1993), p. 6.

Initially, as part of the EEA agreement, the European Community promised the EFTA states a role in political decision making (or "decision shaping," as it was called). In 1990, however, the EC made community membership a requirement for states to have a voice in European institutions. Shortly thereafter, Social Democratic leaders in Norway and Sweden changed their strategy from the pursuit of closer ties with the EC, and a new free trade agreement, to the pursuit of full membership. The 1989 revolutions in Eastern Europe legitimized the revival of the EC membership issue by the Norwegian Social Democratic Party and made this change of strategy possible in neutral Sweden, where pressure on the state to join the EC was particularly strong because of the political power of organized business.

Sweden's corporate sector is dominated by a small number of large, privately held companies. "About twenty international groups account for a third of industrial employment, half of total Swedish exports and almost three-quarters of total industrial R&D expenditure. They also generate more than half of total profits and listed values."[29] In Sweden's manufacturing-dependent economy, the government adopted a "production-oriented" strategy in the early 1980s. The Norwegian government, on the other hand, pursued a "sheltering strategy" by relying heavily on income from the petroleum sector.[30]

In response to the EC's internal market program, Swedish companies relocated their production facilities and purchased subsidiaries in European Community member states. Between 1985 and 1990, foreign direct investment by Sweden increased from Skr 10.9 ($1.4 US billion) to Skr 69.6 billion ($11.8 billion).[31] By 1987, Sweden's thirty largest companies had more employment abroad than at home.[32] According to the managing director of the Swedish corporation Aga, "Sweden needs Swedish companies, but Swedish companies do not need Sweden."[33] No comparable exodus of capital occurred in Norway, where the economy has become less dependent on manufacturing since the 1970s and primarily dependent on petroleum exports. When Swedish employers moved south, the pressure to integrate intensified. Influential representatives of Swedish export firms actively participated in the EC political debate.[34] Three leaders of Swedish "national champion" companies (Antonia Johnson of Axel-Johnson, Pehr

---

[29] Swedish Ministry of Finance, *Medium Term Survey*, p. 296.

[30] Iversen, "Power, Flexibility."

[31] Sveriges Riksbank, 1991.

[32] Pär Trehörning, *Measures to Combat Unemployment: Labor Market Policy in the Mid-1990s* (Stockholm: Swedish Institute, 1993), p. 22.

[33] James Fulcher, "The Social Democratic Model in Sweden," *Political Quarterly* 65 (1994): 212.

[34] Paulette Kurzer, *Business and Banking* (Ithaca: Cornell University Press, 1993).

Gyllenhammar of Volvo, and Peter Wallenberg of the Wallenberg group) were members of Prime Minister Ingvar Carlsson's advisory board on EC relations.[35] In Sweden, the Social Democrats abandoned their traditional reservations concerning European integration and sought to reform the core policies of their political economy at a remarkable speed.

Since the 1960s, the Swedish government had maintained that the policy of "alliance freedom" (nonalignment) prevented the state from joining the EC. Yet the government rapidly revised its position after the end of the Cold War, arguing that changes in the international system required Sweden to join forces with its largest trading partner and to play a role in the new Europe. In July 1991, the Swedish Social Democratic Government applied to join the EC, and on November 13, 1994, 52 percent of the participants in a national referendum on the EC question voted in favor of membership. Just two weeks later, in another national referendum, the Norwegian people rejected their government's initiative to join forces with EC member states, again by 52 percent. Thus Sweden set sail for Europe, while Norway stayed ashore on the northern periphery.

In the 1990s, European integration became a means to an end, enabling governments to reform domestic policies and institutions to revive the economy. As northern European political leaders adopted a strategy of bringing their economies in line with those of EC member states, they charted a course that will be difficult to reverse.

Core Policies Change on the Road to Brussels

Acquiescing to project Europe means giving up national control over core policies—something that until recently Scandinavian governments have been unwilling to do. In the policy areas of currency, external security, and agriculture, Scandinavian governments have, to varying degrees, abandoned traditional remedies and endorsed EC policy regimes. In currency policy alignment, Norway and Sweden have followed a similar path. Despite the public's rejection of EC membership and the government's subsequent decision not to join, Norway has continued to pursue cooperation with the European currency regime, although in security and agriculture, it has resisted the demands of European integration and retained its traditional policies.

Currency Policy

The determination of the value of national currency is at the heart of economic sovereignty. Yet since the 1970s, Scandinavian governments have

[35] "Hemligt råd styr Sverige mot EG," *Svenska Dagbladet* (June 30, 1991): 6.

increasingly adapted their economies to changes in the value of stronger currencies (particularly the deutsche mark), trading off national currency policy for transnational cooperation in currency policy. The European Community is Scandinavia's largest trading partner; thus changes in the currency values of EC member states and in the degree of EC-wide collaboration have "spill-over" effects on Scandinavian political economies.

Denmark was the first of the Scandinavian states to cooperate with the EC in currency policy, joining the EMS in 1979, and since then has sought EC approval to devalue its currency.[36] While a narrow majority of Danes vetoed the Maastricht treaty in June 1992 and the Edinburgh compromise temporarily excludes Denmark from the creation of a currency union, it is likely that the Danish government will schedule a new referendum asking the public to reconsider economic and political union. All major parties in Danish politics endorse participation in the European currency regime.

In contrast to Denmark, the EFTA applicants to the EC (Sweden, Norway, Austria, and Finland) could not join the EC à la carte, and agreed to monetary cooperation in their accession treaties. When the Swedish and Norwegian governments decided to apply to join the EC, they also agreed to trade off national currency policy for European collaboration. While non-EC countries cannot belong to the EMS, both governments transformed their exchange rate policies once they decided to join the EC. The ultimate goal of Swedish and Norwegian exchange rate policy is full participation in the EMS.[37]

Thus Sweden and Norway unilaterally pegged the value of their currencies to the ECU as part of their effort to forge closer ties to the EC.[38] Norway pegged the value of the Norwegian krone to the ECU on October 22, 1990, seven months before Sweden pegged the value of the Swedish krona to the ECU on May 17, 1991. When the fixed exchange rate policy was established, the Swedish Riksbank accepted a narrower margin of currency fluctuation than the Norwegian Central Bank (Norges Bank). The Swedish krona was allowed to fluctuate by a narrow band of 1.5 percent, as compared to the Norwegian krone, which had a wider band of 2.25 percent.[39] By linking the value of Scandinavian currencies to the ECU *before* joining the EC, both governments signaled their willingness to cooperate with the

---

[36] Finn Ostrup, *The Development of the European Monetary System* (Stockholm: Nerenius and Santerus Forlag, 1992).

[37] Hans Lindberg and Christina Lindenius, "The Swedish Krona Pegged to the ECU," *Quarterly Review* 3 (1991): 14–15; and Christina Lindenius, "The Norwegian Krone to the ECU," *Quarterly Review* 1 (1991): 31–32.

[38] Jonathon Moses, "Fixing the Agenda: ECU Linkage and the EU Ambitions of Nordic Elites," paper presented at the annual meeting of the American Political Science Association, New York, September 1–4, 1994.

[39] Lindberg and Lindenius, "Swedish Krona," p. 17.

community. While pegging Scandinavian currencies to the ECU is not as binding as Exchange Rate Mechanism (ERM) membership (in the ERM system, currencies are tied not only to the ECU but also to each other at fixed parities), it marks an important change from a nationally based floating exchange rate policy to a European currency regime. Scandinavian governments have tied their currencies to a group of states that prioritize price stability.

Yet there are additional consequences of trading off a national exchange rate policy for a European regime. The transition from a national to a European exchange rate policy is problematic for small economies that have a share of their foreign trade with non-EC countries. For example, the Norwegian krone's linkage to the ECU has adverse effects on the competitiveness of Norwegian exports. While the previous exchange rate basket was weighted to reflect Norway's most important trading partners (with larger proportions of U.S. dollars and Swedish kronor), the ECU basket is not as representative of Norway's trade balance as the previous exchange rate basket. Thus whenever the German currency strengthens its position relative to the dollar, the competitiveness of Norwegian exports in the American market diminishes.[40]

In addition to effects on export competitiveness, any crisis in the European currency regime is directly passed on to Scandinavian political economies—as experienced in the ERM crisis of the early 1990s. In 1992, Sweden and Norway internalized changes in German monetary policy. As a consequence of German reunification, the Bundesbank introduced an anti-inflationary monetary policy. Higher interest rates were passed on to other EMS members, and to Sweden and Norway. As long as these economies remained tied to German economic policies, the value of national currency appreciated against the U.S. dollar and the Japanese yen.[41]

The Swedish government stubbornly hung on to a pegged currency rate well into the crisis. Approximately Skr 160 billion ($26.7 billion) left the country in less than a week, and the overnight lending rates soared to as much as 500 percent before the government announced that it would abandon European currency cooperation on November 19, 1992.[42] Nor could the Swedes rely on European policy regimes during the crisis. The Swedish government's request to allow the Swedish krona to be fully linked to the EMS, thereby permitting access to the currency support program, was rejected by the Monetary Committee. The Bundesbank, in particular,

[40] Lindenius, "Norwegian Krone," pp. 34–35.

[41] Center for Business and Policy Studies (Sweden) Economic Policy Group, "Sweden's Economic Crisis: Diagnosis and Cure," Occasional Paper 42, February 1993, p. 11.

[42] "Swedish Kronor Devalued," *Sweden Report* 11 (Stockholm: Ministry of Foreign Affairs, December 1992), p. 1.

objected to Sweden's peg to the ECU ("a currency that does not exist" as opposed to a "natural currency") and noted that Sweden was not a full member of the EMS.[43] While Sweden's currency continued to float downward after the crisis, the value of Norway's currency stabilized—largely due to the effect of its petroleum resources. The shift to a floating exchange rate in Sweden led to a 10 percent devaluation, and a sudden increase in the cost of imports.[44] Since the currency crisis of fall 1992, both governments have temporarily returned to the traditional policy of devaluation, and a much less rigid currency regime.

For the Swedish and Norwegian political economies, multilateral currency cooperation has thus far proved costly and destabilizing. Despite immediate benefits in the form of lower interest rates and currency inflows, both economies have experienced greater instability and currency outflow.[45] For Sweden's political economy and the coalition government of Prime Minister Carl Bildt, the crisis was particularly devastating. The economic situation was dreary enough, with a soaring budget deficit, high public debt, and one of the lowest levels of GDP growth in the Organization for Economic Cooperation and Development (OECD). Despite several bailout packages initiated by Bildt in the fall of 1992, the government was unable to get the economy on a stable course.

Despite the costs associated with a European currency regime, Swedish and Norwegian central banks maintain a commitment to linking their currencies to the ECU. According to an official at Norges Bank (the Norwegian Central Bank), even though Norway did not join the EC on January 1, 1995, it will continue to tie its currency to the ECU. According to Swedish economist Marianne Nessen, because of changes in the relative weights of currencies in the ECU basket, Scandinavian currencies will be more dependent than before on the health of other European economies, and face new kinds of exchange rate risk.[46]

There are some interesting paradoxes on the road to European currency union. Norway remains outside the EC for the forseeable future yet is better able to meet the macroeconomic requirements for the first stage of economic and monetary union specified at Maastricht. Sweden's budget deficit (12.9 percent of GDP) and public debt (83 percent of GDP) are well above the Maastricht limits, despite Sweden's desire to be in the inner core of EC policy making.[47] Sweden appears to have more in

[43] David Cameron, "British Exit, German Voice, French Loyalty," paper presented at Columbia University, March 1993, pp. 32–33.
[44] "Swedish Kronor Devalued," p. 1.
[45] Robert Bergqvist and Leif Johansson, "The International Foreign Exchange Market in 1990 and 1991—Expanding EMS Bloc," *Quarterly Review* 4 (1991): 10–13.
[46] Marianne Nessen, "The New Swedish ECU Basket," *Quarterly Review* 1–2 (1992): 29.
[47] "Heading South," A Survey of the Nordic Countries, *Economist* (November 5, 1994): 5.

common with Spain than with Norway in obstacles to full participation in the EMU.[48]

The capacity of Scandinavian states to pursue independent policies has changed—not only in currency policy but also in security policy. In our second policy area, national security, neutral Sweden has readily conformed to the imperatives of EC membership, while Norway remains committed to NATO.

External Security Policy

Under the terms negotiated at Maastricht, EC member states agreed to cooperate in the Western European Union (WEU) and to adopt common external security and foreign policies. The Danes rejected this dimension of EC policy coordination in a referendum held on June 2, 1992. Because a majority of Norwegians voted against EC membership, Norway's security policy will continue to be determined on a national basis and through cooperation with NATO member states. On the other hand, as a condition for joining the EC, Sweden has accepted what the Danes have rejected. Sweden's willingness to overcome its historical aversion to entangling alliances and to redefine its neutrality policy to conform with the Maastricht treaty is another example of political change in Scandinavia resulting from regional integration.

While Norway and Denmark were occupied by German forces from April 1940 until the end of the Second World War, Sweden managed to remain neutral and to avoid occupation; it has maintained a policy of neutrality since the Napoleonic Wars. Neutrality policy is "one of the pillars of Swedish national identity, with the kind of cross-partisan support among the citizens that makes an unorthodox view an affront."[49] Accordingly, prominent security analysts in Scandinavia anticipated few changes in Swedish neutrality policy even after the fall of the Berlin Wall and the breakup of the Soviet empire.[50] To abandon neutrality as a security concept would imply giving up a fundamental Swedish institution. Thus it came as no suprise when Ingvar Carlsson, leader of the Social Democratic Party, proclaimed in the summer of 1990, "If the EC forges ahead with its plans to create a political union, Sweden cannot join the EC. . . . Swedish participation in EC foreign policy forums could influence the credibility

[48] "Spain and the EU: One Speed, Dead Slow," *Economist* (March 4, 1995): 30.

[49] Ulf Lindstrom, "Scandinavia and the EU," Department of Comparative Politics, Bergen, Norway, 1995.

[50] Lauri Karvonen and Bengt Sundelius, "Neutrality Freeze: Explaining Policy Rigidity amidst International Change," paper presented at the annual meeting of the American Political Science Association, San Francisco, August 30–September 2, 1990 (revised 1995).

of our neutrality policy."[51] What did come as a suprise was how rapidly the official Swedish position changed. Virtually overnight, Carlsson's reservations concerning the consequences of Swedish membership in the EC disappeared. Under his leadership, the Swedish government announced its intent to join the EC in a finance bill presented to the parliament.

Why the rapid reversal in Sweden's neutrality policy? If Carlsson had been genuinely concerned with the "high politics" of military security, he would have stood firm. Instead, the imperatives of business interests (to be in the EC) and the public's support for EC membership (one year prior to the national elections) appear to have been more important to the Social Democratic leader.

According to numerous statements made by former Conservative Prime Minister Carl Bildt, Sweden's role in European politics changed fundamentally with the end of the Cold War and with political instability in the former Soviet Union.[52] Sweden's political elite intend to cooperate fully with the ambitions of EC integrationists. Sweden became a member of the EC on January 1, 1995, with a commitment to abide by the foreign and security policy aims outlined in the Maastricht treaty. Paradoxically, given Sweden's traditional policy of "alliance freedom," the Swedes are even more European than the Danes in their willingness to participate in a strengthening of the European defense pillar, the Western European Union (WEU). In the words of Carl Bildt, Sweden's prime minister during a critical period in the EC accession process (1991–94):

> Sweden will be an active and committed participant in the evolution of common foreign and security policy. Foreign observers who think otherwise have not really understood the Swedish mentality. When we join international cooperation, we intend to have influence, and we want to make a difference.[53]

For Norway, an EC outsider and a loyal member of NATO, the Maastricht treaty has not directly affected military planning, although under Prime Minister Gro Harlem Brundtland, Norway's foreign policy strategy has included closer cooperation with the EC in European security policy making. Under her leadership, Norway became an associate member of the WEU. In the EC campaign, Chief of Defense Torolf Rein joined other senior officials in the foreign policy establishment in supporting EC membership to enhance Norwegian security. Rein advocated full membership in the Western European Union "as imperative for the country in the future since the WEU will increasingly take over NATO's role in Europe."[54]

[51] Ingvar Carlsson, "EG-medlemskap omojliggors," *Dagens Nyheter* (May 27, 1990): A4.
[52] Carl Bildt, speech to the Institute of International Affairs in Rome, October 1992.
[53] Carl Bildt, speech in Brussels, September 1993.
[54] "The Case for Defence," *Norway Now* (August 1994): 2.

Yet in the Norwegian debate over EC membership, Brundtland was unable to convince the public of the potential security benefits of integration. Despite changes in the alliance, Norwegians continue to view NATO as the preferred multilateral security forum.

Thus, paradoxically, given their tradition of neutrality, the Swedes have demonstrated a stronger commitment to a unified Europe than the Norwegians. The Europeanization of core Swedish policies is not only visible in security policy, but also in another important regime—agricultural policy.

Agricultural Policy

A Scandinavian innovation in agriculture has been a practice of rewarding farmers above and beyond levels of support given to agricultural producers in EC member states. Reforming agricultural policy goes to the heart of traditional alliances between farmers and Social Democrats, and marks a significant shift from the past, when farmers were of equal status to industrial workers.[55]

Sweden, Norway, and Denmark were traditionally agrarian societies. Farmers are symbolic of northern Europe's peasant past, and closely associated with the historic development and national identity of these nations. The inability of farmers to sustain a livelihood in agriculture led to a mass exodus from Scandinavia during the nineteenth century. The loss of a significant proportion of the population to more fertile (American) soil and the supply disruptions experienced during the First and Second World Wars led to a desire to provide assistance to the farmer. As Gøsta Esping-Andersen explains in *Politics against Markets* (1985), farmers played a unique political role as a partner in the red-green alliances formed in Scandinavia during the 1930s. In exchange for agricultural subsidies, the farmers agreed to offer their support to the Social Democratic Party. This political coalition was unique to northern Europe, and permitted a lengthy period of Social Democratic leadership.[56]

During the postwar period, the Swedish and Norwegian governments protected and subsidized domestic agricultural production in order to maintain a secure supply of basic foodstuffs, to provide employment in the periphery, and to guarantee a decent wage to farm workers. Even though agriculture has diminished in economic importance, agrarian parties continue to play an important role in Scandinavian politics—particularly in Norway.[57] Until recent reforms in agricultural policies, Scandinavian farmers enjoyed higher subsidies than other farmers in Europe.

[55] Esping-Andersen, *Politics against Markets*, p. 37; and Gøsta Esping-Andersen, *Creating Social Democracy* (University Park: Penn State University Press, 1992), pp. 175–212.

[56] Esping-Andersen, *Politics against Markets*, pp. 37, 41–53, 62, 87, and 204.

[57] Christine Ingebritsen, "Norwegian Political Economy and European Integration," *Cooperation and Conflict* 30 (1995): 349–63.

Table 1. Agricultural support

	%share of GDP spent on agriculture	U.S. dollars per full-time farmer	U.S. dollars per hectare farmland
Norway	3.7	39,600	4,240
Sweden	1.3	38,600	950
EU	2.0	17,700	1,120
United States	1.5	36,100	210

SOURCE: *Agricultural Policies, Markets and Trade, Monitoring and Outlook* (Paris: OECD, 1993).

Denmark is the only Scandinavian country blessed with abundant, fertile land suitable for farming. Denmark's export-led growth model depends on international markets for its agricultural products. In Norway and Sweden, on the other hand, agricultural production is primarily for the domestic market; from an economic perspective, subsidizing farmers is a costly, impractical endeavor.

As Europe's northernmost agricultural region, Norway and Sweden share a harsh climate, short growing season, and soils that are often rocky and difficult to cultivate. Yet despite the harsh conditions facing agricultural producers, the level of support to agriculture distinguishes these states from other advanced industrial nations. As indicated in table 1, Norwegian and Swedish subsidies to agriculture exceed the level of support provided farmers in the EC, or farmers in the United States. Defenders of agricultural subsidies often point to the "social rationality" of such policies and the pursuit of noneconomic goals including income equality, environmental quality, dispersed habitation, and national security.[58] During the postwar period, Norway's and Sweden's "socially rational" policies heavily protected agriculture through a mix of price subsidies, import and export regulations, transportation support, and numerous other state transfers. In a comparison of agricultural policies, Norway and Sweden share a commitment to food security, rural development, and income equality between farmers and industrial workers.[59] Thus, from the perspective of Norwegian and Swedish farmers, the EC's Common Agricultural Policy (CAP) constituted a "liberal" market regime, based more on market principles than social rationality.

[58] Johan Marcks Von Wurtemberg, "The Cost of Present Agricultural Policies in the EFTA Countries," Occasional Paper 18 (Geneva: European Free Trade Association, 1987), p. 1.

[59] Michele Micheletti, *The Swedish Farmer's Movement and Government Agricultural Policy* (New York: Praeger, 1990), chaps. 1–3; General Agreement on Tariffs and Trade, *Trade Policy Review: Sweden* (Geneva, August 1990), pp. 163–69; Organization for Economic Cooperation and Development, *National Policies and Agricultural Trade* (Paris: 1990), pp. 11–12, 47, and 53; and Zenon Tederko, "Agricultural Policy and Trends in Norwegian Agriculture," (Oslo: Norwegian Agricultural Economics Research Institute, 1992), pp. 11–24.

In the 1990s, it is better to be a farmer in oil-dependent Norway (outside the EC) than in Sweden. The Norwegians have *increased* subsidies to agricultural districts and have continued to defy the imperatives of liberalization and internationalization.[60] In Sweden, on the other hand, the government initiated major liberalizing reforms in the agricultural sector prior to entry into the EC, so much so that Swedish farmers preferred the EC's CAP to Stockholm's more "liberal" policy.[61] As in the 1972 EC debate, Norwegian farmers actively resisted the liberalizations in agricultural policy represented by EC membership. During the 1994 accession debate, farmers in Norway planted flowers in a pattern that read "No to the EC"; they painted anti-EC slogans on their barns and even on their farm animals in protest of the Social Democratic government's effort to bring Norway into the EC.[62]

The farmers' resistance to European integration became a significant factor in Norwegian party politics. In the fall of 1993, the Center Party emerged as the second largest party in the national parliament by appealing to anti-EC sentiment, particularly in rural areas of the country. By contrast, Sweden's Center Party has broadened its political base to include white-collar workers and environmentalists, and no longer represents strictly agrarian interests, which continue to resist integration. Although there were divisions over EC membership within the ranks of Sweden's Center Party, the leadership supported entry into the EC.

In July 1991, the Swedish government introduced its New Food Policy, which substantially liberalized support to the agricultural sector. According to the EC's report "The Agricultural Implications of EC Enlargement," Sweden's New Food Policy "represents a sharp break with the tradition of agricultural support and this reflects an increasing feeling within Sweden that agriculture does not have a special claim to public support than other sectors."[63] The Swedish government eliminated export subsidies for grain, pork, beef, and milk, and introduced other measures designed at achieving greater "EC compatibility" in the agricultural sector. One of the central aims of the Swedish reforms was to reduce consumer prices by increasing competition in agriculture.[64] Norway, in contrast to Sweden, has moved much more slowly in reforming its agriculture policies to correspond to the level of support provided by the CAP.

[60] Between 1979 and 1988, the producer subsidy equivalent (PSE) more than doubled (Organization for Economic Cooperation and Development, *National Policies and Agricultural Trade*, 1990, p. 13).

[61] Interview at the Swedish parliament with EC policy expert.

[62] "Painted Cows Get the Message Across," *European* (September 2–8, 1994): 20.

[63] Bureau Européen de Récherches, "The Agricultural Implications of EC Enlargement," report prepared for Directorate General VI of the Commission, Brussels, February 1993.

[64] *Det svensk jordbruket i EU* (Jonkoping, Sweden: Jordbruksverket, 1994), p. 3.

Norway has the least desirable farmland and the most generous subsidies to farmers in Scandinavia. Only 2.4 percent of Norway's land has been cultivated for agricultural purposes. The topography is a barrier to efficient land use, since fjords, mountains, rivers and narrow valleys make it difficult, if not impossible, to rationalize production. The average size of the Norwegian farm is about 25 acres (10 hectares), smaller than the EC average of 32 acres (13 hectares) and one-third the average size of farms in Sweden, 74 acres (30 hectares).

Norway's agricultural policy is designed to maintain the population settlement pattern in peripheral areas. "Therefore, Norway is willing, mainly for demographic reasons, to accept smaller farms and lower levels of productivity than other countries where the demographic problems are less important."[65] Income levels for agricultural workers should correspond to the average income of industrial workers, according to Norway's solidaristic policy adopted by parliament in 1975. In order for Norwegian farmers to maintain their livelihood, they depend heavily on support from the state. State subsidies permit farmers to remain in isolated, mountainous regions far from the capital city of Oslo. The elaborate system of tariff and nontariff barriers protects domestic producers from foreign competition. The price system encourages Norwegians to consume the last domestically produced apple or potato before contemplating a much more expensive imported variety. As a consequence, Norwegian food prices exceed the EC average.

While the Norwegian government supports an "efficient, rational" agricultural policy, subsidies to farms and regulations governing the ownership of farm property seem to contradict these stated policy goals. For example, the extent of protection for the small farmer is especially high. In order to prevent the decline of small farms, the state rewards farmers who cultivate small, inefficient plots of land. The more isolated and remote the farm, the higher the subsidy.

Although the Norwegian government approved a new plan to promote a "more cost-efficient agricultural sector" in February 1993, the central aim of regional policy—to keep the population in the periphery—was retained:

> The main objective of national policy is to stimulate economic development through expansion of existing economic activities and the creation of new job opportunities. Agricultural policy plays an important role in this respect. To prevent such areas from becoming too sparsely populated, measures must be taken to sustain a higher number of people in agriculture than otherwise would be necessary.[66]

[65] Tederko, "Agricultural Policy," p. 50.
[66] Von Wurtemberg, "Cost of Agricultural Policies," p. 16.

Despite rhetorical commitments by the government to "enhance market mechanisms," Norway lacked Sweden's political resolve to reform the agricultural sector. Instead, in 1991 the Norwegians slightly reduced their prices for some agricultural products, only to offset this effect entirely by *increasing* direct payments to farmers.[67] In contrast to Sweden, Norway has neither reduced its export subsidies nor changed its elaborate system of direct payments to agricultural producers, but continues to retain lavish subsidies to the agricultural sector and a high level of support for peripheral regions.

Thus where Sweden has reformed state agricultural policy to meet the requirements of the EC's agricultural regime, and redefined its policy of neutrality to conform with the plans for European foreign and security policy cooperation outlined in the Maastricht treaty, Norway, in the face of substantial resistance to agricultural reforms, has made no such sweeping changes in its core policies.

To explain Sweden's accommodation and Norway's resistance to European integration, let us examine differences in each state's dependence on the European economy and in the political power of each state's domestic coalitions for and against the European project.

Explaining Norwegian Resistance and Swedish Reform

The pressures of Europeanization on Norway's raw materials–dependent, oil-exporting economy have been less destabilizing to national institutions and policies than the pressures experienced in Sweden's manufacturing-dependent economy. As Ulf Lindstrom and Lars Svåsand point out, "Norway's affluence was not immediately at stake as the country considered its relationship to Europe. In 1990, petroleum accounted for almost half of the nation's export revenues."[68] The economic dependence on oil has enabled the state to retain more of its traditional policies and institutions. While the Norwegian economic model is changing under the pressures of internationalization, "the resources from the oil sector give the state considerable leverage compared to Sweden."[69] As Sweden entered the EC, the economy was experiencing its worst crisis since the Great Depression. With unemployment and public debt rising to levels more typical of Sweden's southern neighbors, the legitimacy and the capacity to sus-

[67] U.S. Department of Agriculture, *Western Europe: Agriculture and Trade Report* (Washington, D.C.: December 1992), p. 85.

[68] Ulf Lindstrom and Lars Svåsand, "Scandinavian Political Parties and Europe," in John Gaffney, ed., *Political Parties and the European Union* (New York: Routledge, 1996), pp. 205–19.

[69] John D. Stephens, "The Scandinavian Welfare States: Development and Crisis," paper presented at the World Congress of Sociology, Bielefeld, Germany, July 18–23, 1994, p. 22.

Table 2. Norway's "EC election"

Political party	1989 results		1993 results	
	%	Seats	%	Seats
Labor Party	34.3	63	37.1	67
Center Party	6.5	11	18.5	32
Conservative Party	22.0	37	15.6	28
Christian Democrats	8.5	14	8.4	13
Socialist Left Party	10.1	17	7.9	13
Progress Party	13.0	22	6.0	9
Liberal Party	3.2	0	3.6	1
Red Electoral Alliance	.4	0	0.5	1

SOURCE: "Lahnstein's Political Landslide Blocks EC Membership," *Norway Now* 7 (1993): 2.

tain traditional social democratic policies had fundamentally changed. Thus the structural imperatives for reform were far greater in Sweden than in Norway.

In the political process of convincing the electorate to vote in favor of European integration, the two governments faced entirely different coalitions. Strong, centralized economic interest groups in Norway resisted Europeanization, while strong, centralized economic interest groups in Sweden promoted Europeanization.

In Norway, farmers retain a powerful position in national politics. Agrarian organizations are represented by the Center Party in the Norwegian Parliament and have actively opposed Norwegian accession. In the fall 1993 elections, Norway's anti-EC Center Party received more votes than the Conservative Party, as indicated in table 2. According to Norwegian political scientist Henry Valen, this "EC election" split the parliament into two opposing camps: the Euro-supporters and the Euro-opponents.[70] The success of the Center Party in the 1993 national elections made it impossible for the government to obtain parliamentary approval for EC membership.

Sweden and Norway have also differed significantly in the willingness of their political elites to internalize values represented by the European project. With respect to the political power of economic ideas, neoliberalism has been more prominent in Swedish than in Norwegian politics. The EC's neoliberal reform initiative is compatible with the preferences of Sweden's politically powerful business elite. In the debate over European integration, Swedish corporate leaders were influential in convincing the Social Democratic leadership of the advantages of joining the EC. By contrast, Norwegian businesses did not assume a common strategic position but in-

[70] Henry Valen, Institute for Social Research, Oslo, September 1993; and discussions with Valen in Bergen, Norway, May 1995.

Table 3. Election to the Riksdag, 1988 and 1991

	1988		1991	
	% Vote	Seats	% Vote	Seats
Social Democrats	43.2	156	37.6	138
Left Party	5.8	21	4.5	16
Greens	5.5	20	3.4	—
Center Party	11.3	42	8.5	31
Liberals	12.2	44	9.1	33
Conservatives	18.3	66	21.9	80
Christian Democrats	2.9	—	7.1	26
New Democrats	—	—	6.7	—
Others	0.7	—	1.2	—

SOURCE: Diane Sainsbury, "The 1991 Swedish Election: Protest, Fragmentation, and a Shift to the Right," reprinted by permission from *West-European Politics* 15:2 (April 1992): 161, published by Frank Cass & Company, 900 Eastern Avenue, Ilford, Essex, England. Copyright Frank Cass & Co. Ltd.

stead the "no" coalition of farmers and fishermen represented by the Center Party set the terms of the domestic EC debate. Thus the Swedish state has adapted much more readily to the imperatives of regional integration, and social democracy in Sweden is no longer as antimarket or anti-EC as it was in the past.

The ideological shift to the right in Sweden has led to reform initiatives that counter the norms of collectivism once central to the "Swedish Model." Political changes have been visible within the Social Democratic Party, in the election of right-of-center parties that support closer ties to the EC, and in a domestic reform proposal calling for fundamental changes in Swedish institutions and policies.[71] While Sweden has retained the norm of universal, solidaristic social welfare policies, it has reduced the extent of coverage and is likely to undertake further reforms as it struggles toward economic recovery.

In the 1980s, Swedish trade unionists and Social Democratic Party activists nicknamed certain senior administrators and political advisors to government ministers "the Cabinet Right." The neoliberal reforms proposed by the "Cabinet Right" included liberalization, privatization, and deregulation. These officials questioned Sweden's political commitment to the social security system and regarded the trade unions as an obstacle and Social Democratic parliamentary groups as too slow and out-of-date.[72]

In the 1991 elections, the Social Democratic Party suffered its worst defeat since 1928. As indicated in table 3, two parties on the right gained

[71] Lindbeck et al., *Turning Sweden Around*, pp. 171–227.
[72] Knut Rexed, paper presented at the conference "Where is Sweden Heading?" New School, New York, October 1991, p. 4.

seats in the Swedish Riksdag—New Democracy and the Christian Democrats. New Democracy campaigned on a populist platform, promising to reduce the price of alcohol and reassess Sweden's immigration policies. The Christian Democrats appealed to voters concerned about the erosion of moral values in Swedish society. Four nonsocialist parties formed the new government, under Conservative Party Prime Minister Carl Bildt. At the heart of the Bildt government's program was bringing Sweden into the EC.

In December 1992, the Conservative government appointed an economic commission to put forth recommendations on how to improve Sweden's economic performance. The Lindbeck Economic Commission proposed a series of broad-sweeping, remarkably un-Swedish reforms: allowing the Swedish krona to float until participation in an EC-wide currency union was possible, pursuing a long-term policy of price stabilization, liberalizing labor market legislation, reducing employment allowances, abstaining from incomes policy initiatives, decentralizing wage bargaining in the public sector, and limiting wage negotiations to one level (sectoral or firm) to contribute to lower inflation.[73] The commission recommended greater reliance on private sector solutions and on the individual, greater freedom of choice, and political reforms designed to make government officials more responsible to the public.[74] The finance ministry was to be given greater power in relation to other ministries, parliaments were to serve longer terms, and the power of interest groups in politics (particularly trade unions) was to be curtailed.[75] The commission also endorsed more independence for the Swedish central bank and recommended that the bank be made responsible for reducing inflation.

When the Swedish Social Democrats returned to power in the fall of 1994, they were committed to bringing the country into the EC and to revitalizing the moribund Swedish economy. To convince the public of the desirability of joining the EC, Swedish Social Democrats advocated collective solutions at the European level—from closer trade to closer political cooperation. European integration, proclaimed the Swedish elites, represented an opportunity for social democracy. In Norway, the Social Democrats were less successful in overcoming widespread misgivings about European integration.

Norway's former prime minister Gro Harlem Brundtland has been the strongest proponent of the Europeanization of Norwegian Social Democracy. Although her efforts to bring Norway into the European Community were stalemated by opposition within her party, in the Norwegian Confed-

---

[73] Press release, Swedish government, Report on the Lindbeck Economic Commission, Stockholm, March 9, 1993.

[74] Assar Lindbeck, "Overshooting, Reform and Retreat of the Welfare State," paper delivered at the Seventh Tinbergen Lecture delivered at de Nederlandsche Bank, Amsterdam, October 1, 1993.

[75] "Sweden: Ask the Devil," *Economist* (March 13, 1993): 62.

eration of Trade Unions (LO), in the agrarian Center Party, and among a majority of the public, her personal vision was consistent with Danish and Swedish political leaders: to continue the Social Democratic project at the European level.

Before Sweden announced its intent to join the EC, the LO had already established an office in Brussels. In *Swedish Labor Law in a European Perspective*, the LO called for strengthening the European labor movement to balance the increasing power of multinational companies, establishing common principles such as a mimimum wage system for workers, and cooperating closely with other trade unions within the EC's decision-making institutions.[76]

The LO has become increasingly dissatisfied with labor's economic policies and with proposals to align Norway's more solidaristic labor policies to EC policy regimes. In Sweden, on the other hand, the LO shared the pro-integrationist stance of the Social Democratic Party and officially endorsed EC membership—despite protests from within the labor movement.

Thus in the policy areas of currency, external security, and agriculture, we have witnessed important differences in the willingness and in the capacity of Norway's and Sweden's governments to resist the forces of Europeanization. Norway experienced greater societal resistance than Sweden in the EC campaign, and has not liberalized its agricultural policy to the CAP. Both states aligned their currencies to the ECU, yet Sweden, as an EC member state, will have to conform to the convergence requirements for EMU membership to a much greater extent than Norway. In national security policy, Sweden has reformed its conceptions of neutrality policy to permit full cooperation with the EC's efforts to create common foreign and security policies, accepting a greater role in European foreign policy making than in the past. Norway, on the other hand, found no compelling national security reason to join the EC. While its government seeks to keep all options open, and has pursued an associate agreement with the WEU, Norway remains strongly committed to NATO. In closing, let us turn to the changing role of German power in Scandinavia, and the implications of Denmark's experience in the EC for Sweden and Norway.

The Danish Model: Germany, the EC, and Euro-Corporatism

Denmark's experience in the EC is, in many ways, an indicator of where the other Scandinavian states are heading. As this analysis indicates, there

---

[76] Translated from *Svensk arbetsrätt i Europa-perspektiv* (Stockholm: Swedish Confederation of Trade Unions, 1992), pp. 14–15.

are now fewer and fewer differences between the policies of Denmark and those of Sweden and Norway. What has happened to Denmark in the EC? What does this suggest for the other Scandinavian states, now that Germany has become a more important trading partner and a more influential actor within the EC, as well as an important ally within EC institutions?

When Denmark joined the EC in 1973, Britain was Denmark's largest trading partner. The direction of trade has changed, however, and today Germany is a more important trading partner. In 1973, 20 percent of Danish exports went to Britain, as compared to 13 percent to Germany; by 1990, those trade statistics had turned around: 20 percent of Danish exports went to Germany and only 11 percent to Britain.[77] Thus the most significant change in Denmark's political economy is an increased dependence on both the EC and Germany. As Danish historian Hans Christian Johansen argues:

> The dominating position of Germany within the EEC [EC] means that German economic measures are much more important to Denmark, and the more penetrating integration in Europe becomes, the higher the Danish dependency on Germany will be. Typical signs of this process in the 1980s were the fixed exchange rate vis-à-vis the D-mark and the adjustment of wage and interest levels to German standards.[78]

As the Danish experience with European monetary cooperation suggests, a multilateral currency regime requires Scandinavian governments to abandon unilateral devaluations of their national currencies and to submit any revisions of parities for approval by all parties.

Sweden is undergoing what Denmark is long familiar with: EC-level constraints on its economic policies, and a greater dependence on Germany as a consequence of European integration. For example, to participate in the EMU, EC member states must meet specific requirements—the Maastricht convergence criteria. Inflation cannot exceed that of the best three countries by more than 1.5 percent, the budget deficit cannot be greater than 3 percent of GDP, long-term interest rates cannot exceed the two lowest rates by more than 2 percent, total public debt cannot exceed 60 percent of GDP, and the exchange rate of the national currency must remain within the range established by the European Monetary System (EMS) for two years. Swedish economic reports increasingly refer to the Maastricht convergence criteria, and compare Sweden's economic performance to EC imperatives.[79] As Sweden seeks to implement domestic re-

[77] Hans Christian Johansen, "The Danish Economy at the Crossroads between Scandinavia and Europe," *Scandinavian Journal of History* 18 (1993): 55.

[78] Ibid., p. 56.

[79] "Danish-Belgian Scenario," in *Outlook on the Swedish Economy* 1 (April 1995): and "A Brighter Outlook for 1995 and 1996," *Outlook on the Swedish Economy* 2 (June 1995): 1–2.

forms to meet these convergence criteria, dependence on Germany will deepen. As in Denmark, Germany has become Sweden's most important trading partner. When Sweden entered the EC, trade with Germany accounted for approximately 14 percent of 53 percent total Swedish exports to the European Community.[80]

What are the political effects of greater Scandinavian dependence on Germany? In the EC debates in Scandinavia, pro-integrationists advocated a "Nordic bloc" strategy as a way to counter the voting weight of larger states—most notably, Germany—in the Council of Ministers. In the Danish view, it is better to deal with a more powerful neighbor in a multilateral forum than be compelled to negotiate with it bilaterally. The legacy of the Second World War is still felt in Denmark and Norway, with some older members of the population hanging on to images of German militarism. Danes were even more cautious in their attitudes toward German unification than Norwegians, reflecting their historic ambivalence toward their southern neighbor.[81] The contemporary Scandinavian "Germanophobia," however, is based on economic concerns (Will Germany own us? Will Germans buy up our summer homes?). Swedes and Norwegians were encouraged by the Danes' success in establishing restrictions on the purchase of private property within the EC. Thus, in contrast to previous periods of Scandinavian foreign policy, integration is seen as a desirable means to mediate the influence of more powerful nations. Political leaders in Sweden and Denmark endorse intergovernmentalism and express an optimistic view of their capacity to influence the EC from within.

Germany also plays the role of an important political partner in the EC's complex web of institutions. Chancellor Helmut Kohl actively promoted Scandinavian accession, and the German foreign ministry has come to the defense of the Norwegians in tense disputes over fishing rights with the Spanish. In social and environmental policy, Scandinavian ambitions are in many ways compatible with the aims of German political leaders, with Scandinavian governments strongly endorsing Germany's efforts to integrate central European states in EC institutions.

The traditional distinctions made by scholars between the successful Social Democratic institutions and policies of the Swedish model, and the more liberal, less solidaristic institutions and policies of the Danish model are less and less apparent as all three states abide by the EC's internal market program. In the past, Sweden and Norway were committed to the pursuit of full employment; today, like Germany, they pursue anti-inflationary policies and price stability. Sweden has experienced Danish levels of unemployment since it began pursuing closer economic ties with the EC. In

---

[80] General Agreement on Tariffs and Trade, *Trade Policy Review: Sweden* (Geneva: 1995), p. 8.

[81] Christian Søe, "Denmark and Germany: From Ambivalence to Affirmation?" in Dirk Verheyen and Christian Søe, eds., *The Germans and Their Neighbors* (Boulder, Colo.: Westview Press, 1993), pp. 109–13.

Norway, unemployment has doubled, but still lags behind Sweden or Denmark. As the Scandinavian "middle way" between capitalism and socialism changes, Germany serves as an alternative model to Scandinavian corporatism.[82]

Thus pragmatic acceptance of a more powerful Germany and the legitimacy of the European integration project emerged in the midst of a profound crisis in the institutions and policies of the Scandinavian model. The distinctions between the solidaristic Scandinavian political economies and the more market-dependent political economies to the south have diminished, and are unlikely to be revived as European integration deepens.

Conclusion

The breakdown of Scandinavian corporatism was already in progress when Scandinavia's largest trading partner, the EC, introduced its reform measures in 1985. European integration has accelerated and deepened political change by structuring the substance and the direction of Scandinavian reforms. In three critical policy areas (currency, external security, and agriculture), Scandinavian governments have sought to adapt their policy regimes to conform to EC policy regimes. The changes in Scandinavian institutions and policies discussed in this chapter should be distinguished from other core Scandinavian policies (social welfare) facing tremendous domestic pressure for reform, yet only indirectly affected by European integration.

As Scandinavia's relationship to the EC changed, Germany became a more important trading partner and a political ally within the EC policy-making network. For Scandinavia, currency policy is the only area where an independent effect of Germany's influence is visible. In other policy areas, Germany's power is tamed and diffused by the complex network of EC institutions. Scandinavian governments view multilateralism as the appropriate means of mediating German power.

Scandinavians have always defined themselves as separate from the rest of Europe. In contrast to the southern or central European states, European integration could not offer Scandinavians more than national governments could deliver. The distinctiveness of national solutions and Scandinavia's perception of being better off than the rest of Europe has diminished, with important consequences for the acceptance of European integration in Scandinavian politics.

[82] See Jonas Pontusson, "Between Neoliberalism and the German Model," in Colin Crouch and Wolfgang Streeck, eds., *Political Economy of Modern Capitalism* (London: Sage, 1997), pp. 55–70.

Scandinavian governments no longer portray European integration as a threat to Social Democratic principles, and have, to varying degrees, sought to cooperate with the EC as a means of resolving problems at home. Scandinavian citizens, however, have been more skeptical about the Europeanization process than their governments. Since Sweden joined the EC in 1995, the Swedish public's opposition to the EC has increased. Sweden's rapid and surefooted accession has led many Swedes to question their new identity as EC members. Euro-skepticism is even stronger in oil-dependent Norway, where political coalitions seeking to preserve the policy legacies of postwar Scandinavian Social Democracy *outside the EC* remain strong.

CHAPTER SEVEN

Returning to Europe: Central Europe between Internationalization and Institutionalization

Włodek Anioł, Daneš Brzica, Timothy A. Byrnes,
Péter Gedeon, Hynek Jeřábek, Peter J. Katzenstein,
Zuzana Poláčková, Ivo Samson, and František Zich

"Central Europe" is an amorphous concept loaded with historical memories.[1] In the 1960s and 1970s the term had little political currency and was invoked only by a small number of historians specializing in the Habsburg empire or Friedrich Naumann's plans for an economic bloc in central Eu-

This chapter synthesizes the findings of Włodek Anioł and Timothy A. Byrnes, "Poland's 'Return to Europe'"; Daneš Brzica, Zuzana Poláčková, and Ivo Samson, "The Slovak Republic: Bridge between East and West"; Peter Gedeon, "German and EU Influence on the Postsocialist Transition in Hungary"; and Hynek Jeřábek and František Zich, "The Czech Republic: Internationalization and Dependency." These four papers were delivered at the workshop "Europe, Central Europe and Germany: Perspectives for the Future," Bratislava, Slovak Republic, March 7–9, 1996. They constitute the bulk of a forthcoming volume on Germany and central Europe: Peter J. Katzenstein, ed., *Mitteleuropa: Between Europe and Germany* (Providence, R.I.: Berghahn Books). The authors thank Péter Hanák and the participants of workshops in Budapest, Bratislava, at the Institute of World Economy in Budapest, and the colloquium at European University Viadrina in Frankfurt for their comments on prior drafts.

[1] "Central Europe" here refers to Poland, Hungary, and the Czech and Slovak Republics. Naming this geographic area implies a form of identity politics fraught with difficulties. "East central Europe," for example, defines this region so that it includes as well many of the other Eastern European states such as Romania, Bulgaria, and perhaps the Balkan states and Russia. For the purposes of this essay, that definition is too broad. Referring to the region with a capital letter, as "Central Europe," creates an artificial reification that tends toward exclusion. Regions such as central Europe are specific constructs serving particular analytical or political purposes. For a discussion of problems of naming and identity politics, see Iver B. Neumann, "Russia as Central Europe's Constituting Other," *East European Politics and Society* 7 (Spring 1993): 349–69. For brief overviews, see also "Germany, Democracy, and Mitteleuropa," special issue of *German Politics and Society* 28 (Spring 1993); and Tamás Szemlér, ed., *Relations between Germany and East Central Europe until 2000: Prospects and Policy Options* (Budapest: Institute for World Economics of the Hungarian Academy of Sciences, 1994).

rope early in the twentieth century. But by the early 1980s, "central Europe" had come to express the political aspirations of some of the members of the democratic opposition in Poland, Hungary, and Czechoslovakia. During the Cold War there was no center in a world that was divided between East and West. Poland, Hungary, and Czechoslovakia were part of "Eastern Europe," dominated by the Soviet Union. From the perspective of western Europe, all of this changed rapidly when, in the early summer of 1989, the Hungarian government cut the barbed wire on its Austrian border. This created a trickle of refugees that, a few months later, became a flood lapping over the Berlin Wall, rushing through narrow openings, washing away its foundations, and thus leaving open borders and empty spaces in the center of Berlin, Germany, and Europe.

Differences in the roads that the now four central European states have traveled in the 1990s, away from "state socialism" and the Soviet empire, tell us how misleading terms like "Eastern Europe" were then. It was not one version but various national forms of Communism that the Red Army implanted in central Europe after 1945. Today's central European states all face similarly daunting tasks of political and economic transformation. But the similarity in tasks highlights the differences in their political choices. History matters. The role of the Catholic Church in Poland, the Hungarian reforms of 1968–72, and the occupation of Czechoslovakia after 1968—these political experiences are all closely connected to the diversity of political regimes and political strategies that have emerged since 1989. Furthermore, the different experiences with Germany in the 1930s and 1940s, and in the more distant past, have shaped collective memories with noticeable effects on how the central European states have since 1989 reacted in their relations with Germany and Europe to the disjunction between rapid internationalization and slow institutionalization.

Central Europe thus has no objective characteristics that determine its politics either before or after 1989. With the end of the Cold War and the rapid disappearance of Soviet and Russian influence, Germany and Europe have, to varying degrees, affected the central European states through markets and bilateral ties. Although the effects of multilateral European institutions are beginning to be noticeable in some areas for some countries, such as Poland and minority rights, until all four central European states become members of the European Union (EU) and NATO, these effects will remain relatively small.

While waiting for the process of political enlargement to take its course, the central European states are building institutional bridges of their own; the economic failures of the past give special urgency to the experiments of the present. Reform policies in central Europe aim at imitating successful institutions and practices in other European states. Compared to western Europe's, central Europe's average per capita GDP fell from 45 percent in 1913 to 41 percent in 1950; by 1973, it had once again increased to 45 percent, before plummeting to 25 percent in 1990. Put differently, the gap between western and central Europe has widened from 2:1 to 4:1 in less than two decades, one measure of the magnitude of the crisis of state socialism that led to its implosion.[2] Almost by default, the central European states turned for solutions toward the capitalist, democratic, prosperous, and internationalized welfare states in western Europe.

Despite this similarity in their orientation and basic commitment to political reform, important differences exist in the strength of nationalist and internationalist forces in each of the four central European states. In Poland, for example, the main cleavage of the past pits former supporters of the Communist regime against those of Solidarity. But lurking just under the surface is the division between "cosmopolitans" or "internationalists," who seek to move rapidly along all fronts toward Europe, and "true Poles" or "nationalists," who fear too close a link to Europe as a potential threat to Poland's autonomy. The difference between internationalism and nationalism exists not only within states but also between them. In virtually all aspects of its political life, the Czech Republic is steering a strong Western course. For a variety of reasons, the Slovak Republic is not.

Before World War I, the central European states did not exist as such; they were part of the Habsburg empire or, in the case of Poland, divided up among Russia, Prussia, and Austria. Despite political alliances with France and other states, during the interwar years Poland, Hungary, and Czechoslovakia were sucked into Germany's economic, diplomatic, and military sphere of influence. After 1945, they were forced into the orbit of the Soviet Union. Since 1989, these now four states are seizing their first opportunity in this century to buffer international, and especially German, influences through the creation of institutional similarities at home and the gradual forging of multilateral links abroad. Judging by the experiences of states on the western, northern, and southern periphery of Europe, their success will depend less on developing new social and economic relationships with Germany and Europe and more on redefining traditional central European norms and interests through new domestic and international institutions. The varying strength of institutionalization and internationalization in Poland, Hungary, and the Czech and Slovak Republics is most evident in four issue areas: the import and export of institutions, minority rights, national security, and economic and social policies.

[2] Iván T. Berend, "Európa! De miért?" [Europe! But why?], *Népszabadság* [Peoples' Liberty] (January 28, 1995): 17.

Importing and Exporting Institutions

The process of transferring institutions across state borders is of great importance as creating potential buffers that, in the absence of common membership in multilateral institutions such as the EU or NATO, can also soften the impact of rapid internationalization. The central European states have imported some institutional models from the West in modified form, such as Hungary's adaptation of the Bundesbank model. But these states also seek to export some of their own institutions. Poland's Catholic Church, for example, is committed to remake secular western Europe in its own image. In either case, it is not simply a matter of shipping institutional blueprints across state borders. Rather, institutions emerge from contested policies, which, over time, alter both new blueprints and old practices.

Hungary's National Bank

Although, under Communism, the planning bureaucracy of the state dominated the national bank, Hungary began reforming its banking system in the early 1980s. Limited decentralization in monetary institutions created what, in the 1990s, would become Hungary's small- and medium-sized commercial banks; by 1987, a two-tiered banking system had been set up. But it was only with the legislation passed by parliament after 1991 that a fundamentally new framework was created.

After 1989, the economic reformers in all parties agreed on the desirability of creating an autonomous national bank as an essential safeguard for a normally functioning market economy. The national bank drafted the new legislation in-house. Even without German advisors, this draft reflected the German model. Hungarian economic reformers had simply looked around Europe and found in the Bundesbank the most autonomous national bank worth imitating. The attraction of the German model was reinforced when, in the preparations for the Treaty on European Union (TEU), German pressure succeeded in having the Bundesbank serve also as a model for the Central European Bank (CEB). German institutional practices and the Hungarian reformers' strong orientation to Europe thus joined hands. They found concrete expression in the commitment to create an autonomous national bank in Hungary.

In the debate over the new bank legislation, the government, for obvious political reasons, tried to rein in the bank's autonomy, while the opposition pushed hard for a totally autonomous bank. In the end, a political compromise was reached. Government pressure resulted in some specific administrative and political regulations, as well as the provision that the national bank be permitted to engage in limited deficit financing operations.[3] By international standards Hungary's national bank is legally more autonomous than those of France and Italy, while in legal terms, it is less autonomous than the Bundesbank.[4]

Since parliament established the national bank in 1991, the government has looked for ways to diminish the bank's autonomy. For example, Prime Minister Jozsef Antall proposed a member of his inner circle of advisors in the Hungarian Democratic Forum (HDF), Peter Akos Bod, as the first head of the bank in 1991. Although, following the requirements of the law, Bod resigned his seat in parliament and suspended his membership in the HDF, with his appointment the government sought to circumvent the bank's institutional autonomy through informal, personal channels. After its election victory of 1994, the new coalition of socialists and liberals let it be known that it would welcome a change at the head of the bank. Appointed for a term of six years, Bod resigned his post within six months.

At the initiative of the government, and over the bank's determined opposition, parliament modified in 1993 the Act on the National Bank of Hungary and voted the bank a lump sum loan of 80 billion Hungarian Forints ($723 million) to help finance the budget deficit for fiscal 1994. The ceiling limiting the bank's deficit financing operation was raised from 3 to 5 percent of GDP. The net effect of this change in policy was that state bonds and treasury bills crowded out private capital from Hungary's relatively underdeveloped capital markets. As a result, fiscal rather than monetary policy came to dominate the formation of Hungarian interest rates.[5] After several short cycles of stop-go policies, of increasing and decreasing interest rates, and after acrimonious political debates, the liberal-socialist coalition government settled on a policy of austerity that has eroded its legitimacy in the eyes of large segments of the electorate since its 1994 election victory.

The deficits in Hungary's balance of payments and budget as well as Hungary's inflation rate far exceed the convergence indicators that the TEU specifies, with no stable Hungarian exchange rate likely in the foreseeable future. Looking beyond the severe political and economic constraints of the current period of economic transformation, Hungary may

[3] The amendment to the Act on the National Bank of Hungary (NBH) passed in 1993 stipulates that the amount of the loans given to the state budget is unlimited in 1992, is 5 percent instead of 3 percent of GDP in 1993, and will be Ft 80 billion ($722 million) in 1994.

[4] John B. Goodman, *Monetary Sovereignty: The Politics of Central Banking in Western Europe* (Ithaca: Cornell University Press, 1992), p. 11.

[5] Éva Várhegyi, "A monetáris politika és közvetítő rendszere a piacgazdasági átmenet útján," [Monetary Policy and Its System of Mediation on the Way of Transformation toward a Market Economy], unpublished paper, Budapest, p. 48; Éva Várhegyi, "Monetáris és bankpolitika: A rendszerváltozás első kormányának mérlege," [Monetary and Banking Policy: The Balance of the First Government of System Change], *Külgazdaság*, [International Economy] 4 (1994): 39–52.

eventually seek greater exchange rate stability, gradually move toward a harder-currency policy, and thus emulate states like Spain that have walked the same difficult path during the last decade. But for now the time is not right.

The head of the Bundesbank, Helmut Schlesinger, has suggested that, in the interest of exchange rate stability, the Hungarian forint be explicitly pegged to the deutsche mark.[6] But in the 1990s the Bundesbank and German monetary policy offer no workable institutional model or set of policies for Hungary. Hence, to date, Hungary's national bank has not followed the German suggestion. And under current levels of internal and external indebtedness, the monetary targets specified for Hungary's membership in the European Monetary Union (EMU) are simply impracticable. The deep recession accompanying the process of economic transformation and the electoral constraints of democratic politics simply make it impossible for the government to trade in some of its room for maneuver in monetary policy for a more stable national currency.

Poland's Catholic Church

During the Communist era, the Catholic Church was a decisive vehicle of opposition to the political system. The church hierarchy acted as a kind of alternative authority structure to the party-state, an authentically Polish counterpoint to a Soviet-imposed regime. This role had historical antecedents. During World War II, Stefan Wyszyński, chaplain to the Polish underground and future primate of Poland, squarely identified the church with armed resistance to Nazi rule, and with the dramatic resurgence in Polish nationalism that the occupation created. Indeed, for Cardinal Wyszyński, and for the church he led until his death in 1982, Catholicism was an integral element of Polish nationalism. A "Catholic Poland" was an indispensable signal of the limits of twentieth-century totalitarianism. Today, it offers a direct challenge to the conditions now prevailing in Germany and the EU.[7] But in democratic Poland the position of the church has also become problematic. Democratic pluralism raises the prospects of a progressive secularization of society and of an eventual rejection of Poland's deeply Catholic cultural heritage.

The church thus opposes a headlong rush to rejoin what Pope John Paul II has called Europe's "civilization of desire and consumption."[8]

[6] Schlesinger made his proposal in a lecture delivered at the Budapest University of Economics in March 1993. *Népszabadság* (April 2, 1993): 5.

[7] See Ewa Morawska, "Civil Religion versus State Power in Poland," in Thomas Robbins and Roland Robertson, eds., *Church-State Relations: Tensions and Transitions* (New Brunswick, N.J.: Transaction Books, 1987), pp. 221–32.

[8] "Pope Calls Poland to Resist Western Europe's Secular Ways," *New York Times* (June 8, 1991): A3.

Poland's isolation from western Europe over the last fifty years has preserved a cultural distinctiveness the church is committed to preserving
and a pervasive religiosity the church would like to see reignited throughout the continent. For these reasons, Polish Catholic leaders prefer to speak
not of Poland's "return to Europe"[9] but rather of Poland's reassertion of
its historic role as the bulwark of Roman Christianity in central Europe.
Standing astride both the religious and political dividing lines of Europe,
the Polish church wants Poland to serve as an instrument of the reevan-
gelization of the Orthodox East, and as a spiritual and moral exemplar to
the secular West. Poland's responsibility to preserve its distinctiveness, its
"Catholicity" if you will, in the face of the secular commercialism of western Europe is as clear and compelling as its responsibility had been to resist Communism and foreign domination before 1989. Put another way,
the church is not so much interested in Poland rejoining Europe as it is in
inviting Europe to rejoin Poland in a renewed commitment to its shared
Christian heritage.

This grand, even grandiose, vision of Catholic Poland's role in the
emerging new Europe has had a profound effect on the church's approach
to Polish politics in recent years. The church has welcomed the re-creation
of a democratic Poland. But it has aggressively defended its institutional
interests in the new political order, and it has just as aggressively asserted
its views on central political issues from abortion, to economic restructuring, to entrance into the European Union. The church's leaders correctly
view themselves as having been central agents in the political transformation that took place in 1989. They are now insisting that they play an
equally central role in determining the direction that transformation will
take in the future.

John Paul II's election, and his triumphant return to Poland in the Spring
of 1979, played an important part in the creation of Solidarity the following year, the subsequent weakening of the Polish regime, and the eventual
disintegration of the Soviet bloc. The pope's primary role in the transformation of European politics was to reveal the utter failure that Soviet Communism had experienced in the attempt to impose its will on the hearts of
Poles and other central Europeans. If, as Stalin once said, Communism fit
Poland like a saddle fit a cow, then John Paul II's papacy represented the
enduring distinctiveness of the Polish cow. His very existence as a stubbornly independent and fiercely pious Polish Catholic, and the ecstasy with
which his election was greeted in his homeland, symbolized the survival of
a culturally and socially independent Poland, despite more than three
decades of Soviet-imposed Communist rule. The Polish pope would embody, celebrate, and advance that independence with all the considerable
and varied tools available to the modern papacy.

[9] Indeed, the pope has dismissed such a formulation as a "humiliation." Ibid.

The pope has used every conceivable venue to forcefully articulate his views: during his first pilgrimage to Poland after he had been elected pope; in one of his earliest encyclicals, *Slavum Apostoli;* and during his first, triumphant trip back to post-Communist Poland in 1991. His voice has been joined by those of the national leaders of Poland's Catholic Church. In August 1995, Cardinal Józef Glemp, speaking to 100,000 pilgrims at Jasna Góra Monastery in Czestochowa, pronounced Poland's entry into the European Union a "moral issue," not merely an economic one. Poles should be wary of the potential threat EU membership poses to Polish national identity.[10]

Such a vision of the world requires the church's active and sustained participation in Polish political life. On issues of church-state relations, religious instructions in the school, the ratification of the 1993 concordat with the Vatican, on vital social issues such as abortion, and in partisan politics, such as the presidential election of 1995—in all of these the church has chosen a high-profile, relentlessly activist stance.[11] Its mission could not have tolerated less. If the church could not operate freely on what it considers vital issues in Poland, how could it hope to succeed in its broader European mission?

This stance reflected not simply Catholicism in a democratizing polity but, uniquely, Polish Catholicism, as a brief comparison with Spanish Catholicism readily illustrates. The Spanish church, which had, to say the least, a long and storied history of active political involvement in Spain, adopted a very different approach to the rebirth of democracy in its own country during the 1970s. Despite its increasingly vocal, and politically significant, opposition to Franco's regime, the Spanish Catholic hierarchy played a remarkably restrained role in Spanish politics immediately following the transition to democracy.[12]

[10] Cardinal Glemp's sermon was reported on August 16, 1995, under the headline "To Which Europe? At Jasna Góra, Primate Glemp Strongly Criticized the Poles Striving to Join Europe," *FBIS-EEU* (August 17, 1995): 32.

[11] One of the ramifications of Aleksander Kwaśniewski's victory in the 1995 presidential elections is likely to be a reform of Poland's strict antiabortion law. At the moment, abortions are allowed in cases of rape, incest, irreparable fetal deformity, and when the woman's life or health would be threatened by carrying the pregnancy to term. Doctors performing abortions for other, so-called social reasons, face prison terms of up to two years. A bill substantially easing these restrictions on elective abortions was passed by the Sejm in 1994, but was vetoed by then-President Lech Wałęsa. Following the elections, the ruling coalition has announced its support for a law that would permit legal abortions up to twelve weeks of pregnancy if a woman felt she could not afford to give birth to a baby, or if she was experiencing other unidentified personal difficulties. The Sejm approved this limited "abortion on demand" bill in the fall of 1996; President Kwaśniewski signed it into law in November, 1996.

[12] There is a substantial literature on the role of the church in Spanish politics both before and after the transformation to democracy. See, for example, Juan J. Linz, "Religion and Politics in Spain: From Conflict to Consensus above Cleavage," *Social Compass* 27 (1980): 255–77; Richard Gunther and Roger A. Blough, "Religious Conflict and Consensus in

While not quite retreating to a monastic asceticism, the Spanish bishops have limited themselves to what some of them termed an "active neutrality" with regard to both partisan electoral politics and a host of controversial public policy issues."[13] Sensitive to the historically close relationship between the church and right-wing political forces, the bishops were committed to preventing a return of the virulent anticlericalism of the Spanish Republic. As a result, they not only eschewed personal intervention in Spanish politics, they also largely "abandoned [their] traditional attempt to enter political society through the mobilization of the Catholic laity."[14] The bishops were active in encouraging a smooth transition to democracy and in calling for a retention in Spanish society of traditional Catholic values. But they were neutral as to the particular political direction the transition should take. The church, in a sense, turned inward following the change in political regime, and allowed religion and morality to be "privatized" in Spanish society.[15] Thus the active pursuit of Spain's European vocation in the 1980s was not burdened by a domestic Catholic opposition articulating a different ideological view of Europe.

Coming out of a very different national and ecclesiastical history, the Polish bishops have demanded much more than a spiritually forthright but politically neutral role in post-Communist Poland. The church's close identification with Polish nationalism, its powerful role in the dawning of Polish democracy, and not incidentally, its special relationship with a Vatican headed by a Polish pope have all combined to call forward a Polish episcopate deeply involved not only in Polish politics and public policy but also in the fundamental debate over Poland's proper place in the society of European states.

One of the central projects of European integration is the partial assimilation of individual nationalisms into a more encompassing European collective identity. While the general prospects for such a development are, at the very least, uncertain, it is likely that the Catholic Church will pose an especially troublesome barrier in Poland. Like cultural leaders in many other countries, the Polish Catholic bishops are anxious to retain and protect Polish national distinctiveness as they embark upon a new and deeper relationship with the European community of nations. Unlike most other cultural leaders, however, the Polish bishops also want that distinctiveness—namely, Poland's national Catholic identity—to serve as

---

Spain: A Tale of Two Constitutions," *World Affairs* 143 (1981): 366–412; Stanley G. Payne, *Spanish Catholicism: An Historical Overview* (Madison: University of Wisconsin Press, 1984); and José Casanova, *Public Religions in the Modern World* (Chicago: University of Chicago Press, 1994), pp. 75–91.
[13] Payne, *Spanish Catholicism*, p. 216.
[14] Casanova, *Public Religions*, p. 89.
[15] Ibid., p. 90.

the cornerstone of a fundamental transformation of the wider community. Theirs is a vision that is as grand as the idea of European union itself. But it is also a vision that fundamentally challenges the principles and processes on which that union has been based for four decades.

In the absence of common membership in multilateral institutions, importing or exporting national institutions is one way of buffering the effects of internationalization, although attempting to import or export them wholesale, as in the case of the Hungary's national bank and Poland's Catholic Church, is the exception. More typically, national institutions emerge piecemeal from policy experimentations that are informed by the push and pull of daily politics and the strategic calculations of political actors rather than encompassing institutional blueprints.

MINORITY RIGHTS: BETWEEN WESTERN AND CENTRAL EUROPE

In contrast to western Europe, central European states hold to an ethnic rather than a civic definition of national identity. What does this difference tell us about the treatment of ethnic minorities in central Europe? Remembering the Holocaust and brutal, large-scale policies of ethnic cleansing by Nazi Germany, many political observers point to questions of ethnic relations as the acid test by which to judge whether central Europe and Germany really have been "Westernized." The evidence of the 1990s is inconclusive. While the war in Yugoslavia points in one direction, the peaceful breakup of Czechoslovakia points in another. The treatment of national minorities and the consequences for bilateral relations in central Europe show substantial variation between the Western institutional model (Polish-German relations) and a central European model (Slovak-Hungarian relations).

German Minority in Poland

For centuries a multiethnic society, Poland developed a strong sense of collective identity, in the nineteenth century, becoming, for the first time in modern history, a virtually homogeneous state after 1945. Where ethnic minorities amounted to about 30 percent of the Polish population during the interwar period, since 1945 they account for less than 5 percent.[16]

[16] Ethnic minorities in Poland include about 300,000 Ukrainians (scattered around the country), 200,000–250,000 Belarussians (living mainly in the Podlasie region in eastern Poland), 20,000–30,000 Roma, 20,000–25,000 Lithuanians (Puńsk and Sejny districts in the northeast), 20,000 Slovaks (southern Poland), and 10,000–15,000 Jews. This ethnic mosaic is completed by small communities of Russians, Greeks, Armenians, Czechs, and Tatars. *Mniejszości narodowe w Polsce i polityka państwa polskiego wobec nich* [National Minorities in Poland and Polish State Policy] (Warsaw: Office for Culture of National Minorities at the Ministry of Culture and Art, September 15, 1995), p. 1; and Ryszard Walicki, *Mniejszości narodowe w Polsce w*

The most important minority, ethnic Germans number 300,000–500,000, concentrated mostly in Silesia but also in the Warmia and Mazury region. They stayed behind when some three million were expelled from the territories Poland acquired east of the Oder and the Lusatian Neisse as a result of the Potsdam Conference and when another million left between 1955 and 1989. Most of these Germans identified themselves as Silesians, Mazurians, Warmians, or Kashubes first, and as Germans or Poles second. But the postwar policy of assimilation and the exodus of the 1970s and 1980s has revived German ethnic sentiments. The Communist government insisted that no German ethnic minority existed any longer in Poland while, at the same time, issuing exit visas to more than half a million persons who had incontrovertible proof they were German.[17] It took the democratic revolution to change this schizophrenic policy.

European minority rights are predicated on the presumption that the country of residence has the right to expect as much civic loyalty from the members of its minorities as from all other citizens. With the distinctions between individual and collective rights beginning to erode, European norms for the treatment of minorities are in flux. Through its membership in the Organization for Security and Cooperation in Europe (OSCE) since the beginning of the Helsinki process in the mid-1970s, and in the European Council since 1991, Poland has affected, and been affected by, this shift in norms. Although not legally binding, the Commission on Security and Cooperation in Europe (CSCE) document on the "Human Dimension," passed in Copenhagen in June 1990, offers the most advanced protection of minority rights, including an explicit acknowledgment of individual and, less securely, collective minority rights.[18] The Council of Europe has opened for signature two conventions, for regional or minority languages (1992) and for the protection of national minorities (1995). Although Poland is party to the second convention, ratification requirements are so restrictive it may take years before the convention becomes legally binding.

These shifts in European norms, expressed as much as political as legal standards, have affected Poland's bilateral relations with all of its neigh-

---

1992 r. w świetle badań empirycznych [National Minorities in Poland in 1992 in Light of Empirical Studies] (Warsaw: Office for Studies and Expertises, Chancellery of Sejm, 1993), pp. 1–4.

[17] For a more comprehensive treatment of ethnic Germans in Poland, see Cezary Żołędowski, "Mniejszości narodowe w Polsce" [National Minorities in Poland] in Anton Rajkiewicz, ed., *Społeczeństwo polskie w latach 1989–93: Wybrane zagadnienia i dane z zakresu polityki społecznej* [Polish Society in 1989–93: Selected Issues and Data on Social Policy] (Warsaw: Friedrich Ebert Foundation, 1994).

[18] Jan Barcz, "Protection of National Minorities under the CSCE System and European Standards," *Polish Quarterly of International Affairs* 1 (Summer/Autumn 1992): 170. See also Jan Barcz, "European Standards for the Protection of National Minorities with Special Regard to the CSCE: Present State and Conditions of Development," in Arie Bloed and W. de Jonge, eds., *Legal Aspects of a New European Infrastructure* (Utrecht: University of Utrecht, 1992).

bors. Where once Poland had three neighbors (the Soviet Union, Czechoslovakia, and the GDR), now it has seven (Russia, Lithuania, Belarus, Ukraine, the Czech and Slovak Republics, and Germany). In a series of political declarations and through the signing of bilateral treaties between 1991 and 1994, the Polish government affirmed the protection of minority rights with all of its neighbors. In negotiating these treaties, Poland agreed with its partners not to look for "special solutions" or separate provisions modeled on central European, prewar ideas. Instead, western European standards became the foundation for resolving minority questions in bilateral relations; specifically, Poland modeled its treaties after the most advanced standards articulated by the CSCE.

It did this also in cooperation with the German government: through joint declarations during Chancellor Helmut Kohl's November 1989 visit, through the treaty of November 14, 1990, confirming the Oder-Neisse border as definitive, and through the "Treaty on Good-Neighbourly Relations and Friendly Cooperation" of June 17, 1991. Following the Copenhagen Declaration, the second treaty emphasizes the obligations of states to protect their minorities,[19] as well as these minorities' identities; their rights to education, association, and participation in public affairs; and their freedom of religion and of association. In other areas, such as minorities' equal access to legal remedies for asserting their rights, equal access to regional media, and right to use the mother tongue version of their forenames and surnames, the treaty goes even further than the Copenhagen Declaration.[20]

The adoption of international norms in the treatment of minorities was made possible by Poland's democratic revolution. Minority affairs were moved from the jurisdiction of the Ministry of Internal Affairs to the Ministry of Culture and Art,[21] which has resulted in a veritable explosion in the number of publications issued by minority groups, in their access to radio and TV, and in changes in curricula, to include German instruction in kindergarten and vocational schools, as well as in primary and post-primary classes if a minimum number of students so request.[22]

Since the roundtable discussions in spring 1989, all ethnic minorities have the right to form their own unlicensed associations, with independent

[19] The "Document of the Copenhagen Meeting on the Human Dimension" of the CSCE was adopted on June 29, 1990.

[20] Unavoidably, some issues remained unresolved in the June 17, 1991, treaty, for example, German designation of place-names in traditionally German areas of settlement.

[21] See *Mniejszości narodowe w Polsce w 1993 r.* [National Minorities in Poland in 1993] (Warsaw: Ministry of Culture and Art, Office of National Minorities, 1994).

[22] The minimum numbers of students are seven for primary school and fourteen for post-primary schools. Despite these improvements, some doubts have been raised whether these provisions fully meet the language needs of minorities. See *Some Remarks on National Minorities in Poland: The Protection of Their Rights, Achievements and Failures* (Helsinki Foundation for Human Rights: Warsaw, May 1993).

sources of income. By the mid-1990s, a total of 120 such associations existed, half of them for the German minority, compared to only seven during the Communist era. The electoral law for the parliamentary elections of October 1991 reduced the number of signatures required for the registration of candidates representing national minorities, as opposed to ethnic Polish candidates. As a result, representatives of the German minority entered the lower house of parliament (Sejm) with seven deputies, and the Senate with one senator; the German deputies formed the "Parliamentary Group of the German Minority." Moreover, legislation passed in May 1993 exempted minority parties from having to meet a nationwide minimum threshold of 5 percent of the vote to enter the Sejm.[23]

The Europeanization of Poland's minority policy has led to a dramatic improvement in Polish-German relations. In the 1980s, the German government pressed unsuccessfully for the recognition of the German minority in Poland; the Union of German Expellees (BdV) tried to tie that demand to the broader issue of the Oder-Neisse frontier. The Polish reforms of the 1990s have led to a remarkable relaxation in bilateral relations. The German government now provides financial assistance to the German minority, keeping the Polish government informed and directing its aid to regional infrastructure improvements, thus helping non-Germans as well.[24]

Despite the enormous improvements in German-Polish relations and in the political conditions of the German minority in Poland, some serious problems remain. On both sides of the border, extreme German nationalists continue to make Poles in Silesia suspicious that the recognition of a German minority may eventually open the way to the growth of a German fifth column in Poland. The situation is aggravated by some Silesians in Germany who still hope that Silesia will eventually become part of Germany and whose organizations, like the BdV, are subsidized by the German authorities.[25] Some of these radical claims have strongly influenced representatives of the German minority in Poland. The Central Council of German Associations, for example, has asked both the Polish and the

[23] In 1995, the German minority in Poland had four deputies and one senator, while the Ukrainian minority had one deputy.

[24] Some subsidies go only to members of the German minority, for example, benefits for the aged and disabled and salaries for the functionaries of minority organizations. According to information received by the Polish Foreign Ministry, this aid amounted to about DM 46 million in 1993. While the German Foreign Ministry covers expenses for culture and education, the German Ministry of Interior deals with social assistance.

[25] In 1990, for example, Hartmut Koschyk, the secretary-general of the BdV, called on the government of the Federal Republic to secure a clearly privileged status and special rights for the Germans in Opole, Silesia. He wanted the Silesian question to be internationalized, and he demanded assistance in the settlement of this region by descendants of its former inhabitants. He also demanded that the areas along the Oder and Neisse rivers somehow be formally incorporated into the EC. See also Patricia Davis, "Ethnic Germans in Poland: Bridge Builders or a New Source of Conflict," *German Politics and Society* 31 (Spring 1994): 24–46.

German governments to confer dual nationality on Germans domiciled in Poland. And it has also sought special legal protection from the Federal Republic and closer cooperation between German organizations in Poland and refugee associations in Germany. The major complaint of the German minority is not with Poland's legal framework and national politics but with the ill will and hostility of local governments.[26] In sum, while the ethnic politics of the past is still visible, especially at local levels, developments in the 1990s illustrate that Europeanization holds great promise to lead to a permanent improvement of Poland's minority policies and its relations with all of its neighbors, including Germany.

Hungarian Minority in the Slovak Republic

Compared to the strength of European standards in the treatment of the German minority in Poland, the position of the Hungarian minority in the Slovak Republic reflects both the powerful hold of traditional, central European conceptions of nationality as well as intense political infighting in Bratislava. About 15–20 percent of the current Slovak population of 5.3 million belong to ethnic minorities, mostly Hungarians (600,000–800,000), Roma (250,000–500,000), and Czechs (60,000). Spurred by Nazi Germany's atrocities and occupation, Czechoslovakia's forcible resettlement of ethnic Germans after World War II left in 1950 only 6,000 of the more than 150,000 Germans who had lived in Slovakia in 1930.[27]

Hungarians are compactly settled between the Danube and the southern border of the modern Slovak Republic. Incorporated for many cen-

[26] Henryk Kroll, chairman of the German Minority's Parliamentary Caucus, said in an interview: "We have particularly painful relations with the authorities in Opole province. Starting with general matters, this shows itself in the one-sided interpretation of the Polish-German Treaty: not respecting our right to tradition, to have our own schools, and so on." *Warsaw Voice* (July 18, 1993): 9. Specific complaints that Germans in Poland tend to articulate include the right of former Polish citizens of German origin to return to Poland and purchase real estate; the right to form minority-based political parties; the introduction of the use of bilingual versions of the names of localities where the German minority dominates in a region; the right to use the mother tongue in contacts with the Polish state or, more far-reaching, recognition of German as a second official language in areas with a strong minority population; the right of persons forcibly drafted into the Wehrmacht to include their years of service in their calculations of pension rights; as well as claims that some provisions of the Polish-German treaty are inadequate and require revision and calls for changes in the status of Opole Silesia. In sharp contrast, other German minority organizations and German nongovernmental organizations operating in Poland define their principal objective to build more bridges between Germans and Poles. The foundations of Germany's main political parties, for example, seek to act as "catalysts" for the further Europeanization of Poland. See an interview with Gösta Thiemer, head of the Konrad Adenauer Foundation in Warsaw, in *Warsaw Voice* (July 4, 1993): 7.

[27] Georg Brunner, *Nationalitätenprobleme und Minderheitskonflikte in Osteuropa* (Ebenhausen: Foundation for Political Science,1993), p. 117; Dieter W. Bricke, *Minderheiten im östlichen Mitteleuropa: Deutsche und Europäische Optionen* (Baden-Baden: Nomos, 1995), p. 97.

turies in the Habsburg empire, and after 1867 in the empire's eastern half, administered by Hungary, Slovakia became part of Czechoslovakia at the end of World War I. A relatively liberal minority policy during the interwar years is one reason why the Hungarian population in Slovakia has preserved its distinctive identity. The nationalist fervor surrounding the 1993 breakup of Czechoslovakia fed the fears of Slovaks living in the southern part of the country, where they were a minority in their newly constituted state. Slovaks and Hungarians have engaged in a war of symbols that may poison political relations for years to come. For example, while the Slovak Ministry of Transport ordered the removal of Hungarian village signs, the Hungarian minority built memorials commemorating Horthy's occupation of southern Slovakia during World War II. Lurking behind the symbols is the specter of violence. The Hungarian parties in the Slovak Republic have, to date, succeeded in blocking the government's attempt to reorganize the Slovak armed forces so that one of its parts would become a Border Guard.

Slovak-Hungarian relations have been influenced by both European norms and domestic constitutional provisions. The Slovak Republic's constitutional provisions are in full agreement with European standards such as Articles 20–22 of the Council of Europe Framework Convention for the Protection of National Minorities. And the Slovak constitution of September 1992 contains the "Charter for the Protection of Human Rights and Fundamental Freedoms" found also in the Czech constitution.

But these constitutional protections of minority rights have not been free from criticism. Some Slovaks, for example, have criticized a constitutional provision that lets individuals freely choose to join a specific national minority, as especially members of the Roma minority do. Slovak language laws have also met with criticism. The Hungarian minority often criticized a relatively liberal law, in force until November 1995, that regulated the use of minority languages. And it has condemned outright the elimination of many of the provisions protecting minority rights in the new law, which, for example, prohibits bilingualism and restricts the official use of minority languages to instances where the minority constitutes at least 20 percent in a village or town.

The Hungarian minority has insisted on the official recognition of the Hungarian versions of first and family names; on the use of Hungarian street and village signs alongside Slovak ones; on the revocation of a postwar decree that declares the Hungarian minority in Slovakia to have been collectively guilty in their conduct during World War II; and on the redrawing of administrative boundaries. Hungarians point to the silence in the Slovak constitution and relevant legislation about the necessary financial support for the constitutionally mandated educational and cultural affairs of the national minorities in the Slovak Republic. Most important, the Hungarian minority points to the preamble of the Slovak constitution, which enshrines the central European rather than the western European tradition of ethnic and national identity. It reads: "We the Slovak nation," rather than "We citizens of Slovakia."

Hungary's constitutional provisions and domestic and foreign policies tended to aggravate the Slovak situation in the early 1990s. By stipulating that Hungary is responsible for the welfare of ethnic Hungarians living abroad and that the government must support the relations between these minorities and Hungary, the Hungarian constitution introduces an ethnic notion of nationality into Hungarian foreign policy. Indeed, the Hungarian government has consistently intervened on the side of the Hungarian minority in Slovakia, and did so particularly strongly when the Slovak parliament rejected a constitutional revision put forward by the Hungarian minority to reword the preamble of the Slovak constitution. By sending the complaint of four ethnic Hungarian parties in the Slovak Republic to the Council of Europe, the Hungarian government aligned itself with the position of radical elements among Slovakia's Hungarian minority. Given this Hungarian policy, it is not surprising that, since 1990, representatives of the Hungarian minority have engaged the Hungarian MDF (Hungarian Democratic Forum) and its more nationalist successor rather than the Slovak government in a permanent dialogue on the issue of minority rights.

The Liberal and Socialist opposition to Prime Minister Jozsef Antall's government strongly criticized these contacts and insisted that recognition of the inviolability of borders should be part of any agreement seeking to secure Hungarian minority rights in the Slovak Republic. When the socialist-liberal government was elected in Hungary in 1994, it organized its foreign policy around three major goals: European integration, the stabilization of relations with Hungary's neighbors, and bilateral guarantees for Hungarian minorities living in other countries including the Slovak Republic. In this manner, it sought to allay NATO fears it was re-creating for itself a problem of Greco-Turkish dimensions should Hungary and the Slovak Republic be admitted to NATO. Indeed, the fear persists in some Western quarters that a suppression of the Hungarian minority in the Slovak Republic might trigger a crisis of Yugoslav proportions.[28] Hungary and the Slovak Republic concluded a five-year bilateral military cooperation agreement in October 1993. Signed within weeks of the association agreement with the EU, the agreement symbolized the commitment of two of the four central European (Visegrad) states to seek membership in NATO jointly. But neither government took on any onerous, specific obligations.

The Basic Treaty, signed on March 19, 1995, regulates the status of minorities on both sides of the Hungarian-Slovak border, focusing primarily

---

[28] Bennett Kovrig, "Az Atlanti Tanács Megoldást Keres a Kisebségi Kerdésben" [NATO Council Seeks a Solution of Minority Issue], *Népszabadság* (June 18, 1994): 30.

on two issues: Hungarian guarantees of the inviolability of Slovak borders; and Slovak protection of Hungarian minority rights. The border issue has been solved. And because of Hungary's unwavering European commitment, the treaty's ratification met no resistance in the Hungarian parliament. Nevertheless, the issue of minority rights remains mired in ambiguity and controversy. Specifically, in contrast to some of the major international treaties signed and ratified at the end of World War II as well as virtually all domestic legislation, Recommendation 1201 of the Council of Europe speaks of "collective," not "individual," minority rights, permitting both Hungary and the Slovak Republic to present the treaty's obligations to their domestic constituencies in different terms.

In Slovak domestic politics, this game has run quickly into real difficulties. The Hungarian minority, for example, refers to Recommendation 1201 when it defends its claims for greater autonomy. Because they are adamantly opposed to granting the Hungarian minority anything that might resemble collective rights, parties of both the ruling coalition and of the opposition in the Slovak parliament reject this demand. Indeed, the parliament handed Prime Minister Vladimir Mečiar's government its most stinging defeat in December 1995, when it refused to ratify the treaty. It further complicated relations with the Hungarian minority in November 1995, when it passed the controversial State Language Act, revoking the relatively liberal provisions of the Language Act of 1990. In both instances, nationalist forces inside the ruling coalition succeeded in shaping government policy. It took the Slovak parliament until March 1996 to ratify the Basic Treaty. The Slovak National Party (SNS) coupled its support of ratification to the passing of a far-reaching amendment to the criminal code that opens the door wide to administrative abuse and judicial shackling of the political opposition. The amendment was denounced vociferously and in unprecedentedly strong language both by liberal critics of the government and by the Catholic Church. In the view of the Conference of Bishops of the Slovak Republic, the amendment is comparable to legislation passed by the Communists in 1948 that provided the basis for "the conviction and torture of hundreds of thousands of innocent victims."[29]

But it is easy to paint the situation in colors that are darker than the reality. No Hungarian party in the Slovak Republic expresses irredentist demands. Most politicians of the Hungarian minority realize that they would be the first to suffer the serious consequences of any revival of extremist nationalist tendencies in Hungary or among their own members. These lead-

---

[29] "Strafrecht in der Slowakei Verschärft," *Frankfurter Allgemeine Zeitung* (March 27, 1996): 3. Earlier in 1996, in an exchange of letters with the Hungarian Bishops' Conference, the Slovak Bishops expressed their solidarity concerning the rights of the Hungarian minority living in the Slovak Republic.

ers continually emphasize that all they demand is more "autonomy," a term they do not define very precisely, and a greater devolution of responsibilities and power to local levels of government. A much-publicized meeting of mayors and other representatives of the Hungarian minority in 1994 succeeded in easing Slovak fears about the threat of Hungarian separatism. And Hungarian-Slovak relations may well improve following the ratification of the Basic Treaty by the Slovak parliament in March 1996.

Although the minority issue was exploited by important political forces in the Slovak Republic for tactical reasons, the Slovak National Party and its ally, the Movement for Democratic Slovakia, lost a vote of confidence in the Slovak parliament with which they had hoped to bring down the government in March 1994. In the September 1994 election, the party barely won the 5 percent of the national voted necessary to enter parliament. Even if Prime Minister Mečiar and those parties supporting his coalition were to exploit the minority issue for domestic reasons, it is highly unlikely that it would trigger armed conflict between Hungary and the Slovak Republic.

Furthermore, the Hungarian minority has considerable stakes in Slovak politics. It is organized in four different parties and has elected seventeen members to the National Council. Wherever Hungarians are in a majority, they control local government. And they are represented in a variety of official bodies at the national level dealing with minority affairs. The Hungarian minority has a variety of cultural institutions and media at its disposal, with financial subsidies totaling 63 million Slovak korunas ($2.1 million), compared to the 25 million Hungarian forints ($179,000) that the Hungarian government allocates in support of the cultural affairs of the Slovak minority in Hungary.[30] About 80 percent of the children of the Hungarian minority attend kindergarten, elementary, grammar, and vocational schools where Hungarian language is available either as the single or as a second language of instruction.[31] In technical high schools and secondary occupational schools, the proportion declines to 40 percent, while at the university level, Hungarian language instruction is virtually unavailable.[32] It comes as no surprise, therefore, that the educational qualifications of the Hungarian minority lag far behind the levels enjoyed

[30] Slovak Ministry of Foreign Affairs, *Situation of the Hungarian Minority in the Slovak Republic: With International Comparisons* (Bratislava, March 1996), p. 10; interview with Tibor Szabo, director, Slovak Section, Office for Magyars Abroad, Budapest, June 1995. It should be noted that in terms of sheer numbers, the Hungarian minority population in the Slovak Republic (estimated at more than half a million) is probably ten times larger than the number of Slovaks living in Hungary (estimated at about 50,000).

[31] Slovak Ministry of Foreign Affairs, *Situation of Hungarian Minority*, p. 15.

[32] Except for the Department of Hungarian Language and Literature at the Comenius University and three Hungarian departments at the Pedagogical University in Nitra, which trains future teachers.

by the Slovak population. Nevertheless, the Hungarian minority remains strongly opposed to the introduction of alternative education schools that would offer some subjects in Slovak and some in Hungarian. From the Hungarian perspective, this most probably would lead to a policy of forced assimilation, as happened to a substantial part of the Slovak minority in Hungary in the 1960s, and to a reduction in the number of classes offered only in Hungarian.

The political volatility and intractability of minority rights illustrate the extent to which traditional central European notions continue to shape Hungarian, Slovak, and Polish politics at the local, as distinct from national, level. Over time, membership in multilateral European institutions may have the effect of further favoring western European over central European conceptions of ethnicity and minority rights. But judging by the tenacious hold of central European conceptions on the political imagination of Germany in the last forty years, this process will remain very slow, thus leaving the door open to unsettling crises in central Europe's future.

SECURITY POLICIES: NEW AND OLD

With the end of the Cold War, security in Europe has come to include, besides traditional military issues, problems such as terrorism, drugs, organized crime, and migration. In the eyes of policy makers, national security has acquired an explicitly societal dimension. This shift has sharply elevated the importance of the security measures coordinated by the third pillar of the EU, for example, through the Schengen Accords. Because Germany has a special interest in coordinating security policies that have a societal dimension, European and German effects are closely intermingled. But in the absence of Polish membership in the EU, its Western orientation leaves Poland little choice but to adjust unilaterally to changes in German or European policies.

Poland's Migration Policy

The Europeanization of Poland's migration policy offers an instructive example of the societal dimension of security that is intimately connected with the economic integration of Europe.[33] Between 1985 and 1992 western Europe's annual immigration increased from about 1.0 million to 2.7 million persons; and the share of irregular or uncontrolled migrants

---

[33] See, for example, Christopher Mitchell, "International Migration, International Relations and Foreign Policy," *International Migration Review* 23 (Fall 1989): 682; Włodek Anioł, "Poland: From Emigration to Immigration?" *Refugees* 76 (June 1990): 35–36.

increased from 20 to 40 percent.[34] In reaction to these changes, western European states have restricted the right to asylum. Between 1992 and 1994, the number of asylum seekers in western Europe declined by more than 50 percent, from 693,000 to 315,000. And with the apparent end of the war in Yugoslavia, about 600,000 Bosnian refugees are likely to be resettled in the near future.[35] For the traditionally labor-importing countries on the continent, the adoption of more restrictive national migration policies is a high-priority item. Most of them are concerned with halting illegal immigration and have adopted strict repatriation policies. A number of countries have severely curtailed the right to political asylum.

"Safe country" is the core concept that informs the emerging, more restrictive European migration regime.[36] If applicants for asylum are nationals of countries appearing on a list of countries considered "safe," their application is automatically denied. Because the compilation of such lists is often very questionable, human rights organizations view them as worrisome developments. The label "safe country" carries a sort of presumption that contradicts the notion of treating refugees as individuals, rather than as members of groups. Meanwhile, according to the UN Convention on the Status of Refugees of 1951, individual persecution has to be demonstrated to qualify for refugee status. Current western European practice considers only those applicants for asylum who satisfy the narrowest interpretation of the Geneva Convention requirement of having a well-founded fear of persecution on grounds of nationality, race, religion, political opinion, or membership in a particular social group.[37]

The creation of a single European market has spurred harmonization of visa, entry, and readmission requirements among European states, as well as joint development of common, more restrictive external border polices.[38] Since 1987, the EU ministers of immigration have established a number of intergovernmental commissions that address these issues, assisted by the various working groups of an ad hoc immigration group. Two conventions coordinate national policies dealing with the granting of

[34] Jonas Widgren, "The Need for a New Multilateral Order to Prevent Mass Movements from Becoming a Security Threat in Europe," paper prepared for the conference organized by the Center for Strategic and International Studies, Taormina, Italy, April 1–3, 1993, p. 3.

[35] International Migration Bulletin 6 (Geneva: United Nations/ECE, May 1995): pp. 2–5.

[36] Kay Hailbronner, "The Concept of 'Safe Country' and Expedient Asylum Procedures: A Western European Perspective," International Journal of Refugee Law 5 (Spring 1993): 31–65.

[37] Several European countries grant some form of status and residence to "humanitarian" refugees who do not meet this narrow requirement; for example, asylum seekers who would be entitled to protection using other international instruments, such as victims of civil wars who fail to suffer individual persecution.

[38] See, for example, Giuseppe Callovi, "Regulation of Immigration in 1993: Pieces of the European Community Jig-Saw Puzzle," paper prepared for the conference "The New Europe and International Migration," Turin, November 25–27, 1991.

asylum and the crossing of national frontiers. And at the 1992 Edinburgh summit the EU member states formally articulated the principles informing their external migration policies. The TEU, furthermore, specifies that EU member states will decide jointly, if necessary by majority vote, about the conditions under which asylum is granted and about which visitors will need a visa to enter the EU. The Schengen group within the EU comprises the original six members of the EEC and the three Mediterranean member states (Germany, France, Italy, the three Benelux countries, Spain, Portugal, and Greece).[39] The Schengen area is a fully integrated territory in which individuals traveling between countries are no longer legally obliged to show any passports when they cross borders. The elimination of internal borders is accompanied by more intensive control of external borders primarily through the operation of one integrated information system. However, the Schengen Accords are still not fully implemented.

Poland shares with the states in western European increased exposure to a broad range of new security risks. Here, as elsewhere in Europe, organized crime accounts for sharp increases in the illegal shipments of weapons and radioactive materials, drug trafficking, car thefts, and the laundering of illegal funds. And here, as in many other countries, fears of foreigners are overblown. Between 1991 and 1994, for example, only about 1,000 foreigners were arrested or served time in Polish prisons; this was less than 0.5 percent of the total prison population, even though the number of illegal workers from the east may run as high as 200,000.[40] The number of individuals seeking to cross Poland's western border illegally is also high and growing.[41]

Since 1989, Polish policy has been strongly influenced by developments in western Europe and the EU. Specifically, Polish migration policy has aimed to adapt to the increasingly illiberal and restrictive policies of western European states. Since 1991, the Polish government has participated in the "Vienna process," which focuses on East-West migration, and the

[39] Since 1994, Austria has participated in the Schengen group as an observer.

[40] See *Rzeczpospolita* [Republic] (April 21, 1994). See also Jan B. de Weydenthal, "Immigration into Poland," *RFE/Rl Research Report* 3 (June 17, 1994): 40.

[41] In 1992 alone, more than 30,000 people, primarily from Romania and Bulgaria, were arrested for illegally crossing into Poland. *Recent Developments in Policies Relating to Migrations and Migrants,* papers submitted by the members of the European Committee on Migration (CDMG) of the Council of Europe, Strasbourg, September 1, 1993, p. 47. The figure for illegal immigrants in 1993 dropped below 18,000. The 1993 figure was provided by the Ministry of Internal Affairs and reported by the Polish Press Agency (PAP) on February 10, 1994. While Poland is primarily a transit country, further destabilization in the east or the closing of German and Scandinavian borders in the north and west could quickly make Poland a country of destination for those seeking to escape intolerable living conditions further east, especially Russia. This would destabilize Polish labor markets and exacerbate social tensions. Hence, in Polish eyes, migration policy has a substantial security dimension.

"Berlin/Budapest process," which concentrates on illegal migration, and has developed additional contacts in migration matters through its membership in the Council of Europe (since 1991) and in the Organization for Migration (since 1992). Poland's administrative practices and laws are being harmonized with evolving European standards, a difficult and prolonged process, especially for Polish laws dealing with aliens and asylum seekers.[42]

Generally speaking, as in western Europe, Poland has moved gradually from more liberal to more restrictive policies. For example, in 1989–90 the Polish government was very supportive of East German refugees who were seeking to reach West Germany. It expressed its readiness to assist Jewish emigrants from the Soviet Union on their way to Israel. And it assisted the Baltic boat people. When Sweden tightened its liberal asylum policies in 1989–90, the Polish government permitted more than 1,000 individuals deported from Sweden to stay in Poland, and it provided them with humanitarian aid. Legislation subsequently adopted established a firm foundation for Poland's new, liberal approach.

Very soon thereafter, the more restrictive western European policies were beginning to shape as well Poland's approach. Specifically, Poland's 1995 draft legislation for aliens introduces the concept of "safe countries" widely used by western European states to deny refugee status to individuals from states judged to have nonrepressive regimes. Furthermore, the draft legislation does not provide for an independent, impartial, and central organization or decision-making process, thus inviting administrative abuse. The ripple effect by which western European practices are imitated by Poland is also evident in the introduction of visa requirements for citizens of the former Yugoslavia. Within a month of Denmark's and Sweden's adopting new policies in 1993, Poland and the Czech Republic had adjusted their policies as well.[43] And as in western Europe, the Polish government plans to sanction airlines that bring in foreigners with inadequate documents.

Polish policy has been affected most directly by changes in German policy. The enormous influx of ethnic Germans from the east, refugees from the war in Bosnia, and persons from Third World countries seeking better

[42] See Włodek Anioł, "The Europeanization of Polish Politics: The Case of Migration Policies," Working Papers on Transitions from State Socialism, no. 95.3, Mario Einaudi Center for International Studies, Cornell University, July 1995, p. 13.

[43] For example, between January and May 1993, only about 100 of over 23,000 citizens of Yugoslavia and 19,000 citizens of Bosnia who entered Polish territory had applied for refugee status in Poland. Most of them were in transit on their way to Scandinavian countries. See Tomasz K. Kozłowski, "Poland: Between Transit, Asylum Seeking, and Immigration. Legal and Institutional Consequences of the Phenomenon of Involuntary Migration," paper prepared for the Seminar on Protection of Refugees in Central and Eastern Europe, Sofia (June 21–23, 1994), pp. 5–6.

living conditions and individual security from persecution led in the early
1990s to a dramatic increase in the number of migrants into Germany.
This created an explosive, xenophobic backlash and a severe tightening
in German immigration regulations. Because of British opposition to
Germany's preferred EU solution to its migration problem, after much internal debate, Germany amended its Basic Law to restrict asylum status to
political refugees only and to permit the deportation of those coming to
Germany in search of a better economic life. Confirmed by Germany's
Constitutional Court in May 1996, the effect of the law was to cut the
number of applications for asylum in half; of a total of 200,000 requests in
1995, only 18,000 were approved.[44] As part of a compromise with the domestic opponents of this constitutional change, the government negotiated agreements with and granted financial assistance to the neighboring
states most affected by the new German policy (Poland, the Czech Republic, and Austria). Because all of Germany's neighbors, including Poland,
are considered "politically safe," asylum seekers who reach Germany by
traveling through them are now deported unless they can meet the restrictive criteria of being political refugees. A German-Polish agreement,
signed in May 1993, stipulated that illegal asylum seekers entering from
Poland would be sent back to Poland within six months of their arrival in
Germany; that in exceptional circumstances, such as a sudden and massive
surge of migrants into Poland, Germany would authorize entry for certain
defined categories of migrants; and that Poland would receive DM 120 million during 1993–94 to help implement the agreement.

De facto, the 1993 German-Polish agreement modifies a central point in
the agreement Poland had concluded with the Schengen group in 1991.
In return for removing Poland from the Schengen visa list, the Polish government had then agreed to accept the return of illegal Polish immigrants
caught in the Schengen territory. Germany had been intent on having the
1991 agreement cover all unwanted aliens arriving through Polish territory at German borders. But Poland insisted successfully that it was obliged
only to take back Polish citizens who had overstayed their three-month
limits and worked illegally. In signing the 1993 agreement with Germany,
Poland made an important modification in its position and thus became
the first central European state to accept the principle of "safe third
states." But because the consistent implementation of a policy based on
this principle is very difficult for European states bordering areas not necessarily considered "safe" for persecuted individuals, in the summer of
1993 Poland also signed a series of bilateral agreements with all of its neighbors, except Russia and Belarus, which basically spread the new German
policy further east and south. The growing restrictions of European and

---

[44]*International Herald Tribune* (May 15, 1996): 6.

German migration policies have thus cast Poland in the unenviable position of acting as western Europe's eastern filter for migrants. Embedded in multilateral arrangements, bilateral deals have created a new, more restrictive migration regime in which Poland acts as Germany's most important eastern gatekeeper.

Slovak Defense Policy

The Slovak Republic illustrates the continued relevance of traditional conceptions of national security in contemporary Europe. Because the EU is not an actor in national security affairs and because the German military is fully integrated into NATO, European and German effects matter little in this case compared to national, NATO and Russian effects. The relations between central and western Europe are thus nested in a variety of broader international arrangements.

With only 5.3 million inhabitants, the Slovak Republic borders Ukraine, with 50 million; Poland, with almost 40 million; Hungary and the Czech Republic, with 10 million each; and Austria, with 7.5 million. The breakup of Czechoslovakia and political developments in the East and the West has prompted domestic debates about the future position of the Slovak Republic vis-à-vis East and West. A state with no past, confronting bewildering changes both at home and abroad, the Slovak Republic is more open to a nationalist-populist style of politics than are its central European neighbors. Political elites and mass publics remain deeply divided about the international course that the new state should steer. Although Slovak efforts to join NATO, the Western European Union (WEU), and the EU are not at the center of public concern, according to opinion polls taken in the summer of 1995, the Slovak Republic is the only Visegrad country in which a majority of the public is not in favor of entering NATO.[45]

Slovakia has no tradition of state sovereignty, and its domestic politics and foreign policy show a high degree of conflict and indecision. On the one hand, before the parliamentary elections of November 1994, virtually the entire political elite and all of the political parties in parliament favored a defense policy aimed at integrating the Slovak Republic into Western security institutions. Thus President Michal Kováč visited NATO headquarters in Brussels in late 1993 and applied officially for Slovak membership. And as late as 1995, in talks with a Russian parliamentary delegation, the chair of the Slovak Parliamentary Committee for Foreign Affairs stated that while Russia might have reservations about Slovak ef-

[45] This includes undecided respondents. However, a substantial majority of the Slovak public favors joining the EU even though most respondents know precious little about the economic, political, and security dimensions of EU membership.

forts to join NATO, it had to recognize that every post-Communist country had the "right to decide freely its priorities in foreign policy."[46] Slovak membership in NATO depends on meeting five basic criteria: civilian control of the army, compatibility between the military equipment of the Slovak army and that of NATO members, completion of the democratic transformation of society, development of a free-market economy, and friendly relations with neighbors.[47] According to public remarks by the U.S. secretary of defense in September 1995, the Slovak Republic scores high on the first two points.[48] Since Slovakia traditionally has been an exporter, not importer, of military equipment, the rapid progress in weapons compatibility is especially noteworthy. And in line with the Treaty on Conventional Armed Forces in Europe (CFE), Slovak armed forces sharply reduced their equipment in 1993–95, scrapping between one-half and two-thirds of their tanks and heavy artillery.[49]

On the other hand, the Slovak Republic also sees itself as a possible ally of Russia. Since the November 1994 elections, a substantial political constituency in Slovak politics prefers a policy of neutrality between East and West to a Western alignment. Because of its exceptionally close relations with Russia, the Slovak Republic occupies a unique position in central Europe. In August 1993, Russia's President Boris Yeltsin visited Bratislava to sign a bilateral Russian-Slovak treaty, which underlined democratization as a central, defining element in the relationship of these two states, an element that looked much less secure only two years later. At the same time, the Russian and Slovak ministers of defense signed a five-year military agreement that provided for closer bilateral defense and security ties and for the delivery of Russian military equipment to the Slovak army. Following objections from opposition parties in parliament, at the last minute the Slovak government withdrew a controversial clause in the draft treaty stipulating that neither state would assist a military attack on the other by allowing an attacking country's troops on its territory. This clause would, in effect, have obligated the Slovak Republic to remain neutral in any conflict in which Russia might be involved. At the signing ceremonies of the treaty, President Michal Kováč reaffirmed his country's intent to join NATO. This was followed by the Treaty of Friendly Relations and Mutual

[46] Ivan Laluha, as quoted in the *Press Agency of the Slovak Republic* (TASR), September 18, 1993.

[47] "Friendly relations" means relations that go beyond the basic treaties with both neighboring countries and Russia.

[48] William Perry, as quoted in *Pravda* (September 19, 1995).

[49] As of October 1995, the Slovak armed forces had about 47,000 personnel. Interview at the Ministry of Defense of the Slovak Republic, October 24, 1995. The figures for tanks and artillery are taken from "Martin Votruba, Slovak News" (February 27, 1995), *RFE/RL Research Report* (March 5, 1993). The latest reduction of tanks down to 570 was made in the second half of October 1995.

Cooperation (ratified by the Slovak parliament in 1994); an agreement between the Slovak and Russian governments that dealt with a variety of cultural matters, abrogated the visa requirement for travel between the two countries, and facilitated the issuing of working permits (March 1995); and an agreement between the Slovak and Russian ministries of interior on technical cooperation in the arms industry (also March 1995). Indeed, by the end of 1995, the Slovak Republic had signed sixty-eight bilateral treaties with Russia, most of which concerned economic and cultural issues.

Slovak vacillation between West and East is made possible by the ambiguities inherent central Europe's international relations after the Cold War. For example, in an effort to expand its bilateral security arrangements and to demonstrate to NATO its readiness to establish close military ties with its eastern neighbors and support of multilateral arrangements in the region, the Slovak Republic has sought to reach agreements with Ukraine and Romania. NATO has a strong interest in having Russia acquiesce to NATO's eastern enlargement. This puts the Slovak Republic and the other central European states in the peculiar situation of seeking good relations with Russia while working toward NATO membership. Because it would probably not be addressed either by a Western security guarantee or by a national policy of neutrality, instability in Russia and Ukraine is potentially deeply troubling for Slovakia.

Militarily, it is practically impossible to defend the Slovak Republic were it to confront a serious threat from any of its larger neighbors. With a budget of less than $300 million, the Slovak military lacks essential equipment and installations such as airfields, ammunition depots, modern weapons, and accommodations for officers and their families. The country is often described as "two East-West railways and three North-South mountain valleys."[50] The former integration of Slovakia (as a part of Czechoslovakia) into the Warsaw Treaty Organization (WTO) left the country's national defense intermeshed with that of its neighbors. For instance, Czechoslovak pilots who trained in eastern Slovakia had to start descent maneuvers over Hungarian territory. With the breakup of the WTO after 1990, Slovak politicians called for new national "forces for mountain terrain" and also for a "homeguard of territorial defense forces."[51] In the aftermath of the Velvet revolution in February 1992, the Czecho-Slovak armed forces were put under non-Communist control, although the Slovak Republic's first defense minister was a professional military man.[52]

[50] "Central and Eastern Europe: The Challenge of Transition," in Stockholm International Peace Research Institute, *SIPRI* (Oxford: Oxford University Press, 1993), p. 106.

[51] Minister of Interior Jozef Tuchyňa in his speech in Liptovský Mikuláš, as quoted in *Lidové noviny* [People's News] (November 2, 1992).

[52] General Imrich Andrejčák, who was in office until the fall of the Mečiar government in March 1994.

Currently, Slovak territorial integrity is challenged directly only by fringe extremist political groups in Hungary and Ukraine that are urging a revision of the borders negotiated at the end of World War I. But because the ethnic Hungarian and Ukrainian minorities in the Slovak Republic are concentrated in border areas, political extremism abroad might in times of crisis be reinforced by political extremism at home.

Since 1995, statements by Western officials and articles published in the Western press on the possibility of the Visegrad countries being admitted to NATO have ceased to mention the Slovak Republic as a possible candidate. The unprecedented and increasingly bitter conflict between the Slovak president and prime minister since 1995 is one reason why the Slovak Republic's international position in central Europe has deteriorated so sharply. Significantly, Slovak defense policy is beginning to show a quiet tilt toward a more neutral stance. For example, the Slovak Republic's contributions to international peacekeeping, though relatively modest in absolute terms, are disproportionately large in comparison to those of the Czech Republic.[53] Reflecting the general foreign policy orientation of these two states, after the Dayton Agreement the Slovak contingent of about 600 peacekeepers stationed in Croatia was left under the authority of the UNPROFOR, while the Czech contingent of about 1,000 was put under the command of NATO's INFOR. During a visit to the Slovak Republic in September 1995, U.S. Chief of Staff John Shalikashvili indicated that while the Czech Republic is leading the Slovak Republic in seeking convergence with NATO along different dimensions, Slovak armed forces are by no means passive bystanders in this process.[54] This characterization illustrates a growing disparity between the positions of the two states not evident in the statements of U.S. or NATO officials only a few years earlier. Despite Slovak participation in NATO's Partnership for Peace (PFP) program, there is no longer any guarantee that Slovak defense policy is traveling on a road that will eventually turn toward the West. On questions of national defense, the Slovak Republic appears to be charting a course that differs systematically from that of the other three central European states.

ECONOMIC AND SOCIAL POLICIES: INTERNATIONALIZATION WITHOUT INSTITUTIONALIZATION

The central European states are exposed to a mixture of international (German, European, and global) influences that help shape their eco-

---

[53] Interview by Ivo Samson, Martin Kahl, and Phillip Borinský at the Slovak Ministry of Defense, October 24, 1995.

[54] John Shalikashvili, as quoted in *Sme* [Shift] (September 28, 1995).

nomic, regional, and social policies without the buffers that the states along Europe's northern, western, and southern periphery have come to enjoy. The experience of Hungarian and Slovak privatizations, the automobile and media industry in the Czech Republic, the Slovak Republic's extremely rapid conversion of its military industries, and Hungary's social policies illustrate the most important experience that sets central Europe apart from other subregions of Europe: much internationalization of markets and little institutionalization of multilateral institutions. Thus, in contrast to the Netherlands and Belgium, for example, central Europe often experiences and interprets the spreading of German economic influence as German domination.

Privatization in Hungary and the Slovak Republic

Privatization in central Europe is widely considered as a basic means to establish a market economy, to separate economy from polity, to create new economic incentives, and to establish ownership control over corporate managers. But the central European states privatize along different trajectories and at different speeds.[55] Just as western Europe features different types of capitalism—statist in France, liberal in Britain and quasi-corporatist in Germany—the different routes by which the central European states are extricating themselves from Communism will generate different types of capitalist democracies in central Europe. This difference is well illustrated by the different experiences with privatization in Hungary and the Slovak Republic.

Hungarian privatization is a trial-and-error process that reacts to changing conditions; all forms, with the exception of mass voucher privatization, have been tried at one time or another.[56] Hungary's privatization strategy has thus been truly mixed.[57] It has featured centralized privatization through the sale of state assets by governmental agencies; decentralized privatization through the sale of state assets by managers, subject to final approval by government bureaucrats; managerial buyouts; spontaneous privatizations in which managers sell state assets to themselves or other buyers without approval by the public authorities; employee ownership schemes in which state assets are sold at a preferential price to the employees of a given firm; outright gifts; and partial compensations or

[55] See David Stark, "Path Dependence and Privatization Strategies in East Central Europe," *East European Politics and Societies* 6 (Winter 1992): 17–51.

[56] The Hungarian policy of compensation briefly approximated to some extent the mass voucher system. See also David Stark and László Bruszt, *Postsocialist Pathways: Transforming Politics and Property in East Central Europe* (New York: Cambridge University Press, 1998).

[57] See Éva Voszka, "Enyém a vár . . . Privatizáció, 1990–1993," [My Castle . . . Privatization, 1990–1993], *Társadalmi Szemle* [Social Review] 49 (1994): 1–9.

restitutions.[58] This mixed pattern of privatization has not yet run its course. The slowness of the privatization process has had political benefits. Voters tend to attribute negative side effects, such as massive layoffs and growing inequality in income and wealth, to the broad transition to a market economy rather than the specific policies of privatization.

In the interest of preventing old elites from gaining a foothold in the new economy, and backed by a bureaucracy interested in expanding its power, between 1990 and 1991 the government of Prime Minister Antall favored a centralized privatization.[59] Removed from parliamentary oversight, the State Property Agency (SPA) was put in charge of the sale of state-owned firms down to a relatively low value limit.[60] Representatives of the opposition parties who had served on the SPA's board of directors were gradually eased out of office and replaced by individuals considered loyal to the government. The SPA thus became soon a target of attack for the parliamentary opposition. Lacking the expertise to monitor the deals struck by firm managers, the SPA moved slowly and with no more than partial success. The government recognized this weakness and changed gears in 1991, when it launched a new program of decentralized privatization, mostly of small firms, in which the SPA exercised only the final right of overall approval.[61]

Seeking to involve a larger numbers of potential voters directly in the privatization process before the 1994 parliamentary elections, the government changed its policy once more and gave a renewed emphasis to compensation. Those entitled to reprivatization were given compensation vouchers that could be exchanged for real property titles or shares. But because full restitution was infeasible, the majority of former owners received only a fraction of the value of their assets.

Despite its promise to finish privatization within three years, divisions within the newly elected Socialist-Liberal coalition made the government of Prime Minister Gyula Horn move slowly and with great caution.[62] The Free Democrats favored a fast privatization process, even at the cost of

[58] On the history of privatization in Hungary, see David Bartlett, "The Political Economy of Privatization: Property Reform and Democracy in Hungary," *East European Politics and Societies* 6 (Winter 1992): 73–118. On the so-called spontaneous privatization, see Mária Móra, "Az állami vállalatok (ál)privatizációja" [The (Pseudo-)Privatization of State-Owned Enterprises], *Közgazdasági Szemle* [Economic Review] 38 (1991). Hidden or informal privatization is estimated to be as large as official privatization. See also Éva Voszka, "A tulajdonosi szerkezet átalakulásának fél évtizede Magyarországon" [Five Years of the Transformation of Ownership Structure in Hungary], unpublished paper, Budapest, 1993, p. 4.

[59] Bartlett, "Political Economy of Privatization."

[60] Voszka, "A tulajdonosi szerkezet."

[61] In 1992, the government set up the (later privatized) State Holding Company (SHC), which was put in control of 163 mostly large firms the government did not intend to sell.

[62] *Népszabadság* (November 23, 1994): 15.

short-term economic loss or social inequality. The Socialists favored a slower process that seeks to avoid economic losses and minimizes social inequality. In light of enormous budget deficits, the government preferred outright sales over any other form of privatization;[63] it planned to bring to an end Hungary's cautious, mixed privatization policy by 1997.

What are the quantitative dimensions of Hungary's privatization to date?[64] The initial centralized phase of privatization under the auspices of the SPA covered assets valued at Ft 127 billion ($1.7 billion), which dwarfed the second, decentralized wave of privatization.[65] All told, between 1989 and 1993, one-third of the assets of the SPA were sold for Ft 520 billion ($4.7 billion), or about one-quarter of the total value of state assets to be privatized. At the end of 1992, there were still about 6,000 partially state-owned companies, and that figure increased in the following years. And most state-owned assets awaited privatization. In March 1994, the SPA held assets valued at Ft 378 billion ($3.4 billion); the corresponding figure for the State Holding Company (SHC) was Ft 976 billion ($8.8 billion). After four years, the SPA and SHC still needed to privatize 60 percent of the assets initially put under their jurisdiction.[66] By the end of 1994, the government had handled more than 1.8 million claims in the form of compensation vouchers, involving a total value of Ft 114 billion ($7.0 billion). Because, however, there was simply an insufficient supply of corresponding assets to maintain the price of the compensation vouchers, the vouchers had lost 60–70 percent of their nominal value by 1995.

How has privatization been affected by international influences? In Hungary privatization spurred a widespread fear that foreign capital would annex Hungary economically. Economic statistics illustrate a foreign influence that is balanced among Austrian, German, and U.S. investors and that has grown gradually. Among the reasons are Hungary's mixed priva-

---

[63] *Figyelő* [Observer] (September 29, 1994): 18–19.

[64] Quantitative estimates of different aspects of Hungarian privatization are fraught with difficulties. Data are generally unreliable because different sources typically publish different figures that cannot be compared. The values of state-owned assets may be book values, which do not match sales prices. Furthermore, state-owned assets are constantly losing their value. Hence the figures quoted here are useful only for indicating rough trends and orders of magnitude.

[65] György Matolcsy, *Lábadozásunk évei* [The Years of Our Convalescence] (Budapest: Research Institute on Privatization, 1991), p. 226. Of the 423 firms with less than 300 employees and capitalized at less than Ft 300 million, only 147 firms were sold for a mere Ft 5.5 billion ($72.7 million) in the first wave. Of firms capitalized under Ft one billion, 277 took part in the second wave. These figures are tiny compared to the Ft 1,500 billion capitalization of the 163 state firms put under the jurisdiction of the SHC. An additional 60 corporations operate under the authority of branch ministries. Voszka, "A tulajdonosi szerkezet," p. 11. Informal privatization has been estimated to be as important in aggregate terms as all official privatization programs taken together.

[66] According to Prime Minister Gyula Horn, 50 percent of state-owned assets have already been privatized. *Népszabadság* (January 1, 1995).

tization strategy, a lack of suitable investment opportunities, and the fear of foreign takeovers. Foreign investments accounted for 79 percent of total privatization sales in 1990; by 1994 they averaged, for the SPA, around 28 percent of cash revenues, 10 percent of sold companies, and 6 percent of total revenues.[67] The policy that Prime Minister Horn's government has adopted since 1994 led to an increase from 6 to 66 percent of the foreign share in total revenues by 1996. Strapped for cash, the government plans to sell about half of the state-owned assets to foreign investors, who are estimated to provide 80–90 percent of the total privatization income in the policy's next phase. The share of foreign ownership of the Hungarian economy was predicted to reach 25–30 percent by 1997.[68]

Between 1990 and 1993, the share of foreign direct investment not targeted at the state sector averaged about 70 percent.[69] With the German share rising, foreign investment is becoming less diversified. In 1995, German and American capital accounted for, respectively, 29 and 24 percent each, Austrian for about 11 percent, and French for about 9 percent.[70] Neither the process of privatization nor its outcome reflects specific German influences. Hungary's mixed privatization strategy has nothing in common with how the Treuhandanstalt has operated in Germany. And German acquisition of Hungarian assets appears to have been modest in absolute size and balanced by the presence of active American and Austrian investors. On the other hand, international consulting firms have been very prominent in Hungary's privatization process. Specifically, they have helped the government solve problems of asset valuation and of finding buyers for state-owned firms. In the initial phase of privatization, for example, of the eighteen consulting firms working for the government, only two were Hungarian. German firms played a marginal role, while British and American firms dominated.

Slovak privatization is intimately related to that of the Czech Republic, to which the Slovak Republic is often compared. The origin of the privatization programs in both states started before the breakup of Czecho-Slovakia. Because Czecho-Slovakia's public sector constituted 98 percent of all firms, the reformers were looking for as fast and irrevocable a break

[67] Bertalan Dicházi, "Tények és adatok a magyar privatizációról—1993," [Facts and Data about Hungarian Privatization—1993], in Sándor Kurtán, Péter Sándor, and László Vass, eds., *Magyarország politikai évkönyve* [Political Yearbook of Hungary] (Budapest: Center for Democratic Studies, 1993), p. 847; *Privatization Monitor, SPA* (March 31, 1995): 6.

[68] *Népszabadság* (November 23, 1994): 15, and (April 6, 1996): 5; I. Nagy, "Privatizáció, így, úgy,—sehogy?" [Privatization, This Way, That Way—No Way?], *Figyelő* (November 17, 1994): 23.

[69] Andrea Szalavetz, "A külföldi tőkebefektetők részvétele a magyarországi privatizációs folyamatban," [The Participation of Foreign Investors in the Privatization Process in Hungary], unpublished paper, p. 5.

[70] *Népszabadság* (April 6, 1996): 5, and (May 25, 1996): 1.

with the past as possible. While virtually all reformers agreed on the over-all objective, there was considerable disagreement about how this objective should be accomplished. Some favored direct sales and public auctions; others emphasized the advantages of new forms of privatization such as employee or management buyouts; still others argued in favor of a voucher scheme assisted in some cases by investment funds. In the end, the federal Czechoslovak government settled on a three-step process of privatization. First, within a few years most of the small state-owned firms were to be auctioned off; in the case of the Czech Republic, more than 90 percent within three years. Second, large companies were to be sold directly to the public, or joint ventures were to be formed with foreign companies. Between 1990 and 1995, for example, foreign firms invested $5.8 billion in the Czech Republic.[71] Finally, and most importantly, Czecho-Slovakia decided on a process of voucher privatization. The five rounds of the first wave were implemented in 1992, prior to the country's breakup. This program aimed at the privatization of large firms valued at 166.5 billion Czechoslovak korunas ($5.76 billion). The program relied on both direct (12.3 billion korunas, or $426 million, by 1993) and indirect sales (through the issuing of individual vouchers). In addition, a total of 9,667 out of 11,420 economic units were successfully auctioned off as part of the small-scale privatization program. This resulted in total sales of 14.0 billion Slovak korunas ($421 million), more than the original offering price. By the end of 1993, the Slovak Republic's small-scale privatization was virtually complete. That the private sector went from one-fifth to two-thirds of Slovak GDP between 1992 and 1995 is largely due to the success of the privatization process.[72]

In the case of the Czech Republic, voucher privatization gave each adult citizen, for a $35 fee, coupons with an estimated average value of $1,000 in the first round, and a nominal value of $700 in the second, which could be used to purchase shares in hundreds of former state-owned firms. State-owned companies valued at $10 billion, representing 70–80 percent of the public sector, were thus transferred into private hands within a few years. Most Czechs placed their coupons with investment funds, which received 70 percent of the coupons in the first round, 60 percent in the second.

Not so in the Slovak Republic, which has engaged in an acrimonious debate whether to proceed along the Czech path of unrestrained voucher privatization. In a series of policy shifts during 1995, the government scrapped the planned voucher privatization, thus undermining the position of investment funds. Instead, it moved aggressively forward with bond

[71] Hana Píšková, "Přímé zahraniční investice vzrostly" [Direct Foreign Investment Increased], *Hospodářské noviny* [Economic News] (March 1, 1996): 7.
[72] Slovak Ministry of Privatization, 1995 data.

privatization and direct sales. Rooted in domestic power politics, the political struggles over Slovak privatization have clear consequences for the institutional structure of the Slovak Republic's emerging capitalist economy, specifically the position of investment funds and the type of corporate governance system, American or German, that will eventually prevail. After the breakup of Czecho-Slovakia, 2.6 million citizens were registered for the first round of privatization in the Slovak Republic.[73] In this round, 503 Slovak companies, with a book value of 90 billion Czechoslovak korunas ($3.1 billion), were offered for voucher privatization. Slovak citizens could also invest in 988 companies in the Czech Republic.[74]

As was true of the Czech Republic, voucher privatization created investment funds as an important, new type of economic actor in the Slovak Republic. Rather than investing in companies directly, coupon holders relied on these investment funds as financial intermediaries for about 60 percent of their total investment. Affirming the right of shareholders to participate in the control of individual enterprises, nearly one-third of thirty-two fund managers surveyed in 1993 saw corporate governance rather than securities trading as their most important task.[75] The interest in control varied with the degree of a fund's ownership of particular firms; when the stake in a firm exceeded the 10 percent mark, more than one-quarter of the managers wanted to exercise control. Fully one-third of the managers wanted to control more than ten enterprises.

It is thus hardly surprising that the funds meet with considerable opposition from both individual shareholders and corporate managers. Associations of individual shareholders, however rare, are often coordinated by corporate managers or trade union leaders and have no regular legal standing in the Slovak Republic. Investment funds view them as unfair, because legally unregulated, competition. On their list of possible partners for cooperation, the funds put these associations last. Nevertheless, the shareholder associations are seeking to exercise political influence. Under the leadership of the former Minister of Privatization Milan Janičina, for example, an association seeking to protect the rights of individual investment voucher owners organized an unsuccessful petition drive in June 1995 to force a referendum on the stalled second round of voucher privatization. Corporate managers also found themselves in conflict with

---

[73] The number of registrants increased to 3.4 million for the second round of privatization, which, however, remained stalled in 1995–96.

[74] Individual Slovak investors used 90 percent of their coupons to purchase shares in Slovak companies; the proportion of total coupons used by investment funds ran at only about 65 percent. See *Trend 3*, p. 1.

[75] Daneš Brzica and Brigitta Schmögnerová, "Podnikový sektor z pohl'adu investičných spoločností a investičnýcoh fondov," [Enterprise Sector from the Point of View of Investment Companies and Investment Funds], *EÚ SAV* (Bratislava, Slovak Academy of Sciences, Institute of Economics, April 1993).

investment funds. They had expected voucher privatization to leave their prerogatives untouched or to enhance their power through management buyouts or the purchase of shares from individuals. As matters turned out, investment companies soon became serious competitors for power at the level of the firm.

Like Hungary, the Slovak Republic has a Fund for National Property (FNP) to administer state-owned corporations. It is one of the biggest owners of partially privatized Slovak companies. The FNP has become a political football in the 1990s. In the changing political climate, its rights and responsibilities have been radically restructured. An amendment to legislation originally passed in 1991 expanded the fund's role in the privatization process, while at the same time prohibiting any direct links between the FNP and the Slovak government. Until March 1994, for example, Vladimir Mečiar, then prime minister of the Slovak Republic, was also president of the Presidium of the FNP. Top administrators of the FNP are now elected by the Slovak National Council (SNC).

Slovak privatization has led to an intense debate between different political parties, symbolized in the bitter political and personal conflict between the prime minister and the president of the republic. President Michal Kováč has taken a strong position on the issue of voucher privatization, which has stalled Prime Minister Vladimir Mečiar's planned modifications prior to the second wave. Specifically, the president has refused to sign three amendments to what is commonly referred to as the "Large-Scale Privatization Act" (Act no. 92/1991). Specifically, the president objects to legal provisions that would limit the power of investment funds by prohibiting them from putting their representatives on management, as opposed to supervisory, boards of those companies in which they hold significant numbers of shares. And he strongly opposes new legislation that would grant the government a veto right over key corporate decisions such as the sale of a company to foreign investors.

As in Hungary, privatization in the Slovak Republic is a profoundly political process, shaped by considerations of political power and expediency as much as by arguments of economic rationality. The Mečiar government is proposing to sharply reduce, if not eliminate, voucher privatization in the second round, and ultimately, the role of investment funds and international investors in the Slovak economy. But in sharp contrast to Hungary, the evolution of Slovak policy does not feature merely a succession of different approaches to a vexing problem within an agreed-upon political framework. Instead, the future of Slovak privatization is now cast in the terms of a deep personal, political, and constitutional conflict between the prime minister and the president.

Privatization also raises issues of nationalism and internationalism. Motivated by the expectation of short-term profits, the only substantial inflow of portfolio investment into the Slovak Republic occurred in the first quarter of 1994. But voucher privatization and investment funds have also helped create a capital market for foreign investors. As in Hungary, foreign investors in the Slovak Republic have created a market for financial services and alternative investment vehicles such as option agreements. The door is thus open to a variety of forms of foreign participation in the Slovak privatization program. Because they will probably have to sell a portion of their portfolios to foreign investors in order to raise the capital necessary for financing individual companies and paying individual coupon holders, investment funds may find themselves at odds with management, which typically has no interest in ceding control over operations to a foreign owner. In such conflicts, the government, specifically the Ministries for Privatization and Finance as well as the FNP, tend to line up on the side of management. Deputy Prime Minister and Minister of Finance Sergej Kozlik, for example, has argued that a clearance "sale of shares abroad is a menacing possibility. We do not know yet who stands behind whom. Personally I see risks rather than positives."[76] Fears of international investments are one important reason why the second wave of Slovak privatization remains mired in controversy, and why the Slovak Republic is perceived in many European quarters to be sliding back toward a policy that defends an authentic nationalism against a liberal internationalism.

The consequence has been a noticeable cooling of relations between the Slovak Republic and foreign firms and experts. Experts from the World Bank and other international financial organizations reportedly have insisted that for the second wave of voucher privatization to succeed, a minimum of SK 70–80 billion ($2.42 billion) worth of assets must be privatized, a larger proportion of the total state-owned firms than the government may be prepared to sell.[77] The Japanese investment firm Nomura's widely noted decision to sell its stake in one of the largest Slovak investment funds, VUB Kupon, may reflect a declining interest of the international financial community in the Slovak economy.

German influence figures only indirectly in the Slovak Republic's domestically driven privatization policy. Just as the Hungarian national bank actively emulated the Bundesbank model, the Slovak FNP is seeking to actively emulate the German institutional model of statutory corporate bodies. The adoption of German accounting rules reinforce this bias. The corollary is for the Slovak government to work against the American model of corporate governance. Hence it is consistent for the Mečiar government to curtail the role of investment funds in the process of privatization. The government instead favors the role of banks, traditionally an

[76] *Národná obroda* [National Revival] (January 3, 1995): 13.
[77] *Národná obroda* (May 8, 1995): 121.

important part of Germany's "social market economy." Thus, rooted in the domestic struggle for power, policy imitation may eventually forge institutional links between the Slovak Republic, Germany, and Europe, outside of Europe's multilateral settings.

Czech Auto and Media Industries

One need not look for processes of imitation or diffusion across the Czech border, for Germany is the leading foreign investor in the Czech Republic and accounts for about twice as much as either the United States or Switzerland or the Netherlands and more than three times as much as France.[78] The most important of these investment projects in the years 1990–94 was VW's takeover of Skoda.[79] Skoda is the biggest car producer in the Czech Republic. In September 1993, the company had 429 suppliers.[80] It produced about 200,000 cars annually in the early 1990s, half for the export market, accounting for about 7 percent of total Czech exports. Its 17,000 workers in the main Skoda enterprise and more than 60,000 workers employed by its suppliers together make up about 3.5 percent of the total work force of the Czech Republic.[81]

In 1990, Skoda ran a deficit of more than $150 million. Without a dramatic infusion of capital and technology the firm appeared to be doomed in the highly competitive, internationalized automobile industry.[82] The Czech government thus actively sought a strong foreign partner. The choice was eventually narrowed from eight to two companies, VW and Renault, whose offers were comparable along many dimensions. VW prevailed for several reasons. Czech unions had much greater confidence in how German companies dealt with workers. The similarity in German and

[78] Between 1990 and 1995, direct foreign investment totaled $5.797 billion. This figure was divided between Germany ($1.740 billion or 30 percent), Switzerland ($821 million or 14.2 percent), the United States and the Netherlands ($787 million or 13.6 percent each), France ($542 million or 9.3 percent), Austria ($316 million or 5.4 percent), and other foreign investors ($805 million or 13.9 percent). See Písková, "Přímé zahraniční investice vzrostly," p. 7.

[79] The largest foreign investment project in the Czech Republic to date was undertaken in 1995 by a Dutch-Swiss consortium, which invested in the Czech telecommunications monopoly.

[80] Of Skoda's suppliers, 269 (63 percent) were Czech, 39 (9 percent) were Slovak, and 121 (28 percent) were foreign.

[81] "List of Skoda-VW Suppliers," Press Information Skoda, Public Relations, Skoda Works, 1993.

[82] Different sources give different estimates of the size of Skoda's deficit in 1990. On the low end of estimates, about Kčs 2.5 billion ($89.3 million) is Peter Dedek in *Mladá fronta Dnes* [Young Front Today] (March 16, 1991); and Zdeněk Kadlec in *Svobodné slovo* [Free Word] (November 16, 1991). Another source cites a figure of about Kčs 7 billion ($250 million). *Mladá fronta Dnes* (March 23, 1990). Decisive for our estimate is the fact that VW promised to pay, in three installments, a total amount of $150 million (DM 200 million or about Kčs 3.6 billion) as quoted in *Lidové noviny* [People's News] (June 12, 1991).

Czech industrial cultures and the shorter distance to Wolfsburg were also important factors. Furthermore, VW had prepared a much more detailed plan, which promised to shake up old managerial structures, both within Skoda itself and with regard to its subcontractors. And VW was much more assiduous than Renault in cultivating all interested constituencies: managers, union leaders, workers, journalists and politicians.

Although the text of the agreement between Skoda and VW is not in the public domain, VW appears to have committed itself to buy 70 percent of Skoda between 1991 and 1995 in three installment payments totaling $1.2 billion.[83] In 1991 and 1992, reports in the press spoke of investments totaling DM 9 billion ($5.8 billion) by the year 2000. By the end of 1993, as the crisis at VW and in the automobile industry deepened, VW-Skoda proposed a new and lower figure of about DM 3.7 billion ($2.2 billion).[84] This cutback was made over the strong opposition of Tomas Jezek, chairman of the Foundation of National Ownership (which in 1993 still owned 69 percent of the company's stock), and Vladimír Dlouhý, minister for industry and business. In late 1994, the Czech government signed a new agreement with VW, which took account of the reduced scale of the new company. Making no mention of former commitments to develop a new car and engine and to build new production facilities, it specified a level of production of about 340,000 units by the end of the decade, some 100,000 less than had been originally projected.[85]

For its part, the Czech government adhered to the various incentives to which it had agreed in 1991.[86] With business conditions deteriorating sharply in 1991–93, Skoda-VW successfully bargained with the government for additional tax cuts and increased import duties on new cars. Over the determined opposition of the Ministry for Economic Competition, the company increased its prices; by the end of 1992, prices were more than twice as high as in 1990.[87] It defeated the effort of the Office for Economic Competition to reduce import duties from 19 to 10 per-

[83] *Lidové noviny* (June 12, 1991).

[84] News broadcast of Czech TV "Deník ČT" [Daily News], December 16, 1993; *Finance East Europe* 3 (September 23, 1993): 2–3.

[85] *Süddeutsche Zeitung* (October 23, 1994); *Handelsblatt* (November 30, 1993); *Frankfurter Allgemeine Zeitung* (July 22, 1994); *Financial Times* (December 17, 1993).

[86] The Czech government committed itself to a two-year tax holiday and thereafter to a tax ceiling at 40 percent of profits; to tax breaks of 17 percent each year for the first three years for new investments in machinery and of 6 percent each year for the first five years for new investments in construction; to tariff-free import of parts for the production of cars to be sold abroad; to no price restrictions on cars and services as long as the company does not abuse its monopoly position in domestic markets; to a four-year tariff rate of 19 percent for cars imported into the Czecho-Slovak market as well as additional tax barriers for imported cars. These commitments were made in a letter that was eventually published in *Lidové noviny* (May 31, 1991).

[87] The Czech Department of Economic Competition argued that these price increases were due to VW-Skoda's strong position in domestic markets.

cent. And it did not respond to a strike waged in September 1994 to protest a reclassification of production jobs, limitations on the number of full-time jobs for workers, engineers and white collar employees, in apparent violation of the company's initial commitment to job security for 19,000 workers.

In search of quality and efficiency, VW-Skoda has strongly reoriented its subcontracting network toward German firms.[88] Excepting Slovak subcontractors, 71 percent of the foreign subcontractors working for VW-Skoda in September 1993 were German, twice the proportion, for example, of German firms participating in Czecho-Slovak joint ventures in 1992; including Slovak subcontractors, the proportion of German firms still amounts to 54 percent.[89] Furthermore, twice as many domestic subcontractors working for VW-Skoda since 1991 have linkups with German firms as did before. VW's takeover has thus made Skoda highly dependent, especially in hard times. The Czech economy has been opened to international influences few envisaged when the initial deal was signed. Skoda has not become an autonomous hub of product innovation and the site of new production serving central and eastern European markets. Instead, hard times in Wolfsburg have sharply reduced the growth and technological potential of the company.

But VW's new, austere course has had ramifications far beyond Skoda. A cutback in production at Skoda has had serious consequences for the more than 200 suppliers, many of whom do not have alternative outlets.[90] The dependence of Czech parts suppliers has created a production structure in the Czech Republic that to some extent resembles Japan's—except that control over the Czech automobile industry lies beyond national borders. The new distribution system that Skoda-VW has created reinforces this dependence. The reorganization of the company's subcontracting arrangements and distribution systems has reinforced an asymmetric dependence relationship between Skoda and VW and between the Czech Republic and Germany. In good times, it may generate greater profits and investments, but in bad, it may lead to more conflicts of interest and more distributional struggles that neither Skoda nor the Czech Republic can win. Internationalization and dependency, this case illustrates, go hand in hand.

The internationalization of the Czech print media offers a second illustration of the creation of asymmetric dependency, although the presence

[88] "List of VW-Skoda Suppliers," *Hospodářské noviny* (September 9, 1992): 2.

[89] See Hynek Jeřábek, "Internationalization through Investment Partnership or Dependency of Czechia: Two Case Studies of Transformation," Working Papers on Transition from State Socialism, no. 95.7, Cornell University, 1995, p. 44; *Czechoslovak Joint Ventures* (June 1992). *Skoda Foreign Suppliers* (September 1993).

[90] "Dodavatelé Škody žádají o dotace" [Skoda Suppliers Asking for Subsidies], *Lidové noviny* (August 19, 1994): 1.

of other foreign investors in other segments of the media industry, specifically electronic media, circumscribe German influence. Democratization, privatization, and commercialization set the stage for a rapid move from centralized national control under Communist rule to a flourishing, variegated, decentralized media industry open to international participation under democratic, capitalist control. Despite numerous unsuccessful attempts to challenge its most important decision, the independent Radio and Television Board granted the first license for a private, national TV station to a group of investors in which American capital accounted for two-thirds of the total.[91] The Czech electronic media industry is today highly competitive, relying substantially on advertisements to fund its programming costs.

Foreign investors have moved more slowly in the print media; but move they did after 1993. Increasing foreign ownership of the Czech press for the most part affects only the commercial, and not the editorial, side of the business. It is too early to tell whether such contractual arrangements will work as well in harder times as they have in normal times. Internationalization has also seen the import of foreign know-how from different sources. Reuters, for example, has brought not only its capital but also its style of work, a high degree of professionalism, training for Czech journalists, study visits abroad, and other benefits. The French company MAFRA, the long-time owner of *Mladá fronta Dnes* [Young Front Today], has introduced computer typesetting. The Swiss concern Ringier has offered its wealth of experience in publishing to *Lidové noviny* [People's News], *Československý profit* [Czechoslovak Profit], and *Blesk* [Lighting], as well as other newspapers and magazines. In short, foreign influence exists in the national press, although it is divided among several different foreign investors located in different states. Nevertheless, the relative importance of German investors has become very substantial. Two German investors now control papers with 42 percent of the total Czech readership. The Czech ownership share of the national press has declined from 100 percent in 1989, to 48 percent in 1992, to 33 percent in 1995.[92]

At the regional level, the picture is no different. The German news concern Passauer Neue Presse is introducing innovations that tend to give

[91] *Lidová demokracie* [People's Democracy] (February 5, 1993); "Havel o CET21," [Havel about CET21] *Český deník* [Czech Daily] (February 9, 1993).

[92] "Zahraniční kapitál v denním tisku" [Foreign Capital in the Press], *Telegraf* [Telegraph] (November 15, 1993); "Prstenec kolem středu Čech" [The Ring around the Center of Bohemia], *Práce* [Work] (July 30, 1993); "Kdo co ovládal v tisku v roce 1992," [Who Controlled What in the Print Media in 1992], *Český deník* [Czech Daily] (March 26, 1993); "Nejčtenější deníky: Blesk, MfD a Rudé právo" [Dark Red Newspapers: *Lightning, Young Front Today,* and *Red Right*], *Rudé právo* [Red Right] (December 23, 1993). By comparison, foreign investors had a stake in about half of Poland's national and regional publications in 1994, with about 70 percent of the total press run. German publishers are the largest foreign shareholder, owning about 18 percent of both the national and regional press.

Czech regional dailies more national appeal, while at the same time regionalizing the national press. *Labe* in northern Bohemia, *Vltava* in southern and western Bohemia, and the *PN Press* in eastern Bohemia prepare the common core of several regional papers; district editorial offices then augment their dailies with local news and regional advertising. Thus regional dailies maintain a regional form and content while sharing the cost of foreign and national news reporting. Because of its successful acquisitions of regional and local dailies and its innovative management the Passauer Neue Presse enjoys virtually a monopoly position in the regional media markets in southern and western Bohemia.[93] Various estimates put the share of the regional media market controlled by German publishers at about 80 percent.[94] However, the Department for Economic Competition concluded that because tight coupling between national and regional markets prevented the emergence of monopolies, the strong position of German publishers in the Czech Republic's regional press was not putting market competition at risk.[95]

These data suggest that Czech fears of German economic hegemony and Czech dependency are not unfounded. In the 1930s, German economic influence was based on a deliberate political strategy of creating asymmetric economic dependencies between Nazi Germany and its smaller central and eastern European neighbors. It is difficult to detect any coordinated political strategy of the German government to create a position of economic influence in the Czech Republic. But the spontaneous expansion of German business is another matter. In March 1996, half of the Czech public viewed Germany as a danger for the Czech economy, a slight increase compared to 1992. But the proportion of those viewing Germany as a source of political danger jumped from 29 to 39 percent.[96]

Germany favors economic expansion for reasons of prosperity and stability. It is likely to become a strong champion of an early admission of the Czech Republic to the European Union, hoping to use Czech production sites to export to a potentially large eastern market. For the foreseeable

---

[93] *Mladá fronta Dnes* (June 7, 1993).

[94] On November 23, 1992, an article in *Český deník* entitled "Tiskový obchvat" [Press Outmaneuvred] and signed by Kateřina Rollová launched a discussion of the Czech regional press and its new Bavarian owners. Among the most interesting material subsequently published was a table in *Český deník* on March 26, 1993, with the title "Kdo co ovládal v tisku v roce 1992" [Who Controls What in the Press in 1992]. A long article in *Práce* on July 30, 1993, entitled "Prstenec kolem středu Čech" [Ring around the Center of Bohemia] described how the Passauer Neue Presse had obtained nearly 80 percent of the regional press. Relevant figures also were printed in the *Telegraf* on November 15, 1993, in a brief report entitled "Zahraniční kapitál v denním tisku" [Foreign Capital in the Daily Press].

[95] "Fúze PN Press, Vltavy a Labe byly schváleny" [Merger of PN Press, Vltava, and Labe Approved], *Rudé právo* (February 19, 1994).

[96] *Frankfurter Allgemeine Zeitung* (April 10, 1996): 1.

future, Czechs, like Austrians in the late 1950s and 1960s, will debate and worry over the *kalte Anschluss*—economic annexation by the backdoor. Such fears no longer exist in Austria, because it has diversified its dependence among other states, because its economy is growing and vital, and most important, because numerous institutional similarities and overlaps buffer Austria from an acute sense of dependency. Whether developments will turn out so well for the Czech Republic remains to be seen. It will depend in part on European and global developments that the Czech Republic has no chance of controlling directly.

Slovak Military Conversion

The Slovak Republic was exposed to other pressures emanating not from Germany and the EU but from Prague and from Western capitals more generally. The Slovak Republic's radical conversion program for its armaments industry is unprecedented throughout the industrial world. The end of the Cold War in 1989 and the Gulf War of 1990 were a double shock that eliminated most of the demand for Slovak armaments virtually overnight. Sharp reductions in international tensions and in the defense budgets of former Warsaw Pact countries, the loss of export markets in the Third World, a new national policy of sharply restricting arms exports, and the proven inferiority of traditional mechanized forms of warfare in the Gulf War all made inescapable a very rapid contraction of eastern Slovakia's heavy industry in general and its weapons producers in particular.

Czecho-Slovakia's new identity as a democratic state and its wish to join Western international institutions such as NATO, the EU, WEU, and the CSCE were also important reasons for a reorientation in the government's policy. In a new international system, the federal government could no longer afford to neglect the political aspects of Czecho-Slovak weapons exports. This was true in particular of arms shipments to the Middle Eastern countries such as Iran and Syria. The decision of the Czecho-Slovak federal government to sell arms to Syria generated a note of protest from the U.S. government to Deputy Minister of Foreign Affairs Martin Palouš. Democratization and new international allies thus also diminished the market for Czechoslovak weapons exports. During his visit to Hungary, U.S. Assistant Secretary of Defense Donald Atwood declared that the U.S. government had no objections either to a strong defense in former Soviet bloc countries or to arms production or exports, provided these went only to friendly states.[97] Deputy Director of the U.S. Agency for Arms Control and Disarmament Michael Moodie voiced a similar opinion. Interna-

---

[97] *Hospodářské noviny* (July 22, 1991): 14.

tional economic and political developments were reinforced by the federal government's draconian decision to halt arms exports altogether as incompatible with the democratic norms of the Velvet revolution.

As a consequence, production at the thirty-six Slovak arms producers dropped by 9.5 billion Czechoslovak korunas ($665 million) in 1989, compared to further reductions of 8 billion ($286 million) in 1990 and 6.3 billion ($226 million) in 1991.[98] All told, between 1988 and 1992, production dropped by an astounding 90 percent.[99] In 1988, armaments accounted for almost 9 percent of Slovak exports, compared to only 2 percent in 1992. WTO members absorbed about 80 percent of Czecho-Slovak arms exports in the late 1980s. With the breakup of the WTO those exports declined from Kčs 6.1 billion (426 million) in 1988 to Kčs 0.1 billion (35 million) in 1992.[100] And the share of arms production in total Slovak industrial production declined from 6.3 percent in 1988 to 0.9 percent in 1992. The impact at local and regional levels was disastrous. Slovakia's major arms producers laid off thousands of workers.[101] Between 1987 and 1992–93, Slovakia lost between 40,000 and 50,000 jobs in the arms industry, or about 70 percent of all jobs lost in the Czecho-Slovak economy.[102] Regionally, the impact was also highly asymmetric, with northwest Slovakia bearing 70 percent of the total reduction, while south central Slovakia took cuts of "only" 18 percent.[103] These dramatic reductions reinforced the widely shared Slovak sentiment that political decisions in Prague had disastrous consequences only in Slovakia, and that a breakup of Czecho-Slovakia might therefore be in Slovakia's best economic interest. In 1991, 70 percent of the Slovaks were highly critical of the federal government's policies, which they closely associated with the name of President Václav Havel.[104] To be sure, the conversion

---

[98] Karol Droppa, "Conversion of Armaments Production in the Slovak Republic," in *Conversion of the Military Production: Comparative Approach* (Bratislava: Slovak Academy of Sciences, Institute of Economics; and Friedrich Ebert Foundation, Bratislava, 1993), p. 7.

[99] Brigita Schmögnerová, "Konverzia v podnikoch Slovenskej republiky v transformačnom období" [Enterprise Conversion in a Slovak Republic in Transition], *Ekonomický časopis* 41 (April 1993): 265.

[100] Jaroslav Bartl, "Peripetie zbrojárskej výroby" [Peripheral Armaments Production], *Hospodářské noviny* (July 26, 1993): 4.

[101] Oldřich Čehák, Ladislav Ivánek, Miroslav Krč, and Jan Šelešovský, *Zbrojní výroba, konverze, obranyschopnost* [Armament Production, Conversion, and Defense Capacity] (Prague: Magnet-Press, 1993), p. 78.

[102] Droppa, "Conversion of Armaments Production," p. 7.

[103] Ludmila Kormanová, *Conversion of Arms Production at a Regional Level* (Bratislava: Slovak Academy of Sciences, Institute of Economics, and Friedrich Ebert Foundation, 1993), p. 185.

[104] Parol Frič et al., *Aktuálne problémy slovenskej spoločnosti—máj 1991* [Actual Problems of Slovak Society—May 1991] (Bratislava: Institute for Social Analysis, Comenius University, 1991), pp. 49–50.

process led Slovak enterprises toward normal competitive environments; it reduced overmanning; and it created small- and medium-sized firms producing for civilian markets. But whatever the policy's beneficial long-term benefits, its short-term costs for the Slovak economy were enormous.

A number of international actors, many from the United States, were involved in the Slovak conversion process. They provided assistance, mostly at the national level, to specific enterprises and regions. Members of the International Executive Service Corps (IESC), for example, gave advice to both major firms such as ZŤS Martin, ZŤS Dubnica, PS Považská Bystrica, and PPS Detva as well as to the Slovak government. The U.S. Agency for International Development (AID) offered technical support for two Slovak companies undergoing conversion. KPMG Peat Marwick, a large consulting firm, was selected to organize the restructuring of both PPS Detva and ZŤS Hriňová. The Czecho-Slovak-American Enterprise Fund (CSAEF) also engaged a variety of support activities that focused primarily on small- and medium-sized firms. And one Dutch company, START, set up operations in the northwest region to improve the human resource management routines of Slovak firms that are going through the conversion process. The activities of international organizations in which the United States plays a leading role have also been important. The North Atlantic Cooperation Council (NACC), for example, devoted three major meetings to the Slovak conversion problem.[105] And the OECD, the International Monetary Fund (IMF), the World Bank Group, and the Bank for International Settlement also have offered assistance at the regional and enterprise level.

Several European institutions and organizations not directly concerned with economic matters have also been involved in the Slovak conversion; so has the European Bank for Reconstruction and Development (EBRD). Furthermore, should the Slovak Republic choose a western European path in its security policy, it might be able to join the Independent European Programme Group dealing with the coordination of procurement and research and development policies in organizations like the European Cooperation for the Long Term in Defense (EUCLID).[106] In sharp contrast to the involvement of the United States and European actors,

---

[105] "Defense Conversion," May 20–22, 1992; "Interaction between Defense Spending and Economic Development with Particular Emphasis on Defense Budget Issues," September 30–October 2, 1992; and "The Human Dimension of Defense Conversion," December 3–4, 1992. See Daniel George, "NATO's Economic Cooperation with NACC Partners," *NATO Review* 41 (August 1993): 20.

[106] Philip Gummett, "Restructuring of the Arms Industries in Western Europe: Market Rationalization Rather Than Conversion," in *Conversion of the Military Production, Comparative Approach: Papers from an International Conference* (Bratislava: Friedrich Ebert Foundation, 1993), pp. 48, 58.

Germany has played no more than a marginal role in assisting Slovak conversion. Support has typically come from Germany's political foundations, which have organized some seminars; direct German aid was discussed by the Slovak-German Roundtable without any concrete results.

Slovak arms executives and government officials have made it clear that the arms industry should be given a second chance. According to former Deputy Defense Minister Andrej Sobol, the Slovak Republic is committed to exporting weapons in competition with other states.[107] The new policy explains why the Slovak government launched a major advertising campaign in 1994 and sent delegations of officials and executives from major Slovak arms producers to India, Vietnam, Indonesia, and Iran, all former importers of WTO arms. Foreign officials also have visited Bratislava hoping to forge closer ties with Slovak arms producers. The government's objective is to raise arms production to at least 25 percent of the 1989 capacity within a few years.[108] Topping the Slovak Republic's list of military products is a newly designed howitzer code-named "Zuzana" that fires NATO-standard ammunition. Military experts believe this cannon to be the first of its kind intended for Western markets. The arms producer ZŤS Martin has modernized its classic T-72 tank, which is also now available on the world market. According to experts, there are an estimated 8,000 T-72 tanks in use around the world. The modernization of the Slovak arms industry has also contributed to an increasing compatibility with NATO weapons and was a frequent theme of discussions with Western defense officials during 1995.[109]

The Slovak Republic's conversion policy since 1989 shows the primacy of international economic and political developments, which have translated directly, and virtually unmediated by institutions, into a massive dislocation of the Slovak regional economy. Nationalist resentment of Czecho-Slovak federal policy, initially dominated by Czech influence, and of the harsh intrusion of international markets and political pressures is shaping the distinctive political outlook of the Slovak Republic in contemporary central Europe.

---

[107] "We do not want to be known as the gun suppliers of Europe, we just want to provide our citizens with jobs. . . . It is a strategic fight for the arms market out there, and every tactics and means is fair game. We will do what the rest of the world does." Former Defense Minister Andrej Sobol in interview for Reuter, Bratislava, November 24, 1994.

[108] Then Defense Minister Pavol Kanis, as quoted by Reuter, Bratislava, November 24, 1994.

[109] The modernization of the Slovak arms industry was discussed at meetings of the Defense Minister Ján Sitek with the British Defense Minister Malcolm Rifkind on February 15, 1995, as reported in *Národná obroda* (February 16, 1995), and with U.S. Secretary of Defense Perry on September 18, 1995, as reported in "Armáda Slovenskej republiky" [The Army of the Slovak Republic], *Sme* (September 19, 1995): 96–97.

Hungary's Social Policy

Hungary's experience illustrates how international developments affect the partial reorganization of social policies in post-Communist states. The evolution of Hungary's social policy is affected by two contradictory constraints. The first is rooted in the economic crisis of transformation, and the second, in the political crisis of legitimation. The first puts the government under pressure to cut, and the second to expand, social services. Hungary's social policy thus lies at the intersection of an emerging market economy and a consolidating political democracy, within international economic constraints that focus more on international capital markets, the IMF, and the World Bank than on the EU and Germany.

The legacy of Communism was a set of social policies shaped by political, not economic, considerations. Social benefits were generous well beyond the level of productivity of the Hungarian economy. The state provided free health care and education, family allowances, earnings-related pensions, and sick pay to its citizens. In exchange, wages were kept low. Because there was full employment, there was no need to create a social net to protect the unemployed. And because citizens' eligibility for benefits was tied to their employment status, under full employment, social benefits were quasi-universal. Indeed, in the 1970s and 1980s, universal benefits became a right of citizenship. By the late 1980s, Hungary's social expenditure was on a par with that of the "social welfare" states in western Europe, as illustrated by an overall ratio of social income transfers to GDP well above what would have been expected for Hungary's income level.[110] Because real wages were declining in the 1980s, social transfers increased from 23 percent of the nominal income of the population in 1980, to 24 percent in 1985, and 28 percent in 1990.[111] Hungarian social policy was thus approaching the social democratic model based on the principle of inclusive universality.

What model of social welfare system is Hungary heading for in its post-Communist transition? Economic necessities exert a strong pressure to cut

[110] The World Bank names Belgium, Denmark, Finland, France, the Netherlands, Norway, and Sweden as the "Social Welfare States." *A Világbank szociálpolitikai jelentése Magyarországról* [The Report of the World Bank on Social Policy in Hungary] (Budapest: Institute of Sociology of the Hungarian Academy of Sciences, 1992), p. 34. The figure is open to question. Some sociologists have noted we should take into account the informal economy, which produces an estimated 25–30 percent of the Hungarian GDP. With this adjustment in the GDP figures, the overall ratio of social income transfers to GDP is close to that of "Lower Income States." Others argue that the share of Hungary's informal economy does not exceed 10–15 percent of GDP and hence does not deviate from the figures in western Europe.

[111] *Népszabadság* (October 21, 1993): 10. The ratio of social benefits within the monetary income of the population has increased further in the post-Communist period to 31 percent in 1993.

welfare spending and to move toward targeted social services thus making it difficult to turn toward the Scandinavian model. On the other hand, political constraints make it difficult to give up achieved levels of social spending tied either to the occupational system of society or granted universally as a matter of citizenship right. Social expectations generated by the Communist system make a U-turn toward the U.S. system highly implausible, pushing Hungary instead toward a mix of social security and targeted social services.[112]

In 1990, the official program of Hungary's new government stipulated that the economic transition from Communism should eventually lead to a "social market economy."[113] The allusion to the German model was both obvious and deliberate. Parallel historical situations of the two countries made the choice of the Hungarian government plausible. In both cases, the social market economy was seen as a solution to the collapse and failure of a centrally planned economy. Furthermore, the contrast between Germany's successful and Hungary's unsuccessful model made this choice especially compelling. The "social" in "social market economy" expressed Hungary's intent to maintain a system of social protection. The transition to a market economy was not to lead to abdication of government responsibility in safeguarding the security of society. For Hungarian policy makers, it is self-evident that the German pattern is both desirable and viable.

Thus the government of Prime Minister Antall, elected in 1990, acknowledged the right of individuals to a socially determined minimum level of subsistence; it strove to concentrate financial resources to achieve a socially acceptable level of social provisions, while widening the scope of targeted and means-tested schemes.[114] The government's program supported voluntary organizations providing social services; it encouraged

[112] Bob Deacon expects the social policy regime in Hungary to turn toward the liberal welfare state. He argues that the weakness of leftist parties from inside and the strength of international organizations (IMF, World Bank) from the outside, due to the indebtedness of the Hungarian economy, will push Hungary toward the liberal welfare state. Bob Deacon, "Developments in East European Social Policy," in Catherine Jones, ed., *New Perspectives on the Welfare State in Europe* (London: Routledge, 1993), p. 192. The first four years of post-Communist transition, however, showed that internal pressures stemming from democratic politics are balancing external pressures. The irony of the situation is that a new government dominated by socialists appears to move toward liberal reforms of Hungary's social policy. In March 1995, the Hungarian government, at the initiative of then Minister of Finance Lajos Bokros, announced an austerity program that contained proposals aimed at cutting back social expenditures. The program proposed to abolish universal family benefits. Nevertheless, this reform does not signal a general turn toward a liberal welfare state. Put in the context of a former Communist welfare state in need of restructuring, such reforms, we argue, will produce an outcome that may be closer to a corporatist than a liberal, residual welfare state.

[113] *A nemzeti megújhodás programja* [The Program of National Revival] (Budapest, 1990), p. 13.

[114] *A nemzeti megújhodás programja* p. 120.

private initiatives based on the principle of self-help; and it emphasized the importance of the family in Hungary's new social policy. This reflected the strength of a conservative Hungarian tradition and underlined strong similarities with the German model. In 1991, the Hungarian parliament passed a resolution to modernize the social security system. It foresaw a compulsory social insurance system financed through individual contributions and the state budget. Social assistance was to be separated from social insurance.

For understandable political reasons, the Antall government did not dare do more than piecemeal reforms. In hindsight, this proved to be costly for Hungary; the decentralization of the union movement at that time had created a brief window of opportunity for parliament to adopt some of the unavoidable, painful economizing measures.

With delays, these measures became politically much more costly. Nevertheless, the Horn government adopted them after its election victory in 1994. After 1989, social spending grew, even as Hungary's measured GDP contracted. Between 1985 and 1992, social spending increased from 38 percent to 54 percent of the state budget.[115] Since 1994, growing budget deficits have forced the Socialist-Liberal coalition government to deal with social policy in political circumstances more difficult than those confronted by the Antall government. In March 1995, the government announced a new program of austerity that foresaw the reform of social policy and proposed means-tested provisions for some of the existing universal rights on family benefits.

Although dominated by Socialists, the Horn government took one step toward the residual welfare state model. Further reforms in this direction confront serious political constraints, however. First, the Socialist-Liberal government has to face a revived, strong labor movement. And second, Socialist members of parliament are reluctant to vote against their conscience and in favor of a social policy reform that reduces income redistribution. In any case, the economic exigencies of a very large budget deficit and very high levels of employer contribution to social policy simply do not permit an increase in tax revenues and social support at current levels, let alone a growth in social expenditures. Although social policy outcomes can be regulated even if structural reforms do not come about, economic exigencies appear to compel the government to adopt radical reforms that internalize—and in the case of family benefits, that may even overshoot—the recommendations made by the IMF and the World Bank.

---

[115] Part of this growth in social spending is due to a reduction in subsidies and other direct economic expenditures in the state budget. See István Gy. Tóth, "A jóléti rendszer az átmenet időszakában" [The System of Social Welfare in the Period of Transition], *Közgazdasági Szemle* 41 (1994): 316–18.

Hungarian social policy is affected by the IMF, the World Bank, and the EU. The EU has extended in a limited manner its financial support to the field of social policy within the framework of Poland and Hungary Assistance for Economic Restructuring Programme (PHARE). Since 1990, PHARE has helped with a modest grant of 3 million ECU ($2.3 million) in launching a new foundation for the development of social welfare networks that aims at stimulating local self-help initiatives. PHARE also granted 15 million ECU ($11.4 million) for an employment and social policy development program. And the EU provides expertise and information about western European patterns of social welfare policy. In 1993, the World Bank granted a credit of $223 million over fifteen years that must be spent on the development of Hungary's social security system: $91 million for increasing the capacity of health care institutions, for educational programs, and for the development of informatics; and $132 million for upgrading the social insurance system's computers. In exchange, the government and the social insurance funds have promised not to raise social insurance contributions before June 30, 1998.[116]

The EU, IMF, and World Bank have developed separate channels to the Hungarian government and administration. The EU has primarily connections with the ministries and institutions responsible for the different aspects of social policy. The IMF and the World Bank have close connections with the Ministry of Finance. Where the EU influence is dispersed within the government from below, the IMF and World Bank have their greatest effect at the top, in the ministry with the greatest amount of economic power. Until 1994, the piecemeal approach of the Antall government favored the dispersed mode of the EU. But the power has swung to the World Bank and IMF since March 1995, when the Horn government decided to adopt a radical austerity program. The IMF and the World Bank advocate a restructuring of social policy; introducing the insurance principle in health care, pensions, and unemployment; ending the growth of state financing of social services; and redirecting the resources from universal social services to targeted social assistance.[117] The magnitude of the government's budget deficits and the level of debt of the Hungarian economy assure the IMF and the World Bank a very important voice in

---

[116] *Népszabadság* (April 24, 1993): 5.

[117] In an interview, Deputy Director of the IMF Gerard Belanger saw as a key problem of social security the fact that in Hungary, as in other post-Communist countries, insurance and redistribution are linked in one program. Insufficient funds for social insurance are thus distributed according to universal criteria. Because Hungary is already spending too much on social insurance, the amount cannot be further increased. The solution is a targeted redirection of funds to those truly in need. In such a reformed program, people with higher income would receive less than the poor. See Zsuzsa N. Vadász, "Belanger: Az ígéreteknek ára van" [Belanger: Promises Have a Price], *Magyar Hírlap* [Hungarian News] (October 9, 1993): 8.

any future reforms of Hungarian social welfare policy,[118] while the comparatively weak social welfare regime of the EU is likely to exert much less influence.

The advice and requirements of the IMF and the World Bank, on the one hand, and of the EU and the German "social market economy" model, on the other, do not necessarily exclude each other. To date, the recommendations of the IMF and the World Bank do not aim at ridding Hungarian social policy of the principle of universality and solidarity.[119] All international institutions advocate strengthening private actors within the field of social welfare policy. Furthermore, the EU does not insist on maintaining social welfare policies the IMF and the World Bank consider financially unviable in the long term. Hungarian policy makers are inclined to follow the suggestions of the IMF and the World Bank, not because they are under external pressure but because a great number of them have internalized the ideas that dominate current problem solving in this field. Nevertheless, the commitment to the model of a social market economy and the constraints of electoral politics limit the extent to which liberal policy reforms can be implemented in Hungary.

The influence of international actors is mediated through these structural contradictions in Hungary's domestic politics. The institutional model of German social welfare policy is a point of general orientation for policy makers. The influence of the EU offers at best weak institutional constraints. In the future, the IMF and World Bank are likely to exert more direct influence on Hungarian social policy. The more serious the economic problems of Hungary are, the more effective the IMF and World Bank constraints will be. As long as these different international effects are not in clear contradiction with one another, the Hungarian government will remain free to make its own choices, however hard these may be.

Rapid internationalization with little institutionalization is a pervasive phenomenon of the social and economic reform policies that the central European states have adopted in the 1990s. In the Slovak Republic's pol-

---

[118] This point is emphasized by Deacon, "East European Social Policy."

[119] Deacon erroneously views the IMF and the World Bank simply as harbingers of a neoliberal set of social policy proposals, incapable of learning or adapting to the specific central European circumstances. See Bob Deacon, "A nemzetek fölötti és globális szervezetek hatása a közép-eurpai nemzeti szociálpolitikára" [The Impact of Supranational and Global Organizations on the Social Policy of Central European Nations], *Esély* [Opportunity] 6 (1992), and Deacon, "East European Social Policy." A point Deacon overlooks, however, is that the liberal proposals of the IMF and World Bank do not advocate moving to a residual welfare state. For example, when the World Bank proposed in 1991 to transform the Hungarian system of family allowances into a more targeted system, it did not advocate abolishing the universality of this provision. That proposal came actually from within the government which, for its own economic and political reasons, thus overshot the recommendations of these international organizations. See *A Világbank szociálpolitikai jelentése Magyarországról* [The Report of the World Bank on Social Policy in Hungary] (Budapest, 1992), p. 6.

icy of military conversion and in Hungary's social welfare policy, this involves the EU and Germany less than NATO and Russia, the IMF and the World Bank, and national patterns of adaptation. For reasons of domestic politics, Slovak, more than Hungarian, privatization seeks to curtail an Anglo-American model of capital-market-led and boost a traditional German bank-led model of welfare state capitalism. Internationalization without institutionalization captures the essence, not the subtleties, of a process that for historical reasons acquires different meanings in different settings.

REVISITING THE PAST ON THE RETURN TO EUROPE

For the central European states, the road back to Europe goes through Berlin and Bonn. This political reality stirs painful historical memories. Two generations have passed since Nazi Germany invaded central Europe, occupied it, and made it its staging area for a genocidal war and the Holocaust. While memories of these events appear to account for surprisingly little in today's Hungary and Slovak Republic, and while they have had remarkably few political effects on the clear Western course post-Communist Poland is steering, they play a central political role in the Czech Republic and its troubled relations with Germany.[120]

The resettlement of some three million ethnic Germans after 1945 has eliminated the practical problem of how to deal with a German minority in the Czech Republic. But despite an ostensibly strong commitment to cooperate on the part of both governments, their different historical perspectives have made it very difficult to come to a satisfactory resolution of issues involving past crimes and injustices. At the core of the current problem is the legality of what the Czechs see as a "transfer," and the Germans an "expulsion," of three million ethnic Germans from Bohemia. Historians have little difficulty in recognizing in the Beneš decrees an instance of a policy of ethnic cleansing that Nazi Germany practiced with unsurpassed brutality, on a massive scale, and with genocidal consequence throughout Eastern Europe and the Soviet Union in the 1940s, and that in the Yugoslav war of the 1990s, both Germany and the Czech Republic have repeatedly decried as insufferably inhumane.

The national liberation struggles of "old" and "young" Czechs in the Habsburg empire, strongly opposed by an ethnic German population intent on defending its privileged position, finally resulted in Czechoslovak statehood at the end of World War I. Important strata of the German mi-

---

[120] For a good description of the role war memories play in German-Czech relations, see Berthold Kohler, "Ich habe den Eindruck, wir drehen uns im Kreis," *Frankfurter Allgemeine Zeitung* (April 2, 1996): 6.

nority, however, directly and indirectly undermined the new state. In the 1930s, they became willing instruments of the foreign policy of Nazi Germany. And many welcomed the occupation and dismemberment of the Czechoslovak Republic. Election statistics speak an unambiguous language. In 1935, the pro-fascist Sudeten-German Party won 67.2 percent in the border regions mostly settled by ethnic Germans, compared to only 3.6 percent for the Social Democrats.[121] With 44 members of parliament, it became the strongest party in the Czechoslovak Republic. Most Czechs were forced to leave the border areas after the Munich Agreement. When German troops occupied the rest of the country in March 1939, Hitler established a protectorate over Bohemia and Moravia, subject to his political orders and German law enforcement authorities. And he installed a puppet regime collaborating with Nazi Germany in the remaining territory in a newly constituted Slovak state.

Even before Germany was defeated, the Czechoslovak government-in-exile, headed by Eduard Beneš, concluded, together with the Allied powers, that it would be necessary to resettle German populations, and on a vast scale, from postwar Czechoslovakia, Poland, and Hungary to Germany. The idea reflected a broad Allied consensus and was legalized at the Potsdam Conference on August 2, 1945. This policy reflected strong, antifascist currents in Czechoslovak society. Based on their political experiences between 1938 and 1945, most Czechs identified all Germans as Nazis. At the end of the war, this resettlement was carried out immediately and spontaneously in many parts of Czechoslovakia. This phase of "wild transfers" marked the high point of the uncoordinated violence that the Germans suffered at the hands of the Czechs. The resettlement of most of the estimated three million Germans occurred between 1945 and 1947. At the same time, the Czech population that had left the border areas in 1938 or was subsequently expelled by the Germans returned, together with new settlers. When in 1952 the active settlement of the borderlands had ended, the total population of settlers there was only 2.3 million, or about two-thirds of the 1930 figure. By the late 1980s, it still remained 20 percent below the level of the 1930s. The demographic and territorial structure of the population continues to show the effects of the vast population changes that occurred after 1945. The borderlands still have a wider range of different nationalities, and a higher proportion of non-Czechs, than the interior regions of the Czech Republic.[122]

[121] The Sudeten-German party won 15.2 percent of the national vote. *Malý encyklopedický slovník* [Small Encyclopedic Dictionary] (Prague: Prague Academy, 1972), p. 206; Karel Richter, *Sudety* [Sudeten Country] (Prague: FAJMA, 1994), p. 84.

[122] According to the 1991 census, the share of the Czech population in the border regions ranges between 80 and 96 percent; Slovaks account for 2 to 10 percent; and Germans, for less than one-half percent. *Census of Persons, Houses and Apartments as of March 3, 1991* (Prague: Federal Statistical Bureau, 1993), p. 67.

The Velvet revolution and various voucher privatization programs created fundamentally new political and economic conditions in the Czech borderlands. A border-spanning regional economy has emerged, which expresses itself in cross-border Euroregions designed to solve practical problems affecting local communities. The initiative for creating such regions normally comes from the private sector in Germany. For example, projects financed by the EU in northern Bohemia, and a new regional program drawn up in 1995 for the border region linking Bavaria and the Czech Republic, illustrate how a European umbrella can improve bilateral relations in a multilateral framework. The emerging regional economy is marked by a variety of forms of German investment in Czech firms; the illegal and legal short-distance commuting of Czech workers who take both legal and illegal jobs, often in Bavaria, with take-home pay that is less than what German workers receive but more than what equivalent Czech jobs are paying; and a sharp increase in tourism, prostitution, and a variety of illegal business ventures. While the rapidity of economic and social change has brought a flood of complaints on both sides of the border, most observers agree that, in and of themselves, they are not the source of the problems that bedevil German-Czech relations. Those problems are primarily political.

In a widely noted 1990 speech soon after becoming president, Václav Havel apologized for the mass expulsions after 1945. Havel wanted to create a new spirit that would permit both countries to put the past behind them and look forward to creating cordial relations for the future. Because it seemed to create an equality between Nazi atrocities and the injustice of mass resettlement, many Czechs, especially on the Left, were appalled by Havel's speech. On the side of the Sudeten Germans, the speech reactivated some old demands. On February 17, 1995, Havel responded to the increasingly strident demands of the Sudeten Germans, insisting that now that apologies had been made, it was time to look for practical solutions to real problems. "Our republic," Havel said, "will not discuss a revision of any of the results of World War II, and it will not tolerate any intervention in our constitutional order or accept any alterations in the course of history that would harm the present generation."[123] The solution to the bilateral relations between the Czech Republic and Germany, Havel proposed, was a substitution of the western European concept of political citizenship for the central European notion of ethnic nationalism.

The position of the Czech government is that Germany must renounce, also in the name of the Sudeten Germans, all territorial and property claims. In return, the Czech government is willing to acknowledge, as it apparently did in secret bilateral relations that broke down in February

[123] Václav Havel, as quoted in *Rudé právo* (February 18, 1995): 4.

1996, that serious injustices were committed when the Sudeten Germans were forcibly resettled from Czechoslovakia to Germany after 1945. But for reasons of domestic politics, the Czech government's room for maneuver is circumscribed. A public opinion poll conducted in March 1996 showed that 86 percent would not vote for a party committed to a public apology to the Sudeten Germans for injustices allegedly committed at the end of World War II.[124]

Hence a public appeal in February 1996 by nearly one hundred Czech, and some German, intellectuals that criticized the government's policy on resettlement as unrealistic has had virtually no public impact.[125] The Czech government rejects outright the notion that it engage in a dialogue or negotiations with anyone but the legitimate authorities of the German state. Indeed, with the full support of the overwhelming majority of the Czech population, the government rejects the demand that it do so as a violation of the Potsdam Agreement and as a threat to the entire legal order on which the Czechoslovak Republic was founded after 1945. This position was bolstered strongly on March 8, 1995, when the Constitutional Court of the Czech Republic ruled against a descendant of a Sudeten-German family, now living in the Czech Republic, who was trying to reclaim the property of his parents. The court found the Sudeten Germans responsible and active collaborators of Nazi Germany, declared the Beneš decrees to be fully legal and legitimate, and prohibited any attempt to revise them.[126]

Because it is not minority rights but historical memories that are at stake, international and European norms have been less important in Czech-German than in Polish-German relations. The "Good Neighbourhood and Friendly Cooperation Treaty," which Chancellor Helmut Kohl and President Václav Havel signed in Prague on February 27, 1992, left several important issues unresolved, specifically, a clear declaration of the invalidity of the Munich Agreement of 1938. In addition, the treaty uses the term "land frontier" instead of "state frontier," does not cover property issues, and does not address some outstanding issues such as German reparation payments to Czech victims of fascism. The negotiations and the ramifications of the treaty were controversial in both Czech and German parliaments and resulted in the filing of a letter of understanding,

---

[124] *Frankfurter Allgemeine Zeitung* (May 25, 1996): 7.

[125] *Lidové noviny* (February 20, 1996). This was a follow-up to an appeal of "Reconciliation 95," in which over one hundred Czech, German, and Sudeten-German intellectuals, journalists, and students publicly urged the Czech government to start negotiations with the Sudeten Germans. See *Lidové noviny* (March 30, 1995).

[126] Georg Reißmüller presents, among other things, the Constitutional Court's reasoning in some detail in "Verantwortlichkeit von Deutschen und Tschechen," *Frankfurter Allgemeine Zeitung* (March 28, 1996): 12.

appended to the treaty, that leaves unresolved some aspects concerning the specifically Sudeten-German agenda. Because the German government enjoys strong political leverage, the preeminent foreign policy goal of the Czech Republic, full EU membership, will undoubtedly require compromises and German-Czech cooperation.[127]

Who has leverage over the German government domestically is thus of no small consequence for German-Czech relations. For example, Rudolf Hilf, by no means an extremist among the Sudeten Germans, and a proponent of Euroregions as instruments for international cooperation, regarded Havel's 1995 speech as "a step backwards."[128] The Sudeten-German Homeland Society has demanded that the Czech government open a dialogue with it. And it insists that the Beneš decrees were illegal and that the issue of compensation for lost property must be reopened for consideration. The political objective evidently is to use Czech recognition of the Sudeten-German organization as a way to make it the preferred partner for negotiating unresolved property claims and settle open civil cases.[129] It is the geographic and political balance of power inside Germany that is giving the Sudeten Germans' traditional central European notions of ethnic nationalism such weight in the determination of German policy. Most Sudeten Germans live in Bavaria and are an important voting bloc of the conservative Christian Social Union (CSU). Members of the Sudeten-German Homeland Society deny overwhelmingly that they would like to return to the Czech republic (85 percent), or that they insist on the restitution of lost property (75 percent); and they affirm (83 percent) that the time has come to finally settle this issue.[130] Worried

---

[127] Czechs have very well trained ears. When in his 1994 government policy statement Chancellor Helmut Kohl stated that "it is in the interest of Germany and Europe to keep in mind first of all Poland in the future expansion of the EU," without mentioning explicitly any other state, his statement drew public attention and indignation in the Czech Republic. Despite German denials, Czechs perceived Kohl's statement as a signal that there may well be additional German conditions prior to German support of Czechia's admission to the EU.

[128] Rudolf Hilf, "Václav Havel's Speech and its implications," *Rudé právo* (April 7, 1995): 19.

[129] According to one of the leaders of the Sudeten Germans, Professor Kurt Heissig, outstanding issues include, in exchange for waiving claims to territorial autonomy, liberal measures of personal autonomy in Czech territories; the Czech state's officially encouraging Germans to return to Czech lands, especially to regions formerly settled by Germans; the Sudeten Germans' recognizing the right of domicile for all social groups currently settled in the border regions; the return to Germans *in natura* of property currently in the hands of the state; a choice between property or financial compensation in case of property lost or now in private hands, with the understanding that compensation payments will be small and that the recipients will have to pay taxes on their awards; finally, at least for some time, double citizenship or equality of legal position for Sudeten Germans and Czech natives in certain areas. See Kurt Heissig, "Sudeten German Future in Bohemia and Moravia," *Revue Střední Evropa* [Central European Review] 33 (1993): 27–28.

[130] The responses are based on a representative sample of 400 members that a German survey research institute, Emnid, polled between February and April 1996. See *Der Spiegel* 21 (1996): 33.

nonetheless about the possibility of the creation of a credible right-wing alternative in a state that it has dominated electorally for the last four decades, the CSU has embraced the cause of the Sudeten Germans. During the Sudeten Germans' annual meeting in May 1994, Bavarian Minister President Edmund Stoiber insisted that a direct dialogue between the Sudeten Germans and the Czech government was the only missing aspect in the relationship.[131] With the CSU as a central partner in a shaky coalition government in Bonn, Chancellor Kohl, German foreign policy, and German-Czech relations are thus hostage to a constellation of domestic political forces that give enough weight, within Germany's general European orientation, to a political constituency whose views express traditional central European views.[132] This has colored the German government's foot dragging in its negotiation with the Czech Republic over the signing of a joint declaration supposed to resolve at least some of the items left open in the cooperation treaty of 1992. And it was underlined by Foreign Minister Klaus Kinkel's unprecedented pronouncement calling into question the legality of the 1945 Potsdam Agreement, the basis for the expulsion of the Sudeten Germans from Czech territory at the end of World War II.[133] Despite numerous political obstacles in both German and Czech domestic politics, Prime Minister Vaclav Klaus and Chancellor Helmut Kohl signed a declaration that acknowledged the wrongs each had committed against the other in the 1930s and 1940s.[134]

This chapter has explored the wide range of ways central European states seek to import and export institutions, to adapt their institutions through policy reforms, as in the case of privatization, and to treat their national minorities. It has pointed out differences both in the definition of national security and in the degree to which central European states orient themselves in their security policies toward West or East. Finally, it has shown how, in their economic and social policies, central European states adapt differently to a range of international actors. Despite their many differences, during this period of transformation and transition the four central European states share the necessity of having to deal with many

[131] *Revue Střední Evropa* [Central European Review] 41 (Prague, 1994): 37–43.

[132] Chancellor Kohl's great hesitation in recognizing the Oder-Neisse border in 1990 illustrates how beholden he feels to strong political constituencies on the right wing of the Christian Democratic Union/Christian Social Union (CDU/CSU). In the case of Poland, the risk of creating insurmountable obstacles for unification changed Kohl's stance. There is no comparable issue, however, that would make him change his stance in the case of the Czech Republic.

[133] *Frankfurter Allgemeine Zeitung* (January 18, 1996), and *Rude právo* (January 19, 1996): 1, 4.

[134] Craig R. Whitney, "Germans and Czechs Try to Heal Hatreds of the Nazi Era," *New York Times* (January 22, 1997): A3.

international influences that are relatively unmediated by international institutions. This common condition gives them a distinctive position in European integration, compared to the states located along the northern, western, and southern periphery of Europe.

The integration process is evidently so powerful it has marginalized attempts by different organizations to reduce political uncertainties through the development of a variety of links in central Europe.[135] The gradually enlarging Central European Initiative (CEI), for example, now restricts its annual prime ministerial meetings to problems of the environment, culture, agriculture, and scientific research, important issues in and of themselves, but far removed from the strategic choices that central Europe faces at the margin of the European integration process. Nor have the four central European states in their capacity as the Visegrad group achieved any notable results. Although the framework laid out in the declaration following the Prague summit of 1992 was entitled "New Pattern of Central European Relations," by 1995, the group, as originally conceived, had died. The common quest for EU membership as reflected in the association agreements that the EU concluded at different times with all four central European states puts in question even the symbolic value of the Visegrad group. Because none of the central European states wants a subregional grouping as a substitute for what at least three of them regard as their highest foreign policy priority, EU and NATO membership, the pattern of central European relations resembles a competitive race more than a regional arrangement. International competition, not political cooperation, characterizes a sparse political landscape in central Europe, which, if we can trust northern, western, and southern European experience, is likely to be transformed only by several peaceful and prosperous decades. Meanwhile, sometimes comfortably and sometimes precariously, the central European states will have to cope with the pressures of rapid internationalization, softened by slow processes of institutionalization at home and abroad.

[135] Valerie Bunce, "Regional and European Integration in Postcommunist Europe: The Visegrad Group," in Katzenstein, *Mitteleuropa.*

CHAPTER EIGHT

The Smaller European States, Germany, and Europe

Peter J. Katzenstein

This book has shown that, together with Europe, Germany has varying effects on the institutions and policies of the smaller European states. At times, these effects reflect imbalances in power or a spontaneous coordination of conflicting objectives. More typically, they are mediated by a variety of institutions. These institutional effects do not occur in isolation from broader international or domestic developments. For example, both Germany and Europe have been shaped profoundly by the Cold War and the decision to rearm the Federal Republic within NATO. Widespread suspicion of a potential revival of German militarism made it imperative to embed a rearmed Germany fully in a Western and European framework. After the defeat of the European Defense Community (EDC) in the French Assembly, the European Economic Community (EEC) became a plausible option for anchoring Germany in a European economic network that the United States tolerated in the interest of its anti-Communist grand strategy.

For critical comments and suggestions on earlier drafts I thank David Cameron, James Caporaso, Nikiforos Diamandouros, Barry Eichengreen, Peter Gourevitch, Joseph Grieco, Helga Haftendorn, Peter Hall, Gunther Hellmann, Stanley Hoffmann, Mary F. Katzenstein, Robert O. Keohane, Beate Kohler-Koch, Michael Kreile, David Laitin, Stefan Leibfried, Andrei Markovits, Gary Marks, Harald Müller, Elizabeth Pond, Simon Reich, Judith Reppy, John Ruggie, Gian Enrico Rusconi, Wayne Sandholtz, Fritz Scharpf, Gebhard Schweigler, Anne-Marie Slaughter, Wolfgang Streeck, Bengt Sundelius, and Michael Zürn; seminar participants at the University of Bremen, Darmstadt, Geneva, Göttingen, Manchester, Mannheim, the European University Institute at Florence, the Humboldt University Berlin, and the Wissenschaftszentrum Berlin; the project participants; and two anonymous readers for Cornell University Press.

In the 1980s and 1990s, Germany and Europe have also been closely linked to global developments. The rivalry between the United States and the Soviet Union during the Cold War affected deeply all European states, especially those in southern and central Europe. The rise of new competitors and technological challenges in world markets created strong political pressures, especially from Europe's largest corporations, that helped bring about the Single European Act (SEA). The Balladur initiative in 1987–88 for the creation of a European Monetary Union (EMU) extended the SEA into the domain of monetary policy. The EMU became subsequently the center of the Treaty on European Union (TEU), which received further impetus from the end of the Cold War and German unification. Specifically, the TEU was a concerted attempt on the part of France, Germany, and other European states to create a stronger institutional network to further embed a united Germany in an integrating Europe.

This concluding chapter focuses on the interaction between the smaller or peripheral European states, Germany, and the EU.[1] The first section shows how the diversity in policies and politics within and across the various subregions of Europe points to the softness of the institutionalized effects of European integration. The second section specifies the European and German effects uncovered by the case studies, and the third analyzes how institutional effects vary across different issue areas. The fourth section examines what the EMU and German diplomacy in Yugoslavia tell us about German power. And the final section argues that this power is constrained by the collective memories of the past.

International Effects and Domestic Diversity

Contemporary European politics is marked by the coincidence of two disparate facts. International effects are strong and growing in shaping the affairs of various European states, especially the smaller ones. At the same time, across a broad spectrum of institutions and policies, the domestic affairs of many of these states show a remarkably persistent diversity.

The liberalization of the international economy, including Europe's, has had important effects. Christine Ingebritsen illustrates this point in chapter 6, contending that in Scandinavia, the influence of the global economy on the European integration process is clearly apparent. Key elements that defined the Scandinavian welfare state "model"—collectivism rather than individualism, a centralized system of industrial relations aim-

---

[1] Some of these states, like the Netherlands, are small but not peripheral. Others, like Poland, are peripheral but not small. For the sake of simplicity, this chapter refers to all of them as "smaller."

ing at wage solidarity and full employment rather than decentralization, wage dispersion, and unemployment—have gradually weakened since the 1970s. The result has been most noticeable in Sweden, where, by the early 1990s, strong market pressures weakened a solidaristic social welfare regime and thus narrowed the gap between Sweden and the insurance welfare regimes characteristic of its southern neighbors.

We can also trace easily the effects that the international system has on questions of national security. Chapter 7 illustrates the profound effects that the end of the Cold War, the breakup of the Warsaw Treaty Organization (WTO), and the disintegration of the Soviet Union have had on the central European states. These changes have brought forth distinctive forms of democratic capitalism that are fundamentally reshaping the relationship between central Europe and the rest of Europe. Vital for Poland, Hungary, and the Czech Republic, in particular, are close relations with NATO and its European mainstay, the Western European Union (WEU), as an incipient European security institution, as well as the Organization for Security and Cooperation in Europe (OSCE).

But it would be a great mistake to overemphasize the constraints of the international economy and state system. A liberal international economy enabled the smaller European welfare states to generate the economic growth that could finance their generous welfare services. And the Cold War permitted some of these states to occupy a special neutrality niche or to gain access to multilateral security institutions, such as NATO, that are inherently more beneficial to the smaller states than bilateral security treaties. The evolving European polity offers ample space for a variable domestic politics and a broad range of policies. This mixture of variability within a gradually convergent pattern is a central feature of contemporary European politics.

The Scandinavian social welfare model, for example, has accommodated both the redistributive politics of Sweden and a Danish model that provides generous social services but lacks a strong and explicit commitment to redistribution. Over time, the German institutional model of a social market economy has become increasingly relevant, while the Swedish welfare state model has begun to fade, even inside Sweden. Emphasizing this point in chapter 6, Christine Ingebritsen contends that Denmark may well offer a view of Sweden's future.[2] A member of the EU for more than two decades, Denmark is experiencing both growing economic dependence on Germany and high unemployment rates. Exposed to increasing global competition and economic dependence on Germany, many of the

[2] Christine Ingebritsen, "Euro-Politics and the Danish State: The New Europe, Incorporated?" paper presented at the Annual Meeting of the American Political Science Association, Washington, D.C., September 2–5, 1993.

smaller states located on Europe's western, southern, and eastern periphery welcome political integration because it offers them some promising strategies for countering national weakness. The European Union offers a reasonable prospect for negotiating the turbulence of the global economy with some regional support, as well as political opportunities to "tie down the Germans," and thus to diffuse growing bilateral dependence in a variety of multilateral arrangements.

The politics and policies of the smaller European states also vary widely in security affairs. While Poland, Hungary, and the Czech Republic have taken many measures to permit full integration into European security frameworks and NATO, the Slovak Republic has not. As it seeks to maintain traditionally good relations with Russia while forging new links with Europe, the Slovak Republic, in contrast to Poland, is focusing its attention largely on traditional national security issues.

For the smaller states, pervasive international effects are thus compatible with a considerable diversity in their domestic affairs and in their relationship with Germany and Europe. Often comparisons across geographical subregions make more sense than the grouping of states by points of the compass. In their readiness for an institutional and political engagement of the European integration process Sweden, Spain, and the Czech Republic share much in common. So do Norway, Greece, and the Slovak Republic in their relative indifference or disengagement. Furthermore, membership in the EU does not necessarily make mass publics or governments of a state like Germany more. The Netherlands and Greece, for example, both retain a deeply ambivalent attitude toward Germany, even though the unwillingness of the United States to get involved in the Yugoslav war before 1995 has led to an important change in Dutch attitudes toward Germany. Conversely, while political relations with Germany remain cordial, Slovak domestic politics in 1994–95 impeded, if not blocked altogether, the country's growing association with the EU.

Such variation results from the weight of past political choices, as reflected in different domestic structures and as modified only gradually by the uneven impetus of European convergence in different policy domains. In the case of Scandinavia, chapter 6 contends, the dependence of the manufacturing sector on Europe helped drive Sweden toward membership in the EU; conversely, the importance of the energy sector made it financially possible for Norway to stay outside the EU. Economic structures can thus shape domestic coalitions that have a profound effect on public policy. In a similar vein, as Paulette Kurzer explains in chapter 4, both the Netherlands and Belgium belong to the core of the European integration process and thus view European integration and German influence in Europe with a degree of political equanimity not possible in Scandinavia. Nevertheless, afflicted by divisive ethnic politics, saddled with increasingly uncompetitive manufacturing industries, and shunned by increasingly indifferent foreign investors, Belgium in the 1970s and 1980s managed to run up an extraordinarily high level of public indebtedness, compared to the Netherlands.

The concept of "domestic structures" encompasses not only economic or social structures and coalition politics but also collective norms and identities. As Michael Marks notes in chapter 5, Spain has been much more receptive than Greece to a European definition of its identity and a broad definition of its national interests. For Spain, the attraction of Europe was both instrumental and institutional. Seeking to consolidate a fledgling democracy after decades of Francoism, Spain's newly elected leaders turned toward Europe as a source of political support. As in Spain, support for Europe in Sweden and Finland is both instrumental and institutional. But with a collective Nordic identity as a ready alternative, Swedish and Finnish skepticism about Europe has become much stronger in recent years.

More specifically, personified in Prime Minister Felipe Gonzalez, the new democratic elite, both in government and in opposition, conceived of Spain as a core member of Europe. It sought to show political commitment abroad in ways that were at times highly unpopular with important domestic constituencies. In the mid-1980s, for example, in an enormous about-face, Gonzalez and his Socialist Party abandoned their long-standing, vociferous opposition and decided to join NATO. In 1990, for the first time since the Spanish-American war, Spain sent its armed forces abroad, dispatching three warships to the Persian Gulf in support of the war against Iraq. More important, it invoked a clause of the Spanish-U.S. defense treaty to permit the United States to use American air bases in Spain for bombing runs on Baghdad. And throughout the 1980s, in preparation for eventual EC membership, a Socialist government imposed structural changes on Spain's economy that left the country with the highest unemployment rate in western Europe. In brief, enlarging Spanish collective identity by a tangible European component helped Spain quickly become an important force inside the EU, where it put new issues on the European agenda that core states, including Germany, simply could not avoid. There is little indication that the electoral victory of Spain's conservative Popular Party under the leadership of José Maria Aznar in February 1996 and, subsequently, the formation of a new government of the Center Right will create significant changes in Spain's European policy.

Despite a deeply engrained anti-Americanism that should make the EU a natural and welcome partner, Greece is often hostile to a Europe in which "Latin" influences are seen to dominate unduly. Greece, for example, is the only EU member state that has refused to use the Latin-based classification scheme for EU documents. Commission officials acknowledge the existence of a cultural gap separating Greece from an organization suffused by acronyms and terms drawn from Latin civilization. In their view, Greek officials often seem to believe that the Turk's turban is preferable to the pope's tiara (triple crown).[3] In the 1980s, Greece was primarily interested in extracting a maximum of fiscal benefits from Europe, in reinforcing old political habits and practices rather than creating an institutional model that might help establish new ones. This was so, not because of unusual selfishness on Greece's part, but because of a fundamental mismatch between European and Greek interests. The EC/EU was and remains institutionally ill equipped to deal with issues of national security. Yet it was precisely external security issues (Turkey, Cyprus, Macedonia) that mattered most to Greece as it turned to Europe in the 1960s, 1970s, and well into the 1990s. Each time, Greek expectations in Europe were disappointed. From the perspective of the other EU member states, Greece often appeared like an enfant terrible. From the perspective of Greece, Europe has remained consistently indifferent to its vital security concerns. It is thus not surprising that Greece has had neither Spain's encompassing view of what it expected from the European integration process nor a clear vision of its preferred future in Europe.[4] Nevertheless, Greek policy has definitely moved in a European direction during the last two decades.[5]

Differences in domestic structures and policies toward Germany and Europe can have deep historical roots, or they can result from recent policy choices. When, in 1830, Greece became a sovereign state after centuries of Ottoman rule, its structure resembled that of Spain and other European states only on the surface. The façade of a rationalized bureaucracy and a liberal democracy concealed politics of an altogether different kind. For historical reasons, the government's inability to collect taxes and the lack of a regional system of government, for example, have made it impossible for Greece to conduct a prudent fiscal policy and difficult to benefit from

[3] I am indebted for this example to an anonymous reader of Cornell University Press. See also Kevin Featherstone and Kostas Ifantis, eds., *Greece in a Changing Europe: Between European Integration and Balkan Disintegration* (Manchester: Manchester University Press, 1996).

[4] It is probably no accident that, unlike the Spanish Socialists, the Greek Socialist leadership-in-exile lacked close personal contacts with Germany's leadership. While Felipe Gonzalez built links to Willy Brandt, Andreas Papandreou spent some of his time in the late 1950s teaching at the University of California–Berkeley, before returning to Greece and, after 1967, moving to Sweden and Canada. Papandreou's successor, Kostas Simitis, has closer ties to Germany, where he was educated and where his brother lives.

[5] This is illustrated most clearly in the shift of Greek policy toward Israel, which Greece formally recognized in 1990. During the 1973 Arab-Israeli war, the Greek military junta, which had been unusually friendly toward NATO, refused to permit war material to be shipped from Greek bases to Israel. By contrast, despite strong domestic opposition, in the 1991 Persian Gulf War, the Greek government permitted NATO planes to fly sorties over Iraq from Crete, supported the sanctions, and dispatched two warships to the gulf. I thank Susannah Verney for helping me clarify this point.

the structural funds that allocate investment aid to European regions. Conversely, for the central European democracies, it is current policy choices that matter most. In the specific cases of the Czech and Slovak Republics, the sharp divergence in the political leadership of Prime Ministers Václav Klaus and Vladimir Mečiar is creating domestic structures divergently suited to the assimilation of European institutional practices. Stable political arrangements and substantial pockets of state-owned enterprises in the more consensual and democratic Czech Republic contrast with a possibly more rapid and far-reaching privatization process organized around the largest banks in the less consensual, less stable, and less democratic Slovak Republic.

Whether differences stem from the distant past or from present choices, they highlight an important fact. In Europe international effects do not force differing domestic politics and policy choices into a uniform mold. The pattern varies, depending on the specifics of particular countries and policy sectors, global and regional effects, as well as Germany's indirect institutional power within Europe. These effects can operate autonomously from one another, they can be mutually reinforcing, or they can work at cross-purposes. Although the different effects need to be investigated empirically, taken together, they yield a gradually converging pattern in which the smaller states reveal diversity in politics and policy.

SOFT INSTITUTIONAL EFFECTS: EUROPEAN AND GERMAN

Economic liberalization and political integration have shaped the effects that Europe and Germany have had on the smaller European states. The liberalization in the movement of goods, capital, people, and services that the Single European Act (SEA) had brought about by 1993 was spurred by far-reaching changes in the global economy. When, in the mid-1980s, the EC announced its ambitious goals for greater liberalization, the "smart" money, and not only among Euro-skeptics, was betting that in implementing the act's provisions, especially the last third, the EC would fall significantly short of its stated objectives. The smart money was wrong. The European integration process proved to be remarkably resistant to inevitable national pressures against often painful liberalization measures.

By contrast, the TEU responded primarily to political developments within the EC, particularly German unification, rather than economic developments without. It sought to strengthen EU-wide institutional capacity for collective problem solving. Negotiated at a historical moment when political leaders thought that virtually everything was possible, the ratification of the TEU showed that different states had substantially different visions of their own and Europe's political future. Subsequent political controversies, most importantly over the shape of the EMU, have shown that treaty provisions that aim at quickly replacing, rather than gradually supplementing, national institutions are meeting with substantial opposition.

Since the 1950s, European integration has been marked by a permissive consensus that belies striking inconsistencies of public opinion on issues such as political and economic union or European enlargement. During the 1980s, an increasing proportion of respondents in opinion surveys thought that membership in the European Community was a "good thing" for their country, and that their country had "benefited from membership." But that proportion declined sharply after 1991 (by about 15 percentage points, to 56 percent, the level of the early 1980s), while the proportion of those thinking European integration was a bad thing more than doubled (from 6 to 14 percent). General support for European integration runs roughly parallel with the perceived costs and benefits that derive from EU membership; but general support is higher than a utilitarian calculus would suggest.[6] The movement in German public opinion has closely followed these European trends, although the gap between those expecting positive benefits from integration and those favoring European integration in general is much wider than in Europe.[7]

In contrast to ordinary citizens, the elites in most European countries consider the deepening of European institutions, especially in light of German unification, to be a natural and desirable extension of the European integration process.[8] What is largely taken for granted by ordinary citizens are national states that permit a free flow of factors of production, with the possible exception of labor. The elites, on the other hand, take for granted the institutional context of an integrating Europe that seeks to embed firmly a more powerful, united Germany. In Scandinavia, for example, state and business elites, including Norway's, have joined Europe in the 1980s and 1990s; ordinary citizens have not. "Europessimism notwithstanding," Ronald Asmus writes, "Germany's elite remains committed to European integration—more so than the public at large."[9] The Ger-

[6] David R. Cameron, "National Interest, the Dilemmas of European Integration, and Malaise," in John T. S. Keeler and Martin A. Schain, eds., *Chirac's Challenge: Liberalization, Europeanization, and Malaise* (New York: St. Martin's Press, 1996), pp. 345–48.

[7] Michael Kreile, "The Influence of Domestic Political and Economic Actors on Germany's European Policy," unpublished paper, Humboldt University Berlin, n.d., pp. 5–8. More generally, see the regular publication of the European Commission's *Eurobarometer*, which provides a wealth of survey data.

[8] Elite support for European integration is uniformly strong, hovering around the 90 percent mark in all member states of the EU. See European Commission, *Eurobarometer: Top Decision Makers Survey: Summary Report* (Brussels, 1996).

[9] Ronald D. Asmus, "In Germany the Leadership's Vision Goes Beyond the Border," *International Herald Tribune* (April 12, 1996): 10.

man constitution of 1871 opened with the clause "We the princes," thus drawing a sharp distinction to the U.S. Constitution; the Treaty on European Union is part of an elite-centered tradition in Germany's constitutional history.

These crosscurrents between mass and elite politics define the parameters in which Germany's and Europe's soft institutional constraints affect states on the European periphery. Often almost invisible, over time these constraints can gradually transform national regimes and European international relations. Greece, for example, illustrates an excruciatingly slow, often painful, yet undeniable moving away from exclusively national practices toward norms and identities defined in part by the European polity. Greek eligibility for EU funds requires that national institutions meet certain standards in the preparation of proposals and in the disbursement of funds. This has made possible important changes in national practice. Furthermore, Greek conceptions of identity have shifted, especially since the mid-1980s, toward the inclusion of a strong European component.

We can see a similar process in Scandinavia. Straining under the influence of economic globalization, Sweden's political class viewed accession to the European Union as an opportunity to address problems no longer amenable to national solutions. As a result, the Swedish model of a redistributive welfare state has been altered by the dynamics of European integration. Indeed, because it was a member of the EC, Denmark in the 1980s became a model for many Swedes. Similarly, the post-Communist politics of the Slovak Republic resembles to some extent that of Greece during the first half of the 1980s, while Czech politics looks like Swedish politics in the early 1990s. The range of political experience and experimentation in linking distinct national models to the institutional constraints of the European integration process allows for considerable variation. For all of the smaller European states, those institutional constraints are very real, however differently experienced.

Clustered around Germany, these states exemplify in their politics and policies different mixes of European and German effects.[10] This book has analyzed the experience of ten smaller states based on twenty-four case studies that illustrate the presence of German and European effects. Because national patterns often vary substantially within European subregions and by issue area, and because British, French, Italian, and other national and policy effects have been deliberately neglected, this book's empirical findings are preliminary and should be treated with caution.

Germany has had direct effects on the European integration process. First, German unification was a central factor pushing the member states

[10] See Helen Wallace, ed., *The Wider Western Europe: Reshaping the EC/EFTA Relationship* (London: Pinter, 1991); and William Wallace, *The Dynamics of European Integration* (London: Pinter, 1990).

of the EU to commit themselves in Maastricht to further integration in the interest of binding a united Germany to Europe. Second, because of their economic dependence on Germany, all of the smaller European states seek to diffuse and reduce their dependence through closer European integration. Finally, where collective memories of German domination and atrocities are still vivid, political engagement with Germany and Europe is weakened, as illustrated, respectively, by the Czech Republic and Norway.

More significantly, the case studies show that, mediated by institutions, indirect effects of Germany in Europe are more important than direct effects. Emulation or institutional transfers from Bonn-Berlin, Frankfurt, and Karlsruhe offer a number of examples. The similarity and mutual reinforcement between the segmentation of policy making in Bonn-Berlin and Brussels is another. Polities that segment issues reinforce the multidimensionality of politics, which permits multiple trade-offs, crosscutting political alignments, and blurred distinctions. These, in turn, soften the edges of political conflicts and strengthen the hand of those interested in keeping the integration process going, despite the backlashes it elicits from the social sectors and political coalitions that stand to lose out. Exercising indirect influence, as Simon Bulmer tells us in chapter 2, suits German political capacities and predilections. German interests and the gains Germany enjoys from European integration are thus made less visible and hence politically more palatable to the smaller European states. Without these institutional buffers, perceptions of German domination would be more widespread, and political relations between Germany and the smaller states would be more strained. Institutional buffers soften European and German effects.

Institutionalized power, moreover, is also soft because of its origins. Since 1945, Germany has been socialized into embracing multilateralism as the legitimate institution through which European states should conduct their business with one another. The internationalization of German state identity is a clear manifestation of this important political fact. The effects of German power are softened because of Germany's participation in European institutions. To a substantial degree, that participation has come to define Germany's identity and interests. Germany is the good European par excellence. It consistently advocates policies that support European integration, even if these policies reduce Germany's national power or run counter to its short-term interests.

How the smaller states experience the institutional effects Germany and Europe have on them depends on the depth and extent of their embeddedness in the European integration process. As the case studies in chapters 4–7 illustrate, states deeply involved in European integration on many issues (like the Netherlands and Belgium) experience these effects as soft constraints. States whose embeddedness is still very limited and restricted to few issues (as is true of the central European democracies) experience the effects as hard constraints.

In this conjoining of German and European effects on the smaller European states, one can discern three patterns. First, based on similar domestic structures and reinforced by a shared European identity, Belgium and the Netherlands do not experience their dependence on Germany as such, even in areas such as monetary integration. Rather, they subscribe to similar policy objectives and seek to free ride on the reputation of the Bundesbank in the pursuit of hard-currency policies more open to deficit spending. In other areas, such as internal security, these states stand their ground, despite Germany's persistent push for a Europeanization of policing. Second, in the case of the Scandinavian and southern European states, with the partial exception of the EMU, the effects of Germany and the EU are experienced either as European rather than German effects or as a combination of German and European effects. Finally, in the case of the central European democracies, mediated in some instances by the powerful filter of collective memories, the direct effects of Germany loom large, especially on economic and social issues, as opposed to the more noticeable, though contested, European effects in minority rights and security policies. The empirical findings thus suggest that the small European states experience German and European effects according to the duration and depth of their institutional embeddedness in Europe.

This book's institutional perspective views integration as a process (rather than a discrete event with a clear beginning and end), marked by multilevel governance structures (lacking clear demarcations between domestic and international levels of analysis), and distinguished by the mutual constitution of actors and institutions (which demands searching out iterative cause-and-effect relations over time, rather than specifying necessary and sufficient conditions for particular outcomes).[11] Institutional analysis seeks to integrate the insights of rationalism. It highlights neither the reaction of actors to structures nor autonomous actor calculations. Hence, on analytical as well as empirical grounds, an institutionalist perspective is suspicious of rationalist theories that stipulate determinist effects of international structures or unchanging national or actor interests.

---

[11] See Christopher Daase, "Theorie und Praxis des Kleinen Krieges: Ein Beitrag zum Verständnis des Wandels der internationalen Beziehungen," Ph.D. diss., Otto-Suhr-Institute, Free University of Berlin, December 1995, pp. 263–67, 309–19. An eclectic institutionalism aims at an uneasy combination of positivism and interpretivism. In doing so, it moves attention from the discovery of the correlation among "objectively" existing phenomena to the discovery of the principle that is the foundation of the different types of political practice shaping these structures. On the other hand, an institutionalism that focuses on how practice modifies structures does not deny the existence of objective structures, and acknowledges that interpretation is never a primary experience but always an act of reconstruction.

Instead, institutionalism focuses on how social norms and rules and actor identities and predispositions adapt to one another through political practice. While that adaptation creates habits that make a political environment appear to be "normal," it always remains open to innovation and rupture.

Europe

Europe offers a powerful institutional model of proper conduct and collective identity. Europe is an incarnation of a global, cosmopolitan, secular, and science-based model of conduct that transcends regional and national divisions. At the same time, in different national settings Europe is also defined negatively, as "not Arab," "not Turkish," and "not Eastern European." European identities thus cluster around both inclusive notions of democracy and human rights and exclusive notions of xenophobia and nationalism.

For the social and political elites of most European states at the end of the Cold War, European norms have no rivals that could inform the policies of the smaller European states. Respect for human rights, peaceful democracy, an economy based on private property and supported by a generous welfare state, and close connections with neighboring states and NATO as well as other European security organizations define what it means to be a "modern" European state. As institutionalized practices, these norms are so much taken for granted in northern and western Europe that they pass largely unnoticed.

By contrast, because they clash with competing institutional models in southern and central Europe, the norms are experienced more directly and have more visible political effects. Spain and Portugal in southern Europe in the 1970s and 1980s and Poland, Hungary, and the Czech Republic in central Europe in the 1990s illustrate the power of European norms. As chapter 5 shows, Spain in the 1980s and 1990s epitomizes a conscious strategy of building an image as a "good" European. Under the leadership of Prime Minister Felipe Gonzalez, and supported by Catalan and Basque elites seeking greater degrees of autonomy, Spain has taken a decisive turn toward Europe, assuring it a central position in the core of the EU. This reorientation was not a matter of mere rhetoric. The Spanish government incurred high political costs—extraordinarily high unemployment rates and a fundamental change in security policy—in order to play a new and active role in Europe. Similarly, in growing contrast to the Slovak Republic, post-Communist Poland, Hungary, and the Czech Republic also aim at meeting, with a minimum of fuss, the basic institutional demands that come with being a modern European state.

Political alternatives to Europe are always possible. Greece, for example, followed a path that did not lead straight to Europe; in the 1970s and 1980s, its multilateral foreign policy focused not only on Europe but also on the Mediterranean, the Balkans, and the Middle East. Following U.S. leadership, by the mid-1980s, Western media focused on one particular strand of that policy, which sought to form closer ties with "pariah state" Libya. But by then Greek foreign policy had already shifted from the southern to the western Mediterranean and to the members-to-be of the EU. The end of the Cold War and changes in Greek domestic politics have further reinforced the relevance of European institutional practices for Greece.

Similarly, in the 1990s, the Slovak Republic has pursued an uneven foreign policy course. As chapter 7 describes, the Slovak government has largely adhered to the dramatic changes in policy that the Czechoslovak government had initiated prior to the division of that country. Next to the drastic (80–90 percent) cutback of the Slovak arms industry, all other conversion programs in either East or West pale by comparison. Indeed, the Slovak army's sharp (50–60 percent) reduction in heavy armaments had, by the end of 1995, largely met the targets specified by the Treaty on Conventional Armed Forces in Europe (CFE). And despite considerable political wrangling, plans announced in February 1996 to privatize the Slovak Republic's four largest state-owned banks would, if implemented, lead to very rapid privatization of virtually all publicly owned properties. Nevertheless, on the issue of minority rights, for reasons of domestic politics, progress has, at best, been very halting.

Furthermore, as chapter 7 illustrates, there exists a great difference between the Czech Republic's rapid voucher privatization, Hungary's unceasing experimentation with all forms of privatization, and the Slovak Republic's stalled effort to privatize state-owned banks, bogged down in a bitter political feud between its president and prime minister. And compared with Poland's treatment of the language rights of its German minority, Slovak policy has been full of ambiguities, twists and turns, and nasty political controversies. Indeed, as the decade wanes, it is no longer clear whether the Slovak government is still seriously committed to European norms and practices. Hence, for Germany, it has become doubtful whether the Slovak Republic should still be considered as a viable applicant for early, full membership in the EU.

In some instances, the states on the European periphery contain institutional models that may have wider implications for Europe. For example, as chapter 6 points out, liberalizing market reforms in a variety of policy sectors (such as agriculture, labor relations, and monetary policy) have modified the "Swedish model" and embedded it more firmly in a less solidaristic, continental European version of the welfare state. But liberalization has not yet undercut Sweden's norm of universalism, which guarantees to all citizens access to social benefits, or Sweden's traditional stands on issues of employment, consumer protection, gender equality, freedom of information, and relations with the Baltic states, efforts of Sweden's Europeanizing elites to the contrary notwithstanding.

Similarly, as chapter 7 illustrates, Poland's Catholic Church is moved by a powerful religious vision opposed to the secular one of a peaceful integration of democratic, capitalist societies in western Europe. Based on its success in helping bring down the Communist regime in Poland and beyond, the Polish Church aims at eventually leading Europe away from secularism to Catholicism. Although Polish voters rejected this vision in the November 1995 presidential election, it would be very surprising indeed if Catholic Poland were not to retain some of its deep-seated skepticism about central features of the European polity.

Soft institutional constraints are also illustrated by a bargaining process that simply forbids a straightforward imposition of European norms on member states strongly opposed to specific standards or collective modes of operation. For example, on matters of national security, smaller states like Denmark support Britain's adamant opposition to a gradual emergence of EU competence to act collectively either inside or outside of NATO. Thus the EU must operate by an inclusive bargaining process that yields occasional gains for all member states.

This explains why the European Union often has great difficulties in operating like the IMF. It cannot simply impose strict financial supervision that might lead to the delegitimation of the government or political regime of a member state. In extending special credits in the early 1990s, for example, the EU has had great difficulty in making the Greek government adhere to the fiscal reforms it had agreed to on paper. In 1995, the EU sent a special emissary to Athens to negotiate with all the major Greek parties the financial conditions that Greece, ruled by whatever party or coalition government, had to meet. Only after agreeing to meet these conditions did Greece receive, as part of the EU's regional policy, close to 17 billion ECU (\$14 billion) for the years 1994–99.[12] At the EU's insistence, that agreement became a bill duly passed by the Greek parliament after prolonged and difficult negotiations involving both government and opposition parties. Insisting that Greece do more than meet some statistical criteria, the EU aimed at changing institutional practices in Greece. Only time will tell whether this demanding stance will be met by what European governments would regard as a more "sensible" and accommodating Greek policy. But successful or not, the sharp contrast between the institutional models by which the EU and the IMF operate is readily apparent.

[12] Interview with Jean-Claude Thoenig, Cologne, October 30, 1995.

Germany

Even though they are deeply embedded in Europe, distinctive German institutions also affect the smaller European states. German politics since 1949 has reinforced changes in European international relations that have evolved under American leadership. Access to markets has replaced territorial conquest, and multilateral, international contacts are strongly preferred to bilateral, national bargains. Before 1945, Germany adhered to, and helped define, the standard patterns of bilateral influence between states. Since 1945, multilateral arrangements typically channel national patterns of German influence and power. In short, Germany's bilateral dominance structures before 1945 have either been supplemented or replaced by multilateral influence structures after 1945.

Germany's openness toward transnational politics since 1945 has reinforced this regional pattern of politics. It is distinctive of Germany that it has evolved a practice, and subsequently a theory, of societal foreign policy (*gesellschaftliche Aussenpolitik*). Besides the official foreign policy of the government, most of the major institutions of German society also conduct their own foreign relations. Typically, they engage partner institutions in other countries, thus creating or reinforcing a pattern of transnational relations. The system is grounded in publicly funded foundations that are closely affiliated with Germany's four major political parties. Initially, in the 1950s and 1960s, these foundations focused on political education in Germany. Gradually, they moved part of their operations abroad to develop eventually a global presence. These foundations seek out their ideological allies in other states (Christian Democratic for the Christian Democratic Union's Konrad-Adenauer Foundation, Social Democratic or Socialist for the Social Democratic Party's Friedrich-Ebert Foundation, clerical-conservative for the Christian Social Union's Hanns-Seidel Foundation, liberal for the Free Democratic Party's Friedrich-Naumann Foundation, and participatory-environmental for the Greens' Heinrich-Böll Foundation); they initiate projects serving democratic and developmental practices informed by their distinctive world views. The intended by-product of this system is the systematic knitting of relationships between Germany and all sectors of society in a partner country. Hence when a given government falls and the opposition moves into positions of power, the German government and German institutions typically have well-established contacts and ready access. The foundations, for example, were a visible political presence when the southern and central European states achieved their democratic transitions in the 1970s and 1990s.

Many other institutions in German society also conduct their own informal foreign relations. Unions such as the metalworkers' union (IG Metall), the largest industrial branch union in Europe, employer and business organizations, scientific foundations like the Humboldt foundation, publicly funded research institutes and think tanks of conservative, centrist, and progressive stripes, such as the foreign policy research institute in Ebenhausen, outside Munich, the German Society for Foreign Policy (DGAP) in Bonn, or the Hessian Peace Research Institute (HSKF) in Frankfurt all foster important transnational ties. Even Germany's Constitutional Court seeks to strengthen human rights and the rule of law in Europe. Since the 1970s, it has organized a biannual meeting of the European Supreme Court justices. As do many professions in the United States, often bringing their spouses, the justices meet in a congenial location, deliver papers, and socialize. Considering this German practice of conducting an uncoordinated societal foreign policy, it is therefore no accident that the theory of transnational relations was originally formulated by a German political scientist, Karl Kaiser, before it was subsequently developed further by American scholars of international relations.[13] Similarly, it is not surprising that one of the most influential scholarly studies of German foreign policy published in the last four decades focuses consistently on the regional interdependence of Germany, Europe, and NATO.[14]

Generally speaking, German politics adheres to a form that has considerable affinity with the politics of the smaller states in western and northern Europe—despite the greater importance in Germany of legal institutions, an independent central bank, and a strong federal system. A shared commitment to a moderate politics, institutionalized in Christian Democratic and Social Democratic parties as well as in loose corporatist arrangements, makes German, more than, say, French or British, politics resemble the domestic arrangements of the welfare states in western and northern Europe.[15]

These smaller states interact with Germany, often in European networks. For example, as chapter 4 shows, the importance of a hard-currency policy regime and the commitment to a generous welfare state deeply

[13] Karl Kaiser, "Transnationale Politik: Zu einer Theorie der multinationalen Politik," in Ernst-Otto Czempiel, ed., *Die anachronistische Souveränität* (Cologne-Opladen: Westdeutscher Verlag, 1969), pp. 80–109. This appeared in modified form as "Transnational Politics: Toward a Theory of Multinational Politics," *International Organization* 25 (Autumn 1971): 790–817. Just as the political realism of the 1930s was reflected in the writings of Hans Morgenthau in the 1950s, the liberalism of the 1960s was reflected in Kaiser's scholarship. The evolution of the two main analytical positions in American international relations has thus been deeply affected by German scholarship. It is ironic that, typically, these origins are not fully appreciated even by those Germans who in subsequent decades "imported" key insights of American social science. This speaks to the power institutionalized paradigms exercise over the imagination of individual scholars.

[14] *Regionale Verflechtung der Bundesrepublik Deutschland: Empirische Analysen und Theoretische Probleme* (Munich: Oldenbourg, 1973).

[15] Peter J. Katzenstein, *Small States in World Markets: Industrial Policy in Europe* (Ithaca: Cornell University Press, 1985).

rooted in Christian Democratic social thought define the interests of the Netherlands and Belgium much as they do those of Germany. This is true even though, in the case of the Netherlands, public sentiment continues to remain deeply suspicious of Germany. In the case of Belgium, with its unquestioned identity as a core member of Europe, a serious fiscal crisis has moved the government to impose painful fiscal cutbacks and to experiment with reforms shunned, for example, by Greece, which lacks a comparable European identity. Institutional commonalities with Germany and a similarly central position in Europe's numerous multilateral regimes have had the effect of neutralizing the perception in the Low Countries that German institutions or policies are encroaching on national autonomy.

In the absence of such institutional commonalities and networks, as the discussion of the central European states in chapter 7 illustrates, political relations between Germany and smaller states are more difficult. In their reorientation toward Europe after the disintegration of the Soviet bloc, these central European states must cope with a spontaneous growth of Germany's economic influence, while waiting for eventual, full membership in the EU. VW's purchase of Skoda, the first large investment deal in central Europe after 1989, and the sharp growth of German ownership of the regional press in the Czech Republic are two examples. Economic dependence can lead directly to harmful consequences, as in VW's unilaterally scaling back of its planned investments in the face of adverse market conditions. Or it can reinforce a sense of potential political vulnerability, as in the domination of the Czech Republic's regional press by Bavarian publishers. This is true even though, to date, these publishers are much more interested in making money than in influencing Czech regional or local politics.

As chapter 7 also illustrates, despite a sharp increase in regional trade, labor mobility, and tourism across the Czech border with neighboring Bavaria and Saxony, Czech-German relations remain strained. Can one balance the injustices of German aggression during World War II, abetted and actively supported by a majority of the Sudeten Germans, German occupation, dismemberment of the Czech state, and the large-scale deportation and murder of the Czechoslovak population on the one hand, and the injustices committed during the forcible resettlement of about three million Sudeten Germans at the end of the war, on the other? Moral and political differences in interpretations weigh more heavily than legal ones. As is true of the Hungarian minority language issue in the Slovak Republic, the main difficulty is rooted in the domestic politics of both Germany and the Czech Republic. In a situation of a rapidly mounting national debt, the German government is reluctant to create a precedent for future financial claims by those who have been, directly or indirectly, vic-

tims of atrocities committed by Germans. Similarly, the Czech government and population is unanimous in its rejection of any attempt on the
part of the Sudeten Germans or the German government to create, under
whatever pretext, any possibility for reclaiming German properties lost after World War II. The comparatively unproblematic Polish-German accommodation over Silesia suggests that, among a number of reasons, the
political connections of the German refugee organizations deserve special attention. The Sudeten Germans are taken seriously by the CSU as a
potential breakaway party on the Bavarian right. The Silesian Germans
lack comparable political resources.

The lines are thus drawn sharply for reasons of domestic politics. In
Germany, the Sudeten Germans' main ally, the Bavarian CSU, has considerable clout in the coalition government of Chancellor Kohl. The CSU is
afraid that a premature compromise with the Czech Republic might lead
to an exodus of disgruntled, second-generation Sudeten-German CSU
members and voters and the formation of a new Bavarian party to the
right of the CSU. Because the CSU is essential to the governing coalition
in Bonn, its objections on this point weigh heavily.[16] On the Czech side,
room for compromise is also very limited because of the strong consensus
across the entire Czech political spectrum and in Bohemia that the Potsdam Agreement is an internationally binding legal document that legiti-
mates the displacement of the Sudeten Germans after World War II. Both
Czech and German societies are struggling with painful historical memories and the legacy of past practices of ethnic cleansing in central Europe.

In contrast to the Netherlands and Belgium, the citizens and the government of the Czech Republic do not have the benefit of experiencing a
diffusion of dependence on Germany through multilateral institutions.
Public perception of a tight coupling to German interests and policies is
therefore not simply a function of economic statistics; as chapters 4 and 7
show, it depends also significantly on institutional arrangements. Similar
domestic institutions and intensive multilateral links in Europe buffer the
heavy dependence of the Benelux and Scandinavian states on Germany;
and they protect Germany from the political backlash that such dependence might otherwise easily generate in these states. A lack of institutionalization contributes to the troubled state of Czech-German relations.

Since 1945, German institutions have influenced the smaller states in
western and northern Europe largely through the indirect consequences
of a policy of export-led growth, which has been central to the reconstruc-

[16] The CSU example is not the first instance of a noticeable influence of ethnicity on German foreign policy in recent years. The large proportion of Croatians among the 700,000
Yugoslavs living in Germany had an unmistakable effect on the CDU/CSU and Germany's
policy toward the former Yugoslavia, especially in Bavaria.

tion of the economy and the stabilization of the society of the Federal Republic. The institution of Germany's social market economy, including an independent and assertive Bundesbank, shaped domestic and foreign economic policies that set important parameters for, among others, the wage, industrial, and social policies these smaller European states could adopt.

The situation was quite different in southern Europe. Greece, Spain, and Portugal found in the Germany of the mid-1970s a Social Democratic government and numerous corporate actors firmly committed to a foreign policy of actively intervening in their democratic transition. Mindful of its own Nazi past and successful democratic transition in the 1950s and 1960s, Germany pushed for a southern enlargement of the EC and acted as a champion of these fledgling democracies as viable members of the Community. Germany's political influence was direct, though not uniform, in channeling funds, institutional blueprints, and advisors to various groups, especially in Spain and Portugal.

Finally, political revolutions in the fall of 1989 have left the governments of Poland, Hungary and, since 1993, the Czech and Slovak Republics, looking to Europe and Germany as they undertake the difficult double transition from authoritarianism to democracy and from Communism to capitalism. In their economic and political reform policies and emerging institutions, these states are exposed to a combination of direct and indirect influences from both Germany and Europe.

With the lifting of the Iron Curtain, the Federal Republic has had to cope with an enormous influx of Germans from the former GDR, ethnic Germans from Eastern Europe and the Commonwealth of Independent States (CIS), refugees from the war in Bosnia-Herzegovina, and asylum seekers from the Third World. In the early 1990s, on a per capita basis, Germany took in more foreigners than any other European state. This is the latest episode of an astounding history of demographic instability and change in fundamental tension with German legislation, dating back to 1913, that defines German citizenship in exclusive, ethnic terms. The result was a nationalist and xenophobic backlash in the 1990s, including neo-Nazi and skinhead attacks on foreigners and the burning of hostels where asylum seekers were housed. Eventually, the main political parties agreed to a significant tightening of Germany's liberal asylum laws.

The new legislation made it possible to turn back the majority of asylum seekers at the German border and to deport them to the state from which they had entered Germany, provided that state protected human rights. The new policy imposed a heavy burden on Germany's neighbors, primarily Poland, but also the Netherlands and the Czech Republic. In the case of Poland, described in chapter 7, a liberal European immigration policy, adopted after 1990, has become more restrictive. In order to shield itself from being inundated by refugees and asylum seekers turned back at the German border, Poland adopted legislation that in turn exported further a problem Germany had externalized first. Within a few weeks of signing a bilateral agreement with Germany in May 1993, Poland had concluded readmission agreements with all of its neighbors. A change in German immigration policy thus had a ripple effect throughout Europe.

Chapter 4 provides another illustration of Germany's effect on the smaller European states. By October 1981, Europe's central bankers and economic analysts were in agreement that the Belgian franc was overvalued. Yet despite encouragement from the German chairman of the Monetary Committee of the EMS, Horst Schumann, to devalue immediately or lose his support, Belgium's caretaker government was unable to act. When, in February 1982, a new Belgian government asked for a 15 percent devaluation, Schumann was unsympathetic. After some bargaining, the Belgians reduced their request to 12 percent. Schumann and the committee insisted on a maximum devaluation of 9 percent. The Belgian delegation left the deadlocked committee to consult with its government at home and returned to the bargaining table the next day, ready to settle for 9 percent. At that moment the German delegation announced that 9 percent was no longer acceptable. Belgium had to settle for a 8.5 percent devaluation instead.[17]

But the direct exercise of German power is rare on questions of monetary policy. More often, German monetary power operates indirectly and becomes visible through unilateral policy adjustments other states make in multilateral arrangements. Thus, whenever the Bundesbank changes its rates, the central banks in the Netherlands, Denmark, and Belgium, whose small economies are tightly linked to Germany's, follow suit, often in a matter of minutes. Yet Dutch and even Belgian policy makers, as chapter 4 explains, do not interpret the domination of the Bundesbank over the EMS or the emerging EMU as an external constraint but rather as an advantageous institutional arrangement that expresses their own preferences. Indeed, chapter 4 describes how, together with the Low Countries, the German government worked hard, and eventually successfully, to have the EU adopt a works council directive for companies with more than 1,000 employees, the first successful initiative under the Social Protocol of the TEU.[18]

Institutional emulation is one way of seeking to conceal such unilateral adjustments. For example, hoping to establish a monetary policy with low inflation rates, Spain in the 1970s and Hungary in the 1990s designed

[17] Lecture by Peter Ludlow, Harvard University, February 23, 1989.

[18] Britain's opposition was overcome in this instance because it had chosen to opt out of the Social Chapter of the TEU.

central banks modeled after the Bundesbank. But while the numerous political constraints Hungary faces in its economic transformation make further direct emulation of German and European institutions impossible (chapter 7), Spain has proposed a European version of German fiscal federalism (*Finanzausgleich*) as part of a European Cohesion Fund designed to help the poorer members of the EU (chapter 5).

While institutions buffer, they do not eliminate the dependence on Germany characteristic of the smaller European states. As noted in chapter 6, since joining the EC in 1973, Denmark has gradually moved from the British to the German economic orbit. Sweden, Norway, and smaller states throughout Europe, within and without the EU, favor the European integration process as their most attractive option for constraining German power through multilateral arrangements. And the Scandinavian states look to forging coalitions with Germany on a broad range of issues, including social policy, the environment, and the eastern enlargement of the EU. Between the world of hard interests, where German power simply dictates the policy smaller states must pursue, as in the devaluation of the Belgian franc in February 1983 or the downsizing of the Czech automobile industry in 1993–94, and complete convergence with German institutions, as in the hard-currency policy of the Netherlands, the extension of German institutional practices, embedded in multilateral arrangements, typically creates a world of soft constraints.

Conclusion

The effects that European and German institutions have on the smaller European states are important, though circumscribed. Greece is a member of the EU, while Norway has decided not to join. Yet, in different ways, both states have resisted the pull of European and German institutions. Until 1995, neither Sweden nor Austria had been members of the EU. But basic political similarity to EU member-states, numerous indirect links to the union and to Germany, and policy harmonization under the auspices of the European Economic Area (EEA) prepared Sweden and Austria for European integration much better than Greece. Similarly, although the Low Countries were founding members of the (ECSC) and the EC in the 1950s, while Spain joined the EC only in 1986, chapters 4 and 5 show that, since the late 1980s, all three show strong commitments to European integration. Formal EU membership, however important for learning the rules of the political game in Brussels, does not force a full convergence of political practices. Europe and Germany provide a soft institutional environment for the small European states that leaves considerable leeway for distinct national choices within a broadly converging European pattern.

The softness or hardness of these constraints thus depends on the depth and extent of a state's participation in the European integration process. In Belgium, Sweden, and Spain, resistance to the institutional effects of Europe and Germany is comparatively weak. In the Slovak Republic, Greece, and, on some issues, Denmark, resistance is much greater, spurred by contemporary political power struggles (Slovak Republic), historical memories (Greece), and a conception of integration that excludes security and foreign policy issues (Denmark). And Britain's resistance to a further deepening of European integration in the 1980s and 1990s expresses a mixture of all three factors.

INSTITUTIONAL EFFECTS AND DIFFERENT POLICY ISSUES

The institutional effects of Europe vary among different policy issues. Deregulation and mutual recognition are preferred for economic questions that national actors perceive to be necessary for the effective functioning of a single market. Problems touching on social and security issues are far more resistant to European and German effects. Security issues affect other institutions, such as NATO, and matter greatly to national governments in the process of redefining their security policies. Social issues cut to the very core of the European welfare states. This variability by issue area is reinforced by the fact that the EU is considerably stronger on issues of legislation and central decision making than on issues of implementation, which continue to rely on national bureaucracies and courts.[19]

Chapter 2 suggests why. One of the distinctive features of the European Union is the lack of coordination across different policy sectors. The relative independence in the EU's different governance structures is reinforced by procedural differences. The three different pillars of the EU illustrate the point. On economic issues, the regulatory activities of the European Council and the European Commission as well as the decisions of the European Court of Justice are most important. Procedural differentiation is far greater here than on social and security issues. The first pillar covers not only narrow economic issues such as tariff and nontariff barriers, technical standards, and subsidies; it deals also with technology policy, environmental policy, and the creation of the EMU. In contrast, on common foreign policy (CFSP) issues, the consent principle is paramount. Member states tend to adhere to a declaratory policy style. Finally, on questions of internal security, a prerogative of the ministries of Justice

[19] Svein S. Andersen and Kjell A. Eliassen, "Policy-Making in the New Europe," in Andersen and Eliassen, eds., *Making Policy in Europe: The Europeification of National Policy-Making* (London: Sage, 1993), pp. 255–56.

and Home Affairs (JHA), informal cooperation and covert policy making prevails.

Analogously, Jeffrey Anderson points to important variations in the four issues (agriculture, structural funds, competition, and trade) he examines in chapter 3. Where the federal government has retained full control, such as foreign trade, Germany continues to adhere to its traditional liberal stance. The greatest change in German policy has occurred on issues such as the structural funds and regional policy, where the five new *Länder* have enjoyed the greatest access to Germany's policy-making machinery. In these instances, German policy is changing and now tends toward the articulation of shorter-term interests, conceived in narrower economic terms than had been true before.

Developments pointing in the same direction are evident also in competition policy. Although the German government and the European Commission both showed flexibility in how they dealt with the privatization of more than 10,000 East German firms, the employment-oriented sectoral policy that the German government pursued after 1992 created plenty of friction. Resisting further increases in the capacity of the European steel industry, for example, the Commission agreed to the privatization of Eko Stahl in East Germany only after long negotiations, which resulted in the company being bought, not by the German Krupp concern, but by a Belgian steel producer, Cockerell Sambre.

The segmentation of different policy sectors is a source of both weakness and strength for the EU. It complicates parallel advances in integrative policy making in different policy domains, but it also protects the EU from sectoral crises spiraling out of control and thus putting in question its entire institutional fabric. For Germany, as shown in chapter 2, sectoral fragmentation may impair the pursuit of interests; the German government lacks the mechanisms for imposing priorities across a broad spectrum of organizational interests. But sectoral policy making is also a source of strength. It makes Germany's gains less visible, thus sidestepping potential conflicts with its neighbors. And the lack of coordination can also strengthen the hand of the German government in bargaining with the EU. The government can sometimes point to the opposition of vital domestic constituencies, for example the *Länder,* to policies not to their liking. In sum, the variable institutional effects that Europe and Germany have on the smaller European states reflect the interaction between two multitiered polities.

Economic Issues

Among the various policies that the EU enacts, agricultural and regional policy have arguably the strongest institutionalized effects. Together, they account for about three-quarters of the EU's financial outlays; on these issues, the competencies of Brussels are comparatively large. The Treaty of Rome specifies agriculture and foreign trade as policy arenas in which supranational rather than national authority is to prevail. And the EC's resources for regional policy were enlarged as part of the SEA and TEU negotiations. In the 1980s, the Common Agricultural Policy (CAP) was simply becoming too expensive.[20] As part of the Delors I and II packages, the resources for the structural funds were enlarged in 1988 and 1992. And as a quid pro quo for their support of the TEU, the Mediterranean states (Spain, Portugal, and Greece), under Spanish leadership, demanded additional resources for regional development in the form of a new cohesion fund.

In light of the large costs of the CAP, it is ironic that Norway, with its extraordinarily high subsidies for agricultural producers, resisted European integration in large part because of the liberalization effect that CAP would have brought. Protected for the foreseeable future by large oil and gas revenues, economic efficiency was less important in Norway than the entrenched economic interests and national identities represented by Norway's Center Party.[21] For, in Norway, agriculture is defined, not in economic, but in social terms. Norwegian agricultural policy aims at equalizing incomes between rural and urban incomes, and the aesthetic value of farms matters greatly to Norwegian planners.

By contrast, the Swedish Center Party and agricultural organizations have lacked the power to resist the push of the reformers. Agreeing in 1991 to alter long-standing agricultural policies, they helped prepare the way for Sweden's eventual accession to the EU in 1995. Since the 1930s, agriculture had been an integral part of a Red-Green coalition between workers and farmers. Hence, in this instance, European integration helped redefine central aspects of national politics. And in Germany, ironically, the CAP has become an important ingredient in a pattern of East German privatization that will leave most of the agricultural land in the new five *Länder* in the hands of the few thousand former Communists who had managed the state-owned cooperatives.[22]

[20] John T. S. Keeler, "Agricultural Power in the European Community: Explaining the Fate of CAP and GATT Negotiations," *Comparative Politics* 28 (January 1996): 127–496; Stefan Tangermann, "Agricultural Protectionism and the Agricultural Lobby in Germany: International Implications of Domestic Policies," AICGS Seminar Papers, no. 6, Washington, D.C., July 1993.

[21] Christine Ingebritsen, "Norwegian Political Economy and European Integration: Agricultural Power, Policy Legacies and EU Membership," *Cooperation and Conflict* 30 (1995): 349–63.

[22] With current lessees having been granted the first right to purchase agricultural land, in essence, the accumulation of CAP subsidies will suffice for outright purchase within 10–15 years. The end result will be one of the great ironies of recent German history: the replacement of one small, aristocratic landowning class by another, formerly Communist one.

Regional policy is yet another arena in which the EU redistributes substantial resources.[23] In contrast to agriculture, the reason lies less in the union's rhetorical commitment to the principle of regional convergence and more in the emergent properties of the European polity: the political side payments and negotiated bargains of governments, the redistributive norm that has taken hold in the EU, and the interest the European Commission and some regions have in forging new links and creating new actors that might influence public policy. With Spain acting as the locomotive and Britain as the caboose of a train moving along the tracks of a German-style federalism, strong states and rich regions have helped weaker ones in compensating for the costs of integration and increased competition.

In negotiating for stronger regional measures, Greece has reinforced the commitment of the EC to a common regional policy that allocated aid directly to regional authorities, bypassing national governments and thus contributing to the growth of Euroregions. Despite this diplomatic initiative, however, Greece in the 1980s had yet to create the regional level of government it needed to receive the regional funds that the EC made available.[24] At the other extreme, with Spain's relatively strong and autonomous regions potentially in unsupervised cooperation with the European Commission, the centrifugal aspects of the EU's regional policy were anathema to the Spanish government. As part of the negotiations leading to the TEU and the adoption of a common value-added tax (VAT), the Spanish government succeeded in having the EU establish a new and smaller regional cohesion fund, to be controlled directly by central governments rather than by autonomous regions,[25] and to be financed by additional resources and the reallocation of existing funds away from the CAP. As does regional policy in Spain, agriculture has fundamental political consequences in Sweden and Finland, which negotiated as part of

---

[23] Gary Marks, "Structural Policy and Multilevel Governance in the European Community," in Alan W. Cafruny and Glenda Rosenthal, eds., *The State of the European Community* (Boulder, Colo.: Lynne Rienner, 1993), pp. 391–410.

[24] Fouli Papageorgiou and Susannah Verney, "Regional Planning and the Integrated Mediterranean Programmes in Greece," and Susannah Verney and Fouli Papageorgiou, "Prefecture Councils in Greece: Decentralization in the European Community Context," in Robert Leonardi, ed., *The Regions and the European Community: The Regional Response to the Single Market in the Underdeveloped Areas* (London: Frank Cass, 1993), pp. 139–61 and 109–38, respectively.

[25] Jeffrey Anderson sounds a cautious note on the degree of regional autonomy in his "Skeptical Reflections on a 'Europe of Regions:' Britain, West Germany and the European Regional Development Fund," *Journal of Public Policy Studies* 10 (October–December 1990): 417–47. In addition, the EU's Mediterranean members pushed for and were rewarded by special side payments in form of the 1988 Delors I package (reorganization of EC finances, reform of the Common Agricultural Policy, and a strengthening of the structural funds as flanking measures for making the Single European Act work) and the 1992 Delors II package (proposing further reforms along these lines to enhance economic and political "cohesion" in anticipation of closer economic links, including the EMU).

their accession new categories of support for sparsely populated tracts of land and for arctic farming.

In the Czech-German borderlands, as chapter 7 points out, German policy relies in part on Europe's regional policy to improve cross-border relations and policies. Four Euroregions currently exist along the Czech-German border. Their activities focus on the joint resolution of various practical issues including cross-border communications, protection of the environment, cultural and civil cooperation, and development of economic relations. The intensity of regional activities varies. While the cooperation within the Egrensis Euroregion, the first to be established at Germany's initiative, has run into trouble on the Czech side, activities in the Neisse Euroregion are evolving rapidly.[26] For example, the opening of a new Czech-German border-crossing point that partially passes through Polish territory is a substantial success for European regionalism.

Yet Czech national and regional authorities often remain suspicious of Euroregions with their own representative bodies and their cross-border agreements based on what, to many Czechs, appears to be a questionable delegation of authority. Such suspicions are fueled by the unresolved issue of the Sudeten Germans. Significantly, the initiative for the establishment of Euroregions comes from Germany. Along the German border with Belgium, France, and Switzerland, in the eyes of the German *Länder* governments, Euroregions have proven a useful institutional framework for resolving bilateral problems under a European umbrella, at times bypassing national governments.

The role of the *Länder,* furthermore, is increasing more generally in Germany's European policy. In the domestic process of ratifying the Single European Act and the Treaty on European Union, Germany's federal government had to cede significant powers to the *Länder,* which have gained a new co-decision role (*Mitwirkung*).[27] According to the newly reworded Article 23(1) of the Basic Law, future transfers of sovereign powers from Berlin to Brussels will require the consent of the Bundesrat, subject to Article 79(3), which protects the federal character of Germany. Furthermore, on issues affected by European legislation, Article 23(5) has greatly enhanced the role of the *Länder*. On matters where the *Länder* have exclusive power, Article 23(6) stipulates that they, not the federal government, represent Germany in the European Council of Ministers. With each of the *Länder* having opened its own office in Brussels, the in-

[26] Ann Kennard, "The German-Polish Border as a Model for East-West European Regional Integration: Trans-Border Co-operation on the Oder-Neisse Line," *German Politics* 4 (April 1995): 141–49.

[27] This discussion of the *Länder's* expanding power draws on William E. Patterson, "Beyond Semi-Sovereignty: The New Germany in the New Europe," *German Politics* 5 (August 1996): 167–84.

stitutional representation of regional interests within the EU is bound to increase.[28]

Social Welfare and National Security Issues

Compared to issues of economic regulation, here agriculture and regions, European and German institutional effects are different for social welfare and national security issues. While member states focus on the distributional aspects, the EU concentrates on the regulatory aspects of social policy.[29] This is reflected in the qualitative difference between the spending of the EU and its member states. The EU spends about 1.3 percent of the combined GDP and about 4 percent of total government spending of its member states, which disburse about four-fifths of the EU funds.[30] These figures pale in comparison to the spending of the national welfare states, which amounts to about 30 percent of GDP in northern and western Europe (for example, the Netherlands), compared to 15 percent of GDP in southern Europe (for example, Portugal). And direct wage costs differ between north (Germany) and south (Portugal) by a factor of 7 ($20 compared to $3).

The European integration process has never put particular emphasis on the creation of a common social policy. Because of underlying French-German disagreements, the Treaty of Rome made no more than a limited commitment to a common social policy. The 1970s saw limited gains in the Social Action Program of 1974 (affecting health and safety, gender and immigrant rights), the European Company Statute of 1975, and the elimination of the bias against migrant workers in national social security legislation of 1978. But a proposed expansion of workers' rights under the European Company Statute, the Vredeling proposal, failed in 1980.

---

[28] Alberta M. Sbragia, "The European Community: A Balancing Act," *Publius* 23 (Summer 1993): 23–37; Richard Deeg, "Germany's Länder and the Federalization of the European Union," in Carolyn Rhodes and Sonia Mazey, eds., *The State of the European Community*, vol. 3, *Building a European Polity?* (Boulder, Colo.: Lynne Rienner, 1995), pp. 197–220; Barbara Lippert et al., *Die EG und die neuen Bundesländer: Eine Erfolgsgeschichte von kurzer Dauer?* (Bonn: Europa-Union Verlag, 1993).

[29] On social welfare, see the helpful review of Giandomenico Majone's research on the EU as a regulatory state in James A. Caporaso, "The European Union and Forms of State: Westphalian, Regulatory or Post-Modern?" *Journal of Common Market Studies* 34 (March 1996): 39–44; Stephan Leibfried and Paul Pierson, eds., *European Social Policy: Between Fragmentation and Integration* (Washington, D.C.: Brookings Institution, 1995). Wolfgang Streeck offers a dissenting view in his "Neo-Voluntarism: A New European Social Policy Regime," *European Law Journal* 1 (March 1995): 31–59.

[30] Caporaso, "European Union," p. 39; Paul Taylor, "The European Union in the 1990s: Reassessing the Bases of Integration," in Ngaire Woods, ed., *Explaining International Relations since 1945* (Oxford: Oxford University Press, 1996), p. 289.

Due to British opposition, with the exception of health and safety issues, the 1985 white paper and the 1987 Single European Act (SEA) explicitly excluded all social issues. Furthermore, in the 1980s, growing national opposition against the welfare state and increasing fiscal constraints in domestic politics reduced the power of potential coalitions that might favor a more activist stance for the EU. Adopted in 1989, the EU's Social Charter is a solemn declaration that specifies individual rights; because of Britain's opposition, however, it is not a legally binding document. As part of the Treaty on European Union, the Social Protocol was adopted by qualified majority vote. With the exception of Britain, all EU members opted into the Social Policy Community, which is not covered by the Treaty of Rome and on whose decisions the European Court of Justice cannot rule, should any of the eleven members refuse to go along.

As noted in chapter 4, Dutch and Belgian social policy reforms in the 1980s and 1990s remained largely a national affair. Likewise, labor market reforms were debated strictly with reference to national not European considerations. In some limited areas, such as the setting up of works councils in the largest European companies, one can, however, notice the spreading of German institutional models.[31] In the late 1970s, for example, in contrast to the active involvement of the business communities of the other European states, German big business played a passive role in the discussion of the Vredeling proposal. The reason was simple. Because the proposal emulated Germany's works councils, it did not threaten to impose significant costs. But it took another fifteen years before a coalition between Germany and the Low Countries succeeded in pushing through at the European level a measure that creates works councils for the largest European companies. These councils are designed to facilitate dialogues between management and workers. Sharing with Germany a strong Christian Democratic social strain, the Low Countries saw the works council measure as a natural extension of their preferred national policy at the European level.

Hungarian social policy offers an instructive parallel and contrast. On the one hand, Hungary holds to the German model of a social market economy that prizes efficiency and the principle of insurance rather than redistribution. On the other, Hungary is subject to the direct constraints that loans from the IMF and World Bank and, less directly, the confidence of the international business community impose on its maneuvering room as it reorganizes its social welfare system to suit a new, capitalist economy.

---

[31] Lowell Turner, "Prospects for Worker Participation in Management in the Single Market," in Lloyd Ulman, Barry Eichengreen, and William T. Dickens, eds., *Labor and an Integrated Europe* (Washington, D.C.: Brookings Institution, 1993), pp. 45–79; Wolfgang Streeck, "National Diversity, Regime Competition and Institutional Deadlock: Problems in Forming a European Industrial Relations System," *Journal of Public Policy* 12 (1992): 301–30.

The EU affects social policy through its regulations, not through its spending. While the decisions of the European Court of Justice matter, the distributive, redistributive, and symbolic functions of social policy remain the prerogative of the member states. The welfare state is the institution that has shaped Europe more profoundly than any other during the last half century. To date, it remains largely unchallenged by European integration and the institutional effects emanating from Germany, although the accession of Sweden and Finland may alter this situation appreciably in the coming years. To be sure, through the convergence criteria for the EMU, set at Maastricht, which limit budget deficits to 3 percent of GDP, European integration is having a deflationary effect on macroeconomic policy in many European states, including Germany, which is forcing a curtailment in social spending. But this is a relatively small effect that, in the longer term, is dwarfed by the unavoidably fundamental transformation that demographic change is pushing on all European welfare states. From this vantage point, European effects have accounted for little.

It is thus not surprising that, as chapters 4 and 6 contend for the Low Countries and Scandinavia, on social issues, all politics is national. The welfare state consumes more resources than any other European institution. And during the last half century it has shaped collective identities and political expectations more profoundly than any other. Beyond the issuing of regulations that seek to enhance efficiencies, the European integration process appears to have had little effect on social policy. If, as appears increasingly likely, a central political task of European politics will be to adapt the welfare state to new demographic, technological, and international conditions, then, to date, the current European polity is uninvolved in a central political task confronting all European states.

Nor is the EU equipped to deal effectively with national security issues. Throughout the Cold War, these issues were linked closely to the United States and NATO. To be sure, in the 1970s and 1980s, the system of European Political Cooperation (EPC) among EC members made a useful contribution in the coordination of national security policy. Similarly, in the 1980s, a revived WEU contributed to forging a new, albeit contested, European perspective on questions of national security both inside and outside of NATO. But as president of the EC's Commission Jacques Delors seriously underestimated the civilian nature of the Europe he was trying to build when, in one of his rare Gaullist moments, he declared in 1990 that the Yugoslav crisis was a European affair and should be dealt with by Europeans. In the aftermath of the war in Bosnia, and with France taking the lead in 1996, European states are readying their military forces within NATO, with implicit U.S. support, for future out-of-area peacekeeping and peace enforcement actions.

Short of a total withdrawal of the United States from Europe and a collapse of all reform efforts in Russia, it is difficult to conceive of how the EU could extend itself far into the domain of national security policy. Fearing they will be pushed aside by the larger members of the EU, most of the smaller European states in particular resist moves to extend the EU's activity far into the domain of national security. They prefer the continued existence of NATO and a partial counterbalancing of American, French, and German influences, as they pursue their specific national security interests within the context of shifting Atlantic-European coalitions of states.[32] This is true not only of the Low Countries, Spain, and Finland. Denmark and Norway, as chapter 6 points out, have from the start strongly resisted any attempts to create new European competencies. Greece, on the other hand, prefers that the EU develop a common foreign and external security policy. In preparation for the 1996 intergovernmental conference on this issue, Greece has aligned with the "Europeanists" against the "Atlanticists," arguing, specifically for a further development of the WEU as the emergent defense pivot of the EU rather than as a European pillar within NATO. For, in defense of its vital national security interests, especially against Turkey, Greece is likely to wield greater influence in a European than in a North Atlantic arena. Limited European defense cooperation in NATO, the WEU, and the OSCE is gradually gaining wider political acceptance. Greater coordination in foreign and national security policies, crisis prevention, and the relationship between NATO and WEU are issues central to the evolving European security agenda, even though they often fall substantially outside the domain of the EU.

As chapter 5 makes plain, Spain's national security policy in the 1980s, with its newfound international fixation on the United Nations, NATO, and European cooperation, contrasted sharply with Greece's more autonomous policy. History has left Greece mistrustful of Germany (which occupied the country during World War II) and the United States (which intervened in the civil war in the late 1940s). Furthermore, on the question of Cyprus, Greece has remained locked in conflict with Turkey, a more powerful NATO partner. Finally, Greece is more directly exposed to the risk of war in the Balkans than any other member of the EU. Its pro-Serbian line and its anti-Macedonian policy underline the fact that Greece, looking toward Europe for national security reasons, has often been disappointed. A European Union poorly equipped to deal with national security issues and a member state that looks to it for help precisely on those issues are a perfect mismatch. The weakness of Europe's common foreign

[32] Barry Buzan et al., *The European Security Order Recast: Scenarios for the Post-Cold War Era* (Copenhagen: Centre for Peace and Conflict Research, 1990).

and security policy makes European integration, from the perspective of Athens, much less attractive.

In contrast to national security issues, the EU is deeply enmeshed in the formulation of public order issues, such as drugs, immigration, and police cooperation on questions of terrorism, as well as general foreign policy issues, such as the enlargement of the EU. For example, Germany's strong interest in an eastern enlargement of the EU, and thus in stabilizing conditions to the east of Germany, is mirrored in French and Spanish concerns over growing political instabilities in Algeria and throughout northern Africa and the threats that illegal immigration, drug trafficking, and terrorism pose to the eastern Mediterranean and Greece. New security threats at different geographical locations—the eastern and the southern borders of the EU, the western and the eastern Mediterranean—are competing for the limited resources the EU can allocate to countries threatening to destabilize Europe from without.

Throughout the 1980s, in a variety of fora, Germany pressed vigorously for the creation of institutionalized, EC-wide forms of police cooperation. Yet, as chapter 4 notes, this has had virtually no effect on the reorganization of the Dutch and Belgian police systems in the late 1980s. Furthermore, the implementation of the Schengen Accords, which eliminate border controls in Germany and a number of the smaller European states, has been a source of considerable friction. Specifically, German and French officials have sharply criticized the international effects of the Netherlands' liberal drug policy, which chapter 4 describes. Immigration is an important new security threat for Spain and Greece (chapter 5), as well as Poland (chapter 7). And although it remains committed to a common internal security policy in principle, the fear of terrorist attacks has stopped France from implementing to date the Schengen Accords. In brief, persistent efforts to the contrary, public order issues remain deeply problematic for the EU.

National institutions dealing with security and social issues are politically deeply entrenched in the smaller European democracies. To replace or substantially modify them in one fell swoop is proving to be politically impossible. To modify them gradually, over time, as the historical record of the last three decades illustrates, has led to a fundamental shift in the nature of European international relations. Policy options that the most ardent proponents of European integration could not envisage in the 1960s, for example, the integration of national police forces or the creation of a European central bank, have three decades later become the subject of normal policy debates. Thus, however soft the institutional effects of Europe and Germany on the smaller European states across a wide range of policy issues, these effects are clearly real—and deepening.

EUROPEAN MONETARY UNION, YUGOSLAVIA, AND GERMAN
POWER IN THE EUROPEAN POLITY

This chapter's argument about Germany in Europe is illustrated by the EMU and the Yugoslav crisis, two important episodes of European politics in recent years. These two policy domains exemplify the different strengths of German and European effects. The European effects in the first pillar (EMU) of the Maastricht treaty are strong compared to those in the second pillar (CSFP). And Germany's structural position on issues of monetary integration is much stronger than on questions of foreign and national security policy. Yet, in both cases, one finds an intermingling of German and European effects and the embedding of Germany's material and bargaining power in institutional power.

European Monetary Union

For the foreseeable future, both proponents and critics see in the EMU the highest stage of European integration.[33] Contemporary debates evoke historical echoes. Unlike agriculture and foreign trade, for example, the Treaty of Rome had excluded monetary issues from the list of "matters of common concern." But several policy initiatives sought in the 1960s to put monetary integration on the EC's agenda: the Marjolin Report of 1962, the establishment of a Committee of Central Bankers in the wake of the lira crisis of 1963–64, the 1965 declaration by the EC Commission of fixed European exchange rates as a European policy objective, the instabilities that floating exchange rates created for the CAP system in 1969, and the

[33] The literature on Germany, the EMS, and EMU has taken on tidal proportions and cannot be exhaustively listed here. A few central titles include David Marsh, *The Most Powerful Bank: Inside Germany's Bundesbank* (New York: Random House, 1992); Barry Eichengreen and Jeffrey Frieden, eds., *The Political Economy of European Monetary Unification* (Boulder, Colo.: Westview, 1994); Michele Fratianni and Jürgen von Hagen, eds., *The European Monetary System and European Monetary Union* (Boulder, Colo.: Westview, 1992); Peter B. Kenen, *Economic and Monetary Union in Europe: Moving Beyond Maastricht* (Cambridge: Cambridge University Press, 1995); David R. Cameron, "Transnational Relations and the Development of European Economic and Monetary Union," in Thomas Risse-Kappen, ed., *Bringing Transnational Relations Back In: Non-State Actors, Domestic Structures and International Institutions* (Cambridge: Cambridge University Press, 1995), pp. 37–78; Erik Jones, Jeffrey Frieden, and Francisco Torres, eds., *EMU and the Smaller Countries: Joining Europe's Monetary Club* (New York: St. Martin's Press, forthcoming); "Money Talks. Germany and the New Europe," *German Politics and Society* 14 special issue, ed. Kathleen R. McNamara (Fall 1996); Kathleen R. McNamara, *The Currency of Ideas: Monetary Politics in the European Union* (Ithaca: Cornell University Press, 1997); Kenneth Dyson and Kevin Featherstone, "EMU and Economic Governance in Germany," *German Politics* 5 (December 1996): 325–55.

subsequent creation of the Monetary Compensation Accounts (MCA) to defend that system. Finally, there was the ambitious Werner Plan of 1970, considered a significant step toward a "deepening" of Europe,[34] which specified 1980 as the date by which Europe's economic and monetary union would be achieved. But the upheavals in the international economy quickly put an end to this ambitious plan. Instead of monetary integration, the 1970s saw a succession of crisis-coping measures: the 1971 request of Germany, rejected by France and Italy, that the other European states float their currencies with the deutsche mark; the creation of the European "snake" in 1972, which France and Britain joined only for a short time, thus leaving it as a de facto deutsche mark zone linking several of the smaller European states to the Federal Republic; and, most importantly the creation in 1979 of the EMS, based on the political initiative of Roy Jenkins after he became president of the European Commission in 1977.

It is impossible to discern the ultimate outcome of the intense political debates that will define much of European politics in the coming years. But it is possible to establish a plausible argument for the likely zone of agreement. The history of the European integration process over the last four decades suggests that the success or failure of the EMU is unlikely to be a crucial threshold that will either propel Europe toward political union or make it slide back to 1930s-style power politics. It shows instead that the intermingling of European and German institutional effects typically creates grey zones, rather than clear-cut changes.

Germany illustrates the importance of a partial and contested Europeanization of state identity for monetary integration. Realism and liberalism can offer some plausible hypotheses why Germany has come to like the EMS as an indirect means for shaping the environment in which other states must adjust to German preferences. Typically, such hypotheses focus on the role of the powerful Bundesbank and the effects of its low tolerance for inflation. But these perspectives do not offer much help in making us understand why Germany's government has been so strongly committed to achieve full monetary integration in the EMU at an early date. Why should Germany advocate a policy that would greatly reduce German power in Europe's monetary affairs?

Realist interpretations of European integration, in particular, are puzzled by this apparent paradox. The German government has been willing to give up monetary autonomy, even though the net beneficiaries of such

[34] British membership was then the exemplar of how to "widen" Europe. Germany's *Ostpolitik* and the diplomatic initiative of a newly elected President Georges Pompidou created the political climate in which both "deepening" and "widening" were put on the agenda at the same time.

policy are likely to be Germany's partners. And it has committed itself to concrete dates, even though German negotiators have been disappointed by their failure to make significant progress on issues affecting political union, such as the role of the European Parliament, a common foreign and security policy, and a common policy on internal security issues. For realist theory, the concept of self-binding offers a plausible explanation, but only if it lets go of neorealist theory and turns to the analysis of domestic politics.[35] Furthermore, considering Germany a hegemon in this issue area, as the United States was in the Bretton Woods system, also suffers from significant weaknesses. In Europe's monetary relations, military power does not translate into policy leverage; the ability to fashion consensual package deals does. Furthermore, on issues of monetary integration, Germany has not acted like a hegemon. Indeed, its negotiators have displayed an aversion to being isolated and to confronting difficult issues. Far from organizing cooperation, the German Finance Ministry and the Bundesbank often felt they were being organized into cooperation.[36]

Liberal analysis points to the strong support that the EMU has enjoyed in the financial sector, among the major corporations and the unions. It is clearly in the interest of German business and labor to mitigate future erosions of competitiveness through restricting the room for any further appreciation of the deutsche mark (or a further depreciation of the currencies of some of Germany's European trade partners) by tying it to weaker currencies. But this explanation overlooks Germany's strongly backing the EMU well before the historically unique overvaluation of the deutsche mark in 1995–96. In the early 1990s, German business and labor followed, rather than led, the government. Against a rising chorus of skeptical opinions, these economic groups began to defend the government's policy more actively in the mid-1990s, as they began to recognize more clearly some of the benefits it might bring them.

The leading role that the German government (together with the French) took in accelerating the move toward Europe's monetary integration is best explained by the European identity of the German state. The government thought that Germany's long-term interests would be best served by reducing its access to unilateral instruments of power.

---

[35] See especially Joseph M. Grieco, "Understanding the Problem of International Cooperation: The Limits of Neoliberal Institutionalism and the Future of Realist Theory," in David Baldwin, ed., *Neorealism and Neoliberalism: The Contemporary Debate* (New York: Columbia University Press, 1993), pp. 331–35.

[36] Kenneth Dyson developed this point of being organized into cooperation in his lecture delivered at the Annual Conference of the Association for the Study of German Politics, Goethe Institute, London, April 26–27, 1996.

Most of the smaller European states are less affected than Germany by a partial change in state identity yet still manage to find considerable room for national maneuver in the European integration process, as shown in several of the chapters. Chapter 6, for example, makes this point with regard to Scandinavia. Denmark's membership in the Exchange Rate Mechanism (ERM) since 1979 and the unilateral pegging of the Norwegian and Swedish national currencies to the ECU in 1990–91 illustrate how the Scandinavian states found different ways of linking themselves to the European monetary regime that Germany and France had devised in the late 1970s. The pegging of currencies to the ECU marks a significant change from a nationally based, flexible exchange rate. But it falls short of the restraints that the ERM imposes; for beyond the rate to the ECU, the ERM fixes also the value of a currency in relation to a bilateral parity grid with all of the other participating currencies.

But even the looser coupling to the ECU can impose great instabilities, as the currency crisis in the fall of 1992 showed.[37] For a few days in September 1992, Swedish monetary officials raised interest rates to 500 percent in defense of the pegged rate. But after six weeks of calm, some 160 billion Swedish krona ($29 billion), or about 90 per cent of Sweden's foreign currency reserves, flowed out of the country within a single week in November. In response, the Swedish and Norwegian governments moved once again to a floating exchange rate. While the Swedish krona devalued by 20 percent, petroleum reserves helped stabilize the Norwegian krone. The outcome was paradoxical. Norway, which chose not to join the EU, continues to tie its currency to the ECU. And Sweden, which has become a full member of the EU and is clearly more committed than Norway to the European integration process, may not be able to meet the EMU's economic criteria or may decline to join because of an increase in public hostility.

Sweden's experience is not unlike Spain's, analyzed in chapter 5. With Germany's active support, Spain joined the ERM in 1989, although with a wider than normal band of fluctuations in the value of its national currency, the peseta (± 6 instead of ± 2 percent). In this initial period, the link between Spain and the EMS thus fell between the tight coupling of Denmark and the looser coupling of Norway and Sweden. Because of the system's high-interest-rate bias, membership in the EMS permitted Spain to import stability from Germany. Not unlike the United States and Italy in the 1980s, after 1989, Spain adhered to a tight monetary stance while pursuing a lax fiscal policy. By 1992, the Spanish current account deficit

---

[37] Eric Stern and Bengt Sundelius, "Sweden's Twin Monetary Crises of 1992: Rigidity and Learning in Crisis Decision Making," *Journal of Contingencies and Crisis Management* 5 (March 1997): 32–48.

had increased eightfold, to $24 billion.[38] It mattered little that France, Britain, the Netherlands, and, most important, Germany objected vociferously to Spain's policy as detrimental to their national economies and to the credibility of the EMS. For Spain, the attraction was irresistible of financing increasing budget and current account deficits through high interest rates and an appreciation of the peseta that attracted substantial short-term capital inflows.

The monetary crisis of September 1992 ended the perceived import of monetary stability. In contrast to the northern European states, Spain reimposed capital controls. And between September 1992 and May 1993, the Spanish government devalued the peseta three times, by a total of about 20 percent. Despite yet another devaluation of the peseta in March 1995, Spain's currency, like that of the other members of the ERM, has fluctuated comfortably within a narrow band since early 1994.[39] Hence, adverse developments in monetary affairs notwithstanding, Spain has retained close links to European institutions that differ from those of Denmark, Norway, and Sweden.

Like Spain, the Low Countries have used European monetary arrangements to further national objectives. But they also show notable differences in how they relate to the EMS. Seeking to avoid exchange rate adjustments at all costs, the Netherlands has since the early 1970s adhered to a hard-currency policy practically indistinguishable from Germany's. Yet the high rate of public debt, well beyond what the convergence indicators specified in the TEU permit, indicates that for two decades Dutch fiscal policy has been more relaxed on welfare and labor market issues than one might have expected within the constraints of a hard-currency policy so closely modeled after Germany's.[40]

Belgium was more lax than the Netherlands in shadowing the appreciation of the deutsche mark after 1973 and reaffirmed its traditional hard-currency policy only in the late 1980s. Thus markets cannot yet look back on an established track record of stable policy. And confidence in the Belgian franc is also lower because Belgium has acquired an enormous national debt, currently standing at about 135 percent of GDP. Hence, in contrast to the Netherlands, markets have tended to put the Belgian franc under pressure. This has forced up Belgian interest rates and thus increased the government's budgetary squeeze. Yet when the currency crisis of the fall of 1992 made possible a reevaluation of Belgium's restrictive

[38] Sofía A. Pérez, "Imported Credibility and the 'Strong Peseta': Bundesbank Dominance and Spanish Economic Policy in the EMS," paper prepared for the Ninth Annual International Conference of Europeanists, Chicago, March 31–April 2, 1994, pp. 5–6.

[39] That is, once the official band had been widened in order to make speculations against ERM currencies increasingly risky.

[40] The Austrian policy mix has been similar to the Dutch.

monetary stance, none of the major corporate actors and none of the main political parties was willing to let go of the hard-currency policy.[41] For, within Belgium's strong commitment to that policy and to the EMU, an acceptable balance of power between employers, unions, and different political parties had evolved. Thus Belgium continued to adhere to a hard-currency policy even when some of its major trading partners were pursuing a policy of devaluation.

The Belgian example is noteworthy for a second reason. It underlines the diversity of economic experience among smaller states committed to a hard currency, as do the Dutch example and the economic union between Belgium and Luxembourg, and it emphasizes the very considerable diversity in economic policy rooted in their different national economic institutions. These institutions continue to operate underneath the supposedly unifying constraints of an EU-wide hard-currency regime.[42]

The history of the EMS since the currency crisis of September 1992 suggests also that unifying constraints are not driving policy as much as is frequently assumed. Although the bands by which currencies can fluctuate against one another were widened to 30 percent, in point of fact, the values of currencies continuing to participate in the ERM vary only marginally. Nominally flexible, to deflect market pressures especially in times of crisis, the rates remain largely unchanged. Central banks thus continue to shadow the value of the deutsche mark. Participating states are willing to sacrifice an autonomous national monetary policy and to maintain or return to old exchange rate parities, even in the absence of action by the Bundesbank.[43] "The conventional wisdom regarding the state of monetary cooperation in Europe is quite inadequate," writes Rawi Abdelal. "The countries still in the EMS, especially those in its hard-core, have maintained the value of their currencies very close to their pre-crisis parities."[44]

The behavior of the governments and central banks in the member states of the ERM after the currency crisis of August 1993 points to their strong political commitment to the success of the EMU. It is no longer the functioning of the EMS (and the exchange rate) but the political ambition to qualify for the EMU (and the 3 percent deficit criterion) that drives

[41] The open letter that the Leuven group of academic economists wrote to the Belgian finance minister had no effect.

[42] The "stability" pact in the EU that Germany has pressed for since 1995 would make it more costly and difficult for national governments to run excessive national budget deficits in the EMU. This would reduce the latitude in fiscal policy that smaller European states committed to a hard currency policy have enjoyed to date.

[43] Heinrich Matthes, "'Damocles Shadowing': An Innovation in the Second Phase of EMU," *Intereconomics* 29 (1994): 75–77.

[44] Rawi E. Abdelal, "The Politics of Monetary Leadership and Followership: Stability in the European Monetary System since the Currency Crisis of 1992," *Political Studies* (forthcoming): 2.

monetary and economic policies in Europe. For example, in the wake of August 1993, central bankers and political leaders both insisted that the plans for the EMU would not be derailed. In November 1993, Germany and France announced a joint plan to meet the EMU convergence criteria by 1996. In December 1993, the Bank of France was given full independence, as specified by the Maastricht treaty. With the creation of the European Monetary Institute, the forerunner of the European Central Bank, the second stage of the EMU began on schedule on January 1, 1994. Subsequent developments have reconfirmed this trend. In April 1996, the EU finance ministers and central bankers reached an agreement in Verona that reduced the likelihood of a future split between participants in monetary union and other EU member states.

In brief, the ERM is no longer simply a set of imposed constraints. It is an institution that central bankers and politicians react to differently. Some national capitals simply take the EMS for granted and thus do not recognize it as a constraint; other capitals use monetary restraints to impose a deflationary bias on policy so as to qualify their states for EMU membership and to accelerate a structural transformation of national economies that they regard as inevitable, even at the cost of increasing unemployment; finally, still other capitals experience the EMS as a politically contested constraint.

What do these findings imply for the evolution of the EMS to an EMU and, beyond, to an integrated Europe? The constitution and location of the future European Central Bank (ECB) in Frankfurt are evidence of an institutional transfer from Germany to Brussels. If they are interpreted restrictively, even in the best of economic times, the convergence criteria that define membership in the EMU are likely to pose formidable barriers for the membership of core members of the EU, such as Belgium. And even if they are interpreted liberally, these criteria will keep some current members (Greece) and future members (the east central European states) of the EU out of the EMU for many years to come. If it succeeds, the EMU will not mirror a simple European or German blueprint, but will instead help bring about a Europe marked by different tiers, multiple tracks, and inner and outer layers, arranged in a complex and "variable geometry." Even in the most optimistic scenario, Europe would thus be a variable mix of institutional effects that both enable and constrain national elites.

Yugoslavia

More than virtually any other issue, German recognition of Croatia and Slovenia on December 23, 1991, has fueled suspicion of united Germany. Did Germany not abandon its European partners only a few days after the Maastricht conference and embark on a course of reckless diplomacy?

Did the new Germany not look like the old Wilhelminian one, exemplifying unbridled political ambition? Harsh critics likened German recognition of breakaway Croatia to Nazi Germany's creation of an independent Croatia under German trusteeship during World War II.[45] And they saw in the new German assertiveness the old drive to the Balkans, fueled by economic greed and geostrategic calculations. Yet, in 1989, only one percent of German foreign trade was with Yugoslavia. The business community was conspicuously absent in the domestic debates on German policy. And Germany's strategic culture after 1945 has shown a deep, institutionalized aversion to the mere mentioning of national security interests, let alone geostrategic thinking.[46] Moderate critics saw instead policy blunders, personal failings, and political misjudgments.[47] The evidence and this book's argument suggest a third interpretation. Neither a new unilateralism in German foreign policy nor policy blunders, personal failings, and political misjudgments, but rather domestic politics and the weakness of multilateral security institutions in Europe account for the German decision to recognize Croatia and Slovenia.

Domestic opposition against the EC policy of preserving a united Yugoslavia was building by late spring 1991.[48] The main argument was that the right of self-determination in Europe was indivisible. German unification was based on that principle. And it could not be denied to the breakaway republics if independence was the wish of their majorities, expressed in democratic elections. Furthermore, a policy of recognition would internationalize the issue so that it could be taken up in the UN and thus deter further Serbian aggression. These and other arguments were politically consequential. They were made by leading personalities in Chancellor Kohl's CDU, such as Party Secretary Volker Rühe; by the CSU, speaking for many of the half million Croats living in Bavaria; by the young foreign policy elite of the SPD, who, after the debacle of the Gulf War, favored a

---

[45] Marc Fisher, "Yugoslav Violence Puts Focus on Germany," *Washington Post* (July 7, 1991): A21, quoted in Beverly Crawford, "Explaining Defection from International Cooperation," *World Politics* 48 (July 1996): 483.

[46] Wolfgang F. Schlör, "German Security Policy," Adelphi Paper 277, International Institute for Strategic Studies, London, 1993. Michael E. Smith, "Sending the Bundeswehr to the Balkans: The Domestic Politics of Reflexive Multilateralism," *German Politics and Society* 14 (Winter 1996): 49–67.

[47] Wolfgang Krieger, "Toward a Gaullist Germany? Some Lessons form the Yugoslav Crisis," *World Policy Journal* 11 (Spring 1994): 26–38.

[48] My account draws heavily on Crawford, "Explaining Defection"; Krieger, "Gaullist Germany?"; Peter Viggo Jakobsen, "Multilateralism Matters but How? The Impact of Multilateralism on Great Power Policy towards the Break-up of Yugoslavia," *Cooperation and Conflict* 30 (December 1995): 365–98; and Sonia Lucarelli, "The International Community and the Yugoslav Crisis: A Chronology of Events," EUI Working Paper RSC no. 95/8, European University Institute, Florence, 1995.

more activist foreign policy; by the FDP, which by July 9, 1991, had also come to back a policy of recognition; by the representatives of Germany's sixteen *Länder;* by the foreign policy elite more generally; by the conservative elite newspaper, the *Frankfurter Allgemeine Zeitung,* specifically, one of its editors, Johann Reissmüller, who ran a strong anti-Serb campaign; and by the media covering acts of Serbian aggression. On June 18, 1991 the Bundestag articulated a broad elite consensus that was critical of the EC position and that asserted the breakaway republics' right to secession and self-determination; as early as July 1, Foreign Minister Genscher faced a series of such hostile questions from the Foreign Policy Committee of the Bundestag that, thereafter, he reportedly began to reconsider Germany's diplomatic position on recognition. Even though public opinion remained divided and rather uninterested in the issue, Chancellor Kohl followed suit during the summer of 1991.

The intensification of armed conflict in Croatia in the summer of 1991, the regular negotiation and breaking of ceasefires, and the stalemating of the Western response in the face of sharply diverging national preferences, illustrated the weakness of European multilateral security institutions. France preferred a European military intervention in Yugoslavia that excluded the United States; Britain did not. Germany was, for political and constitutional reasons, unable to lend active support to multilateral military interventions under European, transatlantic, or UN auspices. The overlapping diplomatic and security arrangements between the EC, WEU, NATO, and the UN reflected these different national interests. European political cooperation had been institutionalized more firmly at Maastricht, but it was still based on the principle of consensus, required no binding national commitments, and lacked powers of enforcement. These institutions were too weak to make Kohl and Genscher withstand the domestic pressure they confronted on the principle of self-determination and the issue of recognition.

During the summer of 1991, German citizens' preferences for recognition and their government's continued support for the common EC foreign policy were increasingly at odds. During a meeting between President Mitterrand and Chancellor Kohl on September 18, Kohl promised to abstain from unilateral action on Yugoslavia; in return, Mitterrand accepted Slovenia's and Croatia's right to self-determination. This bilateral deal was repeated in modified form a few weeks later. At their October 10 meeting, the EC foreign ministers resolved to withhold the diplomatic recognition of individual Yugoslav states for another two months.[49] With

[49] In an interview conducted in Bonn in May 1993, former Foreign Minister Genscher said that he understood the October 10, 1991, resolution to mean that by December 10, 1991, Germany would have a green light from the EC for its preferred policy of diplomatic recognition. See Crawford, "Explaining Defection," p. 495, n. 51. This view is highly implausible.

the disintegration of the Soviet Union, the EC began to recognize the Baltic republics and other post-Soviet states. By November 15, the Bundestag unanimously adopted a resolution in which the Serbian leadership was held chiefly responsible for the civil war and in which the Bundestag came out squarely for recognition.

By early December, most EC members had accepted that the existing policy on Yugoslavia had failed and that recognition of the breakaway states would probably be the next step, although they continued to disagree sharply about both the modalities and timing of such a move. A few EC member states (Italy, Belgium, and Denmark) supported the German position openly; Britain reportedly backed Germany as a quid pro quo for German support of the British position at the Maastricht conference; France and others fell in line only because they saw no alternative to Germany's declared intention of recognizing Croatia and Slovenia before Christmas. The meeting of the EC foreign ministers on December 16 again produced a compromise. The EC agreed to extend diplomatic recognition by January 15, provided that Croatia and Slovenia met political conditions that largely followed a catalog developed and agreed upon by the CSCE—including the protection of minority rights and the recognition of the borders and territorial sovereignty of neighbors. In the aftermath of the December 16 meeting, there was some bitterness about the heavy-handed pressure that Germany had exerted to push its partners toward a recognition policy. Genscher was reported not only as intransigent but also overly opportunistic, even exploitative. Because a general agreement on foreign policy coordination had been reached at Maastricht only a few days earlier, none of the foreign ministers wanted negotiations dealing with the first concrete issue after Maastricht to fail.

Up to and including the meeting of December 16, 1991, German foreign policy had neither scuttled multilateral processes and the EC nor blundered. Instead, it delayed a unilateral move that domestic politics, specifically elite opinion, had pushed on Chancellor Kohl and Foreign Minister Genscher during the summer. For six months, Kohl and Genscher and Mitterrand and Major worked hard to maintain a common front. Rather than using domestic pressure as an excuse for earlier recognition, time and again, Kohl and Genscher warned against the dangers of unilateralism and used their domestic political predicaments and a rapidly changing international context that increasingly favored recognition to coax and cajole Germany's EC partner states along to their preferred policy. "The principal reason for the German government's delayed recognition until December," writes Peter Jakobsen, "was fear that unilateral

---

It appears improbable that Genscher's colleagues understood the resolution to carry the same meaning, and probable that Genscher knew this to be the case.

recognition would damage the Maastricht summit and hence its Europe policy irreparably."[50] Until December 16, multilateralism figured strongly in German foreign policy.

The real *Alleingang* (unilateral action) occurred in the next seven days. For Germany did not take seriously the conditionality requirement that French and German officials had drafted as part of the compromise. The six Yugoslav republics had until December 23 to petition the Hague Commission, created in September to certify by January 15 whether the conditions were met. Unresolved by the compromise was what would happen if the conditions were not met. In anticipation of such recognition requirements, both Germany and Croatia in December 1991 made some perfunctory efforts to improve Croatia's inadequate record.[51] It was clear all along that Germany would disregard the report of the Hague Commission if it was negative, as indeed the January 11, 1992, report on Croatia turned out to be. The German position was that Croatia and the other republics simply had to commit themselves to the EC's conditions, not fulfill them. As Beverly Crawford put it, "acceptance of the conditions substituted for fulfillment of them."[52] Hence Genscher announced publicly on December 17 the position he reportedly had taken during the negotiations the night before. It was the stance the United States and most Western states took when in January 1992 they recognized Russia and several other successor states of the Soviet Union. For Germany, anything else would amount to a double standard in international diplomacy. Recognition would be automatic and no further German or EC action was required.

Whatever its logical merits, the German position clearly was at odds with the official transcript of the December 16 meeting. For both tactical and substantive reasons, conditionality mattered greatly to other members of the EC. Hence Chancellor Kohl's decision to recognize Slovenia and Croatia on December 23, without awaiting the commission report, broke Germany's multilateral policy stance and the European compromise. Competitive grandstanding and credit taking by Kohl and Genscher do not offer a plausible explanation of this change in German policy. The reason lies deeper. The blindness of Germany's Yugoslav policy to the internal conditions in Croatia dates back to 1990. With 4 million dollar backing from a Croatian émigré community heavily concentrated in Bavaria, in April 1990 the ultranationalist Croatian Democratic Union (HDZ) won Croatia's first democratic election since 1945. As a result, President Franjo Tudjman em-

[50] Jakobsen, "Multilateralism Matters?" p. 377.

[51] On December 4, the Croatian Parliament unanimously passed a statute guaranteeing Serbian minority rights, a document that, in light of the Croatian policy of the preceding two years, neither the Serbs nor anybody else could take seriously. Germany found a human rights lawyer, who on December 13 gave his approval of the Croatian statute.

[52] Crawford, "Explaining Defection," p. 497.

barked on creating a state that would represent the Croatian nation without granting strong minority rights to a large Serb minority, concentrated in the Krajina, that feared a return of Croatian fascism. (Serb demands for greater autonomy radicalized in the spring of 1991, to a secessionist policy by military force.) In August 1990, Chancellor Kohl's premier foreign policy advisor, Horst Teltschik, had a secret meeting with a personal emissary of President Tudjman, who asked for German recognition if it were to break away from Yugoslavia.[53]

It was one of the great failings of Germany's diplomacy in Yugoslavia not to have required Croatia to guarantee unequivocally minority rights for its Serbian population in return for acceptance as a modern democratic state in Europe. But the German government, totally preoccupied by the headlong rush toward unification, did not consider Yugoslavia a serious diplomatic problem in 1990. Amnesty International and the media would later repeatedly report atrocities committed against non-Croat civilians, and the government headed by President Tudjman would refuse to disassociate itself from Croatian fascists. Germany's neglect of the domestic conditions of the regimes it sought to engage and embed in Europe through peaceful means predates unification and is not a sign of a newfound assertiveness. Indeed, throughout the 1970s and 1980s, under SPD-led and CDU-led governments, Germany's search for a durable détente with Eastern Europe and the Soviet Union had been based on a similar, perhaps unavoidable moral obtuseness.

No other foreign policy episode since 1990 has created as much European nervousness about the new Germany as this one. Germany exercised a fair amount of jawboning power in 1991, but did so in a multilateral framework. When it stepped outside of that framework on the question of conditionality, it revealed a feature, both inescapable and problematic, that has marked German foreign policy both before 1989 and after.

German Power

The Europeanization of a common policy on questions of monetary relations is stronger than on questions of security. An internationalized state identity has led the German government to see its long-term interest best served by relinquishing the unilateral power it currently enjoys in the determination of European interest rates. Despite the deflationary bias the EMU will impose, for a variety of reasons most EU member states are willing to go along in its creation. Not so in the area of common and security foreign policy. Here Germany and the other members of the EU seek to coordinate conflicting policy objectives in an environment where norms

---

[53] Horst Teltschik, *329 Tage* (Berlin: Siedler, 1990), pp. 347–48.

are relatively weak, where uncertainty is great, and where sanctions against defection from international cooperation are not clear. German power is evident both in the creation of a regime that institutionalizes power relations and in an arena that remains open to unilateral defection from international cooperation.

From the perspective of material capabilities and institutional efficiencies, German power in Europe takes an odd form. Writing from a neorealist perspective and referring specifically to the EMU, Joseph Grieco is struck by the tact and diplomacy that marks what he regards as an unambiguous domination of Europe by Germany.[54] Giandomenico Majone's liberal interpretation suggests instead that, in the case of monetary integration, Germany had to exert no pressure on other European governments to accept a European central bank exclusively committed to the goal of monetary stability. These governments had been won over to a strategy of disinflation well before the process of monetary integration started in earnest in 1988.[55] The surprising tact and lack of pressure that mark German power in Europe, this chapter contends, flow from the multilateral institutionalization of power relationships.

This institutionalization is facilitated by what in a comparative perspective is a striking equality in the distribution of material power in Europe. In 1990, for example, German GDP amounted to only one-quarter of the EC's. The corresponding figure for Japanese GDP as a share of the combined GDP of the East Asian Economic Caucus (EAEC) was three-quarters. Furthermore, compared to the stability in the European balance of power during the last generation, Japan's dynamic growth has shifted the balance of power quite substantially in Asia. As a share of the EC's combined GDP, German GDP declined from 27 to 25 percent between 1970 and 1990; as a share of the EAEC's combined GDP, Japan's GDP increased from 57 to 73 percent. France has been able to hold its own against Germany in intra-EC trade during the last three decades, while losing some ground to Germany in the external trade of the EC; Japan's trading partners have not done nearly so well in Asia.[56] Finally, compared to Asia, economic

[54] Joseph M. Grieco, "Realism and Regionalism: American Power and German and Japanese Institutional Strategies during and after the Cold War," paper prepared for delivery at the annual meeting of the American Political Science Association, San Francisco, August 29–September 1, 1996, p. 10.

[55] Giandomenico Majone, "Independence vs. Accountability? Non-Majoritarian Institutions and Democratic Government in Europe," EUI Working Paper SPS no. 94/3, European University Institute, Florence, 1994, pp. 1–2; Wayne Sandholtz, "Monetary Bargains: The Treaty on EMU," in Alan W. Cafruny and Glenda G. Rosenthal, eds., *The State of the European Community*, vol. 2 (London: Longmann, 1993), pp. 125–44.

[56] Joseph M. Grieco, "Systemic Sources of Variation in Regional Institutionalization in Western Europe, East Asia and the Americas," in Helen Milner and Edward Mansfield, eds., *The Political Economy of Regionalism* (New York: Columbia University Press, 1997), pp. 164–87.

equality in Europe is striking. The per capita GDP in the wealthier states in the EC exceeded that of the poorer states by a factor of 3 in both 1970 and 1990. In the EAEC, the corresponding factor increased from 9 to 29. Along a number of different economic dimensions besides GDP, Asian regionalism is marked by conditions of asymmetric dependence that contrast with the symmetric interdependence characteristic of European regionalism.[57] Compared to Japan's role in Asia, the institutionalization of German power in multilateral arrangements is furthered by a comparative absence of asymmetric dependence relations.

Germany's material power does not pose the most significant threat for other European states. Instead, German power, normally exercised with tact and without great pressure, but in support of the German model of economy and society, is expressed in a "creeping German colouring" of European institutions.[58] Because that model has remained largely unaffected by German unification, could Germany export it, like so many other products "made in Germany," in a coordinated and coherent grand strategy?[59] The available evidence suggests that, for institutional reasons, this is highly unlikely. German political power and policy making on European issues is polycentric and lacks coherence across different policy sectors. Based on a detailed examination of agriculture and migration, Nisha Malhan concludes that Germany's role in the EU is policy-specific and covers the full range from assertiveness to compliance.[60] The traditional fragmentation of power between different ministries, and between the government and the Bundesbank, has been reinforced by the strengthened position of the German *Länder* and the increased importance of the Constitutional Court. Not a coherent grand strategy implemented from the Chancellery but polyphonous, multilevel, and multiactor interaction processes typify Germany's approach toward the EU.[61]

Across the divide of 1989–91, German unification, and accelerated European integration, Germany has remained a semisovereign state in its re-

[57] Alan Siaroff, "Interdependence versus Asymmetry? A Comparison of the European and Asia-Pacific Economic Regions," paper presented at the ISA-West Meetings, Seattle, October 14–15, 1994. Siaroff supports this generalization with seven indicators: total population, GDP per capita, total GDP, stock of foreign investment, hosting of multinational corporations, total external assets or debts, and research and development spending.

[58] Ole Wæver, "Nordic Nostalgia: Northern Europe after the Cold War," *International Affairs* 68 (January 1992): 81.

[59] See Douglas Webber, "The Second Coming of the Bonn Republic," IGS Working Paper Series, no. 95/1, University of Birmingham, Institute for German Studies, 1995.

[60] Nisha Malhan, "The Implications of Unification for Germany's Role in the European Union," Ph.D. diss., University of Warwick, April 1996, p. 343.

[61] Simon Bulmer and William Paterson, *The Federal Republic of Germany and the European Community* (London: Allen and Unwin, 1987). For an update of this thesis, see Charlie Jeffrey, "A Giant with Feet of Clay? United Germany in the European Union," IGS Discussion Paper Series, no. 95/6, University of Birmingham, Institute for German Studies, 1995.

lations with the EU. There is no compelling evidence suggesting that
united Germany will become what some feared of the Bonn republic, "the
fourth and richest Reich."[62] Rather more plausible is the Europeanization
of "the German problem" and "other German questions."[63] Germany's
"ostentatious modesty," its "culture of reticence," and its "leadership avoidance complex" all describe an institutional reality that has tamed German
power in Europe through transforming its nature rather than its balance.[64] Hence "we should not be surprised," writes Simon Bulmer, "if Germany remains Europe's 'gentle giant.'"[65]

COLLECTIVE MEMORY

European and German effects are intimately connected with history and
memory.[66] History is an objective process, factual and impartial. Memories are contemporary experiences, interpretations, and reinterpretations
of history. By their very nature, collective memories are both intersubjec-
tive and contested. Political leaders can mobilize such interpretations instrumentally to achieve current political objectives. Or they can be moved
by interpretations that are institutionalized, for example, in history books,
school and university curricula, or the content of media. As a rule, collective memory gets deployed instrumentally in institutionalized settings.
Analytical traditions that neglect the effects of collective memory, as variants of realism and liberalism often do, miss crucial determinants of Germany's stance toward Europe. This is true, specifically, of all those who argue that the changes in world politics since 1989 have made Germany a
"normal" state again.[67]

[62] Edwin Hartrich, *The Fourth and Richest Reich* (New York: Macmillan, 1980).

[63] David Calleo, *The German Problem Reconsidered: Germany and the World Order, 1870 to the
Present* (Cambridge: Cambridge University Press, 1978); David Schoenbaum and Elizabeth
Pond, *The 'German Question' and Other German Questions* (New York: St. Martin's Press, 1996).

[64] I take these descriptions of Germany from Charlie Jeffrey, "A Giant with Feet of Clay?
United Germany in the European Union," Institute for German Studies, Discussion Papers
in German Studies, no. IGS 95/6, University of Birmingham, 1996.

[65] Simon J. Bulmer, "Germany and European Integration: Toward Economic and Political
Dominance?" in Carl F. Lankowski, ed., *Germany and the European Community* (New York:
St. Martin's Press, 1993), p. 95.

[66] Maurice Halberwachs, *The Collective Memory* (New York: Harper and Row, 1980).

[67] Andrei S. Markovits and Simon Reich, *The German Predicament: Memory and Power in the
New Europe* (Ithaca: Cornell University Press, 1997). See also Hans-Peter Schwarz, "Rolle und
Identität der zukünftigen deutschen Aussenpolitik," in Karl Kaiser and Hanns Maull, eds.,
Die Zukunft der Deutschen Aussenpolitik (Bonn: Europa-Union, 1994), pp. 73–88; "The Past as
Arsenal: Debating German Unification," special issue of *German Politics and Society* 30 (Fall
1993); Michael Geyer and Konrad H. Jarausch, "The Future of the German Past: Trans-
atlantic Reflections for the 1990s," *Central European History* 22 (September–December 1989):
229–59.

Germany offers ample testimony for the powerful effects that collective memories have for shaping the interests that determine German and European policies in the 1990s.[68] Historical narratives of German political leaders are instructive for understanding how Germany and Europe are linked. Chancellor Kohl, for example, makes sharp distinctions between German and European history before and after World War II: stability versus instability, peace versus war, prosperity versus depression, democracy versus autocracy, and integration versus balance of power politics. Informed by that narrative, Kohl pushed ahead with his plans for Europe's economic and political union. Thus Chancellor Kohl and the German government did not press, within a multilateral framework, united Germany's new interests in central-eastern Europe as actively as other German politicians, such as the CDU's Wolfgang Schäuble or the SPD's Rudolf Scharping might have done.[69]

But historical memory has also enhanced German power. Informed by historical analogies from the interwar years and worried about a possible rupture between Germany and the West, both in the 1950s and 1970s, U.S. policy makers were more willing to accommodate core demands of the Federal Republic on the issue of German unity than they might have been otherwise. Although the memories of Versailles and Rapallo are fading, the possibility of a unilateral German *Ostpolitik,* rather than a multilateral European one, remains a potent bargaining chip on the side of a German government more committed than its French and British partners to a common foreign and security policy of the EU. Former Foreign Minister Hans-Dietrich Genscher has put the issue in the following terms: "We would not like to monopolize relations with Russia and the other states of Central and Eastern Europe. Therefore, we asked our partners not to leave us alone in this policy, because it is one we have to conduct."[70]

The same analysis applies to the other European states as well. The memory of Nazi atrocities has become a defining part of the structure of

[68] I am relying here greatly on the unpublished papers and forthcoming book of Thomas Banchoff. See also Thomas Banchoff, "Institutions, Historical Memory, and the Enduring Transformation of German Foreign Policy," Working Paper 5.33, Center for German and European Studies, University of California (April 1996); idem, "Historical Memory and the Source of German Power," paper prepared for presentation at the Annual Meeting of the American Political Science Association, Chicago, September 1995; idem, "Historical Memory and German Foreign Policy: The Cases of Adenauer and Brandt," *German Politics and Society* 14 (Summer 1996): 36–53; idem, "German Policy toward the European Union: The Effects of Historical Memory," *German Politics* 6 (April 1997): 60–76; idem, *The German Problem Transformed: Institutions, Politics, and Foreign Policy, 1945–95* (forthcoming).

[69] Banchoff, "Institutions, Historical Memory, and Foreign Policy," p. 29. Banchoff applies this analysis also to the contrasting views of Konrad Adenauer and Helmut Kohl, Adenauer and Kurt Schumacher, and Kohl and Rudolf Scharping.

[70] Hans-Dietrich Genscher, quoted in Banchoff, "Historical Memory and German Power," p. 24.

European politics since 1945.[71] The notion of having been victimized by Germany during the twentieth century is constitutive of most European states, helps define their collective identity, and shapes the interests that inform their policies. Even states that arguably were not occupied and victimized, like Austria, invent a founding myth of victimization that is essential to their collective postwar identity. As chapters 4–7 show, the reaction of the smaller European states toward Germany is strongly shaped by collective memories.[72] During World War II, for example, the Greek population shrank by more than 8 percent, due to famine, executions, and the Holocaust. This gruesome legacy has reinforced a deep-seated suspicion about the historical role foreign powers have played in Greece. And this memory has profoundly shaped Greece's stance toward Germany and Europe in subsequent decades. While memories of dismemberment and suffering under German occupation have also left deep imprints on the stance of Poland and the Czech Republic toward Germany and Europe,[73] the historical memories of Hungary and the Slovak Republic are rooted in different experiences that make their relations with Germany less problematic.

Such divergence within particular European regions is also apparent in northern Europe. While Sweden's relations with Germany are not heavily burdened by history, in Norway, shameful memories of the Quisling government have left a powerful legacy. And neither the Netherlands nor Denmark can escape from either their historical memories of Nazi occupation or their economic dependence on Germany. The smaller European states thus live with memories that entangle them deeply and differently with Germany. And these memories are important in shaping current experiences of different European and German influences.

[71] Tony Judt, "The Past Is Another Country: Myth and Memory in Postwar Europe," *Daedalus* 121 (Fall 1992): 83–118.

[72] Dirk Verheyen and Christian Søe, eds., *The Germans and Their Neighbors* (Boulder, Colo.: Westview Press, 1993); Markovits and Reich, *German Predicament*.

[73] The difference between relatively good Polish-German and relatively poor Czech-German relations in the 1990s illustrates that contemporary history has discernible effects on collective memories. Polish society has debated its relations with Germany since the first exchange of letters between Polish and German bishops in the mid-1960s. In the Czech Republic, the debate about the past, specifically the forcible removal of the Sudeten Germans at the end of World War II, began only in 1990. The Polish debate occurred at a time when the territorial borders in Europe were guaranteed by a "Pax Russica"; since 1990, from the perspective of the Czech Republic, European borders are potentially less stable. Furthermore, Germany has shown much greater sensitivity toward Poland than toward the Czech Republic: the devastations that Germany and World War II brought to Poland were much greater, the expulsion of the Silesian Germans occurred during wartime and in an unplanned manner, and Poland itself lost much territory to the Soviet Union. The Czech Republic suffered less, the forcible removal of the Sudeten Germans occurred after the end of the war and was planned, and the territorial integrity of Czechoslovakia was restored. See Petr Příhoda, "Wenn die Erinnerung die Zukunft Blockiert," *Die Zeit* (May 10, 1996): 8.

Neither Germany nor Europe will be able to escape a past that cannot be forgotten and that forever will remain contested politically. Germany's European identity and interests are not the result of a traditional German nationalism that simply seeks to trade institutional for material or bargaining power. But such nationalism may grow in Germany, especially should other European states, such as Britain and France, decide, for whatever reason, to turn their backs on building the European polity that Germany's political elite would endow with as many elements of its own stateness as possible—an independent bank, a powerful court, a cooperative system of federalism, a parliament that carries some, but not too much, weight and a decision making procedure that is consensual and remains attuned to both vital national interests and the requirements of efficiency.

This is asking a great deal of states whose identity is expressed in distinctive political institutions, such as Parliament or the Grand Corps, and that have played an active role in global politics. What is natural for Germany to expect is not natural for other states to give. Interest dictates to both smaller and larger states in Europe a policy of embedding Germany in Europe, lest Germany, at some future time, be tempted or compelled to once again exercise power that is untamed by institutions. But the burden of history makes such adjustments onerous. On the road to unification, Germany could count on the unquestioned support of the United States, not of Britain or France. Although British and French public opinion was considerably more supportive of unification than their governments, in January 1990 about two-fifths of the French and more than half of the British public believed that a return to fascism was possible in Germany and hence did not trust Germany.[74] And Britain's anti-European and anti-German sentiments are indelibly linked at the highest levels of government. To date, collective memories make Germany and Britain travel with different speeds on the path of European integration; there is no assurance that in the future they might not choose different paths.

"The German question is rooted as much in foreign myth as in German reality," wrote Anne-Marie Burley in 1989; "it is time to concentrate on what the Germans themselves . . . think and want, instead of what other nations, based on either their own historical experience or deep-seated beliefs about entrenched national characteristics, assume they must think and want."[75] This counsel is well-taken; but no political community can escape from its own history. This has led Germany to a largely unques-

---

[74] Jakob Schissler, "Perceptions of the 'New Germany' in the International System," in Dirk Berg-Schlosser and Ralf Rytlewski, eds., *Political Culture in Germany* (New York: St. Martin's Press, 1993), p. 306; *Der Spiegel* 14/1994: 78.

[75] Anne-Marie Burley, "The Once and Future German Question," *Foreign Affairs* 68 (Winter 1989–90): 65, 83.

tioned European and international state identity. Institutional power is the coin in which this Germany pays its debts and collects its bills. While others may accept this coin, because they have had other histories, it is not natural that they do. No avenue to Germany's and Europe's future can ever bypass the past.

CONCLUSION

Smaller states look to Europe. "Authority above the level of the nation-state," writes Nicholas Colchester, "paradoxically helps the *amour-propre* of smaller nations and regions. Portugal holds more sway within the European Union than it would outside it."[76] But is membership in the EU the only determinant for the policies of smaller states that reflect and inform European norms? Or do Benelux for the Low Countries and the Nordic Council for the Scandinavian states provide alternatives to the EU and its predecessors?

Even before the end of World War II, the exile governments of the three Benelux countries decided to form a customs union that helped provide a model for the creation of the European Economic Community (EEC), eventually set up in 1958. And wartime experience made the Low Countries reject Franco-British proposals for the creation of traditional bilateral security arrangements after World War II. Instead, even before the establishment of NATO the Netherlands and Belgium signed a Military Cooperation Accord to achieve novel forms of security cooperation.[77] But Benelux was never meant to substitute for a broader European integration. "The Netherlands," concludes Richard Griffiths, "could consider no form of international cooperation which would exclude its largest trading partner," Germany.[78] An instrumental commitment to a wider European integration process over time became institutionalized. In the words of Hans Daalder, writing about the Netherlands, "supranationalism

[76] Nicholas Colchester, "Goodbye, Nation-State. Hello . . . What?" *New York Times* (July 17, 1994): A17.

[77] See James E. Meade, *Negotiations for Benelux: An Annotated Chronicle, 1943–56,* Princeton Studies in International Finance, no.6 (Princeton: Department of Economics and Sociology, 1957); Pierre-Henri Laurent, "Beneluxer Economic Diplomacy and the Creation of Little Europe, 1945–50," *Journal of European Integration* 10 (1986): 23–37; Wichard Woyke, *Erfolg durch Integration: Die Europapolitik der Benelux Staaten von 1947 bis 1969* (Bochum: Brockmeyer, 1985); George J. Stein, *Benelux Security Cooperation: A New European Defense Community?* (Boulder, Colo.: Westview Press, 1990).

[78] Richard T. Griffiths, "Economic Reconstruction Policy in the Netherlands and Its International Consequences, May 1945–March 1951," EUI Working Paper no. 76, European University Institute, Department of History and Civilization, Florence, 1984, p. 33.

was regarded as a good in itself, because it was the instrument which would 'tame' power politics."[79]

The integration of Scandinavia has deep historical roots.[80] The interparliamentary cooperation of the Nordic Council after 1952 has not made any spectacular inroads into the sphere of intergovernmental relations. But after several decades of cooperation between national executives and administrative agencies, there exists an accretion of advances in policy coordination including a passport union, a common employment market, and reciprocal social security arrangements. In many spheres, common legislation extends throughout Scandinavia.[81] When Denmark's joining the EC threatened to split Scandinavia apart in 1971, a Nordic Council of Ministers was set up with a central secretariat, which since then has become the core of governmental cooperation in Scandinavia. "The ups and downs of Nordic cooperation," concludes Johnny Laursen in his review of the literature, "were, thus, immersed in the ebb and flow of European developments."[82]

Whether subregional integration has preceded, run parallel, or lagged the process of Europeanization, it has reacted to the growing dynamism of the EC/EU-wide integration processes, especially after the end of the Cold War. Indeed, the distinctiveness of Benelux, always regarded as the center of the integration process, is threatened by further advances toward the EMU. European Free Trade Association (EFTA) members in Scandinavia have decided to harmonize national policies unilaterally with EC standards after 1987. Intergovernmental negotiations about the European Economic Space (EES) were concluded successfully in October 1991. While Norway decided not to join the EU, in 1995, Sweden and Finland did, and once inside the EU, they were recognized to be as European as

---

[79] Hans Daalder, "The Role of a Small State in the European Community: The Case of the Netherlands," Working Paper 1991/21, Instituto Juan March, Madrid, 1991, p. 7.

[80] Peter J. Katzenstein, "Regionalism in Comparative Perspective," *Coöperation and Conflict* 31 (1996): 130–34.

[81] See Stanley V. Anderson, *The Nordic Council: A Study of Scandinavian Regionalism* (Seattle: University of Washington Press, 1967), p. ix; Barbara Haskel, *The Scandinavian Option: Opportunities and Opportunity Cost in Postwar Scandinavian Foreign Policy* (Oslo: Norwegian University Press, 1976); Bo Stråth, *Nordic Industry and Nordic Economic Cooperation* (Stockholm: Almqvist and Wiksell, 1978); Bernt Schiller, "At Gun Point: A Critical Perspective on the Attempts of the Nordic Governments to Achieve Unity after the Second World War," *Scandinavian Journal of History* 9 (1984): 221–37; Bengt Sundelius and Claes Wiklund, "The Nordic Community: The Ugly Duckling of Regional Cooperation," *Journal of Common Market Studies* 18 (1979): 59–75; Bengt Sundelius, "Coping with Transnationalism in Northern Europe," *West European Politics* 3 (May 1980): 219–29.

[82] Johnny Laursen, "Blueprints and Nordic Integration: Dynamics and Institutions in Nordic Cooperation, 1945–72," EUI Working Paper RSC no. 94/20, European University Institute, Florence, 1994, p. 4. See also Ole Wæver, "Nordic Nostalgia: Northern Europe after the Cold War," *International Affairs* 68, 1 (January 1992): 77–102.

many of the long-standing members. These facts attest to the complementarity between some of Europe's subregional groupings and the wider European integration process.

Socialist and Communist attempts to institutionalize an alternative Mediterranean vision of Europe in the late 1970s and early 1980s were therefore short-lived. And so was the attempt to create a subregional grouping in central Europe after 1990. The Visegrad Quadrangle, as the most prominent of a number of central European integration ventures, has stalled since 1993.[83] It is no coincidence that, at its 1993 Copenhagen summit, the EU specified conditions that states seeking membership would have to fulfill: stabilization of democracy and the rule of law, readiness to adopt all prior EU regulations (*acquis communautaire*), creation of an effective market economy, and the adoption of policies aiming at meeting in good measure the convergence criteria of the Maastricht treaty. If these soft political, legal, and economic conditions were met, the EU would have to be prepared to disburse hard cash. The best estimate available suggests that the total transfer payments from the EU to the four Visgrad states would amount to 60–90 percent of the 18 billion ECU that Spain, Portugal, Greece, and Ireland received annually in the 1990s.[84] The institutions of the EU are embedded in broader collective European and Western understandings, which are consequential even though they do not find concrete organizational expression. But, as the EU, the European polity has increasingly marginalized alternative groupings of European states.

The relations between the smaller states, Germany, and Europe has been influenced by two factors. Was the compatibility between Germany's consolidating democratic welfare state and any of the smaller states large or small? And did firm multilateral links exist, for example, in the EC or NATO? The difference between the Low Countries and Scandinavia was that until the late 1980s Sweden, Norway, and Denmark were affected primarily by policies, while Belgium and the Netherlands were also exposed to institutional effects. By contrast, the states of southern Europe (before 1975) and of central Europe (before 1990) differed greatly from Germany's domestic order and interacted only sporadically in global institutions with Germany and Europe. In both instances, domestic regime change has opened avenues for greater institutional convergence in southern Europe after 1986 and in central Europe after 1991. The com-

[83] Valerie Bunce, "Regional Cooperation and European Integration in Postcommunist Europe: The Visegrad Group," in Peter J. Katzenstein, ed., *Mitteleuropa: Between Europe and Germany* (Providence, R.I.: Berghahn Books, forthcoming).

[84] András Inotai, "From the Association Agreements to Full Membership? The Dynamics of Relations between the Central and Eastern European Countries and the European Union," paper presented at the Fourth Biennial International Conference of the European Community Studies Association, Charleston, South Carolina, May 11–14, 1995, p. 13.

bined gravitational pull of Europe and Germany thus depends greatly on the compatibility of domestic structures.

Europe may well be the solution to the German problem.[85] But Germany's political placement in Europe is just one of a nested set of relationships. Germany and Europe are part of the broader Atlantic Community, which shares many common values.[86] As is true of western Europe, the Atlantic Community, through NATO, is a guarantor of peaceful change, whatever the political disagreements among its members. And like the European polity, as NATO seeks "multispeed" solutions, it begins to exhibit its own version of a "variable geometry." Swedish and Finnish neutrality, for example, may well be hollowed out as both states gradually slide into NATO's framework through arrangements at the operative level. A perceptible shift in Swedish discourse from the language of neutrality in the late 1980s to the language of "not allied at present" suggests as much.[87] It is thus quite plausible that the domain of national security will give rise to soft institutional constraints similar to those characterizing the European polity in other domains. Furthermore, the Atlantic Community is itself part of a world of regions that, like Europe, is defined by the coincidence of economic globalization and cultural decentralization.[88] Processes that nest institutions within each other are thus central to the Europeanization of Germany.

History and the soft institutional constraints posed by the European polity and Germany suggest that the European polity and its various regimes will accommodate and reflect diversity. This undermines the claim that the European polity is a protostate potentially exposed to German domination. Yet European integration is deepening institutionally and

[85] Calleo, *The German Problem Reconsidered.* In contrast to the position of this book, Calleo's prescient argument is traditionally Gaullist. He sees Europe as an alternative to, rather than as an enhanced context for, a broader system of Atlantic association. In my opinion, it would take political changes more radical than the SEA and the TEU on the European side and the Gingrich revolution of 1994 on the American side to weaken that association so much that Germans and Europeans would begin to entertain seriously the need for developing an exclusive European alternative.

[86] Gebhard Schweigler, "Problems and Prospects of the Atlantic Community," in David D. Hale, Moisés Naím, Gebhard Schweigler, and John D. Steinbruner, *Is the Atlantic Widening? Atlantic Area Nations after the Cold War* (Chicago: Chicago Council on Foreign Relations, 1995), pp. 30–62; Thomas Risse-Kappen, "Collective Identity in a Democratic Community," in Peter J. Katzenstein, ed., *The Culture of National Security: Norms and Identity in World Politics* (New York: Columbia University Press, 1996), pp. 357–399; Glenn Chafetz, "Explaining the Persistence of Western Security Cooperation after the Cold War: A Test of a Social Identity Theory of International Relations," paper prepared for delivery at the 1994 Annual Meeting of the American Political Science Association, New York Hilton and Towers, September 1–4, 1994.

[87] I thank Bengt Sundelius for this observation.

[88] For a discussion of Europe, economic globalization, and cultural decentralization, see J. Ørstrøm Møller, *The Future European Model: Economic Internationalization and Cultural Decentralization* (Westport, Conn.: Praeger, 1995).

spreading in scope. Realist and liberal perspectives on the irreducible core of the nation-state and the inherent difficulty of coordinating conflicting political objectives are as compelling in the mid-1990s as they were in the mid-1960s. And therein lies their greatest drawback. Neither perspective can make much out of the fact that the very ground on which European integration evolves has shifted greatly during the last three decades. Thus they overlook a central fact, aptly described by Nicholas Colchester: "Government will become a more stratified affair, with power, and a little identity, shifting up above national capitals—and identity, and a little power, shifting down below them. Westminster, Paris and Washington will detest the sensation . . . Brussels and Bonn/Berlin will smile knowingly."[89]

We can profitably think of Europe as a set of institutional effects with German components that vary in strength and that are partly redefining the identities, and thus the interests, of European states. The legitimate exercise of German power can occur only through Europe's complex institutional arrangements. Like the smaller European states that surround it, Germany must take as a given this consequence of European integration. Conversely, for the smaller states, the natural means for coping with internationalization and restraining German power is through regional integration, at the cost of changing core policies, institutions, and collective identities. What appears as an unwelcome external constraint to states located at the periphery of the European polity appears quite natural for those located at its center. Because institutional integration describes a process in which the character of states also changes, German domination over contemporary Europe is a mirage—both close at hand and receding. The "Germanization of Europe" and the "Europeanization of Germany," this book's central finding suggests, are part of the same political process.

[89] Nicholas Colchester, quoted in *New York Times* (July 17, 1994): A17.

Index

Abdelal, Rawi, 287
Acquis communautaire, 57, 302
Adenauer, Konrad, 14, 27, 30
Agricultural Council (EU), 98–99
Agriculture, 42; efficiency and, 98–99; as
  EU budget item, 36, 71; green exchange
  rates, 95; Scandinavia, 182–187, 274. *See
  also* Common Agricultural Policy
Alliance freedom, 176, 181
Anderson, Jeffrey, 3, 25, 26, 27, 73, 160n,
  273
Antall, Jozsef, 199, 210, 223, 240–242
Asmus, Ronald, 32, 258
Associated sovereignty, 4, 33–46; Britain
  and, 41–43; France and, 41–43; links
  with semisovereignty, 40–45
Atwood, Donald, 235
Aznar, José María, 164, 255

Balkans, 148–150, 280
Basic Law, 40, 63, 217, 276
Basic Treaty, 210–212
Bavaria, 246, 249, 267
Belgium, 254–255, 261; budget cuts, 121–
  122, 125; Christian Democratic Party,
  109, 118, 121, 125; debt crisis, 117–
  122, 267, 270, 286–287; devaluation
  negotiations, 118–119, 270–271; exchange rate, 117–118, 120–122; policing, 131–133, 139; price indexation system, 120–121; social security, 122–126;
  unions, 119, 120, 122; wages, 119, 121–
  122. *See also* Low Countries
Beneš decrees, 244–245, 247–249

Bilateral initiatives, 66, 78–79, 83, 246
Bildt, Carl, 179, 181, 189
Bod, Peter Akos, 199
Borders, 23; Czech Republic, 245–249,
  276; Hungary, 208–211; Poland, 205,
  207; Slovak Republic, 210–211, 220–
  221. *See also* Policing
Bosnia, 214, 216n, 279
Britain, 5, 57, 62–63, 66, 73, 191, 264,
  299; governance, 41–43; industrial relations and, 127; single-market program and, 77; Spain and, 152; state
  identity, 24, 31–33, 42–43; subsidiarity and, 55
Brittan, Leon, 89
Brundtland, Gro Harlem, 181–182, 189–
  190
Bulmer, Simon, 25, 26, 82, 260
Bundesbank, 9, 14, 25, 74, 269, 283–284;
  Bundesbank Act (1957), 75; Hungary
  and, 198–200, 270–271; inflationary
  policy, 178–179; Low Countries and,
  108–109, 111, 270; Spain and, 152–
  153, 270–271; unification and, 70–
  71, 75
Burley, Anne-Marie, 299

Cannes summit (1995), 145, 147
Caporaso, James, 4, 67n
Carlsson, Ingvar, 176, 180–181
Catholic Church, 202n, 211, 264; nation-
  alism and, 200, 202–203; Spain and,
  202–203; vision of, 200–201, 203–204.
  See also Poland